PENGUIN  C

GW00809289

BROTHERS G
MAGIC TAL

JACOB LUDWIG KARL, the elder of the brothers Grimm, was born in 1785, and WILHELM KARL in the following year. They both studied at Marburg, and from 1808 to 1829 mainly worked in Kassel as state-appointed librarians, Jacob also assisting in diplomatic missions between 1813 and 1815 and again in 1848. Both brothers had been professors at Göttingen for several years when in 1837 they became two of the seven leading Göttingen academics dismissed from their posts by the new King of Hanover for their liberal political views. In 1840 they were invited by Frederick William IV of Prussia to settle in Berlin as members of the Academy of Sciences, and here they remained until their deaths (Wilhelm died in 1859 and Jacob in 1863).

Jacob, one of Germany's greatest scholars, is justly regarded as the founder of the scientific study of the German language and medieval German literature. His most monumental achievements were the *Deutsche Grammatik* (1819–37) and, with his brother's assistance, the initiation of the great *Deutsches Wörterbuch*, the many volumes of which were not completed by later scholars until 1961 and which has become the equivalent of the *Oxford English Dictionary*. Between them, and often in collaboration, the Grimms were responsible for pioneering work on medieval texts, heroic epic, legends and mythology, and for many other contributions to the study of ancient German culture. One of their most remarkable publications was the *Kinder- und Hausmärchen* (1812, with many subsequent editions), which remains to this day the most famous collection of folktales in the world.

DAVID LUKE was born in 1921 and is an Emeritus Student (Emeritus Fellow) of Christ Church, Oxford, where he was Tutor in German until 1988. He has published articles and essays on German literature, and various prose and verse translations, including Stifter's *Limestone and Other Stories*, Kleist's *The Marquise of O- and Other Stories*, *Death in Venice and Other Stories* by Thomas Mann, and Goethe's *Iphigenia in Tauris*, *Hermann and Dorothea*, Parts One and

Two of *Faust*, *Selected Verse* (1964), *Selected Poetry* (1999), and a volume of his erotic poems. His translation of *Faust* Part One was awarded the European Poetry Translation Prize in 1989. For his work as a translator, the German Federal Cross of Merit was conferred on him in 1999 and he won a further award from the German-British Forum in 2000.

BROTHERS GRIMM
Magic Tales

Translated with an Introduction and Notes by
DAVID LUKE

PENGUIN BOOKS

PENGUIN BOOKS

Published by the Penguin Group
Penguin Books Ltd, 80 Strand, London WC2R 0RL, England
Penguin Group (USA) Inc., 375 Hudson Street, New York, New York 10014, USA
Penguin Group (Canada), 90 Eglinton Avenue East, Suite 700, Toronto, Ontario, Canada M4P 2Y3
(a division of Pearson Penguin Canada Inc.)
Penguin Ireland, 25 St Stephen's Green, Dublin 2, Ireland
(a division of Penguin Books Ltd)
Penguin Group (Australia), 250 Camberwell Road, Camberwell, Victoria 3124, Australia
(a division of Pearson Australia Group Pty Ltd)
Penguin Books India Pvt Ltd, 11 Community Centre, Panchsheel Park, New Delhi – 110 017, India
Penguin Group (NZ), 67 Apollo Drive, Mairangi Bay, Auckland 1310, New Zealand
(a division of Pearson New Zealand Ltd)
Penguin Books (South Africa) (Pty) Ltd, 24 Sturdee Avenue, Rosebank, Johannesburg 2196, South Africa

Penguin Books Ltd, Registered Offices: 80 Strand, London WC2R 0RL, England

www.penguin.com

This translation first published as *Selected Tales* 1982
Reprinted with a new Chronology and Further Reading 2004
This My Penguin edition published 2006
1

Printed in England by Clays Ltd, St Ives plc
Set in VIP Palatino

ISBN-13: 978-0-140-45543-4
ISBN-10: 0-141-445543-4

CONTENTS

INTRODUCTION

The modest, almost deprecating title under which what are often called the 'Grimm fairytales' appeared in Germany in 1812 and thereafter was *Kinder- und Hausmärchen, gesammelt durch die Brüder Grimm*. This wording may remind us of three things: first, of the still not wholly stale controversy, to which we must later revert, about whether they are in fact stories 'for children and the household'; secondly, of the difficulty of translating the word *Märchen*; thirdly and most importantly, of the fact that they were 'collected by' the brothers Grimm, who were of course their transcribers and editors and not their authors. Etymologically *Märchen* is simply a story or tale, like *conte* in French or *skazka* in Russian, the diminutive *chen* being no more significant than the *ka* of *skazka*. The common English rendering 'fairytale' is misleading. It is not quite true to say that hardly any of these stories concern 'fairies', since in a number of them there is a supernatural being referred to as *Fee* in the 1812 edition, after which the Grimms for reasons of linguistic purism altered it to *Zauberin* (enchantress, sorceress). But they are certainly not peopled by creatures such as those in *A Midsummer Night's Dream*, and the word 'fairy' thus has inappropriate associations for English readers. On the other hand the majority, and nearly all the most interesting and famous of the tales, operate in a world of wish-fulfilments and magic events, usually involving the laying and/or lifting of some magic spell (*Verwünschung*, a bewitching, literally a 'be-wishing'), and the word *Märchen* has by traditional usage taken on this more specialized meaning of a 'magic tale' or 'tale of enchantment' (*Zaubermärchen*, *volshebnaya skazka*); Tolkien indeed, in his well-known essay 'On Fairy-Stories', finds the term acceptable provided that 'fairy' is taken to mean not an elvish creature but simply magic or enchantment, the realm of *féerie*. The word *Märchen* is also more loosely applied to the

category of comic or joke tales (*Schwänke*, jests) which do not
necessarily involve magic; thus if we include both senses it
comes to mean much the same thing as *Volksmärchen*, 'folktale'.
And in fact these stories cannot really be appreciated unless
they are to some extent viewed in the international perspective
of anonymous folklore (which is not to say that they can be fully
understood in that perspective either). We can here, since I am
not a folklorist, take no more than a rather random glance into
this vast field, the exhaustive exploration of which is still being
carried out by experts, the first of whom indeed were the
Grimm brothers themselves. Although deeply Germanophilic,
Jacob and Wilhelm Grimm had no illusions about the folktale
being an essentially German or Germanic phenomenon. As
their own learned annotations to even the first edition of the
tales indicate, they were well aware that the stories they lovingly collected had, as wholes or in part, innumerable parallels
or equivalents outside as well as inside Germany. They were
simply looking for German versions, German variants, of what
they already knew to be not only ancient but very widely
dispersed material.

In their 1822 preface to these annotations the Grimms write:

> We have carefully recorded points of similarity with foreign tra-
> ditions which are often far separated in time and place, for we feel we
> are right to attach importance to such resemblances, precisely because
> they are not easily explicable. In some instances it is possible or even
> probable that there was direct communication, but in the majority of
> cases we cannot suppose this to be so, and the phenomenon thus
> remains unexplained and all the more remarkable . . . Our accumulated
> evidence attests the existence of folktales in different epochs and among
> different peoples . . .

With hindsight it may be said that these were nothing if not
understatements. The sheer extent of the historical and geo-
graphical dispersal of folktales is still not fully appreciated by
the ordinary reader, who may indeed be familiar with this or
that non-German equivalent of some of the more famous of the
'Grimm' tales, but may still be surprised to learn, for instance,
that for the 'Cinderella' story alone analogues are to be found

not only in England, Scotland, Ireland and France, but also in
the Baltic and Scandinavian languages, Icelandic, Faroese,
Dutch, Basque, Spanish, Catalan, Italian, Romanian, Hun-
garian, Czech, Polish, Serbo-Croatian, Albanian, Greek, Turk-
ish and Armenian. There is even a Chinese version (connected
apparently with the admiration of the Chinese for women with
small feet) dating from the ninth century B.C., and another
ancient tale is reported by the Greek geographer Strabo (first
century B.C.) in which a slipper belonging to the beautiful
courtesan Rhodope is dropped by an eagle into the lap of the
Pharaoh of Egypt and so enamours him that he has his entire
kingdom searched until he finds its owner. We meet Cinderella
under an international variety of names, all connected with
ashes or soot or dirt: Cendrillon, Cenerentola, Aschenputtel,
Pisk-i-aske, Askepott, Ashpit, Ashiepattle, Pepeleshka, Chernushka, Zamarashka, and many others. Similarly we
encounter Rumplestiltskin as Tom-Tit-Tot, Trit-a-Trot,
Whuppity-Stoorie, Ricdin-Ricdon, Titteliture, Zorobubù,
Taradandò, and so forth. The Grimms' annotations have been
expanded and updated by two twentieth-century scholars into
a massive five-volume standard work of reference (Bolte and
Polivka, *Anmerkungen zu den Märchen der Brüder Grimm*,
1912–32) which is now basic to world folklore studies. Even
quite cursory consultation of this, or of the equally important
index by Stith Thompson called *The Types of the Folktale* (1961,
based on Antti Aarne's *Verzeichnis der Märchentypen*, 1910 and
1928), reveals that what applies to the Cinderella and Rumplestiltskin stories also applies in comparable degree to all or most
of the others with which we are here concerned. And this is not
simply to say that this or that collection of folktales has been
much translated, but that the various tales themselves are based
on traditional stories which have been endlessly circulating for
many centuries in a manner that defies analysis. It has been
thought that there is a roughly identifiable 'Indo-European'
area, extending all over Europe and into parts of Asia, to which
a complex of recognizably similar stories belongs, but this is
disputed, as is the theory of the 'diffusion' of tales from India or
some other original centre. The possible oral and/or written

lines of transmission are inextricable, and the existence of folk-tales is a world-wide phenomenon. In the case of many basic stories or story-situations ('motifs'), there can be little doubt that for profound human reasons they have come into being independently ('polygenetically') in quite separate cultures.

If we distinguish particular 'motifs' from whole stories, this impression of the antiquity and ubiquity and universality of folklore materials is reinforced, and the distinction is also useful in other ways. The most casual reader of the Grimm collection will notice that the tales are not only often variants of each other, but consist for the most part of combinations and permutations of certain typical constituent elements. Motifs may be situations, actions, events, characters or objects: the motif of the forgotten (but eventually re-acknowledged) bride, the animal bridegroom (eventually rehumanized), the enchantment or disenchantment of the prince or princess, the helpful animal or dwarf, the cruel stepmother, the magic purse which always contains gold. They are abstractions or models, the details being secondary and differing according to the variant: thus the typical situation (motif) of the hero outwitting the stupid giant or giants is the same whether the hero is a prince, a young huntsman, a tailor's apprentice, a retired soldier or Tom Thumb. The purse of gold may be a jug of oil that never empties or a tablecloth that always lays itself with a good meal, and closely analogous to this motif is of course that of the bird that lays golden eggs or the donkey that excretes diamonds or gold coins (as in No. 41 of the present selection from the Grimm tales*). Motifs demand endless classification and sub-classification, and this has been done in Stith Thompson's monumental *Motif-Index of Folk-Literature* (1955–8) in which the gold-giving donkey, for instance, is motif No. B.103.1.1. They constantly recur in all kinds of contexts and often seem to have a kind of autonomy or independence of their own.

Some examples will illustrate the curiously ancient echoes

---

* For convenience I shall here identify these tales simply by the numbers given to them in this selection, which do not correspond to their numeration in the complete editions. The official Grimm number of each tale and its original German title are given in the Notes.

that may be heard in modern collections such as that by the Grimms. We can only guess that folktales already existed in the Babylonian-Assyrian period, but it is notable that the epic of Gilgamesh, dating from about 1700 B.C., contains some elements which we would now think of as folktale-motifs: the hero's fights with monstrous supernatural adversaries, the trees that bear precious stones as fruit (compare Nos. 25 and 30), the quest for a magical means of preserving or renewing life (No. 18). In 1852 a whole story was discovered on an Egyptian papyrus of about 1250 B.C.: this tale of two brothers, Arup and Bata, shows several 'constant' motifs, including that of the magic token which, when the brothers are separated, warns one of the fate or peril of the other (No. 16) and that of the magic flight (that is, the hero and/or heroine escaping from their pursuer by means of magically interposed obstacles, as in No. 35). In another Egyptian papyrus of about 1000 B.C., there is a fragmentary story beginning rather like No. 6: a prince, the first-born after his parents' long childlessness, is cursed at birth by seven supernatural beings who prophesy that he will be killed by a certain animal, a fate which his father tries to prevent, etc. Motifs in the Old Testament narratives include the exposure of a child (Moses) in a boat (Nos. 26 and 51); the father (Jephtha) who promises to sacrifice whatever living creature he first meets on arrival home, only to find that it is his child (Nos. 40, 51 and 56); the king (Saul) promising his daughter to the slayer of the monster (Goliath) (No. 16); Elisha's never-emptying oil-jug (No. 41); the one forbidden act (prohibition-motif) as in the Garden of Eden story (compare the forbidden room in No. 57 and elsewhere, or the forbidden well in No. 37). The tale (No. 4) of Red Ridinghood, the little girl swallowed by the wolf and then cut out alive from inside it, has even been thought to be reminiscent of the story of Jonah being swallowed and disgorged by the whale. It is certainly reminiscent of the ancient Greek myth of Cronos swallowing his children, who are then cut out of his belly and replaced by stones. The Greek classical texts from Homer onwards tell or allude to such stories, strongly suggesting the existence of an oral folktale tradition. Motifs include the magic transformation of Odysseus's men

into beasts by Circe; the mermaid-like Sirens whose song
would lure them to destruction; Odysseus outwitting the giant
Polyphemus. A father, Thyestes, is tricked by his brother
Atreus into eating his own sons in a stew (compare No. 8). The
hero Peleus captures and marries a mermaid, and cuts out the
tongues of slain beasts as proof that he is the slayer (Nos. 16 and
17). Medea helps Jason to perform tasks set by her father (No.
35) and flees with him, throwing down her brother's severed
limbs to hold up their pursuers (magic flight, No. 35).
Oenomaos deters his daughter Hippodamia's suitors with a
task (the chariot-race) and displays the losers' heads on stakes
(No. 24). Aëdon tries to kill an enemy's son as he sleeps but by
mistake kills her own son Itys whose cap, put on to distinguish
the children, has fallen off; this motif occurs not in the Grimms
but in their seventeenth-century French precursor, Perrault,
whose Tom Thumb tricks the ogre into killing his own sleeping
daughters instead of him and his brothers by exchanging their
headwear. Comic motifs such as thumb-size midgets are also
alluded to in Greek comedy and proverbial sayings. The listing
of such motif-analogues could be much further pursued, and
we must here pass over the various possible examples from
medieval (Latin, French, German, English) literature and from
the sagas of the Norse Edda, mentioning only the now (thanks
to Wagner's versions) especially famous stories of Tristan and
Yseult (the fight with the monster, the voyage in the drifting
boat, the forgotten bride) and of Sigurd (Siegfried) and
Brynhild (Brünnhilde): the young man of supernatural strength
(as in No. 47), the fight with the monster, the hero waking the
sleeping heroine after penetrating the obstacle surrounding her
(No. 6; this analogy was one of the first to be pointed out by the
Grimms themselves); and again the forgetting of the bride as in
Nos. 33–5.

For the reader of folktales, the identification of quasi-
autonomous motifs is also illuminating in that these may often
be seen to combine with each other in an apparently random
fashion, making up in some cases a story which is obviously not
one story but a mixture of two or more. Why, for example, is
No. 38 called 'The Frog King *or Iron Harry*'? The concluding

passage about the faithful retainer with 'iron bands ... round his heart' which break with joy at his master's disenchantment seems an inconsequential and scarcely relevant coda to the main story, which should logically end at the happy union of the disenchanted frog-prince with the princess. But the Grimms knew another version continuing beyond this point, in which the prince leaves on a journey, forgets the young princess and is about to marry another. The heroine and her two sisters have set off to find him, disguised as knights, and join his wedding escort: three 'bands' then successively and audibly break from round the supposed retainer's heart, till her prince remembers, acknowledges and marries her. This is in itself a mixture or 'contamination' of the animal-bridegroom-disenchantment motif (as in Nos. 39 and 40) with that of the forgotten bride, but in the version they finally chose the Grimms left out the latter, retaining only a vestige of it in the minor motif (also constantly attested) of the faithful henchman whose heart is constricted, breaks with joy, etc. This final version makes imperfect sense, but illustrates the fact that a certain inconsequentiality is one of the characteristics of the folktale. Only a few have the complete and compelling dramatic unity of the one about the fisherman (No. 1). Other examples of 'mixed' tales here are Nos. 16, 21, 35, 37, 51 and 52; the latter part of No. 17 also makes poor sense because of the variant chosen (see the note to this story on p. 402).

In modern times the publication of collections of stories from local oral tradition seems to have begun in Italy with Giovan-Francesco Straparola, of whom little is known except that his book *Le Tredici Piacevole Notti* ('Thirteen Agreeable Nights') appeared in Venice in the mid-sixteenth century. The tales are set in a 'frame-narrative' in the manner of Boccaccio's *Decamerone*, and a number of them are of the magical and/or comical *Märchen* type. More distinguished than Straparola, and with a claim to be considered the first great European collection, was *Lo Cunto de li cunti* ('The Tale of the Tales') which appeared in Naples in five volumes between 1634 and 1636, shortly after the death of its compiler Giovan-Battista Basile (1575–1632). This book later acquired its better-known title *Il Pentamerone* from the frame-narrative's 'five days' on which ten ladies must each tell one story. Basile, who published under the whimsical anagrammatic pseudonym of 'Gian Alesio Abbatutis', wrote not in standard Italian but in Neapolitan; he seems to have been uninfluenced by Straparola and may not even have read him. The fifty tales, under the no doubt ironic sub-title 'An Entertainment for Children', are vivid, witty and rather Rabelaisian (for instance, in the equivalent of the Grimm No. 10 the haughty stepsister's punishment is to have a donkey's testicle stuck to her forehead). They are evidently quite close to their oral sources, though Basile's style is a highly individual blend of directness and baroque extravagance. They had a great success locally but little immediate influence outside Italy, where for a long time they do not even seem to have been translated into standard Italian, and then very incompletely; there does not seem to have been any French translation in the time of Perrault, who is thus unlikely to have known them unless in some indirect way. There was no English version until the pruned and bowdlerized one by John Edward Taylor in 1848. But a complete and scholarly German translation by Felix Liebrecht was published in 1846; the Grimms in any case had long known the original *Pentamerone* and valued it highly. They knew Straparola too, in a complete Venetian edition of 1573. In both these Italian collections, especially in that of Basile, there were tales which they regarded as corresponding at least in part to tales which they had found in Germany. In some cases these correspondences amount to little more than one or two shared motifs, while in others there is a broadly equivalent story-line; a few examples from the present selection are referred to in the Notes (Nos. 3, 5, 6, 11, 13, 16, 22, 31, 32 and 40).

The work of Charles Perrault (1628–1703) was of course also well known to the Grimms. His *Histoires ou contes du temps passé*, also known popularly as *Contes de ma Mère l'Oye* ('Tales of Mother Goose'), appeared in Paris, anonymously at first, in 1797 and has ever since been hailed as a literary classic. It contained only eight tales, but was the most famous European collection before that of the Grimms themselves, and it is in Perrault's versions that some of the stories are probably best known to English readers – for example, 'La Belle au bois dormant' ('The Sleeping Beauty', No. 6), 'Cendrillon' ('Cinderella', No. 31), 'Le Petit Chaperon rouge' ('Little Red Ridinghood', No. 4) and 'Le Petit Poucet' ('Tom Thumb' or 'Hop o' my Thumb'). Perrault's paradoxical imposition of sophisticated literary artifice on primitive folktale material is especially evident in his 'Peau d'âne' ('Donkey-Skin', the story corresponding to No. 32 about the princess who flees from her father's incestuous advances disguised in animal-skins): this he tells entirely in elegant verse like that of La Fontaine (it appeared before the *Contes*, and was added to later editions of them in a prose rendering). But in any case, in their treatment of the tales, Perrault and the Grimms are worlds apart. Perrault, a retired civil servant and a member of the Académie, was writing for the entertainment of Louis xiv's courtiers and the cultivated public of the golden age of French classical literature. That he made use of traditional oral material seems undeniable. The Grimms wrote with tactful understatement that

details apart, he added nothing to the tales: his style is simple and natural and strikes a childlike note, *so far as this was possible in the polished and rounded literary diction of his time* [my italics].

They go on to quote certain turns of phrase which seem to echo the language of popular story-telling. It has also been pointed out that Perrault's versions have something of the inconsequential structure of genuine folktale: motifs are brought in for some accidental traditional reason and then disregarded or developed in a manner irrelevant to the main plot. 'Le Petit Poucet', for instance, begins by telling us how the hero is no bigger than a thumb, but his tiny size then plays no further part in the story, which continues as a Hansel and Gretel variant: as in No. 3, the children are abandoned in the forest by their parents and captured by a monster who intends to eat them, but the hero tricks the enemy and they escape. Again, 'La Belle au bois dormant' carries on beyond its natural ending, unlike its Grimm equivalent No. 6, into a development of the jealous stepmother motif which is irrelevant artistically (even if perhaps not psychologically). It is interesting that Basile's

version also adds a similar episode, although for reasons mentioned above Basile is unlikely to have influenced Perrault
directly. Perrault, incidentally, omits in the interests of *bien-
séance* the further motif (found in Basile and some other early
versions) that the sleeping princess is raped by the rescuing
prince and even gives birth to his children while still asleep. The
Grimm 'Dornröschen' ('Briar-Rose') is infinitely more simple,
poetic and moving than any of these variants.

Perrault was essentially a brilliant story-teller who, like Basile
before him, did not yet live in an age that took folklore seriously
as an imaginative phenomenon. In offering these tales half-
apologetically to his contemporaries, he adopted the stance of
an urbane, witty, common-sense realist; they reflect the
fashions of his day rather than a kind of timeless past. Irony is as
conspicuous in them as a sense of mystery is by its absence. At
the beginning of 'La Belle au bois dormant' we read for
example:

... It was a splendid christening; as godmothers for the little princess
they appointed all the fairies they could find in the kingdom (they
found seven), so that if each of them were to give her a present, as fairies
customarily did in those days, the princess would acquire every
imaginable perfection ... In came an old fairy who had not been invited
because for the last fifty years she had never emerged from a tower she
lived in, and was thought to be dead or under a spell ...

and so forth. When the heroine falls into her magic sleep, the
fact that the whole palace staff falls asleep as well is explained in
a rationalizing, humorous way by the intervention of the
friendly fairy who has already mitigated her uninvited colleague's original curse and now reflects that it will be embarras-
sing for the princess to wake up after a hundred years and find
that she has no servants (in Grimm the curse operates auto-
matically and mysteriously on every living thing in the palace,
including the king and queen, transporting them suddenly into
another dimension of time as it were). When, in due course, the
prince wakes her, Perrault tells us that

looking at him more tenderly than seemed quite proper at first sight,
she said: Is that you, my prince? What a long time you've been.

In the subsequent ogress episode, the heroine and her children are to be cooked and eaten 'in sauce Robert'; and Perrault closes the Sleeping Beauty story, as he does all the others, with an ironic 'moral' in verse – in this case to the effect that although marriage loses little by postponement, not many modern young ladies would wish to prolong their engagements for a whole century. Similarly 'Le Petit Chaperon rouge' (where the heroine incidentally is simply eaten by the wolf and not cut out of its belly alive as in Grimm) is represented as a warning to little girls not to talk to plausible strangers in the street, and 'Cendrillon' as a lesson on the importance of charm, social graces and influential relatives. The tone of these worldly-wise postscripts is in keeping with Perrault's general unserious approach. We are being most skilfully entertained, but we are not yet in the world of true myth and enchantment.

Mention must also be made here of a famous and classic non-European book of tales, admired by the Grimms, of which a translation was first published in Europe at the beginning of the eighteenth century. The *Book of the Thousand and One Nights* (often popularly referred to in English as the *Arabian Nights*) was translated into French by Antoine Galland (1646–1715) from an Arabic text, though it is of Indian and Persian as well as Arab origin. This heterogeneous corpus of tales, not ascribed to any one author or assignable to any one period of composition, is thought to have originated from a lost Persian book called *A Thousand Legends*, translated into Arabic in the ninth century as *A Thousand Nights*; the number of 'nights' may have been increased by one because of Islamic superstition about round numbers. The tales have an unmistakable folklore character, though artfully composed into a frame-narrative which tells how a certain King Shahryar, in the habit of marrying only virgins whom he then kills after the first night, is beguiled by the wise Shahrazad (Scheherazade) into listening to her series of tales which so arouse his curiosity that he spares her life for a thousand nights and finally altogether. This frame-story is traceable back to Indian folklore, and there are Indian and Persian folklore parallels for a number of the tales, the basic nucleus of which was added to in the course of centuries by

Arab story-tellers, also using folktale material. Recognizable elements from the *Thousand and One Nights* seem to have found their way into the European folklore tradition long before Galland's introduction of these tales to the Western literary scene, and a number of motif-parallels and approximate story-parallels may be traced between them and the German tales collected by the Grimm brothers: two examples are Aladdin's lamp (No. 43) and the riddle-princess Turandot (No. 24).

Jacob and Wilhelm Grimm, born respectively in 1785 and 1786, grew up in the middle of what we roughly call the age of European Romanticism – or, if we prefer a more sceptical terminology, Romanticisms. It is problematic to describe this as the *German* 'Romantic' period, because although the great epoch of revival in German literature and culture generally began just before the emergence of the young Goethe (1749–1832), and although Goethe in his twenties was, in all but name, an early and radical Romantic, he later developed in a quite different direction, and at the end and turn of the century created and constituted, in close association with his friend Schiller (1759–1805), an authentic and highly important German classicism. If then we say that the age of Goethe (*Goethezeit*), as it is often more conveniently called, was that of German Romanticism, we must also say that German Classicism, in a manner unique in Europe, was incapsulated into it as well. Goethe is sometimes said to have embraced both within himself: it would be more correct to say that Romanticism was something in his youth and in his heart from which he self-defensively moved away. In the early 1770s, however, he was also closely associated with another pioneering figure who, in principle and in certain essential respects, anticipated the lifelong preoccupations of the Grimm brothers. The philosopher and critic Johan Gottfried Herder (1744–1803) is sometimes credited with being the first European to have had a genuine sense of history and historical development. His passionate concerns were the idea of the past as a living thing, existing in its own right and with its own character; the need for a rejuvenating return to origins; the value, ignored by the

Enlightenment, of the simple and unsophisticated, the primitive, the folk-traditional. He was convinced that in the language and still current popular lore of the Germans an ancient treasure of precious imaginative material was to be found – the *Volksseele* or folk-psyche – a fresh, unspoilt, inexhaustible source of inspiration for a truly national literature. In 1778 he published a collection of folksongs or folkballads, not using strict criteria of what a 'folksong' was, or confining himself to German sources (much of the material was translated, and the collection was later entitled *Stimmen der Völker*, 'Voices of the Peoples'). But Herder urged his contemporaries to seek out the half-buried masterpieces of German medieval literature such as the lyric poetry of the *Minnesänger* (courtly love poets) and the *Nibelung* epic, which were to be so thoroughly reinvestigated in the Grimms' day; and he pleaded strongly for a revival of interest in the folktale, pointing to the regional variations and calling for collections to be made. Under Herder's influence, the 22-year-old Goethe was for a time an enthusiastic collector of songs and ballads from oral sources in the Alsace countryside, and at certain points in his earlier work he showed himself to be profoundly in touch with the spirit of folklore, including the folktale. This is above all true of the fragmentary unpublished masterpiece of his youth, the Faust-Gretchen episode (written before 1775) which was to remain the core of a work not finished, by a process of modification and accretion, until about thirty years later: the strangely hybrid poetic drama we now know as 'Part One' of *Faust* (published in 1808). The young Goethe had written the 'Gretchen tragedy' in a manner subtly suggesting the themes and even the structure of folkballads; the heroine herself is presented with an unequalled blend of poetry and naturalness, and in her final Ophelia-like scene she sings a version of the repeated song of the magic bird in a story which the Grimms were to publish in 1812 as 'Von dem Machandelboom' (No. 8, 'The Jeniper Tree'). Goethe had evidently known this story in some form, having almost certainly heard it with other tales from his mother when he was a child. After 1775, settling in Weimar, he could still write the daemonic ballads 'Erlkönig' (inspired by a Danish folkballad translated by

Herder) and 'Der Fischer', but his creativity gradually took other forms, and to the last twelve years of the century belong his 'classical' masterpieces, the *Römische Elegien*, *Iphigenie auf Tauris* and the idyllic 'bourgeois' epic *Hermann und Dorothea*. He was joined in the same decade by Schiller, whose own development brought him by a different route to Weimar Classicism and who in his great historical tragedies *Wallenstein* and *Maria Stuart* synthesized the traditions of Shakespearian and French classical drama.

But the late 1790s also saw the formation of the German 'Romantic' schools officially so termed: a ferment of poetry, fiction, criticism and metaphysical philosophy, a movement extending far beyond literature as such. A central feature of this second and explicit phase of German Romanticism was again a passionate interest in the past – especially, in reaction against Napoleon's conquest of Germany and later in the enthusiasm of the Wars of Liberation, the German past. This quest for the roots of a German cultural identity, in default of a political one, was now even more marked than in the 1770s. The cosmopolitanizing classical Goethe had held himself aloof from it and on the whole continued to do so. But the Grimm brothers embodied it more completely and thoroughly and variously than anyone else in the *Goethezeit* or indeed in the whole European Romantic age. In their passionate historicism, their devoted and reverent search for origins of all kinds, they became not only the virtual inventors of systematic folklorism, but also, in their meticulous inquiries into the remotest past of their language and culture, the pioneers of medievalist scholarship and of historical philology. Separately or in collaboration, apart from the *Kinder- und Hausmärchen*, they produced monumental works such as *Deutsche Sagen* ('German Legends',* 1816–18), the great historical German Grammar in four volumes (*Deutsche Grammatik*, 1819–37), *Deutsche Rechtsaltertümer* ('Antiquities of German Law', 1928), *Deutsche Mythologie* ('German Mythology', 1835), *Geschichte der deutschen Sprache* ('History of the German Language', 1848), and

* This has recently been translated into English by Donald Ward (Millington Books, 1981).

above all the massive German Dictionary (*Deutsches Wörter-buch*), of which they compiled only four volumes in their lifetime but which was continued to many more by later scholars until the last appeared in 1961, completing this astonishing lexicographical enterprise after more than a century.

The Grimm brothers were close to each other as children (though they had three other brothers and a sister) and remained so all their lives, the main outlines of which differ only in their slightly different dates of birth and death. They studied law together until 1805 at Marburg, under the great Friedrich Karl von Savigny, the founder of the historical school of jurisprudence, who taught them scholarly method and drew their attention to medieval German culture. For many years their home was in Kassel, and they worked in library administration or the civil service; Jacob had diplomatic assignments in Paris in 1813 and at the Congress of Vienna in 1815. But their literary and academic fame grew, and in 1830 they were both invited to take up appointments at Göttingen, becoming professors almost simultaneously. This period ended when Ernest Augustus (Queen Victoria's notorious uncle the Duke of Cumberland) became King of Hanover in 1837 and immediately revoked the constitution; the Grimms, as liberal intellectuals, joined in a protest against him and lost their jobs. Three years later, however, under the new King of Prussia, Frederick William IV, they were invited to become members of the Prussian Academy of Sciences in Berlin, where they remained until they died (Wilhelm in 1859, Jacob in 1863). Through a turbulent era they had lived the relatively uneventful lives of German academics of the best type, devoted to their family circle (Wilhelm had married in 1825), devoted to each other and above all to their ceaseless individual and collaborative scholarly undertakings.* In an age of increasing mechanization and urbanization they felt themselves to be explorers and preservers of a precious heritage now in danger of disappearing. Of the *Märchen* they wrote in their preface to the first edition:

* For further biographical details reference may be made to the study in English by Ruth Michaelis-Jena (*The Brothers Grimm*, Routledge, 1970).

It was perhaps timely to record these tales, now that those to whom it
falls to preserve them are becoming ever rarer.

They had begun collecting folktales in 1806 or 1807, and in
this field too their work was of crucial importance in that it was
they above all, even among their Romantic contemporaries,
who really did what Herder had so prophetically advocated.
His message had been heard but half forgotten or distorted. He
had envisaged (as a first step at least) the actual collection of
genuine *Volksmärchen*, not merely an enthusiastic theorizing
about the *Märchen* as a literary or metaphysical principle, or a
creation of new artificial pseudo-folktales, *Kunstmärchen* as they
were called, in which folkloristic materials would be freely
mixed with an individual poet's own fantasies, whimsicalities
or allegorical messages. Even the later Goethe, instead of
exploring further the possibilities of the real indigenous folktales he knew, had himself written *Kunstmärchen* strongly influenced by rococo traditions traceable back to Perrault. At the
turn of the century the leading Romantic writers – Tieck,
Novalis, Brentano – were also chiefly using the *Märchen* idea for
their own artistic purposes. Clemens Brentano (1778–1842),
however, was almost an exception to this and played a special
mediating role on the verge of genuine folklore studies. In
collaboration with Achim von Arnim he published between
1805 and 1808 a much acclaimed compilation of largely authentic German folkpoems entitled *Des Knaben Wunderhorn* ('The
Boy's Magic Horn'), on which even Goethe bestowed praise. It
was more nationalistic in emphasis than Herder's *Stimmen der
Völker*, and came at the right time both for its influence on
modern German lyric poetry and as a stimulus to popular
interest and scholarly inquiry. Brentano, who was the brother-
in-law of the Grimms' teacher Savigny, became friendly with
Jacob and Wilhelm at this time. He aspired to do the same thing
for the *Volksmärchen* as he had for the *Volkslied*, and had already
collected some tales from oral sources in Marburg. It was he
who introduced the brothers to Basile's *Pentamerone*, which he
owned in a rare Neapolitan edition of 1749 and had begun to
translate. It was also through him and Arnim that the Grimms

acquired two of the finest tales in their entire collection: 'Von dem Fischer un syner Fru' ('The Fisher an his Gweedwìfe', No. 1) and 'Von dem Machandelboom' ('The Jeniper Tree', No. 8). These stories, both in Pomeranian Low German dialect, had never been told to the Grimms themselves. In response to a published appeal by Arnim in 1805, they were sent to him from Hamburg by the Romantic painter Philipp Otto Runge (1777–1810), who claimed to have heard and recorded them, and in 1809 Arnim made them available to the Grimms for their own use. It is possible that Runge, a gifted man who was born in Pomerania and could write in the dialect, had added some degree of refinement to his source-material; if so, the fusion of nature and art was in both cases masterly, and the Grimms (whether or not they took them to be wholly unedited transcriptions) regarded these two tales as models for their own enterprise. To receive them as contributions was a symbolic piece of initial good luck and a significant stimulus. Brentano and Arnim, to whom they had surrendered in 1807 their collection of old German poems as material for the *Wunderhorn*, were increasingly impressed by the progress the brothers were now making with their collection of folktales. In 1809 and again in 1810 Brentano begged them to send him their tales as well, promising to use them in his own way without prejudice to the Grimms' intentions – which meant that he would freely rewrite them as *Kunstmärchen* according to his idiosyncratic taste. The brothers again generously agreed to let him have their manuscript, though they prudently had a copy of it made before doing so. For a time it thus seemed that two independent folktale projects were pending: one conceived on scholarly and historical lines by the Grimms and a very cavalier literary one by Brentano. Nature and art, *Volk* and *Kunst*, folklore-study and literary creativity, seemed to be moving apart in a polarized way. But in the end this fortunately did not happen. Brentano tired of the idea, and it fell to the brothers to evolve the amicable synthesis of Jacob's scholarship and Wilhelm's literary taste which in the *Kinder- und Hausmärchen* we now have. Brentano, as they had foreseen, never returned their 1810 manuscript to them: it came to light over a century later in the abbey of

Oelenberg in Alsace and is thus known as the 'Oelenberg manuscript'. Some of the tales in it (which include versions of Nos. 2, 3, 6, 7, 13, 14, 32, 38 and 58) are merely sketched or summarized, but it retains a historic interest as the unpublished original draft of the first volume of the first edition of the Grimm collection.

It was Arnim who in 1812 strongly advised the brothers to publish without delay this first volume, based on the material they already had; what is more, he immediately found them a publisher. It was a gloomy and uncertain year, the year before the defeat of Napoleon by the allied armies at Leipzig, but the book was out in time for Christmas, dedicated to Arnim's wife Bettina, Brentano's sister. The response was so encouraging and so much new material now came to hand that a second volume could be contemplated almost at once. These two volumes, that of 1812 and that of 1815, constitute the first of the many editions of the *Kinder- und Hausmärchen*, and together they contained 156 tales, including nearly all of those which were to remain the most popular. The Grimms had been lucky from the start not only about the 'Fischer' and the 'Machandelboom', but also in their initial direct oral sources, which turned out to be virtually on their own doorstep. One of these was Dorothea ('Dortchen') Wild, whom Wilhelm later married; the Wild family were neighbours of the Grimms in Kassel, and Wilhelm had already known Dortchen as a girl of sixteen when in 1811 she told him the story of 'Mother Snowbed' (No. 11). She told him a number of others as well, including 'Rumplestiltskin' (No. 2), 'Hansel and Gretel' (No. 3), and Nos. 10, 15, 32 and 57. There were also her sisters and her mother, but particularly their old housekeeper Marie Müller, known as 'old Marie', who contributed Nos. 4, 7, 9, 38 and others. After the appearance of Volume I, tales told by word of mouth, either directly to the brothers or transmitted to them by enthusiastic readers, continued to accumulate. What the Wild household had been for the first volume, Frau Katharina Dorothea Viehmann (1755–1815), who lived in Zwehrn, a village close to Kassel, became for the second. The brothers met her probably in 1812 and she was perhaps the most remarkable of all their story-tellers. They referred to her affectionately as *die Märchenfrau*, and their preface to the second edition described her talents in words which tell us much about their own conception of the whole enterprise:

> She has retained these old tales firmly in her memory ... she told them carefully, confidently, and with great vividness, clearly enjoying them herself; at first she would be quite fluent, but if asked to she would then repeat them slowly, so that with a little practice one could write them down as she spoke. We have thus been able to preserve a great deal word for word ... Anyone who supposes that tradition is easy to falsify should have heard how exactly she repeated each narrative and how she insisted on the correct version. She never altered anything during a retelling, and if she made a slip she corrected it at once in mid-sentence ...

To Frau Viehmann the brothers owed nineteen of their best tales, including Nos. 13, 17, 22, 26, 29, 36, 40, 60 and 64. Another rich source was the family of Werner von Haxthausen, a highly gifted and versatile man who collected folklore not only in Germany but in England, Holland and Greece. From him and his brothers and sisters and nieces, on their estate at Bökendorf in the Paderborn area, the Grimms heard twenty-nine tales, including Nos. 16, 20, 23, 35, 46, 52 and 59, and twenty versions of tales they already knew. Among their many other sources, women rather than men seem to have been the most rewarding, but mention must be made of the retired sergeant of dragoons Johann Friedrich Krause, who exchanged tales such as No. 42 for discarded clothing and wrote touchingly misspelt letters of thanks to the brothers, his 'dear benefactors', asking when they would next have a pair of breeches to spare.

With contributions coming in not only from all over Germany but also from Austria, Bohemia and Switzerland, it had long been evident that there was more than enough material for a purely and genuinely German collection of folktales, however many parallels and antecedents they might have in other languages. At first the Grimms had even intended their second volume to consist of a translation of the *Pentamerone* and other foreign material; this plan was deferred and in the end abandoned as obviously unnecessary. In 1819 the second, revised

and slightly augmented edition appeared, again in two
volumes, with an engraved portrait of the late Frau Viehmann.
A third volume was added in 1822, consisting not only of the
already elaborate apparatus of notes (indicating sources and
German or foreign variants and parallels) which had appeared
as appendices in the 1812 and 1815 volumes, but also detailed
synopses of all fifty of Basile's stories; these synopses were
dropped when this third volume was re-edited in 1856. The two
volumes containing the actual tales ran to third, fourth, fifth,
sixth and seventh editions, respectively in 1837, 1840, 1843, 1850
and 1857; and Wilhelm was preparing an eighth edition when
he died in 1859. Each time the number of tales was slightly
increased, until from the 156 of 1815 they reached in 1857 the
canonical count of 200 (oddly, there are actually 201 owing to a
reduplication of one of the numberings in the brothers' last
edition, an anomaly which has since been piously preserved).
There was also, from 1825 onwards, a one-volume selection of
fifty of the best-liked tales, illustrated by the Grimms' brother
Ludwig. Of the seven complete editions, none was exactly the
same as the one preceding it, not only because new tales were
added or substituted, but also because the text of those already
included continued to be slightly revised by Wilhelm, who from
1815 onwards increasingly assumed responsibility for the
Kinder- und Hausmärchen as Jacob devoted himself to other
work.

It is clear that the brothers' initial conception of this project
had been dominated by their justified misgivings about what
Brentano's intended *Märchen* collection would be like. Jacob in
particular seems to have wanted to proceed in a strictly objective historicistic manner, ideally using only direct field-work
which today would be done with tape-recorders. In 1811 he
drafted a public appeal addressed to 'all friends of German
literature [*Poesie*] and history', inviting their assistance in the
daunting task of collecting the entire oral tradition of Germany
straight from the common people, no matter whether it might
be old or new, serious or comic, edifying or otherwise, in prose
or in verse, sensible or silly, and 'most especially the tales told
by nurses and children, the talk of winter evenings, the stories

heard in spinning-rooms'. Everything was to be reproduced
exactly, with no corrections, nonsense and all, dialect and
uneducated speech and all, rhymes and old sayings and all. The
aim was to be 'wholly scholarly', to compile 'materials for the
history of German literature', and such aesthetic or entertainment value as the book might have would be merely incidental.
This ambitious appeal remained unpublished, especially in
view of Brentano's defection from the entire enterprise, and the
Grimms in fact never applied its concept strictly. Brentano
predictably reacted to their first edition by declaring that the
book was messy (*versudelt*) and often tedious because the
Grimms had been excessively concerned with fidelity to their
sources; the brothers for their part, in their preface to the
second edition, expressly repudiated the tendency of certain
contemporaries (Brentano is not actually named) to treat the
folktale as mere raw material for free adaptation according to
personal caprice. But neither of these statements should be
taken as implying that the brothers in fact adhered to a policy of
strict documentary fidelity; they did not, in practice, leave the
material raw or eschew all considerations of literary taste. Their
collection was far from being wholly based on oral field-work by
themselves or others. Even in the first edition they occasionally
used literary sources, if they judged them (by the not yet exact
criteria of their day) to have something of a folktale character,
and such sources were not even always German: a medieval
Latin poem, for instance, was the basis of one of the tales in the
1812 volume (No. 39). They also, even in the first edition,
sometimes drew from more than one source in order to con-
struct a clearer or in some other way more satisfactory story;
this too was contrary to strict documentary principle, but in the
successive editions an increasing number of tales were selective
combinations of variants from quite different parts of Germany.
Other editorial processes were also at work: comparison of the
original Oelenberg manuscript with the 1812 volume confirms
that from the outset the material was being not only selected but
tidied and smoothed out, clarified and harmonized. From the
1815 volume onwards Wilhelm's policy of slight stylization
prevailed more and more. His aim was not a scrupulously exact

historical record of raw folk-utterance but an 'essential' objec-
tivity, a 'pure' *Volkstümlichkeit*, an 'ideal' folktale tone. The
naive style of spoken narrative, with uncomplicated sentences
and everyday vocabulary, enlivened by popular sayings and
idioms, occasional asides to the listening children, rhyming
formulae for the ends of stories – all this was to be not just
slavishly preserved but intensified, accentuated, restored if
necessary. Original end-formulae were in practice often
changed, as were original story-titles. In practice, too, not very
many tales were printed in dialect: many more had probably
been heard in dialect but were printed in High German. The
German, moreover, was to be more purely Germanic: foreign-
derived words such as *Bouteille*, *Profession*, *Minute*, *Prinz* and
Prinzessin were in later editions replaced by *Flasche*, *Handwerk*,
Augenblick, *Königssohn* and *Königstochter*, and in particular (as
already mentioned) *Fee* by *Zauberin*, as if to reduce the traces of
the French tradition to vanishing-point. Another factor was
that Wilhelm often felt the need, from edition to edition, to
elaborate and amplify the narrative, inserting this or that vivid
detail or fragment of dialogue, preserving the folk-like paratac-
tic sentence-structure but expanding the sentences or adding
more of them. The first story of the collection for example (No.
38) opens in the 1812 volume as follows:

> Once upon a time there was a princess and she went out into the
> forest and sat down by a cool well.

In the final 1857 version this single sentence has become a
passage over four times as long (see p. 271, 'The Frog King'),
and the rest of the story has been similarly treated. The same
applies in greater or lesser degree to a number of the tales,
though others again have been left almost exactly as in the first
edition. Wilhelm's elaborations are not always improvements,
but neither are the earlier, less finished and polished texts
necessarily superior.

Complaints that the *Tales* were unsuited to the youthful hear-
ers for whom they were presumed to be intended were of
course raised in many quarters as soon as the 1812 volume
appeared. So far as indelicate sexual details were concerned

(references to extra-marital pregnancy, for example) these had almost all been sufficiently veiled even in this first volume. As to violence, the Grimms defended themselves by appealing to nature and pointing out that there was violence as well as impropriety even in the Bible; Jacob in any case insisted that the *Tales* were not intended solely as a children's book. But they did make some further concessions to tender susceptibilities, excising after the first edition, for example, two brief anecdotes – old stories which had already been published for a century and more and were in all probability based on real-life incidents – about young children playing at being butchers. In one, a five- or six-year-old boy in West Frisia pretends to be a sow and actually does have his throat cut by a playmate (the poet Heinrich von Kleist had already reprinted this 'from an old book' in his *Berliner Abendblätter* of 1810, from which the Grimms took it verbatim with due acknowledgement). In the second, a young boy again slaughters another and is himself stabbed to death by their distraught mother, who then hangs herself. These items could well be dispensed with, not really being folktales at all and certainly not tales of magic. Some mitigating emendations were also made to the true *Märchen*: the cruel mothers of Hansel and Gretel and of Snowwhite became their 'stepmothers' after the first edition, and this change was probably also right, though for quite different reasons. A few other examples from stories in the present selection are mentioned in the Notes.

Neither Jacob's ideal nor Wilhelm's was fully realized in any of the editions of the *Tales*, which thus make a not altogether consistent impression and seem to be neither quite one thing nor quite the other. But Wilhelm's stylizations gave the book a certain general unity of tone, only occasionally marred by a too indulgent use of this or that literary source or by some other needless embellishment. If Jacob had retained complete control over the project, it would no doubt have become more like the folkloristic documentation which the annotatory apparatus still suggests; if he had had no influence on Wilhelm, it might have moved further in a literary direction. The final 201 tales are by no means all of equal interest and value, but the work remains a fascinating compromise between two rather divergent purposes. It reflects two different yet compatible temperaments and combines at its best great artistic charm with the strange force of primitive imaginative material.

Goethe, it must regretfully be recorded, showed a disappointing lack of interest in this most poetic of the Grimms' publications. When Wilhelm on his travels met or called on him in 1815 and 1816, the great man was courteous but nothing was said about the *Tales*. In 1816 Goethe sent his friend Charlotte von Stein a copy of one volume of them, recommending them a little patronizingly as reading for children and asking her to let him have the book back some time; yet there is no evidence that he showed any deep appreciation of them, then or later. But of the work's undoubted success and increasing fame, to which its many editions testify, little need now be said. By the end of the nineteenth century very numerous translations had appeared and the *Kinder- und Hausmärchen* were being read all over Europe and outside it. From the mid-century onwards their popularity had begun to be rivalled by that of the *Eventyr og Historier* ('Tales and Stories') of the Danish novelist, dramatist and poet Hans Christian Andersen (1805–75). Andersen's tales (published gradually between 1835 and 1872) were, however, *Kunstmärchen* rather than *Volksmärchen*; they use traditional material but bear the distinctive imprint of his own imagination and curious personality. Yet some were so immediately appealing that they passed into the stream of oral transmission, and the Grimms even included one of them ('The Princess on the Pea') in their 1843 edition, thinking it was a true folktale. Andersen much admired the Grimms and came to be on cordial terms with them. In the field of collection as distinct from invention, however, their outstanding European successor was Alexander Nicolaevich Afanasev (1826–71), who published between 1855 and 1864 what is still the basic collection of Russian folktales (*Narodnye Russkye Skazki*). This was a much larger collection than that of the Grimms, running to about six hundred tales, and only in quite few cases had Afanasev done the actual recording himself; but they are genuine Russian oral versions and variants, and in most cases the source is given in Afanasev's annotations. While looking upon the Grimm collection as his model, Afanasev allowed himself to be influenced much less than Wilhelm Grimm by considerations other than strict fidelity to his sources. He also arranged the Russian tales in a systematic classificatory manner, whereas the Grimms had deliberately avoided this. Comparison of individual tales from these two great collections remains a fascinating study. It is not possible here even to attempt to enumerate the many analogies of story and motif, but a few Afanasev titles may be mentioned as examples: 'Prince Ivan, the Firebird and the Grey Wolf' (closely similar to No. 19), 'Khroshechka-Khavroshechka' (No. 30), 'The Golden Slipper' and 'Chernushka' (No. 31), 'The Swineskin Cloak' (No. 32), 'The Golden Fish' (No. 1), 'The Flying Ship' (No. 22, with a related motif which appears in No. 27) and 'Dawn, Evening and Midnight' (combining leading motifs of Nos. 20 and 21). A one-volume selection of Afanasev tales has been published in English (Pantheon Books, 1945; reprinted by Sheldon Press, 1976).

The Afanasev collection was also the occasion for a notable theoretical breakthrough by the Russian scholar Vladimir Propp, whose short book *The Morphology of the Folktale* (1928) was little noticed at the time and not translated into English until thirty years later,* but can now be seen as a pioneering example of the 'structural' method of literary analysis. Propp took about a hundred of the Afanasev tales, all of them of the 'magic' type (*volshebnye skazki*), and by identifying a limited number of essential motifs abstracted from them a basic algebraic pattern or 'grammar' of this kind of narrative. The motifs he identified were all actions ('functions' as he called them) by characters in the story, these characters or agents being the small number of principal figures such as the Hero, the Enemy, the Helper ('Donor'), the Princess, the False Hero, etc. The basic 'functions' include a treacherous or hostile act by the Enemy (for example, a dragon carries off the Tsar's daughter); the Hero's departure from home, a prohibition imposed on him and violated by him, his encounter with the Helper who provides him (after he has passed some test) with a magic object or

* 1958; a second edition appeared in 1968 (University of Texas Press; reprinted 1975).

other such assistance; his victory over the Enemy; the pursuit and rescue of the Hero, his performance of a difficult task, his return home and exposure of the impostures of the False Hero, who is then punished; the Hero's marriage and enthronement. Propp found that in the Russian tales these functional motifs, or a selection of them, always occurred in a certain order, and that a fundamental invariant structure of such tales could thus be defined. A similar procedure could no doubt be applied to the Grimm tales.

Not unrelated to investigation of the structural grammar of *Zaubermärchen* are inquiries into their psychological grammar. The mystery inherent in such tales, which was perhaps first really appreciated by the Grimms, is not finally resolved and dispelled by any single method. This applies no less to the psychoanalytical approach, which sees the brothers' puzzled exploration of the variants and constants of the folktale as also a journey into yet another world of the past: that of the archaic psyche, the conscious and unconscious imaginative world of childhood fantasies, anxieties and conflicts which can still be powerfully present in the adult mind. We do not have the whole answer to the problem of the tales here either, but nor are they reducible, by Perrault or anyone else, to mere morally improving fables. From the psychoanalytical viewpoint, which Tolkien's essay (as well as being rather blasé about folklorism) ignores altogether, they are educative, but in a less simple sense. Tolkien states categorically of 'The Frog King' that 'the point of the story lies . . . in the necessity of keeping promises'. Clearly this is one of its points; but what does a frog, as such, have to do with keeping promises? As Freud argued nearly a century ago, the fact that I have eaten or drunk too much may answer the question 'Why did I have a dream?' but not the question 'Why did I have *this* dream?' The story is not simply that the young heroine unwillingly keeps a bizarre promise she has made and is then duly rewarded. It is that she is approached by a frog – a cold, clammy, 'horrid' creature which emerges from deep water at the edge of a dark forest; that the frog claims her promise to take it to bed with her, and that after she has overcome and expressed her repugnance she finds that what she has taken to bed with her is a handsome prince. Many might think that it makes more sense of more elements in the tale to see in this particular example of the 'animal bridegroom' motif the story, among other things no doubt, of an immature girl overcoming the disgust she has hitherto felt about 'nasty' male sexuality. Or again, it is perfectly possible and correct to read 'The Fisher an his Gweedwìfe' as a moral lesson about greed and pride coming before a fall; but in addition, particularly if we read it as the Grimms actually published it, with *Pissputt* meaning exactly what it says and not just 'ditch' or 'filthy hovel' or 'vinegar jug' or some other such bowdlerization, and if we consider the childhood associations of the idea of 'living in a piss-pot', and consider further the overpowering infantile (and adult-unconscious) desire to be omnipotent – to be God, not just 'lord of the sun and moon' as Edgar Taylor's version delicately puts it, but actually to be God, able to control everything including the passage of time – then we shall see that the story has other and psychologically important reverberations. The price of insatiable demands, of insistence on being God, is to remain a dirty little child. In the case of Little Red Ridinghood, it may be illuminating to remember the myth of Cronos, or Jonah and the whale, or the monstrous wolf Fenris of Norse mythology who swallows Odin, or the Latin story of the early-eleventh century in which a little girl with a red garment is found among wolves, or the age-old and widespread superstitions about wolves generally; but perhaps we should chiefly think not so much of these things as of a child's primitive fear of being attacked by a monstrous animal, of being swallowed up in darkness for ever ('Oh, how dark it was inside the wolf!'). Nor does Perrault's suggestion, made with a knowing wink to his adult audience, that the wolf is really a child-molester, come near to the centre of this story, which is not just an attempt to scare children into prudent behaviour but a symbolic fantasy which confronts, expresses and (in the Grimm ending at least) relieves a primitive anxiety. The 'great forest' or 'dark forest' which appears in nearly all these tales is as serious a place as the *selva oscura* of Dante in which he begins his spiritual ordeal. It is the forest into which one ventures out after

leaving home in one's quest for independence, but also the
forest in which one's parents leave one to starve or be 'torn to
pieces by the wild beasts', the forest in which one is lost.
'Hansel and Gretel' makes sense as an expression and relief of
one of the deepest of all human fears, that of parental desertion
and consequent starvation. The story is all about food: the
parents who can no longer afford to feed their children, who
have only a loaf of bread left, the mother who plans to abandon
them in the wood in order to 'be rid of them', the trail of crumbs
that fails to lead them home, the gingerbread house which they
eat and where they are fed on milk and apples and pancakes by
another maternal figure who then turns out to be an ogress,
fattens them for her own dinner and ends up baked in her own
oven; after which, with treasure found in the witch's house and
with their rejecting mother now dead, they can happily find the
way back to their father's house.

Some of these points and many others are developed in
Bruno Bettelheim's Freudian study of 'fairytales' (*The Uses of
Enchantment*, Thames and Hudson, 1976). This book has been
scathingly attacked from a Marxist angle by Jack Zipes (*Breaking
the Magic Spell: Radical Theories of Folk and Fairy Tales*,
Heinemann, 1979), who prefers to see Hansel and Gretel and
the witch as symbolizing the struggle of the peasant class
against the brutal gold-hoarding feudal aristocracy. Notwith-
standing which it is, despite presentational and conceptual
weaknesses, a fascinating compendium of interpretative possibilities, at least for anyone capable of taking psychoanalytical
interpretations seriously at all. Among the matters Bettelheim
discusses is of course that of the notoriously violent events
which occur in this world of 'once upon a time, when wishing
still worked'. It is hardly necessary to point out that violence is
characteristic of folktale and myth as such, and that these fantasies were not the Grimms' own or peculiarly German, as
some have naively supposed (in Basile's version of No. 10, for
instance, the stepmother is tricked into boiling her own
daughter to death; and even in Perrault the ogre cuts the throats
of his daughters, and the wicked queen perishes in a vat of
vipers and boiling oil). But the possibility that emerges more

clearly in the psychoanalytical perspective is that for the child, in whom violent impulses and guilt about them exist anyway, repeated encounters with such fictional events, so far from being frightening or disturbing, may be satisfying, guilt-relieving, reassuring and therapeutic. (A seven-year-old to whom a solicitous adult read 'Snowwhite' but censored its ending promptly complained about the omission of the bit about the red-hot slippers.) The point is not merely that the child recognizes the world of the stories to be one of make-believe anyway, but that he also recognizes them to be true, though in a displaced, symbolic way, even if he could not himself put into words the needs which they meet. In a secure world such as he needs to live in, justice must be seen to be done, and the gruesome folktale punishments are always meted out to symbolic 'evil' enemies. In changing Hansel and Gretel's and Snowwhite's mothers to their stepmothers in the later editions, the Grimms were following an instinctively wise convention. A stepmother is near enough to a real mother to represent her, but different enough from her to be hated with a good conscience. In this particular story the cruelly rejecting, food-withholding, undevourable and therefore potentially devouring mother seems also to be represented by the witch, who gets her satisfyingly appropriate deserts, just as the (step)mother also dies at the end. A characteristic feature of the tales is that the original 'all-good' real mother has died at the beginning (and is perhaps buried under a magic tree), her place being taken by her polar opposite, the all-bad 'step'-mother. (It is really not interesting to be told by Professor Zipes in this context that in feudal times mortality in childbirth was high and stepmothers therefore common.) Such polarized externalizations or splittings, simple oppositions of good and bad, are characteristic of this more primitive emotional world. It is also less to the point to say that the world of the tales is animistic, with talking animals and so forth (though of course it is), than to say that it contains Enemies (giants, dragons, wolves, enchanters or witches, the threatening sun and moon) and Helpers (foxes and other animals, little wise men, the 'kind' stars). The listener can recognize the giant or dragon as the male oedipal enemy from whom the 'princess' must be rescued, but who is safely distinct and distant from his real-life counterpart. The female oedipal pattern also interestingly connects at least three of the stories (Nos. 5, 6 and 7): the adolescent heroine's happy-ever-after meeting with the 'prince' is spitefully delayed by the enchantress who imprisons her in a tower, curses her to fall asleep at puberty for a hundred years, or strikes her into a state of suspended animation in a glass coffin. Sibling-rivals in both sexes of course also abound. Here too, the sisters are often distancingly changed into 'stepsisters'; curiously, the brothers do not seem to need to become stepbrothers, though sometimes they appear as travelling companions (as in No. 20). It is psychologically right that stories about any such enemies should end with just revenge being taken on them. Here again, the polarization of 'good' and 'bad' figures is important. Violent acts done to the former can be reassuringly undone: the decapitated brothers in No. 16 have their heads replaced and are healed by a magic herb; the little boy in No. 8, decapitated by his stepmother and mistakenly eaten by his father, is restored to life (evidently with the help of his original 'good' mother, who is buried under the juniper tree); but his cruel stepmother herself is smashed to pulp with a millstone, and similar ends befall other usurpers and impostors who kill or cheat or otherwise victimize the hero or heroine and thus wrongfully try to win the favour of the 'king', marry the 'prince' or 'princess', etc. The sense of justice is increased if the punishment is particularly fitting or is even the impostor's own invention (as when the treacherous companion in No. 36, who has caused the debasement of the heroine and the slaughter of her magic horse Falada, is in accordance with her own sugges-tion dragged to death by horses). The happy ending is not complete, the moral order not fully restored, until the enemy has been unmasked and punished. In No. 9 the murdered queen comes back to life, but her fawn-brother is not disen-chanted until the witch-stepmother has been burnt to ashes and the stepsister 'torn to pieces by the wild beasts' in the forest where the spell was first cast. It is an essential part of the happy ending of No. 31 ('Ashiepattle', alias 'Cinderella') that the

doves should expose the trickery of the stepsisters and peck out
their eyes. In Perrault's version, it may be more *bienséant* and
edifying that Cendrillon should end by forgiving her evil sisters
and setting them up next door to her palace with noble hus-
bands, but it is less emotionally realistic; the same applies, for
that matter, to the similar ending of Grimm No. 30 ('One-Eyes,
Two-Eyes and Three-Eyes') which is a Cinderella variant.

The Cinderella story, or rather the complex of Cinderella
stories to which No. 32 ('Manypelts') and No. 36 ('The
Goosegirl') must also be reckoned to belong, is a particularly
interesting example of a basic oedipal pattern. In its bare essen-
tials the story is that the heroine, originally loved and esteemed,
is debased and disguised as a lowly and dirty servant, but
eventually, after magically displaying herself in her true
beauty, is recognized by a token (slipper, ring, etc.) and exalted
to marriage with the prince. In the better-known variants the
debasement is due simply to the jealousy or envy of the stepmother and stepsisters, but it is notable that in Basile's 'The
Cinder Cat' ('La gatta cenerentola') the father is a prince,
widowed at first, whose love for his daughter is emphasized,
and that she herself murders her first stepmother on the advice
of her governess, who then becomes her second stepmother
and with the help of her own daughters continues the persecu-
tion of the Cinderella figure. In 'Manypelts' the heroine is again
entirely 'good', but her father, the widowed king, falls in love
with her and decides to marry her himself. To escape from this
would-be incestuous situation (which would make her her own
stepmother) the princess runs away in her self-debasing
animal-skin disguise and enters lowly service with another
king; the magic-display, recognition and exaltation sequence
then follows. The stepmother and stepsisters are absent from
this version, but there is a jealous 'false bride' in Nos. 34 and 35.
Other notable motifs in the complex of Cinderella variants are
that of the persecutory tasks set by the oedipal rival, and that of
the helpful role of the dead (pre-oedipal) mother. In No. 31
itself the stepmother sets the debased Ashiepattle impossible
fantastic tasks which can be performed only with magic help,
and the same thing happens in No. 33. These are, as it were,

female equivalents (compare Nos. 23 and 24) of the Oenomaos motif, that of the king who imposes tasks or riddles on his daughter's suitors, as in Nos. 22, 25, 26 and 27, as well as in 35 in which the Cinderella motif is also used. The original good and loving mother, associated with the magic tree, appears as we have already noticed in No. 8, helping the little boy. In 'Ashiepattle' the father, although playing a much reduced role, does at least bring the heroine the present she asks for, the twig which becomes the magic tree; she plants it on her mother's grave, waters it with her tears, and in the end its gifts enable her to meet the prince. A similar sequence occurs in Basile's version. In the Grimm variant No. 30, the debasing persecutors of Two-Eyes are her real mother and real sisters, but as she sits alone weeping a 'wise woman' appears to her and gives her magic help, including a magic animal and advice on how to plant a tree which bears silver leaves and golden fruit and leads to her exalted marriage. Here it is as if the Helper were the original good mother returning to contrast with the bad one, and it might indeed be said that the same 'splitting' procedure underlies Perrault's 'Cendrillon', where the 'fairy godmother' appears suddenly out of nowhere to help the heroine against the stepmother; but as usual his treatment of this motif lacks the poetic depth and primitive strangeness of the German versions.

The essential point which nearly all these examples illustrate is that according to the psychoanalytical view the 'magic story' with its 'imaginative satisfaction of ancient desires' (to adopt Tolkien's phrase) can perform for the still developing psyche, still torn by conflicts and ambivalences, a deeply relieving, *reassuring* function. Above all, the story's Happy Ending is the ultimate reassurance, the ultimate 'consolation' or 'eucatastrophe' as Tolkien called it. The hero or heroine, the *alter ego* with whom one can identify, succeeds in the end against rejection by those who should have provided love and security, against monstrous hostile figures and treacherous rivals; the anguish of desertion is overcome in the winning of an ideal partner; the 'stupid', belittled, outcast child ends by inheriting the kingdom (always a merely symbolic 'kingdom', presumably representing the achievement of adulthood and independence). One's own wrongs are righted in a way that looks like simple objective justice. One's wishes, whether loving or hostile, are externalized and validated. A mistake or 'bad' wish is not finally irreversible; spells can be lifted, damage done to children by rash curses (Nos. 14 and 40) can be healed and made good. Mysterious help is given – at least to the kind and the humble and the persevering. All this happens in a world which is both real and yet not real; the problem is radical, the passionate demands 'unrealistic', and no ordinary 'realistic' solution will do. There must be unexpected 'magic' help or grace; if there is none, then all hope abandon, ye who enter here.

The present selection of sixty-five tales amounts, in actual quantity of text, to a little under half that of the complete 200 (many of the others being very short). Forty of them are from the first edition, which contained most of the best ones anyway (twenty-two of these forty appeared in the 1812 volume and eighteen in that of 1815). Seventeen of the others were first published in the second edition (1819). In all cases, however, I have translated from the final 1857 text, as being the one generally accepted and readily available. As it happens, the text of most of the forty 'first edition' tales here included came through Wilhelm's hands to the last edition substantially unaltered, or revised only in minor details and often for the better; where this is not so or where the revision is of interest in some other way, it is mentioned in the Notes. The selection of the tales has been guided almost entirely by my own preferences, and at the risk of being slightly unrepresentative I have emphasized the 'magic' *Märchen* at the expense of the comic and nonsense pieces which abound in the complete canon; many of the latter in any case seemed to me to be impossible to translate plausibly, and/or simply unfunny. (It may be noted in passing that coarseness, though characteristic of the true comic folktale, was one of the things the Grimms filtered out of their renderings, and probably indeed most of their tale-tellers already eschewed it for their benefit.) The sequence and numbering are my own. The Grimms deliberately presented their tales in a non-order, like a random scatter of wild flowers, and there have

been attempts by later scholars (Von der Leyen, Aarne, Berend-
sohn) to classify and re-order them in a rational manner. Here I
have tried merely to arrange them in such a way as to draw
attention not so much to variety as to affinities and repetitions
of motif, so that the tales (at least if read consecutively) would to
a limited extent annotate themselves; that is to say, I have very
roughly, and so far as it seemed feasible, grouped them according to subject-matter. The selection itself reflects the same aim.
Seven or eight classical and famous stories come first, and this is
not really a group, though the links between Nos. 3 and 4 and
between Nos. 5, 6 and 7 have already been mentioned. Nos. 1, 2
and 8 seem to stand splendidly and almost unclassifiably on
their own, though Nos. 8 to 12 may be seen to be connected by
the motif of the hostile stepmother or stepsister. Between Nos.
13, 14 and 15 there is an obvious family resemblance, and the
curiously long and elaborate No. 16 shares with 17 the motif of
the false hero (impostor). Five 'pairs' of stories follow, each
displaying some analogy (Nos. 18 to 27). Nos. 28 and 29 have
little in common except the motif of the faithful servant, but
seemed too interesting to omit. Then comes the 'Cinderella' or
'true and false bride' group (Nos. 30 to 36). No. 37 is one which
the Grimms themselves described as a 'male Cinderella' variant
(see Note). This is followed by three 'animal bridegroom'
stories (Nos. 38 to 40), four about magic objects (Nos. 41 to 44),
two about amicably competitive brothers, two about specially
small or large heroes, and two about devil's bargains. Nos. 51
and 53 are miscellaneous tales with overlapping motifs, and
Nos. 54 to 58 are linked by the theme of the defeated enchanter
or enchantress. To end with, I have put in half a dozen samples
of the comic tale, one of which (No. 59) is very well known. As
to the translation itself, I have tried to bear in mind the notorious problems to which, for example, Mr Brian Alderson enter-
tainingly drew attention in a review a few years ago (*The Times*,
6 May 1978). As he pointed out, nearly all the English versions
from Edgar Taylor's (1823) onwards fail to achieve a correctly
voiced oral narrative style or an uncensored fidelity to the
German text (astonishing as this may seem when the Grimms
in fact left so little to censor). Both strictures apply to the first

complete English translation, that by Margaret Hunt, first published in 1884 and still available; the Routledge complete *Grimms' Fairy Tales* (first published 1948) is based on it, and although Margaret Hunt's text has been revised by James Stern and others and most of the bowdlerizations corrected, the English is still irremediably archaic and literary. In fact, the first really adequate complete translation into twentieth-century English has been that by Mr Ralph Manheim (*Grimms' Tales for Young and Old*, Gollancz, 1977) to which I am much indebted and to which those wishing to read the rest of the tales may confidently refer. I am also indebted to the brilliant rendering of thirty-three of the tales by Mr Alderson himself, which Gollancz issued in 1978 as an illustrated children's book. In his short selection Mr Alderson gave a regional English colouring to a few of the tales which the Grimms printed in Low German dialect, an idea which I thought worth following up (Mr Manheim's versions are all in standard, slightly American English). I was fortunate enough to be able to persuade my colleague Mr Gilbert McKay to make Scots translations of Nos. 1, 8, 12, 20, 35 and 54 (from Low German originals) and Mr Philip Schofield to put Nos. 27 and 65 (respectively in Swiss and Austrian dialects) into Irish. Mr McKay has used not a literary or eclectic confection but a genuine north-east-Lowland Scots still spoken in Banffshire, and Mr Schofield has also used a genuine Dublin idiom. A Scots glossary has been provided; an Irish one did not seem necessary. For much valuable help and advice in the matter of translation into Scots I must also warmly thank Dr David Murison and Mr Robin Lorimer.

1

THE FISHER AN HIS GWEEDWÌFE

Eence there wiz a fisher an his gweedwìfe an they dwallt thegither in a chantiepot doon bi the sea. Daily-day the fisher he gaed doon wi's rod an's line tae tak fesh; an he fesht an he fesht.

Ae day he wiz sittin there on's doup, caain's line and lookin doon intae the clear watter; an he sat an he sat. Aa at eence his hyuik dyv't deep doon; an fan he heest it up, fit did he heist up but a great muckle fleuk. The fleuk said: 'Harken tae me, fisher, will ye nae lat me live? I'm nae a richt fleuk avà, fit I am is a *glamourt prince. Fit eese wid it be tae you tae kell me? I doot ye windnae fancy me onywey. Pit me back in the watter an lat me sweem awà.' 'Aweel,' said the fisher, 'ye neednae lay doon a lang lagàmachy tae me; a speakin fleuk's ae fish I'll aye lat sweem awà.' An he pat him back in the clear watter again, an the fleuk dyv't doon tae the boddam an left a lang strype o bleed ahin im. Syne the fisher steed up an gaed back tae his gweed-wìfe in the chantiepot.

'Gweedmàn,' said she, 'haev ye nae teen naethin the day?' 'No,' said he, 'I took a fleuk that said he wiz a glamourt prince, so I lat im sweem awà.' 'An did ye nae wesh a wesh?' said the gweedwìfe. 'Na,' said the gweedmàn, 'fit-for wid I wesh a wesh?' 'Weel,' said the gweedwìfe, 'it's nae verra fine bydin here in a stinkin scunnersome chantiepot. Ye could hae wesht for a wee chaumer for's. Gang an cry till im; tell im we're seekin a wee chaumer. I's warran he'll gie's't.' 'Ach,' said the gweed-màn, 'fit-for shaed I gae back there?' 'Weel, efter aa,' said the gweedwìfe, 'ye took im, an ye lat im sweem awà again. He'll gie's't. Awa ye gang, noo!' The gweedmàn wiz a bittie sweir at first, but he didnae wint tae conter his gweedwìfe aether, an aff he gaed tae the seashore.

Fan he got till't, the sea wiz aa green an yalla, nae sae clear as it wiz afore. Sae he steed up an said:

'Mannie, mannie, meenie mee,
Fleukie, fleukie in the sea,
My gweedwifie Izybell
Seeks fit I waednae seek mysèl.'

Syne the fleuk cam sweemin up an said: 'Weel, fit's she seekin?'
'Och,' said the gweedmàn, 'I haed ye teen, ye ken, an my
gweedwìfe says I ocht tae hae wesht a wesh. She'll nae byde in
the chantiepot ony mair, she's seekin a chaumer.' 'Ye gae
hame,' said the fleuk, 'she haes't already.'

Syne the gweedmàn gaed hame, an his wife wiznae sittin in
the chantiepot noo, but there wiz a wee chaumer stannin there,
an his gweedwìfe wiz sittin afore't on a seat. An his gweedwìfe
took him bi the haan an said till im: 'Come awà ben, see noo,
that's mair like it, is't nae?' Sae in they gaed, an inside the
chaumer there wiz a wee trance an a grand wee room an a
bedroom wi their bed in't, an a kitchie an a pantry, aa furnisht
wi pans as braa's ye like, pewter an braess, aathing needfae. An
oot at the back there wiz a yairdie wi hens an deuks an a wee
gairden wi kail an berry-busses. 'See, noo,' said the gweedwìfe,
'is that nae grand?' 'Aye,' said the gweedmàn, 'that'll dee us
braalies, we'll live weel contentit noo.' 'Maybe,' said the
gweedwìfe. 'We'll tak thocht aboot it.' Syne they took their
supper an gaed tae their bed.

Weel, that gaed on for a week or a fortnicht, an syne the
gweedwìfe said: 'Harken tae me, gweedmàn, oor chaumer's far
ower wee, an the yairdie an the gairden is aafa smaa. The fleuk
micht hae gien's a bigger hoose. I'm seekin tae byde in a great
steen castle.' 'Och, gweedwìfe,' said the gweedmàn, 'the
chaumer's gweed aneuch, fit-for waed we wint tae byde in a
castle?' 'Hoot awà,' said the gweedwìfe, 'awà ye gang, the
fleuk can easy dee't.' 'Noo, noo, gweedwìfe,' said the gweedmàn, 'the fleuk haes jist gien's this chaumer. I dinna wint tae
come seekin again, maybe the fleuk'll be ill-pleast.' 'Awà ye
gang,' said the gweedwìfe, 'he can dee't aa richt an he winna
say no; awà wi ye.' The gweedmàn wiz sweir an his hairt wiz
heavy. He thocht till imsèl: 'It's nae richt avà,' but he gaed for aa
that.

Fan he cam till the seashore, the watter wiz aa vylet an dark blue an grey an thick, nae green an yalla noo, but it wiz still quaet. Sae he steed up an said:

> 'Mannie, mannie, meenie mee,
> Fleukie, fleukie in the sea,
> My gweedwifie Izybell
> Seeks fit I waednae seek mysèl.'

'Weel, fit's she seekin?' said the fleuk. 'Och,' said the gweed-màn, 'she's seekin tae byde in a great steen castle.' 'Ye gae hame, she's stannin at the door o't,' said the fleuk. So the gweedmàn gaed awà, thinkin tae gae hame, but fan he got there, there wiz a muckle great steen pailace stannin there, an his gweedwìfe steed on the steps jist gyan in, an she took im bi the haan an said: 'Come awà ben.' Syne in he gaed wi er, an in the castle there wiz a great entrance-ha' wi a mairble fleer, an a wheen of sairvants tae open the muckle doors, an the waas aa shinin an wi tappasteries on them, an in the rooms aa gowden chears an tables, an crystal candelabrums wiz hingin fae the reef an aa the rooms an chaumbers wiz covert wi cairpets; an there wiz mait an the finest wines stannin on the tables ready for them. An oot at the back o the castle there wiz a great yaird wi stables an byres an the grannest coaches ye iver saa, an a muckle gran' gairden wi the bonniest flooers an fine trees an a park a half-mile lang wi reid deer an rae deer an hares an aathing ye could fancy. 'Weel, noo,' said the gweedwìfe, 'is that nae gran'?' 'O aye,' said the gweedmàn, 'that'll dee us braalies, noo we'll byde in the great castle an we'll be contentit.' 'Maybe,' said the gweedwìfe. 'We'll tak thocht aboot it an sleep on't.' An syne they gaed tae their bed.

The next mornin the gweedwìfe she waukent first; it wiz the first blink o licht an fae their bed she saa the bonny country spread oot afore them. The gweedmàn he wiz still sleepin, sae she powkit him in the side wi er elback an said: 'Gweedmàn, rise up an look oot o the windae. Can we nae be the king ower aa this lan'?' 'Och, gweedwìfe,' said the gweedmàn, 'fit-for waed we be seekin tae be the king? I haev nae wesh tae be the king.' 'Weel,' said the gweedwìfe, 'if ye've nae wesh tae be the king, I

haev.' 'Och, gweedwìfe,' said the gweedmàn, 'fit-for are ye
seekin tae be the king? I canna say that till im.' 'Fit-for nae?' said
the gweedwìfe. 'Gang stracht till im, an say that I'm seekin tae
be the king.' Sae the gweedmàn gaed awà rael dooncast that his
gweedwìfe wiz seekin tae be the king. 'That's nae richt, nae
richt avà,' thocht the gweedmàn. He didnae wint tae gyang, but
he gaed for aa that.

An fan he cam tae the seashore, the sea wiz grey-black, an
bylin up fae the boddam an stinkin like tae scunner a body. Sae
he steed up an said:

> 'Mannie, mannie, meenie mee,
> Fleukie, fleukie in the sea,
> My gweedwifie Izybell
> Seeks fit I waednae seek mysèl.'

Syne the fleuk cam sweemin up an said: 'Weel, fit's she seekin?'
'Och,' said the gweedmàn, 'she's seekin tae be the king.' 'Ye
gae hame, she's the king already,' said the fleuk.

Sae the gweedmàn gaed awà, an fan he cam near tae the
pailace, the castle haed groun far bigger, wi a muckle great tooer
wi orniments on't, an there wiz a wheen of sodgers an drums an
trumpets. An fan he cam intae the hoose, aathing wiz mairble
an gowd an velvet coverins an muckle gowden tossels. Syne the
doors of the chaumber opint an the hale coort wiz there, an his
gweedwìfe sat on a heich throne o gowd an diamints wi a
muckle gowden croon on an a sceptre in her haan o pure gowd
an jewels, an at her side sax maidens in twa raws, ilka een a heid
smaaer nor her neebor. An he steed still an said: 'O gweedwìfe,
are ye the king noo?' 'Aye,' said the gweedwìfe, 'I'm the king
noo.' An he cam an lookit at her, an fan he haed lookit at her for
a fylie he said: 'O gweedwìfe, is't nae a gran' thing tae be the
king! An noo we winna wesh ony mair weshes.' 'Na, gweedmàn,' said the gweedwìfe, an she grew richt gurly, 'I think
*lang, I canna be deein wi't ony mair. Gyang tae the fleuk, tell
im that I'm the King an I'm seekin tae be the Emperor.' 'Och,
gweedwìfe,' said the gweedmàn, 'he canna mak ye the
emperor. I canna say that tae the fleuk. There's nae but ae
emperor in the lan'. The fleuk canna mak an emperor, he jist

canna.' 'Fit's that?' said the gweedwìfe, 'I'm the King, an ye're
my man, will ye gang there this verra meenit? Awà ye gang, if
he can mak kings he can mak emperors, an I'll be the Emperor,
that I will! Awà wi ye!' Sae he haed tae gyang. But fan the
gweedmàn wiz gyan, he wiz feart, an as he wiz walkin he
thocht till imsèl: 'Nae gweed'll come o't; tae seek tae be the
Emperor is impident, the fleuk'll grou tỳert bi the end o't.' Syne
he cam tae the seashore, an the sea wiz still black an thick an
began tae byle up fae the boddam, an bubbles blew up on't an a
gale blew ower't an gart it rage. An the gweedmàn wiz feart. An
he steed up an said:

> 'Mannie, mannie, meenie mee,
> Fleukie, fleukie in the sea,
> My gweedwifie Izybell
> Seeks fit I waednae seek mysèl.'

'Weel, fit's she seekin?' said the fleuk. 'Och, fleuk,' said he,
'my gweedwìfe is seekin tae be the Emperor.' 'Ye gae hame,'
said the fleuk, 'she's the Emperor already.'

Sae the gweedmàn he cam awà, an fan he cam hame, the hale
castle wiz o polisht mairble wi alabaster statues an gowden
orniments on't. Afore't there wiz sodgers mairchin, blaain
trumpets an beatin drums. But in the castle there wiz barons an
lords an dukes gyan aboot as sairvints, an they opint the doors
till im, an the doors wiz o pure gowd. An fan he cam ben, there
sat his gweedwìfe on a throne made o ae lump o gowd twa mile
heich; an she had a muckle gowden croon on three ells heich an
covert wi diamints an rubies; in ae haan she held the sceptre an
in the tither the orb o the empire, an at baith her sides steed
flunkeys in twa raas ilka een smaaer nor his neebor, fae the
biggest giant twa mile heich tae the weeest dwarfie the size o my
*cranny. An afore her steed a great wheen o princes an dukes.
An the gweedmàn steed amang them an said: 'Gweedwìfe, are
ye the Emperor noo?' 'Aye,' she said, 'I'm the Emperor noo.'
An he steed still an lookit at her close, an fan he'd lookit for a
fylie he said: 'O gweedwìfe, fit a gran' thing it is tae be the
Emperor!' 'Gweedmàn,' said she, 'fit-for are ye stannin there?
I'm the Emperor noo, but I'm seekin tae be the Pope tee, gyang

tae the fleuk.' 'Och, gweedwìfe,' saîd the gweedmàn, 'fit wid
ye nae seek tae be? Ye canna be the Pope, there's nae but ae
pope in Christendom, an he canna mak ye that.' 'Gweedmàn,'
said the gweedwìfe, 'I'm seekin tae be the Pope, awà ye gang,
for I maun be the Pope this day!' 'Na, na, gweedwìfe,' said the
gweedmàn, 'I canna say that till im, that's vrang, that's ower
great, the fleuk canna mak a pope.' 'Gweedmàn, stop haiverin,'
said the gweedwìfe. 'If he can mak an emperor he can mak a
pope. Awà ye gang this meenit. I'm the Emperor an I'm seekin
tae be the Pope, awà ye gang, I say!' An he wiz feart an gaed
awà, but he wiz nearly in a dwam, shakkin like a leaf an his
knees knockin thegither. An a ween blew ower the lan' an the
clouds wiz fleein an the nicht wiz grouin mirk. The leafs wiz
wheepin aff the trees an the watter wiz roarin like it wiz bylin
ower, an comin thrashin on tae the shore, an hine aff he could
see the ships plungin aboot in their peril an loupin up an doon
in the waves. There wiz still a nairra strype of blue in the lift, but
at the sides it wiz aa reid wi a storm brouwin up. An he steed up
wi his hairt full o fear an said:

> 'Mannie, mannie, meenie mee,
> Fleukie, fleukie in the sea,
> My gweedwifie Izybell
> Seeks fit I waednae seek mysèl.'

'Weel, fit's she seekin?' said the fleuk. 'Och,' said the gweedmàn, 'she's seekin tae be the Pope.' 'Ye gae hame, she's the
Pope already;' said the fleuk.

Sae he gaed hame, an fan he got till't, it wiz like a great kirk wi
pailaces aa roon't. He haed tae tyaav tae get throu all the fowk,
an inside it wiz aa bricht wi thoosans an thoosans o lichts, an his
gweedwìfe wiz dresst in pure gowd on a far heicher throne an
she haed three muckle gowden croons on, an aa roon aboot her
a wheen o ministers o the kirk, an at her side there wiz twa raas
o lichts as thick an as heich as the biggest tooer ye ever saa, doon
tae the weeest little cannel; an aa the emperors an kings they
war doon on their knees afore her an kissin the tae o her slipper.
'Gweedwìfe,' said the gweedmàn, an lookit at her close, 'are ye
the Pope noo?' 'Aye,' said she, 'I'm the Pope.' An he steed an

lookit close at her, an it wiz like lookin stracht intae the bricht saen. Fan he haed lookit at her for a fylie, he said: 'O gweedwìfe, fit a gran' thing it is tae be the Pope.' But she sat as stiff as a byuird an moovit naither haan nor limb. An he said, 'Gweedwìfe, be contentit noo that ye're the Pope, ye canna be mair nor that.' 'Maybe,' said the gweedwìfe, 'I'll tak thocht aboot it.' Wi that they gaed tae their bed, but she wiznae contentit an she couldnae sleep for greed an aye she thocht fit else she micht be yet.

The gweedmàn sleepit *soon' an hairty, he haed come a lang wey that day, but the gweedwìfe couldnae close her een, she gaed fae ae side tae the tither the hale nicht lang, thinkin an thinkin fit else she micht be, but she couldnae think o onything. Syne the saen began tae rise, an fan she saa the first blink o licht she sait stracht up in her bed an lookit at it; an fan she lookit oot o the windae an saa the saen comin up, Aye, noo, thocht she, can I nae gar the saen an the meen rise? 'Gweedmàn,' she said an powkit im in the ribs wi er elback, 'waaken, gyang tae the fleuk, I'm seekin tae be like God imsèl.' The gweedmàn wiz still half dozint, but he got sic a bring-up that he fell oot o the bed. He thocht he had misheert er an opint his een an said: 'Gweedwìfe, fit's that ye said?' 'Gweedmàn,' said she, 'gin I canna gar the saen an the meen rise an yet haev tae see the saen an the meen risin, I canna be deein wi that an I'll never hae a weel day till I can gar them rise mysèl.' An she gied im sic a fearsome look that a shiver cam ower im. 'Awà ye gyang this meenit, I'm seekin tae be like God imsèl.' 'O gweedwìfe,' said the gweedmàn, an gaed doon on's knees afore er, 'the fleuk canna dae that. He can mak emperors an popes; I'm priggin wi ye, think fit ye're deein an byde at bein the Pope.' Syne she gaed till an aafa heicht, her hair flew aboot er heid, she tore at her sark an kickit im an skreichit oot o er: 'I winna be deein wi't, I winna be deein wi't ony mair, awà ye gang!' Sae he pat on his breeks an ran awà like he wiz dementit.

Ootside there wiz a storm ragin, an sic a ween blaain he could hardly stan on's feet; the hooses an the trees wiz faain aboot im an the hills wiz shakkin an rocks wiz rouwin intae the sea an the lift wiz as black as pick an it wiz thunnerin an lichtnin; an the sea wiz gyan wi muckle waves as big as kirk doors an mountains, ilka een wi a fite croon o foam on the tap o't. Sae he skirlt oot o im, an he couldnae hear imsèl skirlin:

> 'Mannie, mannie, meenie mee,
> Fleukie, fleukie in the sea,
> My gweedwifie Izybell
> Seeks fit I waednae seek mysèl.'

'Weel, fit's she seekin?' said the fleuk. 'Och,' said he, 'she's seekin tae be like God imsèl.' 'Ye gae hame, she's sittin in the chantiepot again.'

An there they sit till this verra day.

2

RUMPLESTILTSKIN

Once upon a time there was a miller; he was poor, but he had a beautiful daughter. Now it happened one day that he was talking to the king, and just to impress him he said: 'I have a daughter who can spin straw into gold.' The king said to the miller: 'That's an art I like the sound of; if your daughter is as skilful as you say, bring her to my palace tomorrow and I'll see what she can do.' So when the girl was brought to him he took her to a room that was piled high with straw, gave her a spinning wheel and said: 'Now set to work; you can work all night till early tomorrow morning, and if by then you haven't spun all this straw into gold you shall die.' So saying, he locked the door of the room himself and she was left there alone.

So there the poor miller's daughter sat and couldn't for the life of her think what to do. She had no idea how to spin straw into gold, and she got more and more scared and finally began to cry. But then suddenly the door opened and a funny little man came in and said: 'Good evening, Miss Miller, what are all those tears about?' 'Oh dear,' replied the girl, 'I'm to spin straw into gold and I don't know how to do it.' The little man said: 'What will you give me if I spin it for you?' 'My necklace,' said the girl. The little man took her necklace and sat down at the spinning-wheel; and whirr, whirr, whirr, round it went three times, and the bobbin was full. Then he put on another, and whirr, whirr, whirr, round it went three times, and the second bobbin was full. And so it went on until morning, by which time all the straw had been spun away and all the bobbins were loaded with gold. The moment the sun rose the king turned up, and when he saw the gold he was amazed and delighted, but the greed for it merely grew in his heart. He had the miller's daughter taken to another room full of straw, much bigger than the first, and ordered her to spin this lot too in one night if she valued her life. The girl didn't know what to do and cried, and

for the second time the door opened and the little man appeared
and said: 'What will you give me if I spin this straw into gold for
you?' 'The ring from my finger,' answered the girl. The little
man took the ring, set the wheel whirring again, and by morning he had spun all the straw into glittering gold. The king was
overjoyed to see it, but his appetite for gold wasn't sated yet. He
had the miller's daughter taken to a still bigger room full of
straw and said: 'You must spin this lot too by tomorrow morning – but if you succeed, you shall be my wife.' She may only be
a miller's daughter, he thought, but I'll not find a richer wife in
this world. When the girl was alone, the mannikin came for the
third time and said: 'What will you give me if I spin the straw for
you this time as well?' 'I've nothing left to give you,' answered
the girl. 'Then promise me that when you are queen I shall have
your first child.' Who knows how that'll turn out, thought the
miller's daughter; and besides, she could think of no other way
out of the trouble she was in. So she promised the little man
what he had asked for, and in return he spun the straw into gold
once more. And when the king came in the morning and found
everything as he had wished, he married her, and the beautiful
miller's daughter became a queen.

A year later she had a lovely baby and had forgotten all about
the little man, when suddenly he appeared in her bedroom and
said: 'Now give me what you promised.' The queen was terrified and offered the little man every treasure in the kingdom if
only he would let her keep her child. But the little man said:
'No, a living thing is more valuable to me than all the riches in
the world.' At this the queen began to weep and lament so
desperately that the little man took pity on her and said: 'I'll
give you three days: if by the end of that time you can tell me my
name, you shall keep your child.'

Then the queen lay awake all night thinking of all the names
she had ever heard, and she sent out a messenger with orders to
inquire far and wide all over the country what other names
existed. Next day, when the little man came, she began with
Caspar and Melchior and Balthazar, and recited all the names
she knew one after another, but to every one the mannikin
replied: 'That's not my name.' On the second day she had

inquiries made in the neighbourhood about the names of the
local people, and recited the oddest and most unusual names to
the little man, asking: 'Could it be Twizzlebotham or Hirpleton-
thwaite or Screwthorpe?' But every time he answered: 'That's
not my name.' On the third day the messenger came back and
reported: 'I haven't been able to find a single new name, but at
the corner of the forest I came to a high hill, a place right at the
back of beyond, and there I saw a little house, and there was a
fire burning outside the house, and round the fire the most
ridiculous little man you ever saw was dancing and hopping
about on one foot and shrieking:

'Today I've been baking, tomorrow I'll be brewing,
Next day fetch the baby prince, that's what I'll be doing.
Tee hee, ha ha, isn't it a shame
That none of them can guess Rumplestiltskin's name!'

You can imagine how glad the queen was to hear this. And
when presently the little mannikin appeared and said: 'Well,
my lady queen, and what's my name?' she first asked: 'Is it
Bert?' 'No.' 'Is it Sid?' 'No.' 'Is by any chance Rumplestiltskin
your name?' 'The devil told you, the devil told you!' screamed
the little man, and he flew into such a rage and stamped his
right foot so hard that he drove his whole leg and thigh right
into the ground; then in his fury he seized his left foot with both
hands and tore himself in two right down the middle.

3

HANSEL AND GRETEL

At the edge of a big forest there lived a poor woodcutter with his wife and his two children; the little boy's name was Hansel and the girl's was Gretel. He had precious little to fill his belly, and once when there was a bad famine in the land he could no longer even get bread from one day to the next. At night he lay in bed worrying, and he tossed and turned and sighed and said to his wife: 'What's to become of us? How can we feed our poor children when we've nothing left for ourselves?' 'I'll tell you what, husband,' answered his wife. 'Tomorrow first thing we'll take the children into the forest, into the very thick of it – we'll make a fire for them and give them each one more piece of bread, then we'll go about our work and leave them by themselves. They won't find the way back home and we'll be rid of them.' 'No, wife,' said her husband, 'I'll not do that; how could I have the heart to leave my children alone in the forest? The wild beasts would soon come and tear them to pieces.' 'Oh you fool,' she said, 'then all four of us will have to starve; you may as well begin planing the boards for our coffins.' And she would give him no peace till he consented. 'But I'm sorry for the poor children all the same,' said the man.

The two children were so hungry that they hadn't been able to get to sleep either, and had heard what their stepmother had said to their father. Gretel cried bitterly and said to Hansel: 'Now we're done for.' 'Hush, Gretel,' said Hansel, 'don't be sad, I'll soon find a way.' And when their parents had gone to sleep he got up, pulled on his coat, opened the back door and crept out. There was bright moonlight, and the white pebbles outside the house shone like so many little silver coins. Hansel bent down and filled his coat pockets with as many as would go into them. Then he went in again and said to Gretel: 'Don't worry, little sister, you can go to sleep now, God won't forsake us.' And he got back into bed.

At daybreak, before it was even sunrise, the woman came and woke the two children: 'Get up, you idle brats, we're going into the forest to fetch wood.' Then she gave each of them a piece of bread and said: 'There's something for your lunch, but don't eat it before then because you'll get nothing else.' Gretel put the bread under her apron, because Hansel had the stones in his pockets. Then they all set out together along the path to the forest. When they had been walking for a little, Hansel stopped and looked back towards the house, and he kept on doing this. His father said: 'Hansel, what are you lagging behind for and looking at? Watch what you're doing and get a move on.' 'Oh, father,' said Hansel, 'I'm looking at my white kitten, it's sitting up there on the roof and wants to say goodbye to me.' The woman said: 'You silly boy, that's not your kitten, it's the light of the morning sun on the chimney.' But Hansel hadn't been looking at the kitten; each time he had been throwing one of the shining pebbles in his pocket on to the path.

When they had reached the middle of the forest, their father said: 'Now, you children, gather some wood, I'll make a fire so you won't freeze.' Hansel and Gretel collected firewood and made quite a little pile of it. It was set alight, and when the flames were burning high the woman said: 'Now lie down by the fire, children, and have a rest. We're going into the forest to chop wood. When we're done, we'll come back and fetch you.'

Hansel and Gretel sat by the fire, and at midday they ate their pieces of bread. And hearing the blows of a woodcutter's axe, they thought their father was nearby. But it wasn't the axe, it was a branch he had tied to a withered tree and the wind was blowing it to and fro. And when they had been sitting and sitting, their eyes dropped shut with weariness and they fell fast asleep. When they finally woke up, it was already pitch dark. Gretel began to cry and said: 'How shall we find the way out of the forest!' But Hansel comforted her: 'Just wait a little till the moon rises, then we'll find the way all right.' And when the full moon had risen, Hansel took his little sister by the hand and followed the pebbles; they glistened like new silver sixpences and showed them the way. They walked all through the night and got back to their father's house at daybreak. They knocked

at the door, and when the woman opened it and saw it was
Hansel and Gretel she said: 'You naughty children, why did
you sleep so long in the forest, we thought you would never
come back.' But their father was glad, for he had been heartsore
at having left them behind all by themselves.

Not long after that times got very hard again everywhere, and
at night the children heard their mother saying to their father in
bed: 'Everything's been eaten up again, we've just got half a
loaf of bread left and then that'll be the end of the story. The
children must go, we'll take them deeper into the forest so they
won't be able to find the way out again; it's our only way of
saving ourselves.' The man's heart grew heavy and he thought:
It would be better to share the last bite with your children. But
his wife would not listen to anything he said; she scolded
him and reproached him. Take one step and you must take the
next; and because he had given in the first time, he had to do
so again.

But the children had been still awake and had heard the
conversation. When their parents were asleep, Hansel got up
again and tried to get out to collect pebbles like the last time, but
the woman had locked the door and Hansel couldn't get out.
But he comforted his little sister and said: 'Don't cry, Gretel,
just go to sleep, God will help us.'

Early in the morning the woman came and fetched the children out of bed. They were given their pieces of bread, but they
were even smaller pieces than before. On the way to the forest
Hansel crumbled it in his pocket, and kept stopping to throw a
crumb on the ground. 'Hansel, why are you stopping and
looking behind you?' said his father. 'Keep on walking.' 'I'm
looking back at my little dove. It's sitting on the roof and wants
to say goodbye to me,' answered Hansel. 'You silly boy,' said
the woman, 'that's not your dove, that's the morning sunlight
on the chimney up there.' But little by little Hansel dropped all
the crumbs on the path.

The woman led the children still deeper into the forest, to
where they had never yet been in their lives. A big fire was lit
again, and their mother said: 'Just you sit here and wait, children, and if you're tired you can sleep a little – we're going into

the forest to chop wood, and in the evening when we're done
we'll come and fetch you.' At midday Gretel shared her bread
with Hansel, who had scattered his piece on the path. Then
they fell asleep, and the evening passed, but no one came to
fetch the poor children. They didn't wake up till it was pitch
dark, and Hansel comforted his little sister and said: 'Just wait,
Gretel, till the moon rises, then we'll see the breadcrumbs I
dropped; they'll show us the way home.' When the moon came
they set out, but they didn't find any breadcrumbs, because all
the thousands of birds that fly about in the forest and over the
fields had pecked them away and eaten them. Hansel said to
Gretel: 'Never mind, we'll find the way,' but they didn't find it.
They walked all night and all next day from morning till evening, but they still hadn't got out of the forest, and they were ever
so hungry, for they had nothing to eat but the few berries that
grew on the ground. They were so tired that their legs wouldn't
carry them any further, so they lay down under a tree and fell
asleep.

It was the third morning now since they had left their father.
They started to walk again, but only got deeper and deeper into
the forest, and knew that unless help reached them soon they
would die of hunger. When it was midday they saw a lovely
snow-white bird sitting on a branch, and it sang so beautifully
that they stopped to listen to it. And when it had finished its
song, it flapped its wings and flew along in front of them, and
they followed it till they came to a little house, where it perched
on the roof. And when they came right up to it, they saw that
the little house had walls made of bread and a roof made of cake
and windows made of clear bright sugar. 'Well, here's something for us,' said Hansel, 'and God bless this food to do us
good. I'll eat a slice of the roof, Gretel, and you can start on the
window; it'll taste sweet enough.' Hansel reached out and
broke off a bit of the roof to try how it tasted, and Gretel stood
by the window-panes and nibbled at them. It was then that they
heard a thin little voice calling out to them from the parlour:

> 'Nibble nibble, little rat,
> It's my house you're nibbling at.'

The children answered:

> 'We're the wind, we're the breeze
> That plays in the trees'

and just went on steadily eating. Hansel, who was enjoying the
roof very much, pulled off a big slab of it, and Gretel bashed out
a whole round window-pane and sat down and had a real treat.
Then suddenly the door opened and an aged crone, bent
double on a crutch, came creeping out. Hansel and Gretel were
so scared that they dropped what they had in their hands. But
the old woman wagged her head and said: 'Why, you nice little
things, how did you get here? Come in and stay with me, you'll
come to no harm.' She took them both by the hand and led them
into her little house. Then she set a fine meal before them, milk
and pancakes with sugar and apples and nuts. Afterwards she
made up two lovely little beds with white linen, and Hansel and
Gretel lay down in them and thought they must be in heaven.

But the old woman had only been pretending to be kind, for
in fact she was an evil witch who lay in wait for children and had
only built the little bread house to lure them her way. When a
child fell into her power she would kill it, cook it and eat it, and
that was a day of feasting for her. Witches have red eyes and
can't see far, but they have a keen sense of smell like animals
and notice when people come anywhere near. As Hansel and
Gretel approached, she laughed a wicked laugh and said mockingly: 'Here's two for me who shan't escape.' Early next morning before the children were awake she was already on her feet,
and as she looked down at them sleeping so sweetly, with their
full rosy cheeks, she muttered to herself: 'This will make a tasty
morsel.' Then she seized Hansel with her bony hand and carried him off to a little shed and locked him up behind a door
with iron bars; he screamed his head off but it did him no good.
Then she went to Gretel, shook her awake and shouted: 'Get
up, you idle hussy, fetch water and cook something good for
your brother; he's sitting out there in the shed and I want him
made plump. When he's plump I mean to eat him.' Gretel
began to cry bitterly, but it was all in vain and she had to do as
the wicked witch told her.

Now the best meals were cooked for poor Hansel, but Gretel got nothing but crabshells. Every morning the old woman crept out to the little shed and shouted: 'Hansel, stick out your finger for me to feel whether you're getting plump.' But Hansel held out a little bone to her, and the old woman, who had weak eyes, couldn't see it and thought it was Hansel's finger, and was amazed that he went on and on not getting plump. When four weeks were up and Hansel was still skinny, she lost patience and refused to wait any longer. 'Now then, Gretel!' she shouted to the little girl, 'look alive and fetch water – tomorrow, whether he's plump or whether he's skinny, I'm going to cut Hansel's throat and cook him.' Oh, how his poor little sister wailed as she was forced to carry the water, and how the tears poured down her cheeks! 'Please, God, help us!' she cried. 'If only the wild beasts had eaten us in the forest, then at least we'd have died together.' 'You can stop all that bawling,' said the old woman, 'it'll do you no good.'

Early next morning Gretel had to go out and hang up a cauldron full of water and light the fire. 'We'll bake first,' said the old woman. 'I've heated the oven already and kneaded the dough.' She drove poor Gretel out to where the oven was, and flames were licking out of it already. 'Crawl inside,' said the witch, 'and tell me whether it's properly heated, then we can shove in the bread.' And her plan was to shut the oven door when Gretel was inside, so she could roast Gretel, and then she would eat her too. But Gretel guessed what she was up to, and said: 'I don't know how to do it; how can I get in there?' 'You silly goose,' said the old woman, 'the opening's big enough, don't you see, I could get in there myself.' And she came hobbling up and stuck her head inside the oven. Then Gretel gave her a push so that she fell in, right into the middle; and she slammed the iron door shut and bolted it. Wow! The old woman began to howl, it was quite horrible; but Gretel ran off, and the godless witch burned miserably to death.

But Gretel ran straight to Hansel, opened his shed and shouted: 'Hansel, we're saved, the old witch is dead.' And Hansel hopped out as a bird does when the door of its cage is opened. How glad they were, how they danced around and hugged and kissed each other! And now that there was nothing more to fear, they went into the witch's house and found cupboards all over it full of pearls and precious stones. 'These are even better than pebbles,' said Hansel, and filled his pockets with as much as would go into them, and Gretel said: 'I'll take some home too,' and filled her apron full. 'But now let's go,' said Hansel, 'if we're to get out of this witchy forest.' When they had walked for a couple of hours, they came to a big wide river. 'We can't get across,' said Hansel, 'I don't see any bridge.' 'And there's no boat either,' answered Gretel, 'but there's a white duck swimming along; if I ask it, it'll help us across.' And she called out:

> 'Little duck, little white duck,
> Gretel and Hansel are stuck.
> No bridge, no way to get over,
> Except your back, if you'll do us the favour.'

Sure enough the duck came swimming towards them, and Hansel sat down on its back and told his sister to sit behind him. 'No,' answered Gretel, 'that'll be too heavy for the duck, it shall take us across one at a time.' The kind little bird did so, and when they were safely on the other side and had walked on for a little, they seemed to recognize more and more of the forest, and finally they saw their father's house in the distance. Then they began to run, rushed into the parlour and flung their arms round their father's neck. The man had not had one happy hour since he had left the children in the forest, but his wife had died. Gretel shook out the contents of her apron, making the pearls and precious stones dance about on the floor, and Hansel threw down handful after handful of them out of his pockets. Now all their troubles were at an end, and they lived on together and were ever so happy. So that was that; look! there runs a rat, who'll catch it and skin it and make a fur hat?

4

LITTLE REDCAPE

There was once a sweet little girl who was loved by everyone who so much as looked at her, and most of all her grandmother loved her and was forever trying to think of new presents to give the child. Once she gave her a little red velvet cape, and because it suited her so well and she never again wanted to wear anything else, she was known simply as Little Redcape. One day her mother said to her: 'Come, Little Redcape, here's a piece of cake and a bottle of wine; take them out to your grandmother, she's sick and weak and she'll enjoy them very much. Set out before it gets hot, and when you're on your way watch your step like a good girl and don't stray from the path, or you'll fall and break the bottle and grandmother will get nothing. And when you go into her room, remember to say good morning and not to stare all round the room first.'

'Don't worry, I'll do everything as I should,' said Little Redcape to her mother and promised faithfully. Now her grandmother lived out in the forest, half an hour from the village. And as Little Redcape entered the forest the wolf met her. But Little Redcape didn't know what a wicked beast he was, and wasn't afraid of him. 'Good morning, Little Redcape,' he said. 'Thank you, wolf.' 'Where are you going so early, Little Redcape?' 'To my grandmother's.' 'What are you carrying under your apron?' 'Cake and wine – we were baking yesterday, and my grandmother's ill and weak, so she's to have something nice to help her get strong again.' 'Little Redcape, where does your grandmother live?' 'A good quarter of an hour's walk further on in the forest, under the three big oak trees, that's where her house is; there are hazel hedges by it, I'm sure you know the place,' said Little Redcape. The wolf thought to itself: This delicate young thing, she'll make a plump morsel, she'll taste even better than the old woman. But I must go about it cunningly and I'll catch them both. So he walked for a while beside

Little Redcape and then said: 'Little Redcape, just look at those lovely flowers growing all round us, why don't you look about you? I think you don't even notice how sweetly the birds are singing. You're walking straight ahead as if you were going to school, and yet it's such fun out here in the wood.'

Little Redcape looked up, and when she saw the sunbeams dancing to and fro between the trees and all the lovely flowers growing everywhere, she thought: If I take Grandmama a bunch of fresh flowers, that'll please her too; it's so early that I'll still get there soon enough. And she ran off the path and into the forest to look for flowers. And every time she picked one she seemed to see a prettier one growing further on, and she ran to pick it and got deeper and deeper into the forest. But the wolf went straight to her grandmother's house and knocked at the door. 'Who's there?' 'Little Redcape, bringing you some cake and wine; open the door.' 'Just push down the latch,' said the grandmother, 'I'm too weak to get out of bed.' The wolf pushed down the latch, and without a word he went straight to the old woman's bed and gobbled her up. Then he put on her clothes and her nightcap and lay down in her bed and closed the curtains.

But Little Redcape had been running about picking flowers, and when she had collected so many that she couldn't carry any more she remembered her grandmother and set out again towards her house. She was surprised to find the door open, and when she went into the room everything seemed so strange that she thought: Oh my goodness, how nervous I feel today, and yet I always enjoy visiting Grandmama! She called out: 'Good morning,' but got no answer. Then she went to the bed and drew back the curtains – and there lay her grandmother with her bonnet pulled down low over her face and looking so peculiar. 'Why, Grandmama, what big ears you have!' 'The better to hear you with.' 'Why, Grandmama, what big eyes you have!' 'The better to see you with.' 'Why, Grandmama, what big hands you have!' 'The better to grab you with.' 'But, Grandmama, what terrible big jaws you have!' 'The better to eat you with.' And no sooner had the wolf said that than it made one bound out of the bed and gobbled up poor Little Redcape.

Having satisfied its appetite, the wolf lay down on the bed again, went to sleep and began to snore very loudly. The huntsman was just passing the house at that moment and he thought: How the old woman is snoring; let's see if anything's the matter with her. So he came into the room, and when he got to the bed he saw the wolf lying there: 'So I've found you here, you old sinner,' he said, 'I've been looking for you for a long time.' He was just about to take aim with his gun when it occurred to him that the wolf might have swallowed the old woman and she might still be saved – so instead of firing he took a pair of scissors and began to cut open the sleeping wolf's stomach. When he had made a snip or two, he saw the bright red of the little girl's cape, and after another few snips she jumped out and cried: 'Oh, how frightened I was, how dark it was inside the wolf!' And then her old grandmother came out too, still alive though she could hardly breathe. But Little Red-cape quickly fetched some big stones, and with them they filled the wolf's belly, and when he woke up he tried to run away; but the stones were so heavy that he collapsed at once and was killed by the fall.

At this all three of them were happy; the huntsman skinned the wolf and took his skin home, the grandmother ate the cake and drank the wine that Little Redcape had brought, and they made her feel much better. But Little Redcape said to herself: As long as I live I'll never again leave the path and run into the forest by myself, when mother has said I mustn't.

5

RAPUNZEL

There was once a man and a woman who had long wished vainly for a child. At last the woman began to hope that God was granting their wish. At the back of their house was a little window looking out over a wonderful garden, full of the most beautiful flowers and vegetables: but it was surrounded by a high wall and no one dared enter it because it belonged to a sorceress who was very powerful and everyone was scared of her. One day the woman was standing at this window looking down into the garden, and she caught sight of a bed of very fine rapunzels. They looked so fresh and green that her mouth watered and she longed to eat some. Her craving grew stronger every day, and as she knew she couldn't have any of the rapunzels she began to waste away and looked pale and wretched. Her husband was alarmed and asked: 'My dear wife, what's the matter with you?' 'Oh,' she said, 'unless I can get some of those rapunzels to eat from the garden behind our house, I shall die.' Her husband loved her dearly and thought to himself: Rather than let my wife die I must get some of the rapunzels for her, whatever the cost. So that evening as it was growing dark he climbed over the wall into the sorceress's garden, hastily broke off a handful of rapunzels and took them back to his wife. She made some salad from them at once and ate it up greedily, but it had tasted so delicious that next day her craving was three times as strong. If she was to have any peace, her husband had to climb over into the garden again. So at nightfall back he went, but when he got down the other side of the wall he had the fright of his life, for there was the sorceress standing right in front of him. She glared at him angrily and said: 'How dare you climb into my garden like a thief and steal my rapunzels! You'll be sorry for this.' 'Oh, madam,' he answered, 'be merciful to me! I only dared because I had to: my wife saw your rapunzels from her window, and she has taken so strong a fancy to them that she would die if she couldn't have some to eat.' When the sorceress heard this, her anger lessened and she said to him: 'If it is as you say, then I will allow you to take the rapunzels, as many of them as you like, but on one condition: when your wife gives birth to her child, you must give it to me. It shall be well treated and I will look after it like a mother.' In his terror the man promised her everything, and when his wife was delivered the sorceress appeared at once, gave the child the name 'Rapunzel', and took it away with her.

Rapunzel became the most beautiful little girl in the world. When she was twelve the sorceress shut her up in a tower in the middle of a forest. It had no stairs and no door, only a little window right at the top, and when the sorceress wanted to come in she would stand at the foot of the tower and call out:

> 'Rapunzel, Rapunzel,
> Let down your hair to me.'

Rapunzel had wonderful long hair, as fine as spun gold. So when she heard the sorceress's voice, she would undo her braided hair and wind it round a hook in the window frame: then down it would fall, twenty ells down, and the sorceress would climb up on it.

After a few years it happened that the king's son was riding through the forest, and as he was passing the tower he heard someone singing so lovely a song that he stopped to listen. It was Rapunzel, who in her loneliness used to pass the time making music with her sweet voice. The prince wanted to go up and see her and he tried to find a door into the tower, but there wasn't one. He rode home, but her singing had touched his heart so deeply that he went out every day into the forest to listen to it. One day as he was standing there behind a tree he saw a sorceress approach the tower and heard her call up to the window:

> 'Rapunzel, Rapunzel,
> Let down your hair.'

And Rapunzel let down her tresses and the sorceress climbed up. If that's the ladder that leads up to her, thought the prince,

I'll try my luck as well. And next day, as darkness was falling, he went to the tower and called up:

> 'Rapunzel, Rapunzel,
> Let down your hair.'

Down dropped her hair at once, and up climbed the prince.

At first Rapunzel had the fright of her life when a man came through her window, for she had never seen one before. But the prince spoke very gently to her and told her that his heart had been so moved by her singing that it had given him no peace, and he had had to come and see her. Then Rapunzel wasn't afraid any longer, and when he asked her if she would take him as her husband and she saw that he was young and handsome, she thought: He'll love me better than my old godmama. So she consented and put her hand in his, and said: 'I'll gladly come with you, but I don't know how I'll get down from here. You must bring a silk cord with you each time you come, and I'll make a ladder with them. When it's finished I'll climb down, and you will put me on your horse.' They agreed that until then he would come to her every evening, for during the day the old woman came. And the sorceress didn't notice that anything was happening, until one day Rapunzel went and said to her: 'Tell me, Godmama, why ever is it that you are getting so much heavier for me to pull up than the young prince? It takes him only a moment to get to me.' 'Ha, you godless child!' cried the sorceress, 'what's this you're telling me? I thought I had shut you away from the whole world, and yet you have deceived me!' In her rage she seized Rapunzel's beautiful hair, twisted it a few times round her left hand and grabbed a pair of scissors with her right. Snip, snap, they went, and off came the lovely tresses and dropped to the floor. And she was so hard-hearted that she took poor Rapunzel to a wilderness and left her there to live in great wretchedness and misery.

But in the evening of the same day on which she had banished Rapunzel the sorceress fastened the shorn-off hair to the hook on the window frame, and when the prince came and called:

'Rapunzel, Rapunzel,
Let down your hair,'

she let it down. The prince climbed up, but at the top he found
not his dearest Rapunzel but the sorceress, who glared at him
with malicious rage. 'Ho-ho!' she cried mockingly, 'so you
think you are going to fetch your lady sweetheart! But that fine
bird's no longer in her nest and no longer singing; the cat has
got her, and it'll soon scratch out your eyes too. You have lost
Rapunzel, you'll never see her again.' At this the prince was
beside himself with grief, and in his despair he jumped down
from the tower; he wasn't killed, but the thorns he fell into
poked out his eyes. So he wandered about the forest blind,
eating nothing but roots and berries and doing nothing but
weeping and bewailing the loss of his dearest wife. For some
years he wandered about in wretchedness, till finally he came to
the wilderness where Rapunzel was scraping a bare living for
herself and the twin children she had borne, a boy and a girl. He
heard a voice singing that he thought he knew well, so he
walked towards it, and as he approached Rapunzel recognized
him and fell on his neck and wept. But two of her tears dropped
on his eyes, and the light was restored to them and he could see
again. He took her to his kingdom, where he was joyfully
welcomed, and they lived for many more years happy and
contented.

6

BRIAR-ROSE

Long ago there lived a king and a queen and never a day passed but they said: 'Oh, if only we had a child!' and yet they never had one. Then it happened one day when the queen was taking her bath that a frog crawled ashore out of the water and said to her: 'Your wish is to be granted; before a year is over you will give birth to a daughter.' It happened as the frog had said, and the queen gave birth to a little girl of such beauty that the king was beside himself with joy and ordered a great feast. He invited to it not only his relatives and friends and acquaintances but also the wise-women of the land, in the hope that they would show the child affection and favour. There were thirteen of them in his kingdom, but because he had only twelve golden plates for them to eat from, one of them had to stay at home. The feast was celebrated with great magnificence, and when it was over the wise-women bestowed their magic gifts on the child: one gave her virtue, another beauty, a third wealth, and so on, till she had everything in the world you could wish for. Just as the eleventh of them had spoken her spell, the thirteenth suddenly entered. She meant to avenge herself for not having been invited, and without greeting or looking at anyone she cried out in a loud voice: 'In her fifteenth year the princess shall prick herself on a spindle and fall dead.' And without speaking another word she turned her back and left the hall. Everyone was horrified, but then the twelfth wise-woman, who still had not uttered her wish, stepped forward: she could not cancel the evil spell but only lessen its effect, so she said: 'But it shall not be death the princess falls into, only a deep sleep lasting a hundred years.'

The king, who dearly wished to protect his beloved child from this misfortune, gave orders that every spindle in his kingdom was to be burnt. But the blessings of the wise-women on the girl were all fulfilled, for she was so beautiful, well behaved, kind and intelligent that no one could look at her without loving her. It happened that on the very day she was to reach the age of fifteen the king and queen were not at home and the girl stayed behind in the palace all by herself, so she explored everything, looked at the rooms and bedrooms just as she pleased, and finally came to an old tower. She climbed to the top of the narrow spiral stair and came to a little door. In the lock was an old rusty key; when she turned it the door sprang open and there, in a little room, sat an old woman with a spindle, busily spinning her flax. 'Good morning, old lady,' said the princess, 'what's that you're doing?' 'I'm spinning,' said the old woman, nodding her head. 'And what's this funny little thing jumping about?' asked the girl. And she took the spindle in her hand and wanted to learn how to spin too. But she had scarcely touched it when the spell was fulfilled and she pricked herself in the finger.

The moment she felt the prick she fell down on the bed that was standing there, and lay in a deep sleep. And this sleep spread over the entire palace: the king and queen, who had just got back and entered the hall, began to fall asleep, and so did their whole court with them. And the horses in the stable fell asleep, and the dogs in the courtyard, the pigeons on the roof, the flies on the wall, in fact even the fire blazing in the hearth stood still and fell asleep, and the roast stopped crackling, and the cook, who was in the act of pulling the kitchen boy's hair for something he had done wrong, let him go and fell asleep. And the wind died down, and on the trees in front of the palace not a single leaf stirred.

But round the palace a thorn thicket began to grow, which grew taller every year and in the end surrounded the entire castle and grew up above the top of it so that you couldn't see any castle any more, not even the flag on the roof. But the legend of the lovely sleeping Briar-Rose (for so the princess came to be called) was told in the land, so that from time to time princes would come and try to force their way through the thicket into the castle. But none of them succeeded, because the thorn bushes gripped each other as if they had hands, and the young men got trapped among them and couldn't free

themselves and died a piteous death. After many many years
another prince came to that country and heard an old man tell
the story of the thorn thicket, and of how it was said that a
palace stood behind it in which a most beautiful princess called
Briar-Rose had been sleeping for the last hundred years, and
the king and the queen and the whole court lay asleep there
with her, and of how he had also heard from his grandfather
that many princes had already come and tried to force their way
through the thorns but had got trapped in them and perished
miserably. Then the young man said: 'I'm not afraid, I'll go out
and find this beautiful Briar-Rose.' The kind old man tried his
best to dissuade him, but the prince didn't listen.

Now it happened that the hundred years had just passed,
and the day had come on which Briar-Rose was to wake up.
When the prince approached the thorn thicket, the thorns had
all turned into enormous beautiful flowers, which parted of
their own accord and let him through unharmed, and behind
him they closed up again and made a hedge. In the palace
courtyard he saw all the horses and the brindled hunting-
hounds lying asleep, and on the roof the pigeons were roosting
with their heads tucked under their wings. And when he went
indoors, the flies were asleep on the wall, the cook in the
kitchen still had his hand outstretched as if to grab the kitchen
boy, and the kitchen maid was sitting with a black chicken in
her lap, about to pluck it. Then he went further and saw the
whole court lying asleep in the hall, and up there beside the
throne lay the king and the queen. Then he went still further,
and everything was so silent that he could hear his own breathing; and in the end he came to the tower and opened the door of
the little room where Briar-Rose was sleeping. There she lay,
and she was so beautiful he couldn't take his eyes off her, and
he stooped down and kissed her. As his lips touched hers,
Briar-Rose opened her eyes, woke up and smiled at him. Then
they went downstairs together, and the king woke up and so
did the queen and the whole court, and they looked at each
other in astonishment. And the horses in the yard got to their
feet and shook themselves, the hounds jumped up and wagged
their tails, the pigeons on the roof took their heads from under

their wings, looked about them and flew off over the fields, the flies began crawling up the walls again, the fire in the kitchen revived and blazed up and cooked the dinner, the roast began to crackle again, and the cook gave the boy such a box on the ear that he howled, and the maid finished plucking the chicken. And after that the wedding of the prince with Briar-Rose was celebrated with great magnificence, and they lived happily till the end of their days.

7

SNOWWHITE

Once upon a time, in the middle of winter when the snowflakes were falling from the sky like feathers, a queen sat sewing at a window with a frame of black ebony. And as she sewed and looked up at the falling snow, she pricked her finger with her needle, and into the snow there fell three drops of blood. The red looked so beautiful against the white that she thought to herself: If only I had a child as white as snow, as red as blood and as black as the wood of this window frame! Soon after this she gave birth to a little daughter who was as white as snow, as red as blood and had hair as black as ebony, and for this reason was called 'little Snowwhite'. And when the child was born the queen died.

A year later the king took another wife. She was a beautiful woman, but proud and haughty, and could not bear that anyone else's beauty should excel her own. She possessed a magic mirror, and when she stood in front of it and looked at herself she would say:

> 'Mirror, mirror on the wall,
> Who is the fairest of us all?'

The mirror would answer:

> 'My lady queen is the fairest of all.'

And this satisfied her, for she knew that the mirror spoke the truth.

But Snowwhite was growing up and becoming more and more beautiful, and by the age of seven she was as lovely as the bright day and more beautiful even than the queen. One day when the queen asked her mirror:

> 'Mirror, mirror on the wall,
> Who is the fairest of us all?'

it answered:

> 'My lady queen is fair to see,
> But Snowwhite is fairer far than she.'

At this the queen took fright and turned yellow and green with
envy. From now on, whenever she saw Snowwhite, her heart
turned over inside her, she hated the girl so. And envy and
pride took root like weeds in her heart and grew higher and
higher, giving her no peace by day or night. So she sent for a
huntsman and said: 'Take that child out into the forest, I'm sick
of the sight of her. You are to kill her and bring me her lungs and
liver as proof.' The huntsman obeyed and took Snowwhite with
him, but when he had drawn his hunting-knife and was about
to thrust it into her innocent heart she began to cry and said:
'Oh, dear huntsman, let me live; I will run away into the wild
forest and never come home again.' And because she was so
beautiful the huntsman took pity on her and said: 'Run away
then, you poor child.' The wild beasts will soon have eaten you,
he thought, and yet it was as if a stone had been rolled from his
heart because he did not have to kill her. And when a young
boar happened to come bounding up he slaughtered it, cut out
its lungs and liver and took them to the queen as the proof she
wanted. The cook was ordered to stew them in salt, and the
wicked woman devoured them, thinking she had eaten the
liver and lungs of Snowwhite.

And now the poor child was utterly alone in the huge forest,
and so terrified that she gazed at every leaf on the trees, trying
to think what to do to save herself. Then she began to run, and
she ran over the sharp stones and through the thorns, and the
wild animals bounded past her but did not harm her. She ran on
as far as her feet would carry her, until it was nearly evening:
then she saw a little cottage and went into it to rest. Inside the
cottage everything was tiny, but more dainty and neat than you
can imagine. There stood a little table with a white tablecloth
and seven little plates, every plate with its little spoon, and
seven little knives and forks and cups as well. In a row along the
wall stood seven little beds all made up with sheets as white as
snow. Because she was so hungry and thirsty, Snowwhite ate a

little of the vegetables and bread from each plate and drank a sip
of wine from each of the cups; for she didn't want to take the
whole of anyone's supper. Then, because she was so tired, she
lay down on one of the little beds – but none of them fitted her:
one was too long, the next too short, till finally the seventh was
the right size. So in it she stayed, and said her prayers and went
to sleep.

When it had got quite dark, the owners of the little house
came home: they were the seven dwarfs who worked in the
hills, hacking and digging out precious metal. They lit their
seven lamps, and as soon as there was light in the cottage they
saw that someone had been there, because not everything was
exactly as they had left it. The first said: 'Who's been sitting on
my chair?' The second said: 'Who's been eating from my plate?'
The third said: 'Who's taken some of my bread?' The fourth
said: 'Who's eaten some of my vegetables?' The fifth said:
'Who's been poking with my fork?' The sixth said: 'Who's been
cutting with my knife?' The seventh said: 'Who's been drinking
out of my cup?' Then the first of them looked round and saw
that there was a little hollow on his bed, and he said: 'Who's
stepped on my bed?' The others came running up and
exclaimed: 'Someone's been in mine too.' But when the
seventh looked at his bed he saw Snowwhite lying there asleep.
And he called the others, who came running up and cried out in
amazement; they fetched their seven little lamps and shone
them on Snowwhite. 'Oh goodness me! Oh goodness me!' they
cried. 'What a lovely girl!' And they were so delighted that they
didn't wake her, but let her go on sleeping in the little bed. But
the seventh dwarf slept with his companions, one hour with
each of them, and so the night passed.

When it was morning Snowwhite woke up, and when she
saw the seven dwarfs she was scared. But they spoke to her
kindly and asked her what her name was. 'I'm called Snowwhite,' she replied. 'How did you get into our house?' asked
the dwarfs. So she told them how her stepmother had tried to
have her killed, but that the huntsman had spared her life, and
then she had wandered all day till finally she found their cottage. The dwarfs said: 'If you will keep house for us, and do the

cooking and the beds and the washing and the sewing and the knitting, and keep everything neat and tidy, you can stay with us and you shan't want for anything.' 'Yes,' said Snowwhite, 'I'd like that very much.' So she stayed with them, and looked after their cottage. In the morning they went into the hills and dug for ore and gold, in the evening they came back and their supper had to be ready. The young girl was by herself all day, and the kind dwarfs warned her and said: 'Beware of your stepmother, she will soon find out that you are here; don't on any account let anyone in.'

But after the queen, as she supposed, had eaten Snowwhite's liver and lungs, her first thought was she was again the most beautiful of all women, and she stood before her mirror and said:

> 'Mirror, mirror on the wall,
> Who is the fairest of us all?'

And the mirror answered:

> 'My lady queen is fair to see:
> But Snowwhite lives beyond the hills,
> With the seven dwarfs she dwells,
> And fairer far than the queen is she.'

Then the queen took fright, for she knew that the mirror never told a lie, and she realized that the huntsman had deceived her and that Snowwhite was still alive. So she began plotting and planning again how to kill her; for so long as she was not the fairest of all, her envy never left her in peace. And having finally thought of a plan, she painted her face and disguised herself as an old pedlar-woman, and no one could have recognized her. In this disguise she went over the seven hills to the house of the seven dwarfs, knocked at the door and called out: 'Fine wares for sale, for sale!' Snowwhite peeped out of the window and called to her: 'Good day, old lady, what have you got to sell?' 'Fine wares, lovely things,' she answered, 'laces of all colours' – and she fetched out one that was made of many-coloured silk. I can let in this honest woman, thought Snowwhite, and she unbolted the door and bought the pretty lace. 'My child,' said

the old woman, 'how untidy you look! Come, I'll lace you up
properly.' Snowwhite suspected nothing, stood in front of the
old woman and let herself be laced with the new lace; but the
old woman laced her up very fast and pulled the lace so tight
that Snowwhite's breath was stopped and she fell down as if
dead. 'Now you're no longer the fairest of us all,' said the queen
and hurried out.

Not long after, when evening fell, the seven dwarfs came
home: but what a fright they got when they saw their dear little
Snowwhite lying on the ground, not moving or stirring, as if
she were dead! They lifted her up, and seeing that she was laced
too tightly they cut the laces – then she began to breathe a little,
and gradually she came back to life. When the dwarfs heard
what had happened they said: 'That old pedlar-woman was the
godless queen and no one else – be on your guard and let no one
in here when we're not with you.'

But when the evil woman got home, she went to her mirror
and asked:

> 'Mirror, mirror on the wall,
> Who is the fairest of us all?'

And the mirror answered as before:

> 'My lady queen is fair to see:
> But Snowwhite lives beyond the hills,
> With the seven dwarfs she dwells,
> And fairer far than the queen is she.'

When the queen heard that, she was so startled that all the
blood rushed to her heart, for she saw very well that Snowwhite
had come to life again. 'But now,' she said, 'I'll think out
something that will deal with you once and for all.' And by the
witchcraft she knew she made a poisoned comb. Then she
disguised herself and took the form of another old woman. And
again she went over the seven hills to the house of the seven
dwarfs, knocked at the door and called out: 'Fine wares for sale,
for sale!' Snowwhite peeped out and said: 'Go away, I'm not
allowed to let anyone in.' 'Surely they'll allow you to take a
look,' said the old woman, and pulled out the poisoned comb

and held it up. The young girl liked it so much that she let
herself be fooled and opened the door. When they had agreed
on a price the old woman said: 'Now I'll comb your hair
properly for you.' Poor Snowwhite suspected nothing and let
the old woman have her way; but she had hardly stuck the
comb into her hair when its poison worked and the young girl
fell senseless to the ground. 'That's done for you now, my
beauty queen,' said the wicked woman, and off she went. But
fortunately it was nearly evening and the seven little dwarfs
were coming home. When they saw Snowwhite lying on the
floor as good as dead, they suspected her stepmother at once,
and searched and found the poisoned comb, and as soon as
they had pulled it out of her hair Snowwhite revived and told
them what had happened. Then they warned her again to be on
her guard and not to open the door to anyone.

Back home the queen stood before her mirror and said:

> 'Mirror, mirror on the wall,
> Who is the fairest of us all?'

And it answered as before:

> 'My lady queen is fair to see:
> But Snowwhite lives beyond the hills,
> With the seven dwarfs she dwells,
> And fairer far than the queen is she.'

When she heard the mirror say this, she trembled and shook
with fury. 'Snowwhite shall die,' she cried, 'even if it costs me
my own life.' With that she went to a completely secret remote
room which no one else ever entered, and there she made an
apple filled with deadly poison. Outwardly it looked like a
beautiful white-and-red-cheeked apple which made everyone
who saw it want to take a bite out of it, but anyone who did so
was doomed. When the apple was ready, she painted her face
and disguised herself as a peasant woman, and then she went
over the seven hills to the house of the seven dwarfs. When she
knocked, Snowwhite put her head out of the window and said:
'I can't let anyone in, the seven dwarfs have told me I mustn't.'
'That's all right,' answered the peasant woman, 'I'll have no

difficulty selling my apples. Here, I'll make you a present of one.' 'No,' said Snowwhite, 'I'm not allowed to take anything.' 'Are you afraid it's poisoned?' said the old woman. 'Look here, I'll cut the apple in two: you eat the red cheek and I'll eat the white one.' But the apple was so cunningly made that only the red cheek was poisoned. Snowwhite was longing to eat this lovely apple, and when she saw the peasant woman doing so she could resist no longer, put her hand out and took the poisoned half. But no sooner did she have a bite in her mouth than she fell to the floor dead. Then the queen gazed at her gloatingly and laughed a dreadful laugh and said: 'White as snow, red as blood, black as ebony! This time the dwarfs won't wake you.' And when she got home and asked the mirror:

> 'Mirror, mirror on the wall,
> Who is the fairest of us all?'

it at last answered:

> 'My lady queen is the fairest of all.'

And then her envious heart was at rest, if an envious heart ever can be.

When the dwarfs came home in the evening, they found Snowwhite lying on the ground, and not a breath stirring from her mouth, and she was dead. They lifted her up, looked all over her for something poisonous, unlaced her, combed her hair, washed her with water and wine, but it was all no good: the sweet girl was dead and dead she stayed. They laid her on a bier, and all seven sat by it and mourned her and wept for her for three days. Then they were going to bury her, but she still looked as fresh as a living person and still had her lovely red cheeks. They said: 'This is something we can't bury in the black earth,' and they had a transparent glass coffin made so that she could be seen from all sides; they laid her in it, and on it in letters of gold they wrote her name, and that she was a princess. Then they put the coffin out on the hill, and one of them always sat by it keeping watch. And the animals came too and mourned Snowwhite, first an owl, then a raven, and then a little dove.

So Snowwhite lay in her coffin for a long, long time; she didn't go bad, but just looked as if she were asleep, for she was still as white as snow, as red as blood and her hair was as black as ebony. Then it happened that a prince strayed into the forest and arrived at the dwarfs' house to spend the night there. He saw the coffin on the hill with the lovely Snowwhite inside, and read what was written on it in letters of gold. And he said to the dwarfs: 'Let me have that coffin, I'll pay you whatever you ask for it,' but the dwarfs answered: 'We wouldn't sell it for all the gold in the world.' So he said: 'Then give it to me, for I can't live without seeing Snowwhite, and I will honour her and treasure her as my dearest possession.' When he said that, the kind little dwarfs took pity on him and gave him the coffin. So the prince told his servants to carry it away on their shoulders. And it happened that they stumbled against a shrub and gave the coffin such a jolt that the lump of poisoned apple which Snow-white had bitten off was jerked out of her throat. And presently she opened her eyes, pushed up the lid of the coffin and sat up and was alive again. 'Oh goodness, where am I?' she exclaimed. The prince's heart leapt with joy and he said: 'You are with me.' And he told her what had happened and said: 'I love you more than anything in the world: come with me to my father's palace, and you shall be my wife.' And Snowwhite liked him and went with him, and their wedding was prepared with great splendour and magnificence.

But Snowwhite's godless stepmother was asked to the feast too. So when she had put on beautiful clothes, she stood before the mirror and said:

> 'Mirror, mirror on the wall,
> Who is the fairest of us all?'

And the mirror answered:

> 'My lady queen is fair to see:
> But the young queen is fairer far than she.'

At this the evil woman shrieked out a curse and was beside herself with fear. At first she decided not to go to the wedding at all, but the thing preyed on her mind and she just had to go to

see the young queen. And when she entered she recognized
Snowwhite and stood rooted to the spot with fright and terror.
But already a pair of iron slippers had been heated over glowing
coals and they were brought in with tongs and placed before
her. Then she had to put her feet into the red-hot shoes and
dance till she dropped dead.

8

THE JENIPER TREE

Lang, lang syne, maybe twa thoosan year, there wiz a rich man
that haed a bonny gweed-livin wife, and the twasome lo'ed een
anither weel; only, they haed nae bairns, an they wintit bairns
sairly; an the gweedwife prayt baith day an nicht for bairns, but
neen cam. Afore their hoose wiz a yaird, an in the yaird steed a
jeniper tree, and eence in the winter-time the gweedwife steed
ablò't pairin an aipple tae ait; an as she pair't it she cuttit er
finger, an the bleed fell intae the snaa. 'Alais,' said the
gweedwife, an she secht fae her verra hairt, an lookit at the
bleed afore er and wiz recht sorrafae, 'oh for a bairnie as reid as
bleed an as fite as the snaa!' An as she spak, aa at eence her hairt
wiz lichent, an she wiz sure that something waed come o't. Sae
she gaed intae the hoose, an a month gaed by an the snaa meltit
awà; twa month an the lan' wiz green; three month an the
flooers cam up oot o the grun'; fower month an the trees grew
thick in the waed an the green branches grew aa throuwither,
an there the birds sang till the hale waed wiz full o their soon' an
the verra blossom fell aff o the trees; syne the fift month it gaed
by, an she steed ablò the jeniper tree, an oh but it smelt that
sweet that her hairt loupit for glaidness as she fell doon on her
knees and didnae ken fit tae dee wi ersèl. An fan the sixt month
wiz by, the fruit hung big an thick on the trees an she grew unco
quaet; an the saivent month an she pu't the berries fae the
jeniper tree an ait them richt greedy-like, an syne she wiz dowie
an nae-weel; an the achtth month it gaed by, an she caa'd her
gweedmàn till er an said: 'If I dee, beery me ablò the jeniper
tree.' An at that she took hairt an wiz weel pleast, till the next
month gaed by. Syne she got a bairnie as fite as the snaa an as
reid as bleed, an fan she saa't, she wiz that kinechtit wi ersèl that
she deet.

Sae her gweedmàn beeriet her ablò the jeniper tree, an sair
did he greet; an efter a fylie his grief saftent, an fan he haed

grutten imsèl dry his hairt hailt again an efter a fyle he took anither wife.

Wi his secant wife he got a dother, but his first wife's bairn wiz a little loonie as reid as bleed an as fite as the snaa. Fan the wife lookit at er dother, oh but she lo'ed her, but syne fan she lookit at the loonie, it gaed er a stoun at her hairt, an it wiz like he wiz aye in her wey, an aye she thocht foo she micht gar aa the inheeritance come till er dother. An the Deil imsèl mintit till er tae hate the loonie, an she powkit im fae ae corner tae the tither, an fyles she lickit im, fyles she nippit im, sae the peer bairn gaed in fear o er. Fan he cam hame fae the school, he haednae a meenit's peace.

Eence the gweedwìfe haed gaen tae the pantry, an her quinie cam till er an said: 'Mither, gie me an aipple.' 'Aye, ma lass,' said the gweedwìfe, an gied her a bonny aipple oot o the kist. The kist haed a muckle heavy lid an a great sharp iron lock till't. 'Mither,' said the quinie, 'will ma brither nae get een an aa?' That angert the wife, but she said: 'Aye, fan he comes hame fae the school.' An fan she lookit oot o the windae an saa im comin, it wiz like Auld Nick cam ower er, an she up wi er haan an fuppit the aipple fae er dother an said: 'Ye winnae get een afore yer brither.' An she keest the aipple back in the kist an pat the lid doon. Syne the loonie he cam in, an the Deil gart er say till im freenly-like: 'Laddie, are ye for an aipple?' An she keest an ill look at im. 'Mither,' said the loonie, 'fit-for are ye lookin sae gurly? Aye, gie me an aipple.' At that she began tae fraise at im. 'Come wi me,' she said, an she liftit the lid, 'an tak oot an aipple.' An fan the laddie boo't doon tae get intill't, slap-bang she knockit doon the lid, an his heid flew aff an fell doon amang the reid aipples. An noo she wiz owercome wi fear, an she thocht: Oh, can I get clear o the wyte o't? Sae up she gaed till her chaumber tae her kist o drawers an oot o the tapmaist drawer she took a fite claith, an she set the heid back on the neck an wappit the claith roon't, sae that naething could be seen, an she set im afore the door on a chear an pat an aipple intae his haan.

Syne little Mary-Jeannie cam intae the kitchie till er mither, that wiz stannin at the fire wi a pan o het watter afore er, steerin't. 'Mither,' said Mary-Jeannie, 'my brither's sittin afore

the door aa fite in the face wi an aipple in's haan. I socht im tae
gie me the aipple but he niver gied me an answer, an I'm rael
feart.' 'Gyang back till im,' said er mither, 'an gin he winnae gie
ye an answer, slap im on the lug.' Sae Mary-Jeannie she gaed
back an said: 'Brither, gie me the aipple.' But he niver gied a
myaut, an sae she slappit im on the lug, an his heid fell doon.
That gied her an aafa bring-up, an she began tae roar an greet,
an ran tae her mither an said: 'Oh, mither, I've caa'd my
brither's heid aff,' an she grat an she grat an she couldnae haud
on greetin. 'Mary-Jeannie,' said er mither, 'fit haev ye deen?
Keep it quaet, noo, an naebody'll notice't, it's deen noo. We'll
mak a stew o im.' An the mither took the loonie an hackit im
smaa an pat im in the pan an stew't im. But Mary-Jeannie steed
by an grat an grat, an her tears fell intae the pan an the stew
didnae need saatin.

Syne the father he cam hame an sat doon at the table an said:
'Far's ma loonie than?' An the mither she pat an ashet o stew on
the table an Mary-Jeannie she grat an couldnae haud on greetin.
An the father said again: 'Far's ma loonie than?' 'Oh,' said the
mither, 'he's awà tae his granny tae byde a fylie.' 'Fit's he deein
there? An niver said fare-ye-weel tae me.' 'Oh, he priggit tae
gyang an spiert at me gin he micht byde maybe sax weeks
yonder; they'll be gweed till im, nae doot.' 'Alais,' said the
gweedmàn, 'I'm sair-made at that, it's nae richt o im nae tae say
fare-ye-weel tae me.' An wi that he set tee tae ait, an said:
'Mary-Jeannie, fit-for are ye greetin? Yer brither'll seen be háme
again. Gweedwìfe,' he said, 'my, but this mait's aafa tastie. Gie
me mair!' An the mair he ait, the mair he wintit. 'Gie me mair!'
he said. 'I'm seekin't aa tae mysèl, I maun hae't aa tae mysèl.'
An he ait an he ait, an aye he keest the beens ablò the table, till
he'd aiten ilka morsel. But Mary-Jeannie she gaed till her kist o
drawers, an oot o the naithmaist drawer she took a fine silk
claith an pickit ilka last little been oot ablò the table an bund
them in the silk claith an cairrit them oot, greetin tears o bleed.
An there she laid them in the green girse ablò the jeniper tree,
an as seen as she'd laid them doon, aa at eence her hairt lichent
an she grat nae mair. An the jeniper tree began tae shoogle an
shak, the branches cam apairt an cam thegither again, apairt an

thegither, just like fan ye're glaid an clap yer haans. An a kyn' o mist cam fae the jeniper tree, wi a fire louwin in the mids o't, an oot o the fire there flew a bonny bird that sang a bonny sang an flew hine up intae the lift. An fan the bird haed floun, the jeniper tree wiz jist like it wiz afore, an the claith wi the beens in't wiz vanisht. An noo Mary-Jeannie wiz as lichtsome as could be, as though her brither wiz aye livin. An she gaed back intae the hoose cheerfae-like an sat doon tae ait.

Noo the bird it flew awà an lichtit on the riggin o a gowdsmith's hoose an sang:

> Fa kellt me deid? My mammie-o.
> Fa ait my flesh? My daddie-o.
> Fa gaithert aa my beenies?
> My sister Mary-Jeannie.
> She bund them in a silken claith
> An laid them the jeniper tree anaith.
> Cheeperty-cheep,
> Sic a braa bird am I-o!

The gowdsmith wiz sittin in his warkshop makin a gowden chyne an he heert the bird as it sat on his riggin an sang, an oh but he thocht it bonnie. Up he steed, an as he steppit ower his doorsteen een o his bauchles cam aff; but stracht up the street gaed he wi a bauchle on ae fit an a stockin on the tither. He haed his moleskin apran on, an in ae haan he held his chyne an in the tither his tyangs, an the saen sheen bricht on the street. An he steed up an lookit at the bird. 'Birdie,' said he, 'oh but ye sing bonnily! Sing yer sang tae me again.' 'Na,' said the bird, 'I winnae sing twice for naething. Gie me yer gowden chyne an I'll sing't tae ye again.' 'Tak it,' said the gowdsmith, 'and noo sing tae me again.' An the bird he cam an took the gowden chyne in his richt clook an sattelt doon afore the gowdsmith an sang:

> Fa kellt me deid? My mammie-o.
> Fa ait my flesh? My daddie-o.
> Fa gaithert aa my beenies?
> My sister Mary-Jeannie.

> She bund them in a silken claith
> An laid them the jeniper tree anaith.
> Cheeperty-cheep,
> Sic a braa bird am I-o!

Noo the bird flew awà tae a sooter's hoose, an lichtit on his riggin an sang:

> Fa kellt me deid? My mammie-o.
> Fa ait my flesh? My daddie-o.
> Fa gaithert aa my beenies?
> My sister Mary-Jeannie.
> She bund them in a silken claith
> An laid them the jeniper tree anaith.
> Cheeperty-cheep,
> • Sic a braa bird am I-o!

The sooter heert it an ran oot o's door in his sark-sleeves an lookit up tae the riggin, an he haed tae haud his haan ower his een tae nae be blent wi the saen. 'Birdie,' said he, 'oh but ye sing bonnily!' An he cry't in tae his door: 'Gweedwìfe, come oot, there's a bird, see at the bird, foo bonnily it sings!' An he cried on his dother an his bairns an his men, his prentice-haans an his sairvint-lassies, an they aa cam oot ontae the street tae see the bird; an roon his neck wiz pure gowd an his een glistet lik stars in his heid. 'Birdie,' said the sooter, 'will ye sing yer air tae me again?' 'Na,' said the bird, 'I winnae sing twice for naething; ye maun gie me a gift.' 'Gweedwìfe,' said the man, 'gyang tae the laft; on the tapmaist byuird there's a pair o reid sheen, fess them doon.' An the wife gaed an feess the sheen. 'Tak this, birdie,' said the man, 'an noo sing yon air taé me again.' An the bird cam an took the sheen intil's left clook an flew up ontae the riggin again an sang:

> Fa kellt me deid? My mammie-o.
> Fa ait my flesh? My daddie-o.
> Fa gaithert aa my beenies?
> My sister Mary-Jeannie.
> She bund them in a silken claith

> An laid them the jeniper tree anaith.
> Cheeperty-cheep,
> Sic a braa bird am I-o!

An fan he feeneesht his sang he flew awà wi the chyne in his richt clook an the sheen in his left, an he flew hine awà till a mull, an the mull gaed clipperty clap, clipperty clap, clipperty clap. An in the mull there wiz twinty muller-lads hyowin awà at a mullsteen, nickerty nack, nickerty nack, nickerty nack, an the mull it gaed clipperty clap, clipperty clap, clipperty clap. An the bird lichtit on a linden tree that grew afore the mull, an sang:

> Fa kellt me deid? My mammie-o,
> – een of them stoppit hyowin;
> Fa ait my flesh? My daddie-o,
> – anither twa stoppit hyowin an harkent;
> Fa gaithert aa my beenies?
> My sister Mary-Jeannie,
> – anither fower stoppit;
> She bund them in a silken claith,
> – nae but acht wiz still hyowin;
> An laid them
> – nae but saiven;
> the jeniper tree anaith.
> – nae but een;
> Cheeperty-cheep,
> Sic a braa bird am I-o!

– an the hinmaist een haed stoppit an haed heard the last bittie. 'Birdie,' said he, 'oh but ye sing bonnily. Lat me heer't an aa, sing yon tae me again.' 'Na,' said the bird, 'I dinnae sing twice for naething. Gie me the mullsteen an I'll sing't again.' 'Aye weel,' said he, 'gin it wiz me ma leen that aichtit it, I'd gie ye't.' 'Aye,' said the rest o them, 'gin he'll sing again we'll gie im't.' Sae the bird cam doon, an the mullers aa twinty of them set tee wi widden praps an raizt up the mullsteen, heezy-up, heezy-up, heezy-up. Syne the bird pat his heid throu the hole an pat the mullsteen on like a collar, an flew back on tae the tree an sang:

> Fa kellt me deid? My mammie-o.
> Fa ait my flesh? My daddie-o.
> Fa gaithert aa my beenies?
> My sister Mary-Jeannie.
> She bund them in a silken claith
> An laid them the jeniper tree anaith.
> Cheeperty-cheep,
> Sic a braa bird am I-o!

An fan he haed feeneesht his singin, he spread his wings, an wi the chyne in his richt clook, the sheen in his left and the mullsteen roon his neck he flew hine awà tae his father's hoose.

In the chaumber the father, the mither an Mary-Jeannie wiz sittin at the table, an the father said: 'Oh but my hairt's licht an it's blithe I am.' 'Na,' said the mither, 'I'm dowie and wae, like there's a thunnerstorm comin.' But Mary-Jeannie she sat an grat an grat, till the bird cam fleein, an fan he lichtit on the riggin, 'My,' said the father, 'oh but I'm glaid an the saen's sheenin that bricht oot yonder, I'm thinkin I'm gyan tae see an auld freen again.' 'Na,' said the mither, 'I'm that terrefeart, my teeth's chitterin, an it's like there's a fire gyan throu my bleed,' an she rieve her bodice open an mair o the like, but Mary-Jeannie sat in a neuk an grat, an held her apran tae her een an grat till the apran wiz sappit. Syne the bird lichtit on the jeniper tree an sang:

> Fa kellt me deid? My mammie-o!

At that the mither stappit her lugs and steekit her een an wid naither see nor hear, but there wiz a roar in her lugs like a fearfae storm and a burnin an flashin in her een like lichtnin.

> Fa ait my flesh? My daddie-o!

'Mither,' said the gweedmàn, 'yonder's a braa bird singin sae bonnily, the saen's sheenin sae warm, an it smells like pure cinnemin.'

> Fa gaithert aa my beenies?
> My sister Mary-Jeannie,

An Mary-Jeannie pat her heid on her knees an grat like tae brak er hairt; but the gweedmàn said: 'I'm gyan oot, I maun see yon bird close tee.' 'Oh, dinnae gyang,' said the wife, 'it's like the hale hoose wiz shakkin an louwin!' But the gweedmàn he gaed oot tae see the bird.

> She bund them in a silken claith
> An laid them the jeniper tree anaith.
> Cheeperty-cheep,
> Sic a braa bird am I-o!

At that the bird lat the gowden chyne faa, an it fell richt roon the gweedmàn's neck like it wiz made for im. An he gaed back in an said: 'Isnae that a braa bird noo, that gied me sic a braa gowden chyne, an richt bonny it is!' But the gweedwife wiz in sic a dwam o fear that she fell the length o ersèl on the fleer an her mutch fell aff o her heid. An the bird sang again:

> Fa kellt me deid? My mammie-o!

'Waed I were a thoosand ells ablò the grun', tae nae hear that!'

> Fa ait my flesh? My daddie-o!

The gweedwife drappit doon like she wiz clean cauld deid.

> Fa gaithert aa my beenies?
> My sister Mary-Jeannie.

'Oh,' said Mary-Jeannie, 'I'll gyang oot tee, tae see gin the bird will gie me a gift an aa.' An oot she gaed.

> She bund them in a silken claith
> An laid them the jeniper tree anaith.

An he keest the sheen doon till er.

> Cheeperty-cheep,
> Sic a braa bird am I-o!

Oh than she wiz blithe an merry! She pat on the new reid sheen an cam in dancin an loupin. 'Oh,' said she, 'I wiz that dooncast fan I gaed oot, an noo I'm that happy. Yon bonny bird haes gien me a pair o reid sheen.' 'Na,' said the gweedwife, and loupit up wi er hair stannin up roon er face lik louwin flames, 'weel-I-wyte the hale wordl's comin till an en', I'm gyan oot tae seek remeìd.' An fan she cam oot o the door, slap-bang the bird keest the mullsteen doon on er heid an caa'd her aa till a jeelie. Mary-Jeannie an her father heert it an gaed oot; there wiz reek and louwin flames comin fae the place, an fan that cleart awà, there steed her little brither, an he took Mary-Jeannie an her father bi the haan, an they were fair kinechtit, an they aa gaed intae the hoose an sat doon at the table tae ait their supper.

9

LITTLE BROTHER AND LITTLE SISTER

Little Brother took his Little Sister by the hand and said: 'Since Mother died we haven't had a single happy hour. Our stepmother beats us every day, and kicks us if we go near her. We get stale left-over crusts to eat; even the little dog under the table is better off, she does throw him a nice morsel sometimes. Dear God, what would our mother say if she knew! Come, let's go away together into the wide world.' They walked all day across meadows and fields and over stones, and when it rained Little Sister said: 'God and our hearts are weeping together!' At nightfall they found themselves in a big forest and were so weary with grief and hunger and their long walk that they sat down in a hollow tree and fell asleep.

When they woke next morning, the sun was high already and the heat of it was coming right inside the tree. And Little Brother said: 'Little Sister, I'm thirsty; if only I knew where there was a spring of water I'd go and drink from it – I think I hear one murmuring.' Little Brother got up, took Little Sister by the hand, and they went to look for the spring. But their wicked stepmother was a witch and knew quite well that the two children had left: she had seen them and crept after them secretly, as witches can do, and had put a spell on all the springs in the forest. So when they found a spring, glistening and leaping over the stones, Little Brother was about to drink from it, but Little Sister heard the words it murmured: 'Drink me and become a tiger; drink me and become a tiger.' And Little Sister cried out: 'Please, Little Brother, don't drink, or you'll be turned into a wild beast and tear me to pieces.' Little Brother didn't drink, although he was so terribly thirsty, and he said: 'I'll wait till we come to running water again.' And when they came to the second spring, Little Sister heard this water speaking too, and it said: 'Drink me and become a wolf; drink me and become a wolf.' And Little Sister cried out: 'Little Brother, please don't drink or you'll be turned into a wolf and eat me.' Little Brother didn't drink, and said: 'I'll wait till we come to running water again, but then I'll have to take a drink whatever you say, because I'm too dreadfully thirsty.' And when they came to the third spring, Little Sister heard the words it murmured: 'Drink me and become a deer; drink me and become a deer.' Little Sister said: 'Oh, Little Brother, please, don't drink, or you'll be turned into a deer and run away from me.' But Little Brother had knelt down by the spring as soon as he reached it, and he stooped and drank some of its water, and no sooner had the first drops touched his lips than he lay there turned into a little fawn.

Then Little Sister wept over her poor bewitched brother, and the little fawn wept too and sat beside her ever so sadly. Finally the girl said: 'Don't cry, little fawn, you know that I'll never leave you.' Then she untied her golden garter and put it round the fawn's neck, and picked reeds and wove them into a soft rope. She tied the little animal to it and led it beside her as she went on deeper and deeper into the forest. And when they had gone a long long way, they finally came to a little house, and the girl peeped in and saw that it was empty, so she thought: We can stay and live here. Then she gathered leaves and moss to make a soft bed for the little fawn, and every morning she went out and picked roots and berries and nuts and brought young grass back for the fawn, which ate out of her hand and was quite content and scampered about beside her. At nightfall, when Little Sister was tired and had said her prayers, she laid her head on the little fawn's back, and he was her pillow and she fell asleep ever so softly. And if only Little Brother had had his human shape it would have been a wonderful life.

For a time they were alone in the wilds like this. But it happened that the king of that country was hunting in the forest with many followers. Then through the trees came the sounding of horns and the baying of hounds and the merry cries of the huntsmen, and the fawn heard them and longed to join in. 'Oh,' he said to his sister, 'let me out to join in the hunt, I can't bear this any longer,' and he kept pleading with her till she consented. 'But,' she said to him, 'be sure to come back to me at nightfall, and I'll shut my door to keep out those wild huntsmen; and so that I shall know it's you, you must knock and say: "My Little Sister, let me in," and if you don't say that I shan't open my door.' Then the young deer sped away and felt so happy and high-spirited in the open air. The king and his huntsmen sighted this fine animal and gave chase, but he outran them, and each time they were sure they had caught him he leapt over the bushes and vanished. When it got dark he ran back to the little house, knocked and said: 'My Little Sister, let me in.' Then she opened the little door for him, and he bounded in and slept soundly all night on his soft couch. Next morning the hunt started again, and when the young deer heard the hunting horn and the huntsmen's tally-ho he grew more and more restless and said: 'Little Sister, open the door, I must go out.' Little Sister opened the door for him and said: 'But you must come back here in the evening and say your words.' When the king and his huntsmen saw the fawn with the golden collar again, they all chased him, but he was too fast and nimble for them. The chase lasted all day, but finally, in the evening, the huntsmen had completely surrounded him, and one of them wounded him slightly in one foot so that he limped and couldn't run fast. Then a huntsman stalked him as far as the little house and heard him call out: 'My Little Sister, let me in,' and saw the door being opened and closed again at once. The huntsman took good note of all this, went to the king and told him what he had seen and heard. Then the king said: 'Tomorrow we shall hunt once more.'

But Little Sister got a terrible fright when she saw that her dear fawn was wounded. She washed off the blood, put herbs on the wound and said: 'Go to your bed, dear little deer, and get better again.' But the wound was so slight that next morning the young deer no longer noticed it. And when he heard the merry hunt starting up again outside, he said: 'I can't bear it, I must join in; they'll not catch me so easily.' Little Sister cried and said: 'They'll kill you now, and I'll be here all alone in the forest and I won't have anyone in the whole world – I won't let you out.' 'Then I'll die of melancholy here,' answered the fawn, 'for when I hear the hunting horn I feel like jumping off my feet!' Then his little sister had no choice and with a heavy heart she opened the door for him, and the young deer bounded into the forest hale and hearty. When the king saw him he said to his huntsmen: 'Now hunt him all day until nightfall, but let none of you hurt him.' As soon as the sun was down the king said to the huntsman who had seen it: 'Now come and show me that little hut.' And when he got to the door, he knocked at it and called out: 'Dear Little Sister, let me in.' And the door opened, and the king stepped inside, and there stood a girl more beautiful than any he had ever seen. The girl was terrified when she saw a man with a golden crown on his head coming in instead of her fawn. But the king looked at her tenderly, took her hand and said: 'Will you come with me to my palace and be my dear wife?' 'Oh yes,' answered the girl, 'but my little deer must come too, I can't leave him.' The king said: 'He shall stay with you all your life and shall lack for nothing.' And meanwhile the deer came bounding in, so Little Sister tied the rope of reeds to him again, took it in her hand and they left the hut together.

The king put the beautiful girl on his horse and took her to his palace, where the wedding was celebrated with great magnificence. So now she was queen, and they lived a long time contentedly together; and the fawn was cherished and cared for and went leaping around in the palace garden. But the wicked stepmother, on whose account the children had left home, never doubted that Little Sister had been torn to pieces in the forest by wild beasts and that Little Brother after turning into a young deer had been shot dead by the huntsmen. So when she heard that things had turned out so well for them and they were so happy, envy and malice began stirring in her heart and left her no peace, and she thought of nothing else but how she might still bring misfortune on the two of them. Her own daughter, who was as ugly as night and had only one eye, reproached her and said: 'It's I who deserve to be queen! She has all the luck.' 'Never mind,' said the old woman and spoke to her soothingly, 'you can be sure of my help when it's time.' So when the time came and the queen had given birth to a beautiful little boy and the king happened to be out hunting, the old witch took the shape of the maid-in-waiting, entered the room where the queen lay sick and weak and said to her: 'Come,

madam, your bath's ready, it will do you good and make you
strong again: quick, before it gets cold.' Her daughter was there
too, and they carried the queen to the bathroom and laid her in
the bath: then they locked the door and made off. But in the
bathroom they had set a blazing hot fire going, so that the
beautiful young queen was soon suffocated.

When that was done the old woman took her daughter,
covered her head with a nightcap and put her into bed in place
of the queen. She gave her the queen's form and features too,
except that she couldn't put her missing eye back again. But so
that the king would not notice, she told her to lie on the blind
side of her face. When the king got home in the evening and
heard that a little boy had been born to him, he was delighted
and wanted to go to his dear wife's bedside and see how she
was. But the old woman called out quickly: 'No, no, sir, leave
the curtains closed, the queen mustn't have light on her yet and
must rest.' The king withdrew and didn't realize that there was
a false queen in the bed.

But when midnight came and everyone was asleep except the
nurse who sat by the cradle in the nursery, she saw the door
open and the rightful queen enter. She took the baby out of the
cradle, rested him on her arm and let him drink. Then she
smoothed out his little pillow, put him back in again and tucked
him up under the coverlet. But she didn't forget the little fawn
either, went to the corner where it lay and stroked its back
Then she walked out of the door again in complete silence, and
next morning the nurse asked the guards if anyone had entered
the castle during the night, but they answered: 'No, we saw no
one.' She came and went like this many nights on end, always
without speaking a word; the nurse saw her every time, but
didn't dare tell anyone about it.

When this had been going on for some time, the queen began
to speak in the night and said:

'How is my baby dear? How is my baby deer?
Twice more I'll come and then never again come here.'

The nurse didn't answer, but when the queen had disappeared
again she went to the king and told him everything. The king

said: 'Alas, what can this mean? Tomorrow night I shall keep watch by the child.' Next evening he went to the nursery, and at midnight the queen appeared again and said:

'How is my baby dear? How is my baby deer?
Once more I'll come and then never again come here.'

And then she nursed the child as usual and vanished. The king didn't dare speak to her, but he kept watch on the following night too. Again she said:

'How is my baby dear? How is my baby deer?
Now is the last time, I'll never again come here.'

At this the king could not restrain himself, rushed across the room to her and said: 'Surely you are no one but my dear wife.' And she answered: 'Yes, I am your dear wife,' and at that moment, by God's grace, her life was restored to her again, and she was fresh and rosy and well. Then she told the king of the crime committed against her by the evil witch and her daughter. The king had both of them brought to trial, and they were condemned. The daughter was taken into the forest, where the wild beasts tore her to pieces, but for the witch a fire was lit and she was burnt miserably to death. And when she had crumbled into ashes, the fawn was transformed and his human shape restored; so Little Sister and Little Brother lived happily together till the end of their days.

10

THE THREE LITTLE MEN
IN THE FOREST

Once there was a man and his wife died, and a woman whose husband died; and the man had a daughter, and the woman had a daughter too. The girls knew each other and went out walking together and afterwards came back to the woman's house. And she said to the man's daughter: 'Listen to me: you tell your father I'd like to marry him, and after that you shall wash every morning in milk and drink wine, but my daughter shall wash in water and drink water.' The girl went home and told her father what the woman had said. The man said: 'What shall I do? Marriage is a pleasure and it's a plague as well.' Finally, unable to make up his mind, he took off one of his boots and said: 'Take this boot, it's got a hole in the sole; go to the attic with it and hang it up on the big nail and then pour water into it. If the water stays in it I'll take a wife again, but if it runs through it I won't.' The girl did as she was told; but the water made the hole shrink and the boot stayed full right to the top. She reported to her father how it had turned out. Then he went upstairs, and when he saw that it was true enough he went to the widow and asked for her hand, and the wedding took place.

Next morning, when the two girls got up, the man's daughter found she had been given milk to wash in and wine to drink, but the woman's daughter got water to wash in and water to drink. On the second morning both the husband's daughter and the wife's got water to wash in and water to drink, and on the third morning the husband's daughter got water to wash in and to drink and the wife's daughter got milk to wash in and wine to drink, and that was the way it stayed. The woman came to hate the sight of her stepdaughter and thought of new ways of tormenting her with every day that passed. She was envious, too, because her stepdaughter was beautiful and charming but her own daughter ugly and unpleasant.

One winter day when the ground was frozen stiff as a stone and the snow covered hill and dale, the woman made a paper dress, called the girl and said: 'Put on this dress, go out into the forest and fetch me a basket full of strawberries, I'm feeling like some strawberries.' 'Why, Lord help us,' said the girl, 'strawberries don't grow in winter, the earth's frozen, and everything's covered with snow, anyway. And why am I to go out in this paper dress? It's so cold that your breath freezes; the wind will blow through it and the thorns will tear it off me.' 'Have you done contradicting me?' retorted her stepmother. 'Get out of my sight, and don't come here again till you've got that basket full of strawberries.' Then she just gave her a crust of stale bread and said: 'You can have that for your lunch and supper.' And she thought: She'll freeze and starve to death out there and I'll be rid of her for good.

So the girl was obedient and put on her paper dress and set out with the basket. There was nothing but snow far and wide and not a green blade of grass to be seen. When she got into the forest she saw a little cottage with three little elf-men looking out of it. She wished them good day and humbly knocked at the door. They called out: 'Come in,' and she went into the parlour and sat down on the bench by the stove to warm herself and eat her breakfast. The little men said: 'Give us some too.' 'Gladly,' she said, and broke her crust in two and gave them half of it. They asked her: 'What are you doing here in the forest in winter in that thin dress?' 'Oh,' she answered, 'I'm to look for a basket full of strawberries and I'm not allowed to go home till I've got them.' When she had eaten her bread they gave her a broom and said: 'Sweep the snow away from our back door with this.' But when she had gone out the three little men asked each other: 'What shall we give her for being so good and kind and sharing her bread with us?' And the first said: 'My gift to her is that she shall become more beautiful with every day that passes.' The second said: 'My gift to her is that a gold piece shall fall from her mouth with every word she speaks.' The third said: 'My gift to her is that a king shall come and take her for his wife.'

But the girl did as the little men had told her, swept away the

snow behind the little house with the broom, and what do you
think she found? A whole patch of strawberries, growing deep
red and ripe out of the snow. She was overjoyed and picked
them till her basket was full, then she thanked the little men,
shook hands with each of them and ran back home to bring her
stepmother what she had asked for. The moment she entered
the house and said good evening, a gold coin fell from her
mouth. Then she told them what had happened to her in the
forest, but at every word she spoke gold pieces fell from her
mouth and were soon lying all over the floor. 'Well, aren't
we high and mighty!' exclaimed her stepsister, 'throwing
money around like that!' But secretly she felt envious and
wanted to go out into the forest too and look for strawberries.
Her mother said: 'No, my darling daughter, it's too cold,
you might freeze to death.' But because the girl gave her
no peace she finally consented, made her a splendid fur coat
to put on and gave her sandwiches and cakes to eat on the
way.

The girl went into the forest and straight to the little cottage.
There were the three little elf-men peeping out, but she didn't
say good day to them or look at them or greet them in any way,
she just barged into the room, sat down by the stove and began
to eat her sandwich and her cake. 'Give us some too,' cried the
little men, but she answered: 'There isn't enough for myself;
how can I give any of it to anyone else?' Then when she had
finished eating they said: 'Here's a broom for you, sweep up
behind our back door.' 'Sweep it up yourselves,' she retorted,
'I'm not your maidservant.' When she saw that they weren't
going to give her anything, she went outside the house. Then
the little men asked each other: 'What shall we give her for
being so rude and having such a wicked, envious, selfish
heart?' The first said: 'My gift to her is that she shall become
uglier with every day that passes.' The second said: 'My gift to
her is that with every word she speaks a toad shall jump out of
her mouth.' The third said: 'My gift to her is that she shall die a
cruel death.' The girl looked for strawberries outside the house,
but when she found none she went back home in a bad temper.
And when she opened her mouth to tell her mother what had

happened to her in the forest, a toad jumped from it at every word she spoke, and everyone thought what a disgusting creature she was.

This enraged the stepmother all the more, and she plotted and planned how to inflict further misery on her husband's daughter, whose beauty was indeed increasing day by day. Finally she took a cauldron, set it on the fire and boiled yarn in it. When it was boiled she hung it over the poor girl's shoulder, gave her an axe, and told her to go out on to the frozen river, chop a hole in the ice and rinse the yarn. She was obedient, went as she was told and hacked a hole in the ice; and as she was in the middle of doing this a magnificent carriage came driving up with the king sitting in it. The carriage stopped and the king asked: 'My child, who are you, and what are you doing here?' 'I'm a poor girl and I'm rinsing yarn.' Then the king felt sorry for her, and when he saw how very beautiful she was he said: 'Would you like to come with me?' 'Oh yes, with all my heart,' she answered, for she was glad to be able to get away from her mother and sister.

So she got into the carriage and drove away with the king, and when they arrived at his palace the wedding was celebrated with great magnificence, just as the little men had foretold for her. A year later the young queen gave birth to a son, and when her stepmother heard of her great good fortune she came to the palace with her daughter and pretended that they were paying the queen a visit. But one day when the king had gone out and no one else was there, the wicked woman seized the queen by the head, and her daughter seized her by the feet, and they lifted her from her bed and threw her out of the window into the stream that ran past the castle. Then the hideous daughter lay down in the bed, and the old woman covered her up from top to toe. When the king came back and wanted to talk to his wife, the old woman cried: 'Hush, hush, now is not the time, she's sweating very heavily, you must let her rest today, sir.' The king suspected nothing and didn't come back till the following morning, and then when he spoke to his wife and she answered him, a toad jumped out at every word, where a gold coin had fallen till now. He asked what this meant, but the old woman said it had been brought on by her heavy sweating and would soon get better again.

But during the night the kitchen boy saw a duck come swimming in along the drain-gutter, and it said:

'How sleeps the king tonight?
Wakes he by candlelight?'

And when he gave no answer she said:

'Where are my guests tonight?'

So the kitchen boy answered:

'They are all sleeping tight!'

And she asked again:

'Where is my babe, oh where?'

And he answered:

'Cradled and sleeping fair.'

Then she went upstairs in the form of the queen, let her son drink at her breast, shook down his bed for him, put back the covers and swam out again along the gutter in the form of a duck. She came this way two nights running, and on the third night she said to the kitchen boy: 'Go and tell the king to take his sword and brandish it over me on the threshold three times.' So the kitchen boy ran and told the king, and he came with his sword and brandished it three times over the ghost: and the third time he did so his wife stood before him, as fresh and alive and well as she had ever been.

Now the king was overjoyed, but he kept the queen hidden in a bedroom until the Sunday on which the child was to be christened. Then when it had been christened he said: 'What do people deserve who lift other people out of bed and throw them into the water?' 'Such villains deserve no better fate,' answered the old woman, 'than to be thrust into a barrel that has been hammered full of nails, and rolled down the hill into the water.' Then the king said: 'You have spoken your own sentence.' He sent for just such a barrel, and had the old woman and her daughter pushed into it; then the bottom was hammered on and the barrel was toppled downhill and rolled into the river.

11

MOTHER SNOWBED

A widow had two daughters, one of them beautiful and hard-working, the other ugly and lazy. But she much preferred the ugly and lazy one, because she was her real daughter, and the other one had to do all the work and be the kitchen drudge of the family. She forced the poor girl to sit down every day at a well by the roadside and spin till her fingers bled. Now it happened one day that the bobbin got quite covered with blood, so she stooped down with it over the well and tried to wash it, but it slipped out of her hand and fell to the bottom. She cried, ran back to her stepmother and told her about the mishap. Her stepmother gave her a terrible scolding and was so hard-hearted as to say: 'Since you let the bobbin fall down the well, you can jump in yourself and fetch it up again.' The girl went back to the well and had no idea what to do, and in her terror she jumped in to fetch the bobbin. She lost consciousness, and when she woke up and came to herself again she was in a beautiful sunlit meadow covered with thousands and thousands of flowers. She walked on through this meadow and came to an oven full of bread; and the bread was calling out to her: 'Oh, pull me out, pull me out, or I'll burn – I'm baked to a turn already.' So she went up to it and took the bread shovel and lifted all the loaves out one after another. Then she walked on and came to a tree, and it was covered with apples and called out to her: 'Oh, shake me, shake me – we apples are all ripe and ready.' So she shook the tree, and the apples fell down like rain, and she shook it until there was not one left on the branches; and when she had put them all together in a pile, she walked on again. Finally she came to a little house with an old woman looking out of it; but she had such big teeth that the girl was scared and turned to run away. But the old woman called after her: 'Why are you afraid, my dear child? Stay with me, and if you do all the housework nicely it shall go well with you. You must just be careful to make my bed properly and give it a good shake to make the feathers fly, because that's when it snows in the world; I am Mother Snowbed.' Hearing the old woman speak to her so kindly, the girl plucked up courage, consented to serve her and set to work. And she did indeed look after everything to the old woman's satisfaction and always gave her bed a mighty great shake, making the feathers fly around like snowflakes. In return she was very well cared for, never given a harsh word and fed every day on roasts and stews. When she had been with Mother Snowbed for quite a time she began to feel sad, and at first even she herself didn't know what the matter was; finally she realized that it was homesickness. Although she was ever so many times better off here than she was at home, nevertheless she felt a longing to go back. Finally she said to the old woman: 'I've got sick for home, and although it's ever so nice down here I can't stay any longer, I must go back up to my family.' Mother Snowbed said: 'You are a good girl to want to go home again, and because you have served me so faithfully I will take you back myself.' Then she took her by the hand and led her to a huge gate. The gate was opened, and just as the girl was standing under it a great shower of gold poured down, and all the gold stuck to her so that she was completely covered with it. 'This shall be yours, because you have worked so hard,' said Mother Snowbed, and she also gave her back the bobbin that she had dropped into the well. Then the gate was closed, and the girl found herself up in the world, not far from her mother's house. And when she entered the courtyard, the cock was roosting on the well there, and he sang:

> 'Cock-a-doodle-do, doodle-do,
> Our golden lady is back, doodle-do.'

Then she went into the house, and seeing her arrive all covered with gold her mother and sister gave her quite a welcome.

The girl told them all that had happened to her, and when her mother heard how she had got so rich she wanted to see the same good fortune come to her other daughter, the ugly and lazy one. So she told her to sit by the well and spin; and so that there would be blood on her bobbin, she pricked herself in the

finger and stuck her hand into the thorn hedge. Then she threw
the bobbin into the well and jumped in after it. She landed, like
her sister, on the beautiful meadow and walked along the same
path. When she got to the oven, the bread again called out: 'Oh,
pull me out, pull me out, or I'll burn – I'm baked to a turn
already.' But the lazy girl replied: 'And get myself all dirty? I
should think not!' And she walked on. Soon she came to the
apple tree and it called out: 'Oh, shake me, shake me – we
apples are all ripe and ready.' But she answered: 'The very idea!
One of you might fall on my head,' and with that she walked
on. When she came to Mother Snowbed's house she wasn't
scared, because she'd been told about her big teeth already, and
she entered service with her right away. On the first day she
forced herself to work hard, obeying Mother Snowbed and
doing everything she told her, thinking of all the gold she
would be given. But on the second day she had already begun
skimping her work, and on the third she grew idler still, even
refusing to get up in the morning. Also she didn't make the
snowbed properly or shake it to make the feathers fly. Mother
Snowbed soon got tired of this and dismissed her from her
service. That was well to the sloven's liking, for now, she
thought, the shower of gold will fall; and sure enough, Mother
Snowbed took her to the gate, but as she was standing under it a
great cauldron full of pitch was poured over her instead of the
gold. 'That's your wages,' said Mother Snowbed, and shut the
gate. So the idle sister got home, but she was covered all over
with pitch, and when the cock that perched on the well saw her,
he sang:

> 'Cock-a-doodle-do, doodle-do,
> Our dirty black slut is back, boo-hoo.'

And the pitch stuck fast to her, so that she was never able to rub
it off for the rest of her life.

12

THE THREE BIRDIES

A thoosand or mair year syne there wiz nae ae king in Scotland but a wheen o little kingies, an een o them dwallt on Benachìe, an he was daft on huntin. Eence as he rade oot o's castle wi his huntsmen, there wiz three quines herdin their kye ablò Benachìe, an fan they saa the king wi aa his mengie, the auldest quine cryet tae the ither twa, pintin tae the king: 'Halloo! Gin I dinnae get him for a man, I'll hae nane avà.' An the secant answert fae the ither side o the hill, pintin tae the man at the king's richt side: 'Halloo! Gin I dinnae get him for a man, I'll hae nane avà.' An the youngest pintet tae the man at the king's left side an cryet: 'Halloo! Gin I dinnae get him for a man, I'll hae nane avà.' (That wiz the king's twa ministers.) The king he heert aathing, an fan he cam hame fae the hunt, he sent for the three quines an spiert at them fit they haed said bi the hill the day afore. They waednae say, but the king spiert at the auldest quine gin she waed hae hem for a man; an she said aye, an the twa ministers socht her twa sisters, for they war bonny-face't lassies aa three o them, the auldest afore them aa, an she haed hair lik lint.

Noo the twa sisters they war bairnless; an eence fan the king haed tae ride furth he brocht them tae the queen tae keep her cheerie, for she wiz expectin a bairnie. She gied birth tae a loon-bairnie, an reid, reid wiz the star at his birth. An the twa sisters said the teen tae the tither: 'We'll tak the bonny laddie an throw im in the watter.' An fan they haed thrown im in the watter (I wyte it wiz the Gaudie watter), a birdie flew up intae the lift an sang:

> Daith-bund am I
> Till the Lord say aye
> The lilly's my sign
> Is that you, lad o mine?

An fan they heert that, a fear cam ower them an awà they ran; an fan the king cam hame, they tellt im that the queen haed fulpit a doggie. 'The Lord's will be deen,' said the king.

But there wiz a fisher that dwallt bi the watterside, an he fesht the loonie oot o the watter still livin; an seein his gweedwìfe wiz bairnless, they brocht im up. A year aifter that the king rade furth again, an the queen gat anither loonie, an again the fauss sisters took im an threw im in the watter, an again the birdie flew up intae the lift an sang:

> Daith-bund am I
> Till the Lord say aye
> The lilly's my sign
> Is that you, lad o mine?

An fan the king cam hame, they tellt im that the queen haed fulpit a doggie again, an eence mair he said: 'The Lord's will be deen.' But the fisher took this secant loonie oot o the watter an brocht im up.

Syne the king he rade furth again, an the queen haed a quinie that the fauss sisters threw intae the watter likewise. Eence again the birdie flew up intae the lift an sang:

> Daith-bund am I
> Till the Lord say aye
> The lilly's mỳ sign
> Is that you, lass o mine?

An fan the king cam hame, they tellt im that the queen haed haen a kitlin; an the king gaed gyte an threw his wife in the dungeon, an there she lay for mony a year an day.

In aa thes time the bairns haed groun big, an eence the auldest gaed oot wi the ither loons tae tak fesh; but they warnae seekin im wi them an said: 'Ye tinker's geet that ye are, gyang yer weys.' At that he wiz sair dooncast, an he spiert at the auld fisher gin it wiz true. He tellt im foo he haed eence been fishin an haed pullt im oot o the watter. An the loon said he waed awà an seek for his daddie. The fisher he priggit wi im tae byde, but there wiz nae haudin im, sae in the en' the fisher haed tae say aye. Oot he set, an aifter he haed traivelt a twarthree days he cam till a muckle stretch o watter, an an auld wife sittin at it takin fesh. 'Gweedday, mistress,' said the loon. 'Thank ye kindly.' 'I wyte ye'll sit lang there afore ye tak a fesh,' quo he. 'An I wyte ye'll seek lang afore ye fin' yer daddie,' quo she. 'Foo will ye cross thes watter?' 'Gweed only kens,' said he. An the auld wife took him up on er back an cairrit im ower; an lang he socht but couldnae fin' his daddie. Syne a year gaed by an the secant loon he gaed oot tae seek for his brither. He cam tae the watter, an the same thing happint tae him that happint tae his brither. Sae there wiz nae but the dother left at hame, an she grat that sair for her brithers that in the en' she priggit wi er father tae lat er gyang tae seek for er brithers. Sae she cam tae the great watter an she said tae the auld wife: 'Gweedday, mistress.' 'Thank ye kindly.' 'The gweed Lord help ye tae tak yer fish.' Fan the auld wife heert that, she grew richt freenly-like an cairrit er ower the watter an gied er a stick an said: 'Noo, my lass, keep tae thes road, an fan ye come till a muckle black dog, ye maun gyang past im quaet an fearless, an naether lauch nor look at im. Syne ye'll come tae a great open castle, an on the doorsteen o't ye maun drap yer stick an gyang stracht throu the castle an oot at the tither side. There ye'll see an auld *waull wi a muckle tree grouin oot o't, an a birdie in a cage hingin on the tree; lift it doon. An syne tak a gless o watter fae the waull an gyang back the same wey cairryin them. At the doorsteen pick up yer stick again, an fan ye come past the dog again hit im in the face, but see an gie im a proper dunt, an syne come back tae me.' She fund aathing jist as the auld wife tellt er, an on her wey back she fund her twa brithers that haed been seekin een anither the hale wordl ower. Thegither they gaed on tae far the black dog lay bi the road, an she struck im in the face an he turnt intae a bonny prince an gaed back wi them tae the watter. The auld wife wiz aye stannin there, an richt glaed wiz she tae see them aa thegither again; an she cairrit them ower the watter an syne she pairtet fae them, for she wiz lowsed fae the spell. But the rest of them gaed back tae the auld fisher, an richt weel-pleast they war that they haed fund een anither again; an they hung the birdie in his cage on the waa.

But the secant saen he couldnae bide in peace at hame, an he

took his bou an arraws an gaed huntin. Fan he gat tỳert, he took
oot his pipe an playt an air on't. Noo, the king he wiz huntin tee,
an he heert it an cam ower, an fan he saa the loon, said he: 'Fa
gied ye leave tae hunt here?' 'Naebody.' 'Fa yaves ye?' 'I'm the
fisher's loon.' 'He has nae bairns.' 'Gin ye dinnae believe me,
come wi me an see.' That the king daed, an he spiert at the
fisher, and the fisher gied im the hale lagàmachy, an the birdie
bi the waa began tae sing:

> My mammy lies her leen
> The prison waas atween.
> Sir King, my noble Sire,
> These are thy bairns dear.
> Thy fauss gweedsisters baith
> They socht thy bairns' daith.
> The watter were their grave
> But the fisher did them save.

They war aa dumbfoonert; an the king took the birdie, the fisher
an the three bairns tae his castle an gart open the dungeon an
brocht his wife oot o't, an a peer shilpit crayter she haed groun.
But her dother gied her the watter fae the waull tae drink an she
grew canty an weel again. But the twa fauss sisters they war
burnt tae daith, an the dother she mairrit the prince.

13

THE TWELVE BROTHERS

Once upon a time there was a king and a queen who lived peaceably together and had twelve children, but the children were all boys. Then the king said to his wife: 'If the thirteenth child you are going to have is a girl, then all the twelve boys shall die, because I want her to have great wealth and the kingdom to be inherited by her alone.' Accordingly he had twelve coffins made, with wood shavings and a pillow all ready in each of them; he had them taken to a locked room, gave the key to the queen and forbade her to tell anyone about it.

The mother sat sorrowing all day, till her youngest son, who was always with her and whom she called Benjamin as in the Bible, said to her: 'Dear mother, why are you so sad?' 'My dearest child,' she replied, 'I'm forbidden to tell you.' But he left her no peace till she went and unlocked the room and showed him the twelve caskets filled with shavings all ready. Then she said: 'My dearest Benjamin, your father had these coffins made for you and your eleven brothers, because if I bring a girl into the world you are all to be killed and buried in them.' She wept as she said this, but her son comforted her and said: 'Don't cry, mother dear, we'll save ourselves all right, we'll run away.' But she said: 'Go out into the forest with your eleven brothers, and let one of you always be sitting on the tallest tree you can find, and keeping watch and looking towards the tower here in the castle. If I give birth to a little son, I shall run up a white flag, and then you may come back; but if it is a little daughter I shall run up a red flag, and then you must escape as fast as you can, and may God protect you. Every night I shall get up and pray for you; in winter I'll pray that you may have a fire to warm yourselves at, and in summer that you may not be languishing in the heat.'

So after she had blessed her sons they went out into the forest. They took turns keeping watch, sitting on the tallest oak tree and looking towards the tower. After eleven days, when it was Benjamin's turn, he saw a flag being run up: but it was not white, it was the blood-red flag announcing that they were all to perish. When the brothers heard this they were angry and said: 'Why should we be put to death because of a girl! We swear we shall be avenged – when we meet a girl, her red blood shall flow.'

Then they went deeper into the forest, and in the middle of it, where it was darkest, they found a little enchanted house standing empty. And they said: 'We'll live here, and you, Benjamin, are the youngest and weakest, so you shall stay at home and keep house; the rest of us will go out and fetch food.' So they went into the forest and shot hares and wild deer and birds and pigeons and whatever was eatable, and then took it home to Benjamin, and he had to get it ready for them so that they could eat their fill. They lived ten years together in the little house, and found plenty to do.

The little daughter who had been born to their mother the queen was now growing older, and she had a kind heart and a beautiful face and a golden star on her forehead. One day when there was a big wash being done she saw twelve shirts among the washing and asked her mother: 'Whose are those twelve shirts? They're much too small for father.' Then her mother answered with a heavy heart: 'My dear child, they belong to your twelve brothers.' The girl said: 'Where are my twelve brothers? I've never heard of them till now.' Her mother answered: 'God only knows where they are – they're wandering about in the world.' And then she took the girl and unlocked the room for her and showed her the twelve coffins, each filled with shavings and with the pillow placed ready. 'These coffins,' she said, 'were intended for your brothers, but they went away secretly before you were born.' And she told her how it had all happened. Then the little girl said: 'Dear mother, don't cry, I'll go and look for my brothers.'

So she took the twelve shirts and set out and went straight into the deep forest. She walked all day, and in the evening she came to the little enchanted house. She entered it and found a young boy and he asked her: 'Where are you from and where are you going?' He was amazed that she was so beautiful and was wearing royal clothes and had a star on her forehead. She answered: 'I'm a princess and I'm looking for my twelve brothers, and I will go to the ends of the earth to find them.' And she showed him the twelve shirts that belonged to her brothers. At this Benjamin realized that she was his sister, and said: 'I'm Benjamin, your youngest brother.' And she began to cry with joy and Benjamin did too, and they kissed and hugged each other very lovingly. Then he said: 'Dear sister, there's still a problem: my brothers and I had agreed that any girl we met would die, because we had to leave our kingdom on account of a girl.' So she said: 'I will gladly die if that will save my twelve brothers.' 'No,' he answered, 'you shan't die; sit down under this barrel till our eleven brothers come, then I'll get round them, never fear.' So she did that, and when night fell the others came back from hunting and the meal was ready. And as they were sitting at table and eating they asked: 'What's new?' Benjamin said: 'Don't you know what?' 'No,' they answered. So he said: 'You've been in the forest, and I've stayed at home, and yet I know more than you do.' 'Then tell us!' they exclaimed. He answered: 'But will you promise me then that the first girl we meet shall not be killed?' 'Yes,' they all cried, 'she shall be spared, go on, tell us.' So he said: 'Our sister is here,' and lifted the barrel, and the princess came out in her royal clothes, with the golden star on her forehead, looking so beautiful and dainty and neat. Then they were all overjoyed and embraced her and kissed her and loved her with all their hearts.

So now she stayed at home with Benjamin and helped him with the housework. The eleven went out into the forest and caught game and deer and birds and pigeons as food for them all, and their sister and Benjamin saw to the preparation of it. She fetched the wood for the cooking and picked fresh vegetables and put the pots on the fire, so that there was always a meal ready when the eleven came home. She looked after the little house in other ways too, and made up the beds with spotless white linen, and her brothers were always contented and they all lived very peaceably with her.

One evening she and Benjamin had prepared a lovely meal, and when the others got back they all sat down together and ate and drank and had a fine time. But there was a little garden behind the enchanted house, and in it there grew twelve lilies, narcissus-flowers some folk call them – and to please her brothers she picked these twelve flowers, thinking she would give one to each of them to go with his supper. But at the very same moment as she picked the flowers, her twelve brothers had been changed into twelve ravens and flown away over the forest, and the house and its garden had vanished as well. So now the poor girl was all alone in the wild forest, and as she looked this way and that she saw an old woman standing beside her, who said: 'My child, what have you done? Why didn't you leave these twelve white flowers alone? They were your brothers, and now they're changed into ravens for ever.' The girl wept and asked: 'Then is there no way of saving them?' 'No,' said the old woman, 'no way in the whole world except one, but it's so difficult that you'll not be able to free your brothers that way. For you must be dumb for seven years, you mustn't speak and mustn't laugh, and if you say a single word or if even one hour of the seven years is lacking, then all will have been in vain, and that one word will kill your brothers.'

Then the girl said in her heart: 'I know for certain that I shall save my brothers.' And she went and looked for a tall tree, climbed up into it and sat there spinning, and neither spoke nor laughed. Now it happened that a king was hunting in the forest, and he had a big deerhound with him which ran up to the tree where the girl was sitting and bounded round it, howling and barking up into it. So the king approached and saw the beautiful princess with the golden star on her forehead, and he was so enchanted by her beauty that he called out to her and asked if she would be his wife. She gave no answer, but nodded her head a little. Then he climbed up the tree himself and carried her down and put her on his horse and took her home with him. The wedding was celebrated with great magnificence and joy, but the bride did not speak and did not laugh. When they had been living happily together for a time, the king's mother, who was a wicked woman, began to slander the young queen and said to the king: 'This girl you've married is a common beggar; who knows what godless mischief she does in secret. She may be dumb and unable to speak, but she could at least laugh, and anyone who never laughs has a bad conscience.' At first the king wouldn't believe it, but the old woman kept on at him for so long and accused the queen of so many wicked things that in the end he let himself be persuaded and condemned her to death.

So a great fire was lit in the courtyard for her to be burnt, and the king stood looking down from the window with tears in his eyes, because he still loved her so much. And when they had already tied her to the stake and the red tongues of fire were licking at her clothes, the last moment of the seven years passed. Then a whirring of wings was heard and twelve ravens came flying through the air and swooped to the ground; and the moment they touched it they were her twelve brothers, and she had released them from the spell. They pulled the fire apart and stamped out the flames, freed their dear sister and kissed and hugged her. But now that she was allowed to open her mouth and speak, she told the king why she had been dumb and never laughed. The king was overjoyed when he heard that she was innocent, and from then on they all lived together peaceably till their lives' end. The wicked stepmother was put on trial; they thrust her into a barrel filled with boiling oil and poisonous snakes, and she died an evil death.

14

THE SEVEN RAVENS

There was a man who had seven sons, but he had no daughter, greatly though he longed for one. At last his wife told him that they could again expect a child and, sure enough, when it was born it was a baby girl. There was great rejoicing, but the child was weak and puny, so weak that it had to be christened at once. The father told one of the boys to go quickly to the spring and fetch christening water; the other six ran along with him, and because each of them wanted to be the first to dip the jug into the well, it fell in and sank. So there they stood and didn't know what to do, and none of them dared go home. When they didn't come back their father got impatient and said: 'I'll wager they've been playing some game again and forgotten all about it, the godless brats.' He was afraid the little girl would have to die unbaptized, and in his rage he cried out: 'I wish those boys would all turn into ravens.' He'd scarcely spoken the words when he heard a whirring of wings in the air overhead, looked up and saw seven coal-black ravens flying away.

The parents were unable now to take back the curse, and yet, grief-stricken as they were at the loss of their seven sons, they took some comfort from their beloved little daughter, who soon got well and strong and became more beautiful with every day that passed. For a long time the little girl didn't even know that she had had brothers, for her parents took care not to mention them, but one day by chance she heard some people talking about her. 'The girl's beautiful, of course,' they were saying, 'but she's to blame really for her seven brothers' misfortune.' This made her very sad, and she went to her father and mother and asked whether it was true then that she had had brothers and what had become of them. So now it was no longer possible for her parents to conceal from her what had happened, though they told her that it had been God's will and that her birth had only been the innocent occasion for it. But day after day she was

conscience-stricken about it, and felt that it was her duty to free
her brothers from the spell again. The thought gave her no
peace, so in the end she left home secretly and went off into the
wide world to try and trace her brothers wherever they might
be, and rescue them at whatever cost. She took nothing with
her but a ring belonging to her parents to remember them by, a
loaf of bread for when she was hungry, a jug of water for when
she was thirsty, and a little chair for when she was tired.

She went on and on, further and further, till she reached the
end of the world. There she came to the sun, but it was too hot
and terrible and it devoured little children. Quickly she ran
away and went to the moon, but it was too cold and it was grisly
and evil, and when it noticed the child it said: 'I smell human
flesh.' So she hurried off as fast as she could and came to the
stars, and they were friendly and kind to her, and each of them
was sitting on its own little chair. But the morning star got up
and gave her a little chicken's leg and said: 'If you don't have
this chicken's leg, you won't be able to unlock the glass mountain, and inside the glass mountain is where your brothers are.'

The girl took the leg, wrapped it up well in a piece of cloth,
and set off again and went on and on until she came to the glass
mountain. The gate was locked, and she tried to take out the
chicken's leg; but when she unwrapped the cloth it was empty,
and she had lost the gift of the kindly stars. What was she to do
now? She wanted to rescue her brothers, but she had no key to
the glass mountain. The good little sister took a knife, chopped
off one of her little fingers, stuck it in the lock and successfully
opened the gate. When she got inside, a little dwarf came to
meet her, saying: 'My child, what are you looking for?' 'I'm
looking for my brothers, the seven ravens,' she answered. The
dwarf said: 'My masters the ravens are not at home, but if you
would like to wait here till they get back, then come in.' Then
the dwarf brought in the ravens' supper on seven little plates
and in seven little cups, and the little sister ate a morsel from
each plate and drank a sip from each cup; but into the last cup
she dropped the ring she had brought with her.

Suddenly she heard a whirring and fluttering noise in the air,
and the dwarf said: 'Here come my lords the ravens flying

home.' And they came, asked for food and drink and looked for their plates and cups. Then one after another of them said: 'Who's been eating from my plate? Who's been drinking out of my cup? This must have been a human mouth.' And when the seventh of them had got to the bottom of his cup, the ring rolled out towards him. Then he looked at it and recognized it as a ring belonging to his father and mother, and said: 'May God grant that our little sister is here; if she were, we should be freed from the spell.' The girl was standing listening behind the door, and when she heard him speak this wish she stepped out, and as she did so the ravens recovered their human shape. And they hugged and kissed each other and went happily home.

15

THE SIX SWANS

A king once went hunting in a great forest, and he was chasing a stag so fast that none of his men could keep up with him. When evening came, he stopped and looked round and realized that he was lost. He searched for a way out but could find none. Then he saw an old woman walking towards him, wagging her head. Now this woman was a witch. 'Old lady,' he said to her, 'can you perhaps show me the way through the forest?' 'Oh yes, my lord king,' she answered, 'that I can, but on one condition: if you don't agree to it, you'll never get out of the forest and you'll starve to death.' 'What condition?' asked the king. 'I have a daughter,' said the old woman, 'who is as beautiful as any you'll find in the world and well deserves to become your wife. If you will make her queen, my lord, I will show you the way out of the forest.' In his mortal fear the king consented, and the old woman took him to her hut, where her daughter was sitting by the fire. She received the king as if she had been expecting him, and he saw that she was indeed very beautiful, but nevertheless he didn't like the look of her and she filled him with a kind of dread. After he had lifted this girl on to his horse the old woman showed him the way, and the king got back to his palace, where the wedding was celebrated.

The king had been married before and by his first wife he had seven children, six boys and a girl. He loved them more than anything in the world, and fearing now that their stepmother might ill-treat them or even harm them, he took them to a solitary castle in the depths of a forest. It was so well concealed and the way to it was so hard to find that he would never have found it himself if a wise-woman had not given him a ball of thread that had magic properties: when he threw it down in front of him, it would unwind itself and show him the way. But the king went out there so often to visit his dear children that the queen noticed his absences and became curious to know

what he was up to all by himself out there in the forest. She
bribed his servants and they betrayed the secret to her, telling
her also about the ball of thread which was the only thing that
could show her the way. So now she had no peace till she had
found out where the king kept the thread. Then she made little
white silk shirts, and by witchcraft that she had learnt from her
mother she sewed a spell into them. And one day when the
king had gone out hunting she took the shirts and went into the
forest, and the ball of thread showed her the way. When she
came within sight of the castle the children saw someone
approaching, and thinking it was their beloved father they
rushed out joyfully to meet him. At once she threw one of the
shirts over each of them, and the moment the shirts had
touched their bodies they were changed into swans and flew
away over the trees. The queen went home feeling very pleased
and thinking she had got rid of her stepchildren, but the little
girl had not run to meet her with her brothers and the queen
didn't know of her existence. Next day the king came to visit his
children, and found no one there except the girl. 'Where are
your brothers?' asked the king. 'Alas, dear father,' she
answered, 'they've gone away and left me here alone.' And she
told him how she had looked out of her little window and seen
her brothers flying away over the forest in the form of swans,
and showed him the feathers they had dropped into the courtyard and she had picked up. The king was grief-stricken, but he
didn't suspect that it was the queen who had done this wicked
deed, and fearing that the girl would be stolen from him as well
he wanted to take her away with him. But she was afraid of her
stepmother and begged the king to let her stay just this one
more night in the castle.

The poor girl thought: I can't stay here any longer now, I will
go and look for my brothers. And when night fell she ran away
and went straight on into the forest. She walked all night and
the next day too without stopping, till she was so tired she could
go no further. Then she saw a huntsman's hut, went up into it
and found a room with six little beds; she didn't dare lie in any
of them, but crawled under one and lay down on the hard floor,
meaning to spend the night there. But just before sunset she

heard a beating of wings and saw six swans come flying in through the window. They settled on the floor and blew at each other until all their feathers were blown off, and their swan-skins peeled off like shirts. When the girl looked at them, she was overjoyed to recognize her brothers and crawled out from under the bed. Her brothers were no less overjoyed to see their little sister, but their joy was brief. 'You can't stay here,' they told her. 'This hut is a robbers' hideout, and if they come home and find you they'll murder you.' 'But can't you protect me?' asked their sister. 'No,' they replied, 'because we can only take off our swan-skins and regain our human shape for a quarter of an hour every evening; then we're turned back into swans.' Their sister wept and said: 'But can't you be freed from the spell?' 'Alas, no,' they replied, 'the conditions are too difficult. You must neither speak nor laugh for six years, and during that time you must make six shirts for us out of starflowers. If you were to speak a single word, all your work would be in vain.' When her brothers had said this the quarter of an hour was up, and they turned into swans and flew out of the window again.

But the girl firmly made up her mind to save her brothers, even if it should cost her her life. She left the hut, went right into the middle of the forest, climbed a tree and spent the night in it. Next morning she went out and gathered starflowers and began to sew. There was no one for her to talk to and she didn't feel like laughing; she just sat there looking only at her work. She had already been there for a long time when one day it happened that the king of that country was hunting in the forest and his huntsmen rode up to the tree where she was sitting. They called out to her and said: 'Who are you?' But she didn't answer. 'Come down to us,' they said, 'we'll do you no harm.' She merely shook her head. When they went on pressing her with questions, she threw her gold necklace down to them, thinking that might satisfy them. But they still persisted, so she threw down her girdle and then, when that did no good either, her garters; and gradually she threw down everything she was wearing and could spare, till she had nothing on but her shift. But the huntsmen wouldn't be put off; they climbed up into the tree, lifted the girl down and took her to the king. The king asked: 'Who are you? What are you doing in that tree?' But she made no reply. He asked her again in every language he knew, but she remained as silent as a fish. She was so beautiful, however, that the king's heart was touched and he fell deeply in love with her. He threw his cloak round her, seated her on his horse, mounted behind her and took her back to his castle. There he had her dressed in fine clothes, and her beauty was as radiant as the bright day, but not a word could be got out of her. He put her next to him at table and was so attracted by her gentle and modest bearing that he said: 'This is the girl I want to marry, and no other in the world,' and a few days later they were married.

But the king had a wicked mother who was not pleased by this marriage and spoke ill of the young queen. 'How do we know what the girl's origins are?' she said. 'She can't even talk, she's not worthy of a king.' A year later, when the queen's first child was born, the old woman took it from her when she was asleep and smeared blood on her mouth. Then she went to the king and accused her of being an ogress who ate children. The king would not believe it and would not allow any harm to come to her. The queen sat on, stitching the shirts together and paying no attention to anything else. The next time, when she again gave birth to a fine boy, the deceitful mother-in-law played the same trick, but the king could not bring himself to believe what she said. He answered: 'She's too gentle and kind to be capable of doing such a thing; if she were not dumb and could defend herself, her innocence would be proved.' But when on a third occasion the old woman stole the new-born child and accused the queen, who uttered not a word in her own defence, the king was forced to have her put on trial, and the judges condemned her to be burnt to death.

When the day came on which the sentence was to be carried out, it was also the last day of the six years during which she was not allowed to speak or laugh, and she had freed her dear brothers from the power of the spell. She had finished the six shirts, except that the last one still had its left sleeve missing. So when she was led out to be burnt she carried the shirts over her arm, and when she was standing at the stake and they were just about to light the fire, she looked this way and that and saw six swans flying towards her. Then she realized that rescue was at hand and her heart leapt for joy. The swans came rushing through the air and swooped to the ground, so that she was able to throw the shirts over them, and the moment they touched them their swan-skins fell off, and there were her brothers standing before her alive and well and handsome; only the youngest of them had his left arm missing and a swan's wing growing out of his back instead. They hugged and kissed each other, and the queen went to the king, who was overcome with amazement, and spoke to him for the first time. 'My dearest husband,' she said, 'now I am allowed to speak and to tell you that I am innocent and falsely accused.' And she told him how he had been deceived by the old queen, who had taken her three children from her and hidden them away. Then to the king's great joy they were brought out of hiding, and the wicked mother-in-law was punished by being tied to the stake and burnt to ashes. But the king and queen and their six brothers lived for many years in peace and happiness.

16

THE TWO BROTHERS

Once upon a time there were two brothers, one rich and the other poor. The rich one was a goldsmith and had a wicked heart, the poor one scraped a living as a broom-maker and was kind and honest. The poor brother had two children; they were twin boys and as like each other as two drops of water. Sometimes the two little brothers would go to their rich uncle's house and get some of the left-overs to eat. One day it happened that when the poor man went into the forest to fetch firewood, he saw a bird that was golden all over and so beautiful that he had never seen one like it. He picked up a pebble and threw it at the bird and managed to hit it, but only a golden feather fell down and the bird flew away. The man picked up the feather and took it to his brother, who looked at it and said: 'It's pure gold,' and gave him a lot of money for it. The next day the man climbed up a birch tree to chop off a few branches: the same bird came flying out, and when the man searched he found a nest with a golden egg in it. He went home with the egg and took it to his brother, who said again: 'It's pure gold,' and gave him what it was worth. Finally the goldsmith said: 'I'd like to have that bird itself.' The poor brother went into the forest a third time and again saw the golden bird perching on the tree: so he threw a stone at it and brought it down and took it to his brother, who gave him a whole lot of gold for it. Now I'll be able to make ends meet, thought the broom-maker, and went home content.

The goldsmith was clever and crafty and knew very well what sort of bird this was. He called his wife and said: 'Roast me this bird and take care not to lose any part of it: I have a mind to eat the whole of it myself.' Now this was no ordinary bird, but one so miraculous that anyone who ate its heart and liver found a gold·piece under his pillow every morning. The wife prepared the bird and put it on a spit to roast. Now it happened that while it was roasting by the fire and the woman had to leave the kitchen to do some other work, the poor broom-maker's two children ran in and stopped beside the spit. They turned it round a few times, and as they did so two small pieces fell out of the bird into the pan. Then one of the brothers said: 'Let's eat these two little bits, I'm so hungry, and after all no one will notice.' So they both ate the pieces; but the woman came in, saw that they were eating something and said: 'What have you eaten?' 'Two little bits that fell out of the bird,' they answered. 'That was its heart and liver,' exclaimed the woman in alarm, and, not wanting her husband to miss anything and get angry, she quickly slaughtered a chicken, took out its heart and liver and added them to the rest of the golden bird. When it was done she served it up to the goldsmith, who ate it all by himself, leaving nothing over. But when he put his hand under his pillow next morning thinking he would find a gold piece, there was no more a gold piece there than on any other morning.

But the two children didn't know what a stroke of luck had come their way. Next morning when they got out of bed something fell to the floor with a clink, and when they picked it up they found it was two gold coins. They took them to their father, who said in astonishment: 'How can this have happened?' But when they found another two on the following morning and this happened every day, he went to his brother and told him the strange story. The goldsmith realized at once what had happened and that the children had eaten the heart and liver of the golden bird, and in order to have his revenge, being an envious and hard-hearted man, he said to the father: 'Your children are in league with the Devil; so don't take the gold and don't let them stay in your house any longer – he has them in his power and may bring ruin on you as well.' The father was afraid of the Devil, and hard though it was for him to do it, he took the twins out into the forest and with a heavy heart left them there.

The two children wandered round in the forest looking for the way home, but they couldn't find it and only got more and more lost. Finally they met a huntsman who asked them: 'Who do you two boys belong to?' 'We're the poor broom-maker's two sons,' they answered, and told him how their father had refused to let them stay at home any longer because they kept finding gold pieces under their pillows every morning. 'Well,' said the huntsman, 'that's no great misfortune, provided you stay honest and don't become idlers.' And because he was a kind man who liked the look of the children and had none of his own, he took them back home with him and said: 'I'll be father to you and bring you up.' So they stayed with him and learnt how to hunt, and as for the gold coins they both kept finding when they got out of bed, he saved them up for them in case they should need them in the future.

When they were grown up, their foster-father took them with him into the forest one day and said: 'Today you shall make your trial shot, and then I'll be able to end your apprenticeship and declare you huntsmen.' They went with him and took cover and waited for a long time, but no game appeared. Then the huntsman looked up and saw a skein of snowgeese flying in triangular formation, and he said to one of the brothers: 'Now shoot down one from each corner.' The young man did so and thus passed his test. Soon another skein appeared, in the shape of the figure two, so the huntsman told the other young man to shoot down one bird from each corner, and he passed his test as well. Then their foster-father said: 'I declare you free; you are now master huntsmen.' Then the two brothers took a walk in the forest together, talked things over and agreed what to do. And that evening when they sat down to supper they said to their foster-father: 'We shan't touch the food or take a bite till you have granted us a request.' He said: 'Well, what's your request?' They answered: 'We've finished our training now and must try our luck in the world, so give us permission to set out and go on our travels.' The old man was delighted and replied: 'Now you're talking like two fine huntsmen! What you ask is the same as what I have wished for you. Go out into the world, and you will have good luck.' And then they ate and drank merrily together.

When the appointed day came, their foster-father gave each of them a good shotgun and a dog and let them take as many of the saved-up gold pieces as they wanted. Then he accompanied them for a bit of the way, and when they parted he gave them one more thing, a knife of bright steel, and said: 'If one day you decide to separate, stick this knife into a tree at the parting of the ways, and then when one of you comes back it will show him how things have gone with his absent brother, because the side of the blade that faces the way he went will rust if he dies, but so long as he is alive it will stay bright.' The two brothers walked on further and further and found themselves in such a big forest that it was impossible for them to get out of it again that day. So they stayed in it overnight and ate the provisions they had brought with them in their hunting pouches; but when they had walked all next day they were still in the forest. As they had nothing to eat, one of them said: 'We must shoot something for ourselves, or we'll starve.' He loaded his gun, had a look round and when an old hare came running out he took aim, but the hare cried out:

> 'Huntsman, huntsman, let me live,
> And two little hares I'll give!'

and at once it bounded off into the undergrowth and brought back two of its young; but the little animals skipped about so merrily and were so endearing that the two huntsmen hadn't the heart to kill them. So they kept them and took them along, and the young hares followed at their heels. Soon after this a fox was slinking by and they were about to shoot it, but the fox cried out:

> 'Huntsman, huntsman, let me live;
> Two of my young cubs I'll give!'

and sure enough he brought two fox cubs, and the huntsmen hadn't the heart to kill them either, but took them along as company for the hares; so they followed them too. Presently a wolf came out of the thicket, the huntsmen took aim at him, but the wolf cried out:

> 'Huntsman, huntsman, let me live;
> Two of my young cubs I'll give!'

The huntsmen added the two wolf cubs to the procession, and they followed them as well. Presently a bear appeared; he also wanted to go on padding around for a while longer and cried out:

'Huntsman, huntsman, let me live;
Two of my young cubs I'll give!'

The two bear cubs were added to the other animals, and that
made eight already. And who came last of all? A lion, shaking
his mane. The huntsmen kept their heads and aimed their
guns, but the lion made the same speech:

'Huntsman, huntsman, let me live;
Two of my young cubs I'll give!'

And he went and fetched the cubs; so now the huntsmen had
two lions, two bears, two wolves, two foxes and two hares
following them to heel and serving them. But all this hadn't
satisfied their hunger, so they said to the foxes: 'Listen, you sly
slinkers, go and get us something to eat, you know plenty of
tricks.' They answered: 'There's a village not far from here,
we've taken quite a few chickens from it already; we'll show
you the way there.' So they went to the village, bought themselves something to eat and had their animals fed as well; then
they continued their journey. The foxes were well informed
about all the chicken-runs in the district, and were able to guide
the huntsmen to the right place every time.

They travelled around for a while like this, but couldn't find
any employment in which they could have stayed together, so
they said: 'There's nothing for it, we must separate.' They
divided the animals so that each of them got a lion, a bear, a
wolf, a fox and a hare; then they said goodbye to each other,
promised to love each other like brothers till their dying day,
and stuck the knife their foster-father had given them into a
tree. After this one of them set off eastwards and the other
westwards.

Now the younger brother and his animals came to a city that
was draped all over with black. He went into an inn and asked
the landlord if he could put his animals up. The landlord gave
them a stable with a hole in the wall: the hare crawled out
through the hole and fetched itself a cabbage; the fox went out
and caught a hen, finished it off and then ate the cock as well;
but the wolf and the bear and the lion were too big and couldn't
get out. So the landlord had them taken out to where a cow

happened to be grazing, and they made a fine meal of that. Having provided for his animals, the huntsman now asked the landlord why the city was all draped in mourning. The landlord replied: 'Because tomorrow our king's only daughter will die.' The huntsman asked: 'Is she mortally ill?' 'No,' answered the landlord, 'she is hale and hearty, but she must die nevertheless.' 'How can that be?' asked the huntsman. 'Out there beyond the city walls there's a high mountain, and on it there's a dragon, and he has to be given a pure virgin every year; otherwise he lays the whole country waste. All the maidens have been sacrificed already by now, and there's no one left but the princess, but even she isn't spared, she is being handed over to him; and that's to happen tomorrow.' The huntsman said: 'Why doesn't someone kill the dragon?' 'Oh,' answered the landlord, 'many knights have tried to do so, but every one of them forfeited his life; the king has promised his daughter in marriage to whoever conquers the dragon, and after his death he is to inherit the kingdom too.'

The huntsman said no more about this, but next morning he took his animals and climbed the dragon's mountain. At the top there was a chapel, and on the altar stood three chalices filled to the brim, and an inscription said: 'He who drinks these cups shall become the strongest man on earth and shall wield the sword that lies buried outside the threshold.' The huntsman didn't drink them; he first went out and looked for the buried sword, but he couldn't move it from its place. So he went back and drained the chalices, and that made him strong enough to pick up the sword and wield it easily. When the time came for the maiden to be sacrificed to the dragon, she was led out accompanied by the king and his marshal and all the courtiers. From a long way off she saw the huntsman on top of the dragon's mountain and thought it was the dragon standing there waiting for her, and didn't want to go up; but in the end, since otherwise the whole city would have been destroyed, she had to set out on her sorrowful way. The king and the courtiers went back home grief-stricken, but the king's marshal was ordered to stay and watch from a distance everything that happened.

When the princess came to the top of the mountain, it was not
the dragon standing there but the young huntsman, and he
comforted her and said he intended to save her. He took her to
the chapel and locked her in. Presently the seven-headed
dragon came swooping down with a great roar. When it saw the
huntsman it was surprised and said: 'What are you doing up
here on this mountain?' The huntsman answered: 'I want to
fight with you.' The dragon said: 'Many a knight-at-arms has
lost his life here, I'll soon deal with you too.' And it began
breathing fire out of its seven jaws. It meant to set the dried
grass on fire so that the huntsman would choke to death in the
heat and smoke, but his animals came running up and
stamped out the flames. Then the dragon rushed at the huntsman, but he swung his sword, making it sing through the air,
and struck off three of its heads. At this the dragon got even
more enraged, rose up into the air, spewed out fiery flames over
the huntsman and was just about to fall on him when he swung
his sword again and cut off three more of its heads. The monster
weakened and sank to the ground, yet it still tried to attack the
huntsman again, but with the last of his strength he struck off
its tail, and because he couldn't fight any more he called to his
animals, who came and tore the dragon to pieces. When the
fight was over, the huntsman unlocked the chapel and found
the princess lying on the ground, for she had swooned with fear
and terror during the battle. He carried her out, and when she
came to herself again and opened her eyes he showed her the
dismembered dragon and told her that now she was saved. She
was glad and said: 'Now you will become my dearest husband,
for my father promised me to the man who would kill the
dragon.' So saying, she undid her coral necklace and divided it
up among the animals as their reward, and the lion was given
the little golden clasp. But to the huntsman she gave her handkerchief on which her name was embroidered, and he went and
cut the tongues out of the dragon's seven heads, wrapped them
up in the handkerchief and kept them carefully.

When that was done, he felt so tired and wearied by the fire
and the fight that he said to the princess: 'We're both so tired
and weary, let's sleep a little.' So she consented, and they lay

down on the ground and the huntsman said to the lion: 'You're
to keep watch and see that no one attacks us while we are
asleep.' Then they both went to sleep; the lion lay down beside
them to keep watch, but he was tired too after the fight, so he
called the bear and said: 'Lie down beside me, I must sleep a
little, and if anything comes wake me up.' So the bear lay down
beside him, but he was tired too, so he called the wolf and said:
'Lie down beside me, I must sleep a little, and if anything comes
wake me up.' So the wolf lay down beside him, but he was tired
too, so he called the fox and said: 'Lie down beside me, I must
sleep a little, and if anything comes wake me up.' Then the fox
lay down beside him, but he was tired too, so he called the hare
and said: 'Lie down beside me, I must sleep a little, and if
anything comes wake me up.' So the hare sat down beside him,
but the poor hare was tired too and had no one to call on to help
him keep watch, and he fell asleep too. So there lay the princess, the huntsman, the lion, the bear, the wolf, the fox and the
hare, and they were all sound asleep.

But when the marshal who had been told to watch from a
distance saw that the dragon hadn't flown off with the princess
and that all was quiet on the mountain, he plucked up courage
and climbed to the top. There on the ground lay the dragon,
dismembered and torn to pieces, and not far from it the princess
and the huntsman with his animals, and they were all lying fast
asleep. And because he was wicked and godless he took his
sword and cut off the huntsman's head, then took the princess
in his arms and carried her down the hill. When she woke up
she was frightened, but the marshal said: 'You're at my mercy,
and you're to say that it was I who killed the dragon.' 'I can't say
that,' she replied, 'because a huntsman with his animals did it.'
Then he drew his sword and threatened to kill her if she didn't
obey him, and so she was forced to promise. Then he took her
before the king, who was overjoyed to see his beloved daughter
again safe and sound, for he thought she had been torn to
pieces by the monster. The marshal said to him: 'I have killed
the dragon and saved the maiden and the whole kingdom, and I
therefore claim her as my wife, as was agreed.' The king asked
the maiden: 'Is what he says true?' 'Oh yes,' she answered, 'I

suppose it must be: but I make it a condition that the marriage shall not take place for a year and a day.' For by that time she hoped she might hear some news of her beloved huntsman.

But on the dragon's mountain the animals were still lying asleep beside their dead master. Presently a big bumble-bee came and settled on the hare's nose, but the hare brushed it off with his paw and slept on. The bee came a second time, but the hare again brushed it off and carried on sleeping. Then it came a third time and stung him on the nose, waking him up. As soon as the hare was awake he woke the fox, and the fox woke the wolf, and the wolf woke the bear, and the bear woke the lion. And when the lion woke up and saw that the maiden had vanished and his master was dead, he let out a terrible roar and cried: 'Who can have done this? Bear, why didn't you wake me?' The bear asked the wolf: 'Why didn't you wake me?' The wolf asked the fox: 'Why didn't you wake me?' And the fox asked the hare: 'Why didn't you wake me?' The poor hare was the only one without an excuse, and he got all the blame. They were all about to set on him, but he pleaded with them and said: 'Don't kill me, I'll bring our master back to life again. I know a mountain where a certain root grows; put it in anyone's mouth and it will cure them of any sickness or wound. But the mountain is two hundred hours away from here.' The lion said: 'You must run there and back within twenty-four hours and bring the root with you.' The hare bounded off, and in twenty-four hours he was back with the root. The lion put the huntsman's head back on and the hare stuck the root into his mouth, and at once he grew together again, his heart started beating and his life came back to him. The huntsman woke up and saw with dismay that the maiden had disappeared. 'She must have gone away while I was asleep,' he thought, 'because she wanted to be rid of me.' The lion had been in such a hurry that he had put his master's head on the wrong way round, but the huntsman was so taken up with sorrowful thoughts about the princess that he didn't notice this. Not until lunch-time, when he tried to eat something, did he see that his head was looking out over his back. He couldn't understand this and asked the animals what had happened to him while he was asleep. Then the lion told

him that they had all been so tired that they had fallen asleep as
well, and then when they had woken up they had found him
dead with his head cut off; the hare had fetched the healing
plant, but he, the lion, had been in such haste that he had put
his head on backwards, but he would now set this mistake to
rights. So he tore the huntsman's head off again and turned it
round, and the hare used the healing root to make it grow back
where it belonged.

But the huntsman was sad; he wandered around in the world
and showed his animals to people as performing dancers. It so
happened that exactly a year later he came again to the very
same city in which he had saved the princess from the dragon,
and this time it was all decorated with scarlet hangings. He said
to the landlord: 'What's the meaning of this? A year ago this city
was draped in black, what's the cloth of scarlet for?' The landlord answered: 'A year ago our king's daughter was about to
be handed over to the dragon, but the marshal fought with it
and killed it, and tomorrow their wedding is to be celebrated;
that's why the city was draped with black then as a sign of
mourning, and why it's draped with scarlet as a sign of joy
today.'

Next day, when the wedding was to take place, the huntsman said to the landlord at lunch-time: 'Would you believe it,
landlord? Today I shall be eating bread from the king's table
here in your inn!' 'Well,' said the landlord, 'I'd even wager a
hundred gold pieces that you'll be doing no such thing.' The
huntsman took on the bet and put down a purse with the same
number of gold pieces in it to match the stake. Then he called
the hare and said: 'Be off with you, little bounder, and fetch me
some of the bread the king eats.' Now the little hare was the
smallest of the animals and had no one to pass this errand on to,
so he had to set out on it himself. Oh dear, he thought, when
I'm bounding through the streets all by myself the butcher's
dogs will be after me. And that was exactly how things turned
out, and the dogs chased him, eager to make alterations to his
good, sound hide. But away he leapt – did you ever see the
like! – and took refuge in a sentry box, without the soldier
noticing. Along came the dogs and tried to flush him out, but

this wasn't to the soldier's liking and he set about them with the butt of his musket till they ran off yelping and howling. When the hare saw that the coast was clear, he bounded into the palace and went straight to the princess, sat down under her chair and scratched her foot. 'Get away from me!' she said, thinking it was her dog. The hare scratched her foot a second time, and again she thought it was her dog and said: 'Get away from me!' But the hare wasn't to be put off and scratched her a third time; then she looked down and recognized the hare by its necklace. So she took him on her lap, carried him to her bedroom and said: 'Dear hare, what can I do for you?' He replied: 'My master who killed the dragon is here and has sent me to ask for a loaf of the bread the king eats.' At this she was overjoyed, and sent for the baker and ordered him to bring a loaf of the bread the king ate. The hare said: 'But the baker must carry it there for me too, so that I'll be safe from the butcher's dogs.' The baker carried it for him right to the parlour door of the inn; here the hare stood on his hind legs, took the loaf at once between his front paws and brought it to his master. Then the huntsman said: 'There you are, landlord, the hundred gold pieces are mine.' The landlord was astonished, but the huntsman went on to say: 'Well, landlord, I've got the bread, but now I intend to eat some of the king's roast.' The landlord said: 'I'd like to see you manage that,' but he wasn't willing to bet on it again. The huntsman called the fox and said: 'My little fox, go and fetch me some roast meat, the kind the king eats.' The redskin knew a thing or two, and he went slinking along byways and alleyways so that no dog caught sight of him; and he sat down under the princess's chair and scratched her foot. So she looked down and recognized the fox by his necklace, took him with her into her bedroom and said: 'Dear fox, what can I do for you?' He replied: 'My master who killed the dragon is here and has sent me to ask for some roast meat, the kind the king eats.' So she sent for the cook and ordered him to prepare a roast, the kind the king ate, and carry it for the fox to his master's door; here the fox took the dish from him, and after first swishing his tail over it to drive away the flies that had settled on the meat, he took it to his master. 'You see, landlord,' said the huntsman, 'here we have bread and meat, but now I want vegetables to go with it, the kind the king eats.' So he called the wolf and said: 'My dear wolf, go and fetch me a dish of vegetables, the kind the king eats.' So the wolf went straight into the palace, because he wasn't afraid of anyone, and when he got to the princess's room he gave the back of her skirt a little tug and made her look round. She recognized him by his necklace, took him to her bedroom and said: 'Dear wolf, what can I do for you?' He replied: 'My master who killed the dragon is here, and has told me to ask for a dish of vegetables, the kind the king eats.' So she sent for the cook, and he had to prepare a dish of vegetables, the kind the king ate, and carry it for the wolf to his master's door; here the wolf took the dish from him and carried it in to his master. 'Well, landlord,' said the huntsman, 'now I've got bread and meat and vegetables, but I want some pastries too, the kind the king eats.' He called the bear and said: 'My dear bear, I know you rather fancy sweet things, so go and fetch me some pastries, the kind the king eats.' So the bear padded off to the palace, and everyone he met on the way steered well clear of him: only when he came to the sentries, they raised their muskets and tried to stop him entering the royal palace. But he reared up on his hind legs and gave a cuff or two with his forepaws right and left, knocking the whole sentry guard over, and having done this he went straight to the princess, stood behind her and gave a little growl. She looked round and recognized the bear and invited him into her bedroom and said: 'Dear bear, what can I do for you?' He answered: 'My master who killed the dragon is here, and has told me to ask for some pastries, the kind the king eats.' So she sent for the pastry-cook and he had to bake some pastry, the kind the king ate, and carry it for the bear to his master's door; here the bear first licked up the sugar plums that had rolled off, then he stood upright and took the dish in to his master. 'Well, landlord,' said the huntsman, 'now I've got bread, meat, vegetables and pastries: but I want wine too, the kind the king drinks.' He called his lion and said: 'My dear lion, I know you like an occasional tipple, so go and fetch me some wine, the kind the king drinks.' Then the lion strode along the street, and everyone ran a mile from him, and when he came to the guards they tried to stop him, but he just gave one roar and they all took to their heels. The lion then went to the door of the royal apartment and knocked on it with his tail. The princess came out and nearly took fright when she saw the lion, but she recognized him by the golden clasp of her necklace, asked him to come with her to her bedroom and said: 'Dear lion, what can I do for you?' He replied: 'My master who killed the dragon is here, and has told me to ask for some wine, the kind the king drinks.' So she sent for the royal cup-bearer and ordered him to give the lion some wine, the kind the king drank. The lion said: 'I'll come with you and make sure I get the right kind.' So he went down to the cellars with the cup-bearer, and when they got there the fellow was about to draw off for him some of the ordinary wine that was drunk by the king's servants, but the lion said: 'Stop! I want to taste that wine first.' And he drew himself a half-measure and swallowed it at one gulp. 'No,' he said, 'this isn't the right wine.' The cup-bearer gave him a dirty look, but he went and was about to draw from another barrel that was reserved for the king's marshal. The lion said: 'Stop! I'll taste that wine first.' And he drew himself a half-measure and drank it. 'This is better,' he said, 'but it's still not the right stuff.' At this the cup-bearer got angry and said: 'So you think you know about wine, do you, you stupid brute!' But the lion gave him a bang on the side of the head that knocked him right over flat, and when he had picked himself up again, he said not another word but took the lion into a special little cellar where the king's own wine was stored, wine that was never served to anyone else. The lion first drew himself a half-measure and tasted it, then he said: 'I should say this was the right stuff.' And he told the cup-bearer to fill half-a-dozen bottles. Then they went upstairs, but when the lion stepped out of the cellar into the open air he was slightly tipsy and swayed to and fro. The cup-bearer had to carry the wine for him to his master's door, and here the lion took the handle of the basket in his jaws and carried it in to his master. The huntsman said: 'Well, landlord, now I've got bread, meat, vegetables, pastry and wine – all of them the kind the king gets; so now I'll have dinner with my animals.' So he sat down and ate and drank, and gave the hare and the fox and the wolf and the bear and the lion food and drink as well and was in high spirits, for he knew now that the princess still loved him. When he had had dinner, he said: 'Landlord, now I've eaten and drunk as the king eats and drinks, and now I'm going to go to the king's court and marry his daughter.' The landlord asked: 'How will you manage that, when she's already got a bride-groom and the wedding's to take place today?' So the hunts-man pulled out the handkerchief that the princess had given him on the dragon's mountain and that he'd used to wrap up the monster's seven tongues, and he said: 'I'll do it with the help of what I have here in my hand.' And the landlord looked at the handkerchief and said: 'I'll believe anything, but I'll not believe that, and I'll wager my house and home against it.' But the huntsman took a purse with a thousand gold pieces, placed it on the table and said: 'I'll match your stake with this.'

Now as the king sat at the royal table with his daughter he said to her: 'What did all those wild animals want that have been visiting you and padding in and out of my palace?' And she answered: 'I mustn't tell you; but you will do well to send to the master of these animals and have him fetched here.' The king sent a servant to the inn to invite the stranger, and the servant arrived just as the huntsman had made his bet with the landlord. So the huntsman said: 'Well, landlord, here's the king sending his servant to invite me; but I'm not going yet, not like that.' And to the servant he said: 'Ask my lord the king to send me royal garments and a carriage with six horses, and servants to attend on me.' When the king heard this answer he said to his daughter: 'What shall I do?' She said: 'You will do well to have him brought here as he asks.' So the king sent royal garments, and a carriage with six horses, and servants to attend on him. When the huntsman saw them coming he said: 'Well, landlord, now I'm being fetched the way I asked.' And he put on the royal garments, took the handkerchief with the dragon's tongues in it and drove to the palace. When the king saw him coming he said to his daughter: 'How shall I receive him?' She answered: 'You will do well to go and meet him.' So the king went out to meet him and led him upstairs, and his animals

followed him. The king showed him to the table and put him
between himself and his daughter, and on the other side of her
sat the marshal as her bridegroom, but he didn't recognize the
huntsman. Now just then the seven heads of the dragon were
carried in to be displayed, and the king said: 'The dragon's
seven heads were cut off by the marshal, and for this I give him
my daughter in marriage today.' At this the huntsman rose,
opened the seven jaws and said: 'Where are the dragon's seven
tongues?' The marshal started and turned pale and didn't know
what to answer; finally in his panic he said: 'Dragons don't
have tongues.' The huntsman said: 'It would be better if liars
didn't have them. But dragons' tongues are the trophies of the
dragon-killer.' So saying, he unfolded the handkerchief, and
there lay all seven of them. He stuck each tongue into the mouth
it belonged to, and each of them fitted exactly. After this he took
the handkerchief that had the princess's name embroidered on
it, and showed it to the maiden and asked her to whom she had
given it. She answered: 'To the man who killed the dragon.'
Then he called his animals, took the necklace off each of them
and the golden clasp from the lion and showed them to the
princess and asked whose they were. She answered: 'The necklace and the golden clasp are mine; I divided them among the
animals who had helped to conquer the dragon.' Then the
huntsman said: 'When I was tired out by the fight and was lying
asleep, the marshal came and cut off my head, then he carried
off the princess and pretended it was he who had killed the
dragon; and that he lied I now prove, with the tongues and the
handkerchief and the necklace.' Then he told everyone how his
animals had healed him with the magic root, how he had
wandered about with them for a year and finally returned to
this place, where he had learnt of the marshal's trickery from
what the innkeeper had told him. Then the king asked his
daughter: 'It is true that this man killed the dragon?' And she
answered: 'Yes, it is true; now I may reveal the marshal's
shameful deed, since it has come to light through no action of
mine: for he forced me to promise to say nothing about it. And
that was why I asked that the marriage should not take place for
a year and a day.' Then the king had twelve councillors sum-

moned and told them to pronounce judgment on the marshal;
and their sentence was that he should be dragged apart by four
oxen. Thus the marshal was put to death, but the king gave his
daughter to the huntsman and appointed him his viceroy in the
whole kingdom. The wedding was celebrated with great rejoicing, and the young king sent for his father and foster-father and
loaded them with treasures. Nor did he forget the innkeeper,
but sent for him and said: 'Well, landlord, I have married the
princess, and your house and home are mine.' The landlord
said: 'Yes, that should be so by rights.' But the young king
answered: 'It shall go by grace and favour instead: you shall
keep your house and home, and I make you a present of the
thousand gold pieces as well.'

So now all was well with the young king and the young
queen and they lived together happily. He often went hunting,
because that was his favourite occupation, and his faithful
animals always had to accompany him. But nearby there was a
forest that had the reputation of being uncanny: once you were
in it, they said, it wasn't so easy to get out again. But the young
king had a great desire to hunt in it and gave the old king no
peace till he consented to let him do so. Then he rode out with a
large retinue, and when he came to the forest he saw a snowwhite deer among the trees and said to his men: 'Wait here till I
get back, I'm going to hunt that noble beast.' So saying, he rode
into the forest in pursuit of the deer, with only his own animals
following him. His men waited there till nightfall, but he didn't
return; so they rode home and told the young queen: 'The
young king has been hunting a white doe in the magic wood,
and he hasn't come back.' When she heard this she was very
worried about him. Meanwhile he had ridden further and
further in pursuit of the beautiful deer, but was never able to
overtake her: each time he thought she was within range he
would see her bounding away into the distance again, and in
the end she disappeared altogether. Then he noticed that he
had got deep into the forest, and took his horn and sounded it,
but he got no answer, because his men were too far away to hear
him. And since night was falling too, he realized that he
wouldn't be able to get home that day, so he dismounted and

made a fire under a tree, intending to spend the night there. As he sat by the fire, with his animals lying beside him, he thought he heard a human voice: he looked round but could see no one. Presently he heard it again, a kind of moaning that seemed to come from above him; so he looked up and saw an old woman sitting on the tree, who was whining over and over again: 'Ow, ow, ow, I'm so cold!' He said: 'Come down and warm yourself if you're so cold.' But she said: 'No, your animals will bite me.' He answered: 'They won't touch you, old lady, come on down.' But she was a witch and she said: 'I'll break a wand off the tree and throw it down to you, and if you strike them on their backs with it they won't touch me.' So she threw him down a wand and he struck them with it, and at once they all lay motionless and were turned to stone. And when the witch was safe from the animals, she jumped down and struck him with a wand as well, and turned him to stone. Then she laughed, and dragged him and his animals to a ditch in which she had collected quite a few such stone figures already.

When the young king didn't come home at all, the queen grew more and more worried and anxious about him. Now it happened that just at this time the other brother, the one who had gone east when they had separated, arrived in the kingdom. He had looked for employment and found none, then he had wandered from place to place and used his animals as performing dancers. Then it occurred to him to go and take a look at the knife he and his brother had thrust into a tree when they parted, and so find out how his brother was faring. When he got there, his brother's side of the blade was half rusted and half of it was still bright. When he saw this he was alarmed and thought: Some great misfortune must have happened to my brother, but perhaps I can still save him, because half of the blade is still bright. He went westwards with his animals, and when he got to the city gate the soldier on guard came out and asked him whether they were to announce his arrival to his wife: the young queen, he said, had been in great anxiety these last few days since he had not come home, for she feared he had perished in the magic wood. The fact was that the guard had mistaken him for the young king himself, so like each other were they, and, besides, he had the wild animals running after him. Then he realized that they were referring to his brother, and thought: It will be best if I pretend to be him, because then it may be easier for me to save him. So he let the guard take him to the palace, where he was received with great joy. The young queen mistook him for her husband, and asked him why he had stayed away so long. He answered: 'I had lost my way in a forest and it took me all this time to find it again.' That night he was conducted to the royal bed, but he placed a two-edged sword between himself and the young queen. She had no idea what the meaning of this could be, but didn't dare ask him.

He stayed for a few days, during which he made careful inquiries about the magic forest; finally he said: 'I must go out hunting there again.' The king and the young queen tried to talk him out of it, but he insisted and rode out with a large retinue. When he had entered the forest, the same things happened to him as to his brother. He saw a white doe and said to his men: 'Stay here and wait till I come back, I'm going to hunt that noble beast.' Off he rode through the forest, and his animals ran after him; but he couldn't overtake the deer, and got so deep into the wood that he had to stop there for the night. And when he had made a fire, he heard someone above him moaning: 'Ow, ow, ow, I'm so cold!' He looked up, and there in the tree sat the same witch. He said: 'If you're so cold, old lady, come down and warm yourself.' She replied: 'No, your animals will bite me.' But he said: 'They won't touch you.' And she called to him: 'I'll throw down a wand for you, and if you strike them with it they won't touch me.' When the huntsman heard this, he mistrusted the old woman and said: 'I'll not strike my animals; come down yourself or I'll climb up and fetch you.' At this she cried: 'Who do you think you are? You'll never harm me.' But he answered: 'If you don't come down I'll shoot you down.' She said: 'Shoot away, I'm not afraid of your bullets.' Then he took aim and fired, but the witch was proof against all bullets made of lead, and she just yelled with laughter and shouted: 'You'll never shoot me.' The huntsman knew how to deal with this: he pulled three silver buttons off his coat and loaded them into his gun, for her witchcraft was vain against silver: and sure enough, when he pulled the trigger she fell shrieking to the ground. Then he put his foot on her and said: 'You old witch, if you don't confess at once where my brother is, I'll lift you with my two hands and throw you into the fire.' She was in great terror, begged for mercy and said: 'He's lying turned to stone with his animals in a ditch.' Then he forced her to take him there, threatened her and said: 'Now, you old baboon, you are to bring my brother and all the other creatures here back to life, or it's into the fire with you.' She took her wand and touched the stones, and his brother and the animals came to life again; and so did many other people, merchants and craftsmen and herdsmen, who stood up and thanked the huntsman for freeing them and went home. But when the twins saw each other again they kissed each other and their hearts were overjoyed. Then they seized the witch, tied her hand and foot and put her on the fire; and when she had burned to death, the thick forest at once opened up and became clear and sunlit, and you could see the royal palace three hours' walk away.

Then the two brothers set off back together and told each other their adventures as they went. And when the younger one said he was ruling over the whole country as viceroy, the other answered: 'So I noticed, because when I arrived at the town and was mistaken for you I was treated with every royal honour: the young queen thought I was her husband, and I had to sit beside her at dinner and sleep in your bed.' When the other brother heard that, he was so enraged with jealousy that he drew his sword and struck his brother's head off. But when he saw him lying dead there and his red blood flowing, he was terribly sorry he had done it. 'My brother saved me,' he exclaimed, 'and I've rewarded him by killing him!' And he wept and wailed. But his hare came and offered to fetch some of the life-giving root, and bounded away and came back with it in good time; and the dead man was brought to life again and didn't notice the wound at all.

Then they continued on their way, and the younger brother said: 'You look like me, you're wearing royal garments like me, and you've got a set of animals following you as I have; let's enter the city by opposite gates and arrive at the old king's palace from both sides at once.' So they separated, and the sentries from the two gates both presented themselves before the old king at the same time and announced that the young king and his animals had returned from hunting. The king said: 'This isn't possible, the gates are an hour's walk apart.' But meanwhile both brothers entered the palace courtyard from opposite directions, and both came upstairs to the king. Then the king said to his daughter: 'You tell me: which of them is your husband? They both look alike, I don't know them apart.' This made her really scared, because she couldn't say which was which; but finally she remembered the necklace she had given to the animals. She looked for it, and on one of the two lions she found her little golden clasp, and at this she cried out in delight: 'The one this lion follows is my rightful husband.' And the young king laughed and said: 'Yes, he is indeed.' And they all sat down to dinner together and ate and drank and had a merry time. That night when the young king went to bed his wife asked him: 'Why have you been putting a two-edged sword in our bed these last few nights? I kept thinking you were going to kill me.' Then he realized how loyal his brother had been to him.

17

THE MASTER HUNTSMAN

Once upon a time there was a young fellow who had learnt the locksmith's trade, and he told his father that he would like to go out into the world now and try his luck. 'Yes,' said his father, 'that suits me,' and he gave him some money to take with him. So he travelled around looking for work. After a time he began to find that the locksmith's trade was not to his liking and no longer suited him, but he fancied the idea of hunting. On his wanderings he met a huntsman in a green coat, who asked him where he had come from and where he was going. The lad replied that he was a journeyman locksmith, but that he no longer cared for the trade and would like to learn hunting instead; would the huntsman take him on as an apprentice? 'Oh yes, if you'll come along with me.' So the young lad went with him, signed on with him for several years and learnt hunting. After that he wanted to go out and try his luck again, and the huntsman gave him an air-gun instead of wages, but it was a special kind of gun: if he shot with it he would never miss. So he set off and presently came to a very large forest. There was no reaching the end of it in one day, so when evening fell he perched on a tall tree to be out of reach of the wild beasts. At about midnight he thought he saw a faint light gleaming some way off; he peered at it through the branches and noted carefully where it was; then he took off his hat and threw it down in the direction of the light, to mark which way he should walk when he got down from the tree. Then he climbed down, walked towards his hat, put it on again and continued in the same direction. The further he walked the bigger the light grew, and when he got near it he saw that it was an enormous fire, and round it sat three giants who had spitted an ox and were roasting it. And one of them said: 'Let me just taste whether the meat's done yet.' And he tore off a piece and was about to put it in his mouth when the huntsman shot it out of his hand. 'Well, look at that,' said the giant, 'the wind blew the meat right out of my hand.' And he pulled off another piece, but just as he was going to take a bite the huntsman shot it away too. At this the giant slapped his neighbour's face and exclaimed angrily: 'Will you stop snatching my food!' 'I didn't snatch it,' said the other, 'I think it was shot down by a sniper.' The giant took a third piece, but the moment he had it in his hand the huntsman shot it down too. The giants said to each other: 'That must be a good marksman if he can shoot the meat right out of our mouths; he'd be useful to us.' And they shouted: 'Come on over here, sharpshooter, sit down at the fire with us and eat your fill, we won't touch you; but if you don't come and we fetch you by force, that'll be the end of you.' So the lad came over to them and told them he was a trained huntsman, and that whatever he took aim at with his gun he would hit it without fail. Then they said that if he would go along with them he would be well looked after. They told him that on the far side of the forest there was a wide river, and beyond it stood a tower, and in the tower lived a beautiful princess whom they intended to carry off. 'All right,' he said, 'I'll soon get hold of her for you.' 'But there's a snag in it,' they added. 'There's a little dog there, and it starts barking as soon as anyone comes near the place, and as soon as it barks everyone at the king's court wakes up, and that's why we can't get in. Will you undertake to shoot the dog?' 'Yes,' he answered, 'that's child's play to me.' Then he took a boat and crossed the water, and when he was about to land the little dog came running towards him and was just going to bark when he seized his gun and shot it dead. When the giants saw this they were delighted, thinking the princess was as good as theirs; but the huntsman first wanted to see how things stood, and told them to wait outside till he called them. Then he went into the castle; there was not a sound to be heard and everyone was asleep. In the first room he entered there was a sword hanging on the wall: it was made of pure silver, and on it was a golden star and the king's name, and beside it on a table lay a sealed letter. He opened the letter, which said that whoever had the sword would be able to kill any enemy he met. So he took the sword from the wall, buckled it on and went further till he came to the room where the princess was lying asleep: and she was so beautiful that he stopped and gazed at her and held his breath. He said to himself: 'It would be wrong to let those savage giants get an innocent maiden into their power: they have wicked intentions.' He looked round again and saw a pair of slippers under her bed: on the right slipper was her father's name and a star and on the left her own name and a star. And she was wearing a long silk kerchief embroidered in gold, with her father's name on the right side and on the left her own name, all embroidered in golden letters. Then the huntsman took a pair of scissors and cut off the right-hand end of the kerchief and put it in his knapsack, into which he also put her right slipper with the king's name on it. Now the maiden was still lying there asleep, and she was all sewn into her nightgown: so he cut off a small piece of her nightgown and put it with the other things, but all this he did without touching her. Then he left her to sleep on in peace, and when he got back to the gate the giants were still out there waiting for him, thinking he would bring the princess to them. But he called out to them to come in, saying that the princess was already in his power, and that he couldn't open the door for them but that there was a hole they must crawl through. So when the first of them came to the hole the huntsman wound the giant's hair round his hand, pulled his head through, drew his sword and cut it off with one blow; then he pulled the whole body in. After this he called to the second giant and cut his head off too, and finally he did the same to the third. Feeling glad to have saved the beautiful princess from her enemies, he cut out the giants' tongues and put them in his knapsack. After that he thought: I'll go home to my father and show him what I've done already, then I'll travel about in the world; if God has good fortune in store for me, it'll come to me sooner or later.

But in the castle the king woke up and saw the three giants lying there dead. He went to his daughter's bedchamber, woke her up and asked her who it could have been that had killed the giants. She said: 'Father dear, I don't know, I was asleep.' Then when she got up and was going to put on her slippers she found the right slipper missing, and when she looked at her kerchief she found that the right-hand end of it was missing, and when she looked at her nightgown a piece had been cut out of that too. The king ordered the whole court to be assembled, including his soldiers and everyone who was there, and asked who had saved his daughter and killed the giants. Now in his army he had a captain, an ugly one-eyed fellow, and he claimed to have done it. Then the old king said that if he had done such a deed he must also marry his daughter. But the princess said: 'Dear father, rather than marry that man I will go as far away into the world as my legs will carry me.' The king said that if she refused to marry him she must take off her royal garments and put on peasant's clothes and leave the court; and he ordered her to go to a potter and set herself up selling earthenware pots and plates. So she took off her royal garments and went to a potter and borrowed a lot of earthenware crockery from him, promising that if she had sold it by evening she would pay him for it. The king also ordered her to sit down at a street corner and offer it for sale there, and then he arranged with some carters to drive right through the middle of it and break it into a thousand pieces. So when the princess had put out her wares on the street, the carts came and smashed them to smithereens. She began to cry and said: 'Oh God help me, how shall I pay the potter now!' The king had done this in order to force her to marry the captain; but instead she went back to the potter and asked if he would lend her some more things. He refused to do so until she had paid for the first lot. So she went to her father and wept and lamented and said she would go away into the world. So he said: 'I'll have a hut built for you out there in the forest, and you shall live in it for the rest of your life and cook meals for everyone, but you are to accept no payment for them.' When the hut was ready a sign was hung out over the door, and on it was written: 'Free meals today, tomorrow you pay.' She lived in the hut for a long time, and word went round in the world that here was a young lady who cooked free meals and that this was written up over the door. The huntsman heard this story too and thought: This is a chance for me; after all, I'm poor and I've no money. So he took his air-gun and his knapsack, which still had in it all the things he had once taken away from the castle as proofs, and went into the forest; and sure enough he found the hut with the sign: 'Free meals today, tomorrow you pay.' Wearing the sword with which he had cut off the heads of the three giants, he went in and asked for something to eat. He was delighted to see the beautiful girl; and beautiful she certainly was. She asked where he came from and where he was going and he told her that he was travelling about in the world. Then she asked him where he had got the sword, because it had her father's name on it. He asked if she was the king's daughter. 'Yes,' she answered. 'With this sword,' he said, 'I cut off the heads of three giants.' And as proof he fetched their tongues out of his knapsack, then he showed her the slipper and the pieces he had cut from her kerchief and her nightgown. At this she was overjoyed and said he was the man who had saved her. So they went together to the castle and asked to speak to the old king, and she took him to her bedchamber and told him that it was the huntsman who had really rescued her from the giants. And when the old king saw all the proofs he could no longer doubt it, and said that he was glad to have found out what had happened, and that he would now give his daughter in marriage to the huntsman. The princess consented to this very gladly. Then they gave him fine clothes as if he were a visiting lord, and the king ordered a banquet. At table the captain sat down on the princess's left and the huntsman on her right, and the captain supposed that he was a gentleman from abroad who was visiting them. When they had eaten and drunk, the old king told the captain that he would like to set him a riddle to guess. 'If a man,' said the king, 'were to claim to have killed three giants, and were to be asked where the giants' tongues were, and were to be shown their heads and see that the tongues were missing, what would be the reason for that?' The captain replied: 'I suppose the giants had no tongues.' 'Not so,' said the king, 'every creature has a tongue.' And then he asked the captain what fate such a man would deserve. The captain answered: 'He would deserve to be torn to pieces.' Then the king said: 'You have passed sentence on yourself.' So the captain was arrested and torn apart by four horses; and the

princess was married to the huntsman. After the wedding he
went and fetched his mother and father, and they lived happily
with their son, and after the old king's death he inherited the
kingdom.

18

THE WATER OF LIFE

Once upon a time there was a king who was ill, and no one thought his life could be saved. But he had three sons, and they were sad about this and went down into the palace garden and wept. Here they met an old man who asked the cause of their grief. They told him that their father was so ill that he would probably die, for nothing did him any good. The old man said: 'I know of another remedy: it's the Water of Life. If he drinks some of that he'll recover. But it's difficult to find.' The eldest brother said: 'I'll find it all right.' And he went to the sick king and asked his permission to set out and look for the Water of Life, for only that could heal him. 'No,' said the king, 'that quest is too dangerous; I would rather die.' But he kept on pleading till the king gave his consent. In his heart the prince was thinking: If I bring him the Water, I shall be my father's favourite son and inherit the kingdom.

So he set off, and when he had ridden for a while he met a dwarf standing in his path who called out to him: 'Where are you riding so fast?' 'You stupid midget,' said the prince very haughtily, 'that's no business of yours.' And he rode on. But this had angered the little man, and he had wished evil on him. Very soon the prince found himself in a mountain gorge, and the further he rode along it the nearer the mountains closed in, until at last the path was so narrow that he couldn't ride a step further; it was impossible to turn his horse or even dismount, and there he sat imprisoned. The sick king waited for him a long time, but he didn't come. Then the second son said: 'Father, let me go out and look for the Water,' thinking to himself: If my brother is dead, the kingdom will fall to me. At first the king wouldn't let him go, but in the end he gave way. So the prince set off along the same road as his brother had taken, and he too met the dwarf, who stopped him and asked him where he was off to in such a hurry. 'You little midget,' said the prince, 'that's no business of yours.' And he rode on without so much as looking round. But the dwarf put a curse on him, and he got stuck in a mountain gorge like his brother and could move neither forward nor back. That's what comes of being high and mighty.

When the second son didn't return either, the youngest offered to set out in search of the Water of Life, and in the end the king had to let him go. When he met the dwarf and the dwarf asked him where he was off to in such a hurry, he stopped to give him an answer and said: 'I'm looking for the Water of Life, because my father's mortally ill.' 'And do you know where it is to be found?' 'No,' said the prince. 'Since you have behaved in a proper manner and not been arrogant like your two false-hearted brothers, I will give you information and tell you how to get the Water of Life. It springs up from a fountain in the courtyard of a bewitched castle; but you will not be able to make your way in unless I give you an iron wand and two loaves of bread. Strike on the iron gate of the castle three times with the wand and it will spring open; inside there are two lions with gaping jaws, but if you throw each of them a loaf they'll become tame. Then you must hurry and fetch some of the Water of Life before the clock strikes twelve, otherwise the gate will slam shut again and you'll be locked in.' The prince thanked him, took the wand and the bread and went on his way. And when he got there everything was just as the dwarf had said. The gate sprang open at the third stroke of the wand, and when he had tamed the lions with the bread he entered the castle and found himself in a beautiful great hall: in it were sitting princes bound by a spell, and he took the rings from their fingers; and then he found a sword and a loaf of bread lying there, and took them with him. Next he came to a room in which a beautiful maiden was standing; she was glad when she saw him, and kissed him and told him that he had freed her from the spell and she would give him the whole of her kingdom, and that if he returned in a year's time they would celebrate their wedding. And then she told him where the fountain was from which the Water of Life sprang, but reminded him that he must hurry and draw from it before the

clock struck twelve. So he went on until he finally came to a
room that had a beautiful freshly made bed in it, and as he was
tired he thought he would rest a little first. So he lay down and
fell asleep; and when he woke up the clock was striking a
quarter to twelve. He jumped up in great alarm, ran to the
fountain, drew some water from it in a cup that stood beside it,
and hurried to escape. Just as he was passing through the iron
gate twelve o'clock struck, and the gate slammed shut with
such a crash that it sliced off a piece of his heel.

But he was glad that he had got the Water of Life, and set out
back home and passed the dwarf again. When the dwarf saw
the sword and the loaf of bread he said: 'You have got possession of very valuable things there, for with that sword you can
defeat whole armies, and you can go on eating that bread and
never finish it.' The prince didn't want to go home to his father
without his brothers, and he said: 'Dear dwarf, can you not tell
me where my two brothers are? They left in search of the Water
of Life before I did, and they never came back.' 'They are stuck
in a gorge between two mountains and can't get out,' said the
dwarf. 'I wished this on them because they were so haughty.'
Then the prince pleaded with the dwarf till he released them
again; but he warned him and said: 'Be on your guard against
them, they have wicked hearts.'

When his brothers came he was glad to see them and told
them what had happened to him, how he had found the Water
of Life and brought a cupful of it with him and had released a
beautiful princess from a spell, who was going to wait a year for
him and then they would be married and he would get a great
kingdom. After this they rode off together and found themselves in a country where there was famine and war and the
king already thought he was on the verge of ruin, the trouble
was so great. But the prince went to him and gave him the loaf
of bread, and with it he fed his whole kingdom and everyone
ate their fill. Then the prince gave him the sword too, and with it
he defeated the enemy armies, and after that he was able to live
in peace. Then the prince took back the loaf and the sword, and
the three brothers rode on. But they came to two more countries
that were ravaged by famine and war, and each time the prince

gave his loaf and his sword to the king; so now he had saved three kingdoms. After that they boarded a ship and sailed over the sea. During the voyage the two elder brothers said to each other: 'Our youngest brother found the Water of Life and we didn't, so our father will give him the kingdom that's due to us and so he'll rob us of our fortunes.' And they sought revenge and plotted together to destroy him. They waited for a time when he was fast asleep, and then they took the Water of Life from him, emptying it out of his cup and pouring salt sea-water into it instead.

So when they arrived home the youngest son took his cup to the sick king for him to drink out of it and get well. But he had hardly tasted a mouthful of the salt sea-water when he fell even more ill than before. And as he was lamenting about this, his two elder sons came in and accused the youngest of having tried to poison him, but told him that they had brought the real Water of Life. So they gave it to him, and no sooner had he drunk some than he felt his sickness leave him and grew strong and healthy as he had been in his youth. After this the two went to their youngest brother and mocked him: 'Oh yes, you found the Water of Life,' they said, 'but you've had the trouble and we've got the reward! You should have been cleverer and kept your eyes open: we took it from you when you'd fallen asleep on the ship, and a year from now one of us will fetch that beautiful princess. But mind you say nothing about this; our father wouldn't believe you anyway, and if you utter a single word you'll lose your life as well, but if you hold your tongue we'll spare it.'

The old king was angry with his youngest son, believing he had tried to kill him. So he summoned all his courtiers and made them pass judgment, and it was decided that the prince should be secretly shot. So one day when he was out hunting and suspected nothing, the king's huntsman was ordered to accompany him. When they were out there in the forest quite alone and the huntsman was looking very sad, the prince said to him: 'Dear huntsman, what's the matter?' The huntsman said: 'I can't tell you, and yet I must.' Then the prince said: 'Tell me right out what it is, I'll forgive you.' 'Oh sir,' said the huntsman, 'I'm to shoot you dead, it's the king's orders.' The prince was startled and said: 'Dear huntsman, let me live! Look, I'll give you my royal clothes, give me your plain ones in exchange.' The huntsman said: 'I'll gladly do so, I just couldn't have brought myself to shoot at you.' So they changed clothes, and the huntsman went home, but the prince went deeper into the forest.

Sometime later, the old king received three wagon-loads of gold and precious stones for his youngest son: they had been sent by the three kings who had defeated their enemies with the prince's sword and fed their peoples with his loaf of bread, and who wanted to show their gratitude. Then the old king thought: Can it be that my son was innocent? And he said to his servants: 'If only he were still alive! How sorry I am now that I had him killed.' 'Sir, he is still alive,' said the huntsman, 'for I didn't have the heart to carry out your orders.' And he told the king what had happened. At this a great weight fell from the king's heart, and he had it proclaimed in every kingdom that his son might come home and that he would be graciously welcomed.

But the princess had a road made leading up to her castle, and it was of pure shining gold; and she told her servants that whoever came riding straight up the middle of it to visit her would be her rightful bridegroom and they were to let him in. But if anyone came riding alongside the road he would not be the right man, and they were not to let him in. So when the year was nearly over, the eldest brother decided that he would hurry off to the princess and claim to be her rescuer, and then he would get her for his wife with her kingdom as well. So he rode off, and when he got near the castle and saw the beautiful golden road, he thought: It would be a crying shame to ride on a road like that. So he turned aside and rode up on the right of it. When he came to the gate, the servants told him he wasn't the right man and that he must go away again. Soon afterwards the second prince set out, and when he came to the golden road and his horse took the first step on it, he thought: It would be a crying shame, his hooves might damage the surface. So he turned aside and rode up on the left of it. But when he came to the gate, the servants said he wasn't the right man and he must go away again. Then when the year had fully passed, the third brother decided to leave the forest and ride to his beloved and forget his sorrows with her. So he set out and thought of nothing but her and wished he were there already, and didn't even notice the golden road. So his horse went straight up the middle of it, and when he reached the gate it was opened to him and the princess received him with joy, telling him he was her rescuer and the lord of her kingdom. Their wedding was celebrated with great happiness, and when it was over she told him that his father had sent for him and forgiven him. So he rode home and told the king everything, and how his brothers had deceived him but he had said nothing about it. The old king wanted to punish them, but they had boarded a ship and set sail and never showed their faces again.

19

THE GOLDEN BIRD

Long ago there was a king who had a beautiful garden behind his palace, and in it stood a tree that bore golden apples. When the apples ripened they were counted, but the very next morning one was missing. This was reported to the king, and he ordered a watch to be kept every night under the tree. The king had three sons, and at nightfall he sent the eldest of them into the garden; but when midnight came the prince could not keep himself awake, and next morning another apple was missing. On the following night the second son had to keep watch, but he fared no better; when the clock had struck twelve he fell asleep, and an apple was missing in the morning. Now it was the third son's turn to watch, and he too was willing, but the king had no great confidence in him and thought he would be even less successful than his brothers. But in the end he allowed him to try. So the young man lay down under the tree, kept watch and fought off his drowsiness. When it struck twelve something came whirring through the air, and in the moonlight he saw a bird flying towards him with its feathers all shining like gold. The bird settled on the tree and had just picked off an apple when the young man shot an arrow at it. The bird flew away, but the arrow had struck its plumage and one of its golden feathers fell to the ground. The young man picked it up, took it to the king next morning and told him what he had seen during the night. The king summoned his councillors, and they all declared that a feather such as this was more precious than the whole kingdom. 'If the feather is so precious,' declared the king, 'then it's no good to me just to have one, and I shall and must have the whole bird.'

The eldest son set out, trusting in his wits and confident that he would soon find the golden bird. Before he had gone very far he saw a fox sitting at the edge of a wood, so he raised his gun and took aim at it. The fox cried out: 'Don't shoot me, and I'll reward you with good advice. You have set out to find the golden bird, and this evening you will come to a village with two inns on opposite sides. One of them is brightly lit and full of people making merry; but don't go in there, go into the other one, even if you don't care much for the look of it.' How can this silly brute be giving me sensible advice! thought the prince and fired his gun, but he missed the fox, and it stuck out its tail and darted off into the wood. Then he continued on his way and in the evening he reached the village with the two inns: in one there was singing and dancing, the other looked wretched and gloomy. I'd be a proper fool, he thought, if I went into that shabby old inn instead of this fine smart one. So he went into the inn where the merrymaking was and settled down there to a life of dissipation, and forgot the bird and his father and all the good things he had ever been taught.

When some time had passed and there was still no sign of the eldest son coming home, the second one set out to try and find the golden bird. Like the first he met the fox, who gave him the same good advice, and he paid no heed to it. He came to the two inns and out of one of them came sounds of revelry, and there was his brother standing at the window calling out to him. He couldn't resist, went in and gave himself over to a life of pleasure.

Again some time passed, and now the youngest prince wanted to leave home and try his luck, but his father was unwilling to let him go. 'It's useless,' he said, 'he's even less likely to find the golden bird than his brothers, and if some ill luck befalls him he won't know what to do; he's simple in the head.' But the boy gave him no peace and in the end he let him go. There was the fox sitting again at the edge of the wood, asking for its life to be spared and giving its good advice. The prince was a good-natured young man and said: 'Don't worry, little fox, I'll not hurt you.' 'You'll not regret that,' answered the fox, 'and I'll help you on your way: climb up behind me on my tail.' And he had scarcely done so when the fox began to run, and off he was carried helter-skelter with the wind whistling through his hair. When they came to the village the young man dismounted, followed the fox's good advice and went into the poorer inn without a second glance and slept peacefully there. Next morning as he walked out into the fields, again the fox was already sitting there, and said to him: 'Now I'll tell you what you must do next. Keep going straight ahead, and finally you'll come to a castle with a whole company of soldiers lying outside it, but don't bother about that for they'll all be asleep and snoring; go right through between them and straight into the palace. Walk through all the rooms; in the last room you come to there will be a golden bird hanging in a wooden cage. Beside it there will be an empty ornamental golden cage, but beware of taking the bird out of its plain cage and putting it into the fine one, or things may go badly for you.' So saying, the fox stuck out its tail again and the prince sat down on it; and off he was carried helter-skelter with the wind whistling through his hair. When he reached the castle, he found everything just as the fox had said. The prince reached the room where the golden bird was sitting in a wooden cage, and beside it stood a golden one; and there were the three golden apples lying around on the floor. Then he thought to himself: It would be ridiculous to leave that beautiful bird in this common ugly cage. So he opened the cage door, seized the bird and put it in the golden one. But at that very moment the bird let out a piercing cry. The soldiers woke up, rushed in and dragged him off to prison. Next morning he was brought before a court, and since he confessed everything he was condemned to death. But the king said he would spare his life on one condition, namely if he would fetch him the golden horse that ran faster than the wind; and then he could keep the golden bird too as a reward.

The prince set out, but he sighed and was sad, for where was he to find the golden horse? Then suddenly he saw his old friend the fox sitting at the roadside. 'You see,' said the fox, 'this is what happened because you didn't do as I said. But don't despair, I'll look after you and tell you how to get to the golden horse. You must carry straight on and you'll come to a castle, and there in a stable will be the horse. The grooms will be lying outside the stable, but they'll be asleep and snoring and you'll be able to lead the golden horse out without difficulty. But you must beware of one thing: whatever you do, saddle him with the plain wood-and-leather saddle and not with the golden one that will be hanging beside it, otherwise things will go badly with you.' Then the fox stuck out its tail, the prince mounted and off he was carried helter-skelter with the wind whistling through his hair. Everything turned out just as the fox had said, and he reached the stable where the golden horse was standing. But as he was about to put on the plain saddle, he thought: It'll be a disgrace for such a beautiful animal not to wear the fine saddle he deserves. But no sooner had the golden saddle touched the horse than it began to neigh loudly. The grooms woke up, seized the young man and threw him into prison. Next morning the court condemned him to death, but the king promised to spare his life and to let him have the golden horse as well if he could bring back the beautiful princess from the golden castle.

The young man set out with a heavy heart, but luckily he soon found the faithful fox. 'I ought just to leave you to your fate,' said the fox, 'but I'm sorry for you and I'll help you again out of your trouble. Your way will lead you straight to the golden castle: you'll get there in the evening, and at night when everything is quiet the beautiful princess goes to the bath-house to bathe there. And when she enters, go up to her suddenly and give her a kiss, and then she will submit to you and you can take her with you; but don't allow her to say goodbye to her parents first, or things will go badly with you.' Then the fox stuck out its tail, the prince mounted and off he was carried helter-skelter with the wind whistling through his hair. When he arrived at the golden castle, everything was as the fox had said. He waited till midnight; and when everyone was fast asleep and the beautiful maiden entered the bath-house, he leapt out and gave her a kiss. She said she would willingly follow him, but begged and implored him with tears to let her say goodbye to her parents before leaving. At first he resisted her pleas, but when she wept more and more and fell at his feet he finally gave way. But no sooner had the maiden reached her father's bedside than he woke up, and so did everyone else in the palace, and the young man was arrested and thrown into prison.

Next morning the king said to him: 'Your life is forfeit: I will only pardon you if you can dig away that mountain in front of my window that blocks my view, and you must get that done within eight days. If you succeed you shall have my daughter as your reward.' The prince began to dig and shovel and didn't stop for seven days, but when he saw how little he had done by then, and how all his work had achieved almost nothing, he fell into a great sadness and gave up all hope. But on the evening of the seventh day the fox appeared and said: 'You don't deserve my help; but go and lie down and go to sleep, I'll do the work for you.' When he woke up next morning and looked out of the window, the mountain had vanished. Overjoyed, the young man hastened to the king and reported to him that the condition was fulfilled, and the king had no choice but to keep his promise and give him his daughter.

Now they both set off together, and before long the faithful fox appeared and said: 'Now of course you possess the best thing of all; but with the maiden from the golden palace you should have the golden horse too.' 'How am I to get it?' asked the young man. 'I will tell you,' answered the fox. 'First take the beautiful maiden to the king who sent you to the golden castle. They'll be overjoyed as they've never been before; they'll willingly give you the golden horse and they'll lead it out for you. Mount it at once and reach down your hand to say good-bye to all of them, and lastly to the beautiful maiden; but when you have gripped her hand, swing her up quickly beside you and gallop away – no one can possibly overtake you, for that horse runs faster than the wind.'

All this worked very well, and the prince carried off the beautiful maiden on the golden horse. The fox was by their side again and said to the young man: 'Now I'll tell you how to get the golden bird too. When you're not far from the castle where they keep the bird, set down the maiden and I'll look after her. Then ride the golden horse into the palace yard; they'll be overjoyed to see it, and they'll bring out the golden bird for you. As soon as you have the cage in your hand, gallop back to us and fetch the maiden.' When this plan had succeeded too and the prince was about to ride home with his treasures, the fox said: 'Now I want you to reward me for my help.' 'What reward

shall I give you?' asked the young man. 'When we get into the
wood there, shoot me dead and chop off my head and my
paws.' 'That would be a fine way of showing my gratitude,' said
the prince. 'That I can't possibly do for you.' The fox said: 'If
you will not do it, then I must leave you; but before I go I'll give
you one more piece of good advice. Beware of two things: buy
no gallows-meat, and don't sit down at the edge of a well.' So
saying, it ran off into the wood.

The young man thought: What a strange animal he is, what
peculiar ideas he has! Who would ever think of buying
gallows-meat? And it's never even occurred to me to sit down at
the edge of a well. He rode on with the beautiful maiden, and
his way took him back through the village where his two
brothers had stayed behind. Here there was great excitement
and hubbub, and when he asked what was the matter he was
told that two men were to be hanged. On coming nearer he saw
that they were his brothers, who had done all sorts of wicked
things and spent all their money. He asked if there wasn't some
way of getting them set free. 'If you're willing to pay for them,
sir,' answered the people. 'But why should you waste your
money ransoming this pair of scoundrels?' But he didn't hesitate and paid for them, and when the two were released they all
continued their journey together.

They came to the wood where the fox had first met them, and
as it was cool and pleasant here and the sun was very hot, his
two brothers said: 'Let's rest here by the well for a little and
have something to eat and drink.' He agreed, and as they talked
he forgot the warning and sat down on the rim of the well,
suspecting nothing. But his two brothers pushed him over
backwards into the well, took the maiden and the horse and the
bird, and went home to their father. 'We've brought you not
only the golden bird,' they said, 'we captured the golden horse
and the maiden from the golden castle as well.' At this there
was great rejoicing, but the horse wouldn't eat, the bird
wouldn't sing and the maiden sat and wept.

But the youngest brother wasn't dead. Luckily the well was
dry and he fell on to soft moss without injuring himself, only he
couldn't get out again. But the faithful fox didn't forsake him in

this peril either: it jumped down into the well beside him and scolded him for forgetting its advice. 'But I must just carry on helping you,' it said, 'and I'll get you up into the daylight again.' It told him to seize its tail and hold on tight, and then it pulled him up out of the well. 'You're still in danger,' it said. 'Your brothers weren't certain you were dead, and they've put guards all round the wood who are to kill you if you show your face.' They came to a poor beggar sitting by the wayside. The young man changed clothes with him and so made his way to the courtyard of the king's palace. No one recognized him, but the bird began to sing again, the horse began to eat and the beautiful maiden stopped weeping. The king asked in surprise: 'What does this mean?' And the maiden said: 'I don't know, but I was so sad and now I'm so happy. I feel that my rightful bridegroom has come.' She told him everything that had happened, although the other brothers had threatened to kill her if she uttered a word. The king had everyone who was in his castle brought before him: the young prince came too, as a beggar in rags, but the maiden recognized him at once and embraced him. His godless brothers were seized and put to death, but he was married to the beautiful maiden and appointed as heir to the kingdom.

But what about the poor fox? Long after this the prince happened to go into the wood again, and there he met the fox and it said: 'Now you have got everything you could wish for; but my misfortune's still not at an end, and yet it's in your power to save me.' And again it implored him to shoot it dead and chop off its head and paws. So he did this, and scarcely had he done it when the fox changed into a man, and who should he turn out to be but the beautiful princess's brother, released at last from the spell that had bound him. And after that there was nothing to mar their happiness for the rest of their lives.

20

THE DWARFIE

There wiz eence a rich king that haed three dothers, an they gaed for a danner daily-day in the castle gairden. The king he wiz a fancier o aa kyn' o fine trees, an there wiz ae tree that he haed sic a *notion o that ·he keest a spell on't, that fa'iver pluckit an aipple fae't waed be beeriet three hunner ells deep ablò the grun'. Weel, fan the hairst-time cam, the aipples on that tree grew as reid as bleed. The three dothers gaed daily-day tae the tree tae see gin the ween haed blawn doon an aipple, but niver an een did they fin', an the tree steed there that heavy-laden that it wiz like tae brak, an the branches hung doon tae the grun'. An the youngest princess she langt sairly for an aipple, an she said tae her sisters: 'Oor daddie loo'es us ower weel tae cast a spell on's; I jalòuse he's deen't tae keep freemt fowk awà.' An wi that the bairn pluckit a bonny big aipple, an ran till er sisters an said: 'Oh, jist tak a tastie o that, sisters dear, I've niver tastit the like in aa my days.' Sae the ither twa princesses they took a bite o the aipple an aa, an the three o them sunk intae the grun' oot o aabody's kennan.

Dennertime cam, an the king he waed cry till his dothers tae come in tae their mait, but there wiz naether sicht nor soond o them. Sairly he socht for them in the castle an the gairden but couldnae fin' them. An he wiz that dooncast that he offert his hale kingdom, an fa'iver brocht his dothers back till im shaed get een o them for a wife. An that mony young men gaed seekin them that the like wiz niver seen, for aabody likit the three bairns, they war freenly tae aa an bonny tae look upon. An three young huntsmen set furth, an fan they haed traivelt a week they cam tae a great castle wi fine chaumbers; and in ae chaumber a table wiz laid wi tastie mait still warm an steamin, though nae a sowl could be haird or seen in the hale castle. They baid there anither half-day an the mait wiz aye warm an steamin, an bi the

en' they war that hungry that they sat doon an ait; an they
agreet tae byde in the castle, an they waed draw lots so that een
waed byde in the castle an the ither twa waed seek for the
princesses. That they daed, an the lot fell on the auldest. Sae the
next day the twa younger lads set aff on their quest an the
auldest he maun byde at hame. At dennertime there cam a wee
mannikie an beggit for a crust o bried, an the huntsman took
some o the bried he haed fund there an cuttit aff a bit roon the
ootside o the loaf tae gie till im; but fan he held it oot till im, the
mannikie lat it faa an socht im tae gie im't again. He wiz ready
tae dee that an boo't doon till't, an losh, the mannikie took im by
the hair an gied im a gweed lickin.

The next day the secant lad he baid at hame an he fair't nae
better. In the evenin fan the ither twa cam hame, the auldest
said: 'Weel, foo did it gyang?' 'Oh, it gaed gey ill.' An they tellt
een anither their throuwcome, but they tellt the youngest een
naething, for they mislikit im an aye caa'd im *Feel Jock, for he
wisnae aa there. Weel, on the third day the youngest een baid at
hame, an the mannikie cam an beggit for a crust o bried; an fan
he gied it till im he lat it faa again an socht him tae kindly haan't
till im again. An said he tae the mannikie: 'Fit? Can ye nae pick
up the crust yersèl? Gin ye cannae be bathert tae tak care o yer
mait, ye dinnae deserve tae ait it.' An the mannikie wiz sair
ill-pleast an said he maun dee his biddin; but he wastit nae time
but took the mannikie an gied him a gweed lickin. The mannikie
he skirlt: 'Haud yer haan! Lat me come tae mysèl an I'll tell ye
far the princesses are.' Fan he heert that he stoppit lickin im, an
the mannikie tellt im he wiz a dwarfie an there wiz mair nor a
thoosand o them; an gin he waed come wi im he'd lat im see far
the princesses war. He showt im a deep waull wi nae watter
in't; but, said the mannikie, he kent that his twa pairtners wesht
im nae gweed, an gin he wintit tae save the princesses he maun
dee't on his leen; the twa lads nae doot wintit tae get them back,
but they waed tak nae risks an rin nae danger for't. Sae he maun
tak a muckle creel an sit imsèl in't wi his huntin-knife an a bell
on't an get imsèl lowert doon in't. Doon ablò, said he, there wiz
three chaumbers, an in ilka chaumber wiz ae prinçess sittin an
gart tae pick the 'lice aff the hunner heids o a dragon; an he

maun cut the dragon's heids aff. An fan the mannikie haed tellt im aa, he vanisht.

Fan the evenin cam, the ither twa cam back an spiert at im foo it haed gaen, an he said: 'Oh, nae that ill.' He tellt foo he haednae seen a sowl till dennertime, syne a wee mannikie haed come seekin a crust o bried, and fan he gied it till im the mannikie lat it faa an socht im tae pick it up, an syne he'd said he waednae an the mannikie haed turnt naisty, but he haednae unnersteed im richt an haed gien im a lickin, an syne the mannikie haed tellt im far the princesses war. The ither twa wiz that mad that the colour gaed fae their faces.

The next mornin they gaed tae the waull an drew lots tae see fa shaed sit in the creel first, an again the lot fell on the auldest; sae in he sat an took the bell wi im. An he said: 'Gin I ring the bell, pull me up fast.' Fan he wiz half-wey doon, they heert ringin an pullt im up again. Sae the secant lad he sat in till't an the same happint tae him. An noo it wiz the youngest een's turn, but he gaed richt tae the boddam. He clomb oot o the creel, took his knife wi im an gaed an steed afore the first door an harkent at it; an he could hear the dragon snorin loud. Sae he opint the door canny-like, an there sat a princess wi nine dragon's heids on er lap, pickin the lice aff o them. Sae he up wi his knife an hackit at them an the nine dragon's heids came aff. Up loupit the princess an threw er airms roon is neck an kisst im ower an ower an took er chyne o pure gowd an pat it roon is neck. Syne he gaed tae the secant princess, an she wiz pickin the lice aff saiven dragon's heids, an he saiv't her an aa, an syne the youngest, an she haed fower dragon's heids tae pick the lice aff o, an he saiv't her an aa. An they haed muckle tae tell an spier, an they kisst an cuddelt an niver devàult. Syne he rang loud aneuch for the lads tae hear im, an he sat the three princesses een aifter the ither in the creel an gat them pullt up; but fan his turn cam, he mine't the wards o the dwarfie, that his pairtners wesht im nae gweed. Sae he took a muckle steen that wiz lyin there an pat it in the creel, an fan the creel wiz half-wey up the fauss pairtners cuttit the rope, an the creel an the steen in't fell tae the boddam. An they thinkin he wiz deid ran awà wi the three princesses an gart them promise tae tell their father that they twa haed saiv't them. Sae they cam tae the king an socht tae mairry his dothers.

Meantime the youngest huntsman he wannert recht sorrafae throu the three chaumbers, thinkin he maun dee, fan he saa a pipe hingin on the waa an said: 'Fit-wey are ye hingin there fan there's neen here tae mak merry?' An he lookit at the dragon's heids an said: 'Aye, ye cannae help me aither.' An but an ben he walkit till the verra fleer wiz polisht wi his step. But at last he bethocht imsèl, took the pipe fae the waa an blew an air on't, an aa at eence there cam dizzens o dwarfies, an ilka note he blew brocht anither een; sae he blew an he blew till the chaumber wiz packit full o dwarfies. They aa spiert at im fit his will wiz, an he said he wiz seekin back tae earth an daylicht; an they aa took haud o im bi ilka hair on his heid, an that wey they clomb up tae the earth wi im. Eence there, he made stracht for the king's castle, for een o the king's dothers wiz jist gyan tae be mairrit, an entert the chaumber far the king sat wi his three dothers. As seen as the lassies saa him they fell awà in a dwam; an the king gaed gyte an threw im in the dungeon, for he thocht he haed deen his bairns some ill. But the princesses cam tae themsèls an fleetcht an priggit wi im tae lat im oot. The king spiert fit-for, an they said they daurnae tell; but their father said they micht tell't tae the fireplace. Syne he steppit ootside an harkent at the door an heert aathing. Sae he haed the twa lads hangt on the gallows an he gied his youngest dother tae the youngest een for a wife. And

> As I wiz weerin gless sheen
> I haet my faet upon a steen:
> Chink, said the sheen,
> an they war deen.

21

JACK THE STRONG MAN

Once upon a time there was a man and his wife who had only one child, and they lived all by themselves in a remote valley. It happened one day that the mother went into the wood to collect pine twigs, and with her she took little Jack, who was only two years old. It was springtime and there were flowers of all colours that attracted the little boy. So she went further and further with him into the forest. Suddenly two robbers jumped out from the thicket, seized the mother and her child and took them deep into the dark forest, to a place where no one ever went from one year's end to another. The poor woman implored the robbers to let her and her child go, but their hearts were of stone: they ignored all her pleadings and drove her on with them by force. After they had had to struggle through bushes and briars for about two hours, they came to a cliff with a door in it; the robbers knocked on the door and it opened at once. They were taken through a long dark tunnel and finally came to a huge cave lit by a fire that was burning in the hearth. On the wall hung swords and sabres and other deadly weapons, glittering in the firelight, and in the middle stood a black table with four other robbers sitting at it playing cards, and the robber captain at the head of it. When he saw the woman he came up and spoke to her, telling her to calm herself and have no fear: they would do nothing to hurt her, but she must do the housework for them, and if she looked after everything properly they would treat her well. Then they gave her something to eat and showed her to a bed where she could sleep with her child.

The woman lived with the robbers for many years, and Jack grew big and strong. His mother told him stories and taught him to read from an old book of romances of chivalry that she found in the cave. When Jack was nine years old he made himself a big club out of a pine branch and hid it behind the bed;

then he went to his mother and said: 'Mother dear, will you tell me now who my father is, I want to know and I must know.' His mother was silent and wouldn't tell him, fearing he would grow homesick; in any case she knew that the wicked robbers wouldn't release Jack. But it nearly broke her heart to think that he would not be able to go to his father. That night, when the robbers came back from their maraudings, Jack fetched out his club, stood in front of the captain and said: 'Now I want to know who my father is, and if you don't tell me at once I'll knock you down.' The robber captain laughed and gave Jack a box on the ear that sent him spinning under the table. Jack stood up again, said nothing and thought: I'll wait another year and then try again; perhaps I'll do better. When the year was up he fetched out his club again, wiped the dust off it, took a good look at it and said: 'This is a fine sturdy club.' At night the robbers came home, drank wine by the jugful, and their heads began to droop. Then Jack fetched out his club, stood before the captain again and asked him who his father was. This time too the captain gave him such a clout over the ear that he rolled over under the table, but at once he was on his feet again and went to work with his club on the captain and the robbers till he had laid them all flat. His mother stood in a corner, amazed by his courage and strength. When Jack had finished the job he went to his mother and said: 'This time I meant it, but now you have got to tell me who my father is.' 'Dearest Jack,' answered his mother, 'come with me, let's go and look for him till we find him.' She took the key of the door from the captain, and Jack fetched a flour sack, stuffed it full of gold and silver and all the other valuable things he could find, and slung it over his back. They left the cave, and Jack fairly goggled when he came out of the darkness into the daylight and saw the green forest and flowers and birds and the morning sun in the sky. He just stood and gazed at everything – you might have thought he was a bit simple. His mother tried to find the way back home, and when they'd been walking for a few hours they arrived safe and sound at their little house in the lonely valley. Jack's father was sitting by the door, and he wept for joy when he recognized his wife and heard that Jack was his son, for he had long since given them both up for dead. But Jack, though only twelve years old, was a whole head taller than his father. They went together into the parlour, but no sooner did Jack put his sack down on the bench by the stove than the whole house began to crack, the bench split and so did the floor, and down went the heavy sack into the cellar. 'God preserve us,' exclaimed his father, 'what's going on? Now you've gone and smashed up our house!' 'Don't let that worry you, father dear,' replied Jack, 'that sack contains more than we need to build a new house.' And indeed Jack and his father began to build a new house straight away, and bought livestock and land and set up in farming. Jack ploughed the fields, and when he walked behind the plough pushing it into the soil the oxen hardly needed to do any pulling. When spring came again Jack said: 'Father, keep all the money and have a hundred-pound cudgel made for me, so that I can go out into the world.' When the cudgel he wanted was ready, he left his father's house, set out on his journey and was soon in a deep, dark forest. Presently he heard something rustling and crackling, looked about him and saw a fir tree being twisted round and round like a rope from bottom to top; and as he looked up and up, he saw a great big fellow who had seized the tree and was spinning it round like a willow wand. 'Hey!' shouted Jack, 'what are you doing up there?' The fellow replied: 'I'm trying to twist a rope to tie up some firewood I've collected yesterday.' I like that, thought Jack, he's a strong man. And he called out to him: 'Never mind that, and come along with me.' The strong fellow climbed down from the top of the tree; he was a whole head taller than Jack, and Jack wasn't small either. Jack told him: 'Your name is now Firtwirler.' Then they walked on, and as they walked they heard a banging and a hammering, and it was so violent that the ground shook at every blow. Presently they came to an enormous cliff, and in front of it stood a giant who was knocking great lumps off it with his fist. When Jack asked him what he was up to, he answered: 'When I try to get some sleep at night, bears and wolves and other vermin of that sort come sniffing and snuffling at me and keep me awake; so I'm going to build a house and lie inside it to get some peace and quiet.' Well, fancy that, thought Jack; he might come in useful too. And he said to him: 'Never mind about building a house and come along with me. I shall call you Cliffclipper.' The giant consented, and off they wandered through the forest, all three of them, and everywhere they went the wild beasts took fright and ran away from them. In the evening they came to an old deserted castle, climbed up into it and lay down in the main hall to sleep. Next morning Jack went down into the garden, which was all neglected and over-grown with shrubs and thorn bushes. And as he was looking around a wild boar came charging at him; but he gave it a blow with his cudgel that knocked it dead. Then he put it on his shoulder and took it upstairs, where they spitted and roasted it and had a fine meal. After that they agreed that every day, by turns, two of them should go hunting and the third stay at home and cook, nine pounds of meat for each of the three. On the first day it was Firtwirler who stayed in, and Jack and Cliffclipper went out to hunt. While Firtwirler was busy cook-ing, a little old shrivelled-up man came into the castle and asked for some meat. 'Clear off, you little ninny,' he answered, 'you don't need meat.' But to Firtwirler's great surprise this incon-spicuous little mannikin jumped up at him and so belaboured him with his fists that he couldn't fight him off, and he fell to the floor gasping like a fish. The little man didn't leave till he had vented his full fury on him. When the two others came back from hunting, Firtwirler told them nothing about the little old man and the beating he had had, for he thought: When they stay at home they can try their luck with the prickly little beast themselves; and the very thought gave him great satisfaction. On the following day Cliffclipper stayed at home, and he fared no better than Firtwirler: he had the life half beaten out of him by the little man for refusing to give him any meat. When the others came home that evening, one look at him told Firtwirler how things had gone, but they both held their tongues and thought: Jack shall have his taste of it too. Next day it was Jack's turn to stay at home, and he duly did his work in the kitchen. And as he was standing there skimming the pot, the mannikin appeared and without further ado demanded a piece of meat. And Jack thought: He's a poor little runt, I'll give him some of

mine so that the others will get their full share. And he handed a
piece of meat to him. When the dwarf had devoured it he asked
for some more, and good-natured Jack gave it to him. 'Here's
another nice piece,' he said, 'and now you just be content.' But
the dwarf asked for meat a third time, and Jack told him he was
being impertinent and didn't give him any more. At this the
wicked little dwarf tried to jump up and treat Jack as he had
treated Firtwirler and Cliffclipper; but this time he had met his
match. Jack, without exerting himself at all, gave him a couple
of such blows that he took a running jump down the castle
stairs. Jack tried to chase him but tripped over him and fell his
full length. By the time he got up again the dwarf was away
ahead. Jack rushed after him right into the forest and saw him
disappear into a cave. Then Jack went home, but he had taken
good note of the place. When the two others got back they were
surprised to find Jack in such good shape. He told them what
had happened, and then they confessed how things had gone
with them. Jack laughed and said: 'It serves you right, you
shouldn't have been so stingy with your meat. But what a
disgrace for big fellows like you to let a dwarf beat you!' Then
they took a basket and a rope and all three of them went to the
cave in the rock where the dwarf had disappeared, and Jack was
lowered into it in the basket with his cudgel. When he got to the
bottom he found a door, and when he opened it there sat a
really beautiful maiden, really beautiful beyond words, and
beside her sat the dwarf grinning at Jack like a baboon. But she
was bound with chains and looked at him so sadly that Jack felt
terribly sorry for her and said to himself: You must rescue her
from the power of this wicked dwarf. So he fetched the dwarf
one with his cudgel and the dwarf fell down dead. But at once
the chains dropped from the maiden as well, and Jack was fairly
entranced by her beauty. She told him she was a princess and
that she had been carried off from her native land by a fierce
count who had imprisoned her there in the rock because she
had refused his love; and she had been tormented and ill
treated by the dwarf, who had been set by the count to keep
watch over her. Then Jack put the maiden into the basket and
got the others to pull her up. The basket came down again, but

Jack didn't trust his two companions and thought: They've already played you false by saying nothing about the dwarf; who knows what they may be plotting against you. So he put his cudgel in the basket, and that was lucky for him, because when the basket was half-way up they let it drop, and if Jack had really been sitting in it that would have been the end of him. But now he didn't know how he was to get up out of this cave; he racked his brains about it but couldn't think of any way. 'It's a shame,' he said to himself, 'to have to starve to death down here.' And as he walked up and down he went again into the little room where the maiden had been sitting, and noticed that the dwarf had a ring on his finger, shining and glittering. So he pulled it off and put it on himself, and when he turned it round on his finger he suddenly heard something whirring above his head. He looked up and saw spirits of the air hovering about, who told him he was their master and asked for his orders. At first Jack was flabbergasted; but then he told them to carry him up to the surface. At once they obeyed, and he felt himself flying upwards. But when he got to the top there was no one to be seen any more, and when he went into the castle he found no one there either. Firtwirler and Cliffclipper had hurried away and taken the beautiful maiden with them. But Jack turned his ring, and the spirits of the air came and told him that his two companions had put out to sea. Jack ran like mad till he got to the seashore; and there he saw, far across the water, a little boat with his faithless friends sitting in it. And in a great rage, without thinking what he was doing, he jumped into the water, cudgel and all, and began to swim; but his hundred-pound cudgel dragged him deep under the water, so that he was nearly drowned. Just in time, however, he turned the ring; and at once the spirits of the air came and carried him to the boat as quick as lightning. So he swung his cudgel and gave his wicked companions their well-deserved reward, and flung their bodies into the sea. But then he rowed away in the boat with the beautiful maiden, who had been in a great state of terror and whom he had now rescued for the second time. He took her home to her father and mother and was married to her, and everyone was delighted.

22

THE SIX WHO WENT FAR IN THE WORLD

Once upon a time there was a man who knew how to do all sorts of things. He served in the war and was loyal and courageous, but when the war was over he got his discharge and a shilling to take on his way as pocket-money. 'We'll see about this,' he said to himself. 'I'll not be treated like this; and if I can find the right people to help me, I'll make the king hand me over all the treasure in his kingdom.' And he went off into the forest in a great rage, and there he saw a fellow standing who had just plucked six trees out of the ground as if they were ears of corn. So he said to him: 'Would you like to be my servant and come along with me?' 'All right,' said the man, 'but first I must take this little bundle of wood home to my mother.' And he took one of the trees and wound it round the other five, then lifted the bundle on to his shoulder and carried it off. Then he came back and went along with his master, who said to him: 'You and I are sure to go far in the world.' And when they had walked on a little further, they met a huntsman who was down on his knees taking aim with his gun. The master said to him: 'Huntsman, what are you trying to shoot?' He replied: 'Two leagues from here there's a fly sitting on the branch of an oak tree, and I'm going to shoot out its left eye.' 'Oh,' said the man, 'you come along with me: the three of us together are sure to go far in the world.' The huntsman consented and came with him. Presently they got to a place where there were seven windmills with their sails going round pretty fast, although there was no wind blowing on either side and not a leaf stirring. The man said: 'I don't know what's driving these windmills, there's not even a breath of wind.' And he travelled on with his servants, and when they had walked for two leagues they saw a fellow sitting on a tree who was holding one nostril shut and blowing through the other. 'Bless me, what are you doing up there?'

asked the man. The fellow answered: 'Two leagues from here there are seven windmills, you see, and I'm blowing at them to make them turn.' 'Oh, you come along with me,' said the man. 'The four of us together are sure to go far in the world.' So the blowhard came down and joined the company, and after a while they met a fellow standing on one leg, who had taken off his other leg and put it down on the ground beside him. 'That's a nice comfortable way of taking a rest,' said the master. 'I'm a runner,' replied the man, 'and because I don't want to go bounding along so quickly I've unbuckled one of my legs; when I run with both legs, I go faster than a bird flies.' 'Oh, you come along with me! The five of us together are sure to go far in the world.' So he came with him, and before very long they met a fellow with a hat, but he was wearing it right down over one ear. The master said: 'Come, come, that's no way to wear a hat, hanging down over one ear! You look a proper fool.' 'I can't help it,' said the man, 'because if I put my hat on straight a tremendous frost begins, and the birds in the sky freeze and fall down dead.' 'Oh, you come along with me!' said the master. 'We six together are sure to go far in the world.'

The six of them now went to a city where the king had had it proclaimed that any man who ran a race with his daughter and won it was to become her husband; but if he lost it he was to lose his head as well. The man presented himself as a competitor, but said: 'I want my servant to run for me.' The king answered: 'In that case you must pledge his life as well, so that both his head and yours are staked on your winning.' When that had all been agreed and made binding, the man fastened the Runner's other leg on and said to him: 'Now be quick about it and make sure we win.' The agreement was that the winner would be whichever of them was first to bring back some water from a very distant well. So the Runner was given a jug, and the princess got one too, and they both began running at the same time; but in a moment, when the princess had covered only a short distance, all the spectators had already lost sight of the Runner and it was just as if the wind had whistled past. In a very short time he reached the well, filled his jug full of water and started back. But half-way back he was overcome by a fit of weariness, so he put down the jug, lay down and went to sleep. He had, however, found a horse's skull lying there on the ground, and used it as his pillow, so that he would not be too comfortable and would wake up again soon. Meanwhile the princess, who was a fast runner too by ordinary human standards, had reached the well and was hurrying back with her jug full of water; and when she saw the Runner lying there asleep she was delighted, and said: 'My enemy is delivered into my hands.' And she emptied out his jug and bounded on. Now all would have been lost if it hadn't been for the Huntsman, who luckily was standing up on the castle tower and had seen everything with his sharp eyes. So he said: 'The princess shall still not get the better of us.' And he loaded his gun and fired it so skilfully that he shot away the horse's skull from under the runner's head without hurting him. At this the Runner woke up, jumped to his feet and saw that his jug was empty and the princess already far ahead of him. But he didn't give up, he ran back to the well with the jug, drew some more water and still got home ten minutes before the princess. 'You see,' he said, 'I really stirred my stumps this time, you couldn't really call it running before.'

But the king felt aggrieved, and the princess even more so, that she was to be given in marriage to a mere common discharged soldier; and they plotted together how they might get rid of him and his companions. Then the king said to her: 'I've thought of a way, don't worry, they'll not get home again.' And to the six he said: 'Now you must eat and drink and make merry together.' And he took them to a room that had an iron floor, with iron doors and iron-barred windows as well. In this room a table had been laid with a variety of delicious food, and the king said to them: 'Go in and enjoy yourselves.' When they were inside, he had the door locked and bolted. Then he sent for the cook and ordered him to light a fire under the room and keep it burning till the iron was red hot. The cook did so, and as the six of them in the room sat at table they began to feel rather warm, and thought it was the effect of their dinner; but when the heat got worse and worse, and they tried to get out but found the doors and windows barred, they realized that the king had had evil intentions and that he was trying to suffocate them. 'But he shan't succeed,' said the Man with the Hat. 'I'll make such a frost that the fire will crawl away in shame.' So saying, he put his hat on straight, and in an instant such a frost set in that all the heat disappeared and the food in the dishes began to freeze. Then when a few hours had passed and the king thought they must all have perished in the heat, he decided to see for himself and had the door opened. But as soon as he looked inside he saw all six of them standing there in the best of health, and they said how glad they were to be able to get out and warm themselves, because it was so cold in the room that their dinner had frozen solid on their plates. At this the king went down to the cook in a great rage and shouted at him, asking him why he had not done as he had been ordered. But the cook answered: 'There's plenty of heat here, sir, see for yourself.' And the king saw that an enormous fire was raging under the iron room, and realized that he would not be able to get the better of the six that way.

So now the king started pondering again how to get rid of his unwelcome guests. He sent for their master and said: 'If you will renounce your right to my daughter and accept gold instead, you shall have as much of it as you please.' 'Very well, my lord king,' he answered. 'Give me as much gold as my servant can carry and I'll not claim your daughter.' And when the king agreed to this he added: 'I shall come and fetch it in fourteen days.' Then he summoned every tailor in the whole kingdom, and they all had to sit sewing for fourteen days making a sack. And when it was ready he told the strong man who could uproot trees to put the sack on his shoulder and go with it to the king. Then the king said: 'What's this enormous fellow with a bale of canvas on his shoulder as big as a house?' And he was alarmed and thought: How much gold will he be able to drag off! So he had a barrel of gold brought, and it took fifteen of his strongest servants to carry it; but the Strong Man picked it up with one hand, put it into the sack and said: 'Why don't you bring some more? Look, this hardly covers the bottom!' So little by little the king had to have the entire contents of his treasury brought, and the Strong Man stuffed it all into his sack, and the sack was still not even half full. 'Fetch some more,' he cried, 'these few lumps won't fill it!' Then another seven thousand wagon-loads of gold from the entire kingdom had to be brought, and the Strong Man shoved them all into his sack, wagons and oxen and all. 'I'll not be particular,' he said. 'I'll take it as it comes, just to get the sack filled.' When everything had been crammed in, there was still room for a lot more; but he said: 'I'll just call it a deal; I suppose it's possible to tie up a sack even if it isn't full.' So saying, he humped it onto his back and off he went with his companions.

Now when the king saw this one single man carrying off the entire wealth of his kingdom, he flew into a rage and ordered out his cavalry to pursue the six of them and take back the sack from the strong man. Two regiments soon overtook them and called out to them: 'You are prisoners: put down that sack with the gold or we'll cut you to pieces.' 'What's that you say?' asked the Blowhard. 'Prisoners, are we? I'll see you all dancing around in the air first!' And closing one of his nostrils he blew through the other at the two regiments, making them scatter in all directions, sky-high and over hill and dale. A sergeant cried out for mercy, saying he had been wounded nine times and was a decent fellow who didn't deserve to be so disgraced. So the Blowhard blew a little less hard and let him come down to earth uninjured; then he said to him: 'Now go home to your king and tell him just to send for more cavalry, and I'll blow the whole lot sky-high.' When the king heard this message he said: 'Let the fellows go, they obviously know a thing or two.' So the six took home the loot, divided it between them and lived happily for the rest of their lives.

23

THE SIX SERVANTS

Long ago there lived an old queen who was a sorceress and her daughter was the most beautiful maiden under the sun. But the old queen's one idea was to lure people to their destruction, and when a suitor came she would say that any man wanting to marry her daughter must first perform a task, or his life would be forfeit. Many were dazzled by the maiden's beauty and did try their luck, but they failed to perform the task the queen set them, and then they were shown no mercy: they had to kneel at the block and have their heads cut off. Now there was a prince who had also heard of the maiden's beauty, and he said to his father: 'Let me go and try to win her hand.' 'No, no!' said the king, 'if you go, you will be going to your death.' Then his son took to his bed and became mortally ill and lay there for seven years, and no doctor could help him. When his father saw that there was no more hope, he said to him very sorrowfully: 'Go and try your fortune, for I know no other way to help you.' When his son heard that, he rose from his bed fully restored to health, and joyfully set out on his journey.

It happened that as he was riding over open country he saw something on the ground some way off that looked like a huge haystack, and when he got nearer he could see that it was the belly of a man lying on his back, a paunch the size of a small mountain. When the Fat Man saw the traveller he sat up and said: 'If you need someone, sir, then take me into your service.' The prince answered: 'What use can I make of a great unwieldy fellow like you?' 'Oh,' said the Fat Man, 'that's a mere trifle: when I feel really expansive, I'm three thousand times this size.' 'If that's so,' said the prince, 'then I can use you, come along with me.' So the Fat Man came along with the prince, and after a while they found another man lying on the ground with one ear pressed against the grass. 'What are you doing there?' asked the prince. 'I'm listening,' answered the man. 'What are you

listening for so attentively?' 'I'm listening to what's going on in
the world at this moment, for nothing escapes my ears, I can
even hear the grass growing.' The prince asked: 'Tell me, what
do you hear at the court of the old queen who has the beautiful
daughter?' The man answered: 'I can hear the whistling of a
sword through the air as it strikes off a suitor's head.' The prince
said: 'I can use you, come along with me.' So they travelled on,
and presently they saw a pair of feet lying on the ground, and
part of the legs as well, but they couldn't see the other end of
whoever they belonged to. When they had gone on quite some
distance they came to the body, and finally to the head. 'Well!'
said the prince. 'What a tall whopper you are!' 'Oh,' said the
Tall Man, 'this is nothing: when I really stretch my limbs I'm
three thousand times this height, taller than the highest mountain on earth. I'll be glad to serve you, sir, if you'll take me on.'
'Come with us,' said the prince, 'I can use you.' They travelled
on and found a man sitting at the roadside with his eyes blindfolded. The prince asked him: 'Have you got such weak eyes
that you can't look at the daylight?' 'No,' answered the man, 'I
can't take off the blindfold because my eyes are so powerful that
when they look at anything it explodes. If that's any use to you,
sir, I'll gladly serve you.' 'Come with us,' answered the prince,
'I can use you.' They travelled on and found a man lying in the
full heat of the sun but shivering with cold and shaking in every
limb. 'How can you be shivering in this hot sunshine?' asked
the prince. 'Oh dear me,' replied the man, 'I have a quite
different constitution: the hotter it is, the colder I get and my
bones freeze to the very marrow, but the colder it is the hotter I
get. If there's ice all round me I can't bear the heat, and if it's fire
I can't stand the cold.' 'You're a strange fellow,' said the prince,
'but if you'd like to serve me, come along with us.' They travelled on and saw a man standing and craning his neck, gazing in
all directions and away into the distance. The prince asked:
'What are you so busy looking for?' The man replied: 'I've got
such sharp eyes that I can see right beyond all the forests and
fields and valleys and mountains and right through the whole
world.' The prince said: 'If you'd like to, then come along with
me, because you're just what I still needed.'

The prince with his six servants now entered the city where the old queen lived. He didn't tell her who he was, but said: 'Madam, if you will give me your beautiful daughter, I will perform whatever you command me.' The sorceress was glad to have such a handsome youth falling into her snares again, and she said: 'I will set you three tasks, and if you succeed in each of them you shall become my daughter's lord and husband.' 'What is the first task to be?' he asked. 'I want you to fetch me back a ring I dropped into the Red Sea.' So the prince went home to his servants and said: 'The first task's not easy, I'm to fetch a ring out of the Red Sea; now tell me how to do that.' The Sharpsighted Man said: 'I'll find out where it is,' and after looking down into the sea he told them: 'There it is, caught on a jagged piece of rock.' The Tall Man carried them to the shore of the Red Sea and said: 'I could fetch it out all right if I could only see it.' 'Well, if that's the only problem!' exclaimed the Fat Man, and he lay down and put his mouth to the water. The waves poured into it as if into a bottomless pit, and he drank up the whole sea till it was as dry as a field. The Tall Man stooped down slightly and picked up the ring. The prince was delighted once he had it, and he took it to the old queen, who was astonished and said: 'Yes, that's the right ring. You've been successful with your first task, but now here is the second. You see there on the field in front of my castle, there are three hundred fat oxen grazing, and these you must devour, skin and bone and hair and horns and all; and down in my cellar there are three hundred casks of wine, which you must drink with the meat; and if you leave so much as one single ox-hair or one little drop of the wine, your life will be forfeit.' The prince said: 'And may I invite no guests? No meal is tasty without company.' The old woman laughed maliciously and replied: 'You may invite one guest to keep you company, but not more than one.'

So the prince went to his servants and said to the Fat Man: 'Today you are to be my guest and eat your fill for once.' So the Fat Man expanded and ate up the three hundred oxen, leaving not so much as a hair, then asked if breakfast was all he was to get. The wine he drank straight from the barrels without needing a glass, and finished it right to the last drop. When the meal was over, the prince went to the old queen and told her that he had performed the second task. She was amazed and said: 'You have done better than any of the others; but there's still one task left.' And she thought: You'll not escape me, you'll not keep your head on your shoulders. 'Tonight,' she said, 'I shall bring my daughter to you in your room, and you shall put your arm round her; but as you sit there with her beware of falling asleep, for I shall come at exactly twelve o'clock, and if she's no longer in your arms then, you will have lost.' The prince thought: This task is easy, I'm sure I'll be able to keep my eyes open; but he called his servants and told them what the old queen had said, adding: 'Who knows what tricks she may be up to? We had better be cautious, and you must keep watch and see to it that once the maiden is in my room she doesn't get out of it again.' When night fell the old woman came with her daughter and left her in the prince's arms; then the Tall Man made a ring of himself and lay down round both of them, and the Fat Man stood in front of the door so that no living soul could get in. So there they both sat, and the maiden didn't speak a word, but the moon shone through the window on to her face so that he could see her wonderful beauty. He did nothing but gaze at her, full of joy and love, and his eyes never once felt weary. That lasted till eleven o'clock; and then the old queen cast a spell on all of them that made them fall asleep, and at the same moment the maiden vanished.

They remained fast asleep till a quarter to twelve, and then the spell lost its power and they all woke up again. 'Alack and alas!' cried the prince, 'now I am lost!' And his faithful servants began to lament as well, but the Listener said: 'Be quiet, let me listen.' And he listened for a moment, then said: 'She's sitting inside a rock three hundred hours journey from here, bewailing her fate. Only you can help her, Tall Man; if you stretch yourself you'll be there in a couple of steps.' 'Yes,' answered the Tall Man, 'but our friend with the powerful eyes must come along as well, so that we can get rid of the rock.' So the Tall Man hoisted the Blindfolded Man on to his back, and in an instant, before you could snap your fingers, they had arrived in front of the enchanted rock. At once the Tall Man unbound the eyes of his

companion, who merely had to look about him and the rock
exploded into smithereens. The Tall Man picked up the princess and carried her back to the palace in no time, then he
fetched his companion with equal speed, and before the clock
struck twelve they were all sitting there as before, wide awake
and in high spirits. When twelve struck, the old sorceress came
creeping in with a mocking expression on her face, as if to say:
'Now I've got him.' For she thought her daughter was sitting
inside the rock three hundred hours away. But when she saw
her daughter in the prince's arms, she was dumbfounded and
exclaimed: 'This is a man with more power than I have.' But
there was nothing she could say, and she had to consent to let
him marry the maiden. But she whispered into her daughter's
ear: 'What a disgrace for you to have to obey a common man,
and not to be able to take a husband of your own choice.'

At this the maiden's proud heart was filled with anger and
she began to plan revenge. Next morning she had three
hundred cords of wood piled up, and said to the prince: 'You
have performed the three tasks, but I'll not become your wife
until one of you is willing to sit in the middle of a fire made of
that pile of wood.' She thought: None of his servants will burn
himself to death, and for love of me he will sit in it himself, and
then I shall be free. But the servants said: 'We've all done
something now except the Freezer, so it's his turn to help.' And
they seated him in the middle of the pile of faggots and set it
alight. The fire began to burn, and it burnt for three days till it
had burnt up all the wood; and when the flames died down,
there was the Freezer standing among the ashes trembling like
an aspen leaf and saying: 'I've never endured such cold in all
my life, I'd have frozen to death if it had gone on longer.'

After this no further excuse could be found, and the beautiful
maiden had to accept the unknown young man as her husband.
But as they were driving to the church the old queen said: 'I'll
not bear the disgrace of it,' and she sent troops after the bride
with orders to shoot down all opposition and bring her
daughter back to her. But the Listener had pricked up his ears
and heard these secret instructions. 'What shall we do?' he
asked the Fat Man. The Fat Man knew what to do: he gave

one or two belches and spewed out behind the carriage some of
the sea water he had drunk. The result was a huge lake in which
the troops got stuck and drowned. When the sorceress heard
this she sent out her armoured cavalry, but the Listener heard
the clanking of their armour and uncovered the eyes of the
Blindfolded Man, who gave the enemy a rather sharp look that
made them disintegrate like glass. After that they drove on
without further interference, and after the pair had been wedded in the church the six servants took leave of their master,
saying: 'You've got what you wanted, sir, and you no longer
need us: we'll travel on and try our luck.'

Half an hour's distance before the royal palace was a village,
and outside it a swineherd was tending his pigs. When they
arrived here, the prince said to his wife: 'Do you actually know
who I am? I am not a prince but a swineherd, and that man there
with the pigs is my father. The two of us will have to do our
share of the work too and help him to look after them.' Then he
stopped with her at an inn, and secretly told the innkeeper and
his wife that during the night they were to take her royal clothes
away from her. When she woke next morning she had nothing
to put on, and the landlady gave her an old skirt and a pair of old
woollen stockings, even acting as if this were a great favour and
saying: 'If it weren't for your husband, you'd have got nothing
from me at all.' Then she believed that he really was a
swineherd and kept the pigs with him, and thought: I've
deserved this by my pride and arrogance. That lasted a week
and she couldn't bear it any longer, for her feet were all covered
with sores. Then some servants came and asked if she knew
who her husband was. 'Yes,' she answered, 'he's a swineherd
and he's just gone out to try and sell some ribbons and laces.'
But they said: 'Come with us, we'll take you to him.' And they
took her up into the palace, and when she entered the hall her
husband was standing there in royal clothing. But she didn't
recognize him till he fell on her neck, kissed her and said: 'I
suffered so much for you, so I wanted you to suffer a bit for me.'
And now the wedding was really celebrated, and your story-
teller wishes he'd been there too.

24

THE SEA-RABBIT

Once upon a time there was a princess, and high up under the battlements of her castle she had a hall with twelve windows facing north, south, east and west; and when she came up here and looked round, she could see the whole of her kingdom. Even through the first window she could see more clearly than other people, and still better through the second, and still more sharply through the third, and so on increasingly until through the twelfth window she could see everything above ground and below ground and nothing could be hidden from her. But because she was proud and would not submit to anyone and wanted to be the sole mistress, she had it proclaimed that she would marry no man unless he could hide from her in such a way that it was impossible for her to find him. But if anyone were to try this and she were to discover him, his head would be cut off and put up on a stake. The castle was already surrounded by ninety-seven stakes with dead men's heads on them, and for a long time no one made the attempt. The princess was pleased and thought: Now I'll live free for the rest of my life. Then three brothers presented themselves to her and declared that they wished to try their luck. The eldest brother thought he would be safe if he crawled into a lime-pit, but she saw him through the very first window and had him pulled out and beheaded. The second stowed himself away in the castle cellar, and him too she saw from the first window, and that was the end of him: his head was put on the ninety-ninth stake. Then the youngest son came before her and begged her to let him have a day to think about the matter, and also to be so gracious as to give him two chances if she discovered him: if he failed on the third try, he said, then he would care no longer for his life. And because he was so handsome and begged her so earnestly, she said: 'Yes, I will grant you this favour; but you won't succeed.'

Next day he racked his brains for a long time to think of a way of hiding himself, but all in vain. Then he took his gun and went out hunting. He saw a raven and took aim at it; but just as he was going to press the trigger the raven called out: 'Don't shoot, I'll reward you for my life!' He lowered his gun, walked on and came to a lake, where he caught sight of a big fish which had just swum up from the bottom to the surface of the water. As he pointed his gun at it the fish called out: 'Don't shoot, I'll reward you for my life!' He let it dive down, walked on and met a fox that was limping. He fired a shot and missed it, and then the fox called out: 'Don't do that; come here instead and pull this thorn out of my paw.' This indeed he did, but then he was just about to kill the fox and skin it when it said: 'Let me be, I'll reward you for my life!' The young man let it run away, and then as it was evening he went back home.

On the following day he was due to go into hiding, but ponder as he might he couldn't think of a suitable place. He went to the raven in the forest and said to it: 'I spared your life, so now tell me a place to hide where the princess won't see me.' The raven put its head down and thought for a long time, and finally it croaked: 'I have it!' It fetched an egg out of its nest, broke it in two and put the young man inside, then closed up the egg again and sat on it. When the princess looked out of her first window she couldn't see where he was, and she couldn't spot him through the following windows either; she began to get anxious, but she saw him through the eleventh window. She had the raven shot and the egg brought to her and cracked open, and the young man had to come out. She said to him: 'You've had your first chance; if you can't do better than that, it'll be the end of you.'

Next day he went to the lake, called the fish and said to it: 'I spared your life, so now tell me where I can hide so that the princess won't see me.' The fish thought about it, and finally exclaimed: 'I have it! I'll put you inside my belly.' It swallowed him and swam down to the bottom of the lake. The princess looked through her windows, and when she couldn't see him even through the eleventh she was greatly alarmed, but finally she discovered him through the twelfth. She had the fish caught and killed, and there was the young man. You can well imagine how he felt. She said: 'You have had your second chance, but I think your head will be on the hundredth stake.'

On the last day he walked across the fields with a heavy heart and met the fox. 'You know how to find all sorts of hidy-holes,' he said to it. 'I spared your life, so now advise me where I am to hide so that the princess won't find me.' 'It's a difficult task,' answered the fox, looking very serious. Finally it exclaimed: 'I have it!' It took the young man to a spring, plunged in and came out of the water in the form of a pedlar and animal-seller. The young man had to dip down into the water too, and was changed into a little sea-rabbit. The pedlar went into the town and put the nice little animal on show. A lot of people crowded round to look at it, and finally the princess came too. She liked the sea-rabbit so much that she bought it and gave the pedlar a lot of money for it. Before he handed it to her he said to it: 'When the princess goes to the window, creep quickly under her pigtail.' Then the time came when she was due to look for him. She went to all the windows in turn from the first to the eleventh and couldn't see him. When she couldn't see him through the twelfth window either, she was scared and furious, and banged it shut so hard that the glass in all the windows shivered into a thousand pieces and the whole castle shook.

She turned away and felt the sea-rabbit under her pigtail, and seized it and hurled it to the ground exclaiming: 'Get away, get out of my sight!' It ran to the pedlar and they both hurried to the spring, where they plunged in and got back their proper shapes. The young man thanked the fox and said: 'The raven and the fish are dunderheads compared to you; you know all the tricks, I must say!'

The young man went straight to the castle. The princess was already waiting for him and resigned herself to her fate. The wedding was celebrated and now he was king and master of the whole kingdom. He never told her where he had hidden the third time or who had helped him; and so she believed that he had done everything by his own skill, and held him in respect, for she thought to herself: He's a match for me after all!

25

THE WORN-OUT DANCING-SHOES

Once upon a time there was a king who had twelve daughters, and each of them was more beautiful than the next. They slept together in a big room with their beds standing all in a row, and every night when they had gone to bed the king locked them in and bolted the door. But when he opened it again next morning, he always saw that their shoes had been danced to pieces, and no one could ever make out how this had happened. So the king had it proclaimed that whoever could discover where his daughters spent the night dancing should marry whichever of them he chose and become king after his death: but if anyone were to undertake this and not make the discovery after three days and nights, his life would be forfeit. Before long a prince came and offered to undertake this venture. He was well received, and in the evening they took him to a room next to the bedchamber of the twelve princesses. Here he was given a bed and told to keep watch and see where they went dancing; moreover, the door between his room and the bedchamber was left open so that they wouldn't be able to get up to anything or go anywhere without his noticing. But the prince's eyes grew heavy as lead and he fell asleep; and when he woke in the morning all twelve of them had been dancing, for there were their shoes with the soles worn through to nothing. On the second and third nights the same thing happened, and then he was beheaded without mercy. He was followed by many others who came to try their luck, but they all lost their lives. Now it happened that a poor soldier, who was wounded and could no longer serve in the army, was on his way to the city where the king lived. He was met by an old woman, who asked him where he was going. 'I don't really know myself,' he said, and added jestingly: 'I think I might try to find out where the princesses wear out their shoes dancing, and then I'll become king.' 'That's not very difficult,' said the old woman, 'you just mustn't drink the wine that will be brought to you that evening, and you must pretend to be fast asleep.' Then she gave him a cloak and said: 'If you put this on you'll be invisible, and then you'll be able to follow the twelve princesses on the quiet.' When the soldier had heard this good advice, he made up his mind in earnest and went boldly into the king's presence announcing himself as a suitor. He was received no less well than the others and given royal clothing to wear. In the evening, when it was time to go to bed, he was taken to the antechamber, and when he was about to lie down the eldest sister came in bringing him a goblet of wine; but he had tied a sponge under his chin and he let the wine run into it, not drinking a drop. Then he went to bed and after a little while began to snore as if he were sound asleep. The twelve princesses heard him and laughed, and the eldest of them said: 'There goes another who might have saved his skin.' Then they got up, opened their cupboards and fetched out magnificent clothes. They sat before looking-glasses beautifying themselves, and skipped about with excitement in anticipation of their dance; only the youngest of them said: 'I don't know what it is, you're all enjoying your-selves but I feel so strange; I'm sure some misfortune is going to happen.' 'You're a little white goose,' said her eldest sister, 'you're always scared. Have you forgotten how many princes have come here already all in vain? I needn't even have given that soldier a sleeping draught, the lout wouldn't have woken up anyway.' When they were all ready they first took a look at the soldier, but he had shut his eyes and lay there without stirring, and now they thought they were quite safe. So the eldest of them went to her bed and knocked on it: at once it sank into the ground, and one after another they went down through the opening, with the eldest leading. The soldier, who had seen everything, didn't hesitate, but put on his cloak and climbed down too just behind the youngest sister. Half-way downstairs he stepped on the hem of her dress, and she was startled and exclaimed: 'What was that? Who's tugging at my dress?' 'Don't be such a simpleton,' said her eldest sister, 'you caught it on a nail.' So they went right down, and when they reached the bottom, there they were in a marvellous avenue of trees with

leaves all of silver, glittering and sparkling. The soldier
thought: I'd better take something to prove this. So he broke off
a twig, but as he did so the tree cracked like a pistol shot. The
youngest sister cried out again: 'There's something wrong,
didn't any of you hear that noise?' But the eldest said: 'They're
firing a salute, because soon we'll have released our princes
from the spell.' Then they walked on into an avenue where all
the leaves were of gold, and finally into a third where they were
of pure diamond; the soldier broke off a twig of each kind, and
each time there was a crack that made the youngest sister jump
with fright, but the eldest kept insisting that a salute was being
fired. On they went till they came to a wide river, and drawn up
at the edge of it were twelve boats, and in every boat sat a
handsome prince. They had been waiting for the twelve sisters,
and each took one of them on board, and the soldier went on
board with the youngest. 'I don't know why this boat's so much
heavier tonight,' said the prince, 'I'm having to row as hard as I
can to get it to move.' 'I suppose it can only be the warm
weather,' said the youngest sister, 'I'm feeling quite hot too.'
Now on the far side of the river stood a splendid, brightly lit
castle, and you could hear drums and trumpets making merry
music inside it. They rowed across and went into the castle, and
each of the princes danced with his sweetheart. But the soldier,
still invisible, danced among them, and whenever one of them
had a goblet of wine in her hand he would drink it, so that it was
empty when she raised it to her lips; and the youngest princess
was scared by this too, but her eldest sister kept silencing her.
There they danced till three o'clock next morning, when all their
shoes were worn through and they had to stop. The princes
rowed them back across the river, and this time the soldier sat
up front in the eldest sister's boat. On the bank they said
goodbye to the princes and promised to come again the following night. When they reached the stair the soldier ran ahead of
them and jumped into his bed, so that by the time the twelve
princesses dragged themselves wearily into their bedroom he
was again snoring noisily for all of them to hear, and they said:
'We're safe from him, anyway.' Then they took off their beautiful dresses and put them away, and put their worn-out shoes

under their beds and lay down to sleep. Next morning the soldier decided not to say anything but to see some more of these strange goings-on, so he followed the princesses on the second and third nights as well. Everything happened just as on the first occasion, and each time they danced till their shoes were worn through. On the third night he brought back a goblet as proof of his story. When the time came for him to give his answer, he took the three twigs and the goblet with him and appeared before the king; but the twelve princesses stood behind the door listening, to hear what he would say. When the king put the question: 'Where did my twelve daughters wear out their dancing-shoes last night?' he answered: 'With twelve princes in an underground palace.' And he reported all that had happened and produced the proofs. Then the king sent for his daughters and asked them whether the soldier had spoken the truth; and realizing that they had been found out and that denials would be useless, they had to admit it all. Then the king asked the soldier which of them he wanted as his wife. He answered: 'I'm no longer young, sir, so give me the eldest.' So the wedding was celebrated that very day, and the king promised to leave the kingdom to the soldier at his death. But the princes were spellbound for a further period, one day for every night they had spent dancing with the twelve princesses.

26

THE DEVIL'S THREE GOLDEN HAIRS

Once upon a time there was a poor woman who gave birth to a little son, and because he came into the world with a caul it was prophesied that in his fourteenth year he would marry the king's daughter. Soon after this it happened that the king came to that village and no one knew it was the king, and when he asked the people what had been happening recently, they answered: 'There was a child born the other day with a caul, and that'll bring him luck in everything he does. It's even been prophesied that in his fourteenth year he'll marry the king's daughter.' The king, who had a wicked heart and was angered by this prophecy, went to the parents, pretended to be very friendly and said: 'You poor folk, let me have your child, I'll look after him well.' At first they refused, but the stranger offered to pay a lot of money for the boy, and they thought: He's a fortune-child, so it's bound to turn out all right for him anyway. So in the end they consented and handed him over.

The king put the child in a box and rode off with him till he came to a deep river; and here he threw the box into the water, thinking: Well, I've rid my daughter of that unexpected suitor. But the box didn't sink, it floated like a little boat, and not a drop of water got into it. It drifted downstream as far as a mill within two leagues of the king's capital, and here it got caught against the dam. Luckily a miller's boy was standing there and noticed it, and he pulled it ashore with a hook, thinking he had found a treasure chest; but when he opened it, there lay a fine little boy looking as fresh as a daisy. He took him to the miller and his wife, and as they had no children of their own they were delighted and said: 'He's a gift from God.' They took good care of the foundling, and he grew up as good as gold.

It so Happened that one day the king came into the mill to

shelter from a storm, and he asked the miller and his wife whether the big sturdy boy was their son. 'No,' they answered, 'he's a foundling. Fourteen years ago he came floating down to the mill dam in a box, and our servant pulled him out of the water.' Then the king realized this was the very same fortune-child he had thrown into the river, and he said: 'Good people, could the lad not take a letter for me to the queen? I'll pay him two gold pieces.' 'As my lord the king commands,' they replied, and told the boy to be ready to leave. Then the king wrote a letter to the queen which said: 'As soon as the boy carrying this letter arrives, he is to be killed and buried, and all that is to be over and done with before I get back.'

The boy set out with this letter, but lost his way and in the evening found himself in a great forest. In the darkness he saw a faint light, made his way towards it and came to a small house. When he entered, an old woman was sitting by the fire all by herself. She was startled to see the lad and said: 'Where are you from and where are you going?' 'I'm from the mill,' he answered, 'and I'm on my way to the queen with a letter I have to take to her; but I've lost my way in the forest, so I'd like to stay the night here.' 'You poor boy,' said the woman, 'this house belongs to a gang of robbers, and when they get home they'll kill you.' 'I don't mind who comes,' said the boy, 'I'm not afraid; but I'm so tired that I can't go any further.' And he lay down on a bench and went to sleep. Presently the robbers came in and asked angrily what strange boy this was lying there. The old woman said: 'Oh, he's just an innocent child, he's got lost in the wood, so I felt sorry for him and let him stay. He's been told to take a letter to the queen.' The robbers opened the letter and read it, and found that it said that as soon as the boy arrived he was to be put to death. At this the hard-hearted robbers took pity on him, and their leader tore up the letter and wrote another which said that as soon as the boy arrived he was to be married to the king's daughter. Then they let him lie there in peace till the next morning, and when he woke up they gave him the letter and showed him the right way. But when the queen had received the letter and read it, she did what it told her to do: she ordered a magnificent wedding feast and the princess was married to the fortune-child. And since he was a handsome and good-natured young man, she was quite happy and content to live with him.

After a time the king came back to his palace and saw that the prophecy had been fulfilled and that the fortune-child was married to his daughter. 'How did this come about?' he demanded. 'I gave quite different orders in my letter.' So the queen handed him the letter and invited him to see for himself what was in it. The king read the letter and saw at once that it had been exchanged for the other one. He asked the young man what had happened to the letter he had been given, and why he had brought a different one instead. 'I know nothing about it,' the boy answered. 'It must have been exchanged during the night, when I was sleeping in the forest.' The king said in a rage: 'You shan't get away with it as easily as that. Anyone who wants my daughter for his wife has got to go down into Hell and fetch me three golden hairs from the Devil's head. That's what I want, and if you bring them to me you shall keep my daughter.' The king hoped in this way to be rid of him for ever. But the fortune-child answered: 'I'll fetch the golden hairs, I'm not afraid of the Devil.' With that he took his leave and began his journey.

His road took him to a great city, where the watchman at the gate questioned him about his trade and about what he knew. 'I know everything,' replied the fortune-child. 'In that case you can do us a favour,' said the watchman. 'You can tell us why the fountain in our market place that used to have wine running out of it has dried up, so that we don't even get water from it now.' 'I'll tell you that,' he answered, 'but you must wait till I return.' Then he went on and came to another city, and again the watchman at the gate asked him what his trade was and what he knew. 'I know everything,' he answered. 'Then you can do us a favour and tell us why a tree in our city that used to bear golden apples doesn't even grow leaves any more.' 'I'll tell you that,' he answered, 'but you must wait till I return.' Then he went on and came to a wide river that he had to cross. The ferryman asked him what his trade was and what he knew. 'I know everything,' he answered. 'Then you can do me a favour,' said the ferryman, 'and tell me why I have to keep on pushing this boat to and fro and no one ever takes over the job from me.' 'I'll tell you that,' he answered, 'but you must wait till I return.'

When he had crossed the river he found the entrance to Hell. Everything inside was black and sooty, and the Devil wasn't at home, but there sat his grandmother in a big armchair. 'What do you want?' she asked him, and she didn't look all that fierce. 'I'd like three golden hairs, please, from the Devil's head,' he answered, 'otherwise I won't be allowed to keep my wife.' 'That's a bold request,' said she. 'If the Devil comes home and finds you here, you'll be for it; but I'm sorry for you, so I'll see if I can help you.' She changed him into an ant and said: 'Crawl into the fold of my skirt, you'll be safe there.' 'Yes,' he answered, 'that's all right, but there are three things I'd like to know as well: why has a fountain that used to flow with wine dried up, so that it doesn't even give water now? And why has a tree that used to bear golden apples even stopped growing leaves? And why is it that a ferryman has to keep on crossing the river and no one ever takes over the job from him?' 'Those are hard questions,' she answered, 'but just keep quiet and stay still and pay attention to what the Devil says when I pull his three golden hairs out.'

When evening fell the Devil came home, and he'd no sooner entered than he noticed that things were not as usual. 'I smell human flesh, I smell it,' he said. 'There's something going on here.' Then he searched in every corner but couldn't find anything. His grandmother scolded him. 'I've only just done the sweeping,' she said, 'and tidied the whole place, and now you're messing it all up again. You're forever smelling human flesh! Sit down and eat your supper.' When he had eaten and drunk, he felt tired and lay down with his head in his grandmother's lap and told her to pick some of the lice out of his hair. It wasn't long before he fell asleep and started puffing and snoring. Then the old woman seized a golden hair, tweaked it out and laid it down beside her. 'Ow!' shrieked the Devil, 'what do you think you're doing?' 'I had a bad dream,' his grandmother answered, 'so I grabbed at your hair.' 'Well, what were

you dreaming about?' asked the Devil. 'I dreamt there was a
fountain in a market place, and wine used to come from it, but
now it's dried up and won't even give them water; what can be
the reason for that?' 'Ho, ho, if only they knew!' answered the
Devil. 'There's a toad sitting under a stone in the well; if they
kill it the wine will flow again all right.' His grandmother picked
out some more of his lice till he fell asleep and started snoring fit
to shake the windows. Then she tweaked out the second golden
hair. 'Ow-wow! What are you doing?' shrieked the Devil in a
rage. 'Never mind, never mind,' she said. 'I did it in my sleep, I
was dreaming.' 'What were you dreaming about this time?' he
asked. 'I dreamt about a kingdom where there was a fruit-tree
that used to bear golden apples, and now it won't even grow
leaves. I wonder what can have caused that?' 'Ho ho, if only
they knew!' answered the Devil. 'There's a mouse gnawing at
its root; if they kill the mouse the golden apples will soon grow
again, but if it goes on gnawing the whole tree will wither. And
now leave me in peace, you and your dreams; if you wake me
up again I'll box your ears.' His grandmother spoke to him
soothingly and picked out some more lice till he was asleep and
snoring. Then she seized the third golden hair and tweaked it
out. The Devil jumped up with a yell and began to set about her,
but she calmed him down again and said: 'How can one help
having bad dreams!' 'What have you been dreaming now?' he
asked, his curiosity getting the better of him. 'I dreamt there
was a ferryman complaining that he has to keep on crossing the
river and no one takes over the job from him. What can be the
cause of that?' 'Ho ho, the stupid lout!' answered the Devil.
'When someone comes and wants to cross, he must just put the
oar into his hand, and then the other man will have to do the
ferrying and he'll be free.' So now that his grandmother had
plucked out the three golden hairs and the three questions had
been answered, she left the old dragon in peace, and he slept till
daybreak.

When the Devil had gone out again, the old woman took the
ant from the fold in her skirt and gave the fortune-child his
human form back. 'Here are the three golden hairs,' she said,
'and I expect you heard what the Devil said about your three

questions.' 'Yes,' he answered, 'I heard it all and I'll remember it well.' 'So that's your problem solved,' she said, 'and now you can be off.' He thanked the old woman for her much needed help and climbed up out of Hell, feeling very pleased with his success. When he came to the ferryman, he was asked for his promised answer. 'First take me across,' said the fortune-child, 'and then I'll tell you how you can be released.' And when he had got to the opposite bank, he gave him the Devil's advice: 'Next time someone comes to be ferried across, just put the oar into his hand.' He went on and came to the city where the barren tree was, and there too the watchman demanded his answer. So he told him what he had heard from the Devil: 'Kill the mouse that's gnawing at its root, and it'll bear golden apples again.' The watchman thanked him, and as a reward gave him two donkeys laden with gold and told them to follow him. Finally he came to the city where the fountain had dried up. So he told the watchman as the Devil had said: 'There's a toad sitting in it under a stone; you must look for it and kill it, and then you'll get plenty of wine from the fountain again.' The watchman thanked him, and he gave him two donkeys laden with gold as well.

Then at last the fortune-child got home to his wife, who was delighted to see him again and to hear how well everything had gone. He took the king what he had asked for, the Devil's three golden hairs, and when the king saw the four donkey-loads of gold he was very pleased indeed and said: 'Now that you have fulfilled all the conditions you can keep my daughter. But, my dear son-in-law, won't you tell me how you came by all that gold? You have brought back very great treasure!' 'I crossed a river,' he answered, 'and that's where I got it from; it's lying all along the bank instead of sand.' 'Could I fetch some for myself as well?' asked the king with great eagerness. 'As much as you want, sir,' replied the young man. 'There's a ferryman on the river, get him to ferry you over and you'll be able to fill your sacks at the other side.' The king, his heart filled with greed, set off in great haste, and when he came to the river he beckoned to the ferryman to take him across. The ferryman came and told him to get into the boat, and when they reached the opposite bank he handed him the oar and jumped out. And after that the king had to go on ferrying as a punishment for his sins.

'Is he still doing it?' 'Why not? I don't suppose anyone has taken the oar from him.'

27

THE GRIFFIN

There was this king, but oi couldn't ever tell you where he rualed or what they called him. He hadn't a son, only a darter, and she only one, and she was always after bein sick and there wasn't a doctor in it that could help her at all. Well, it was propheysied to yer man the king that his darter would be cured by eatin an apple. So he publisoised truout his kingdom that whoever it was brought his darter apples that'd cure her, wouldn't he marry her and become the king himself. A farmer wit tree sons at him heared of it, and sez he to the eldest: 'Owt into the gerden wit yez, pick yerself a basket of them luvly red-cheeked apples and bring them to the caert; maybe they'll cure the princess and yez'll be marryin her and be made king.' Well now, didn't the lad do loik he was told and him on his wey. Then, when he had gone a moile or two, who should he meet but a little leprechaun, and him all in oirn, that ups and asks him what he's got in his basket there. And sez Paddy (that bein the name on him): 'Isn't it frags' legs.' 'Roight yez are,' sez the leprechaun, and him on his wey. So Paddy came to the pallis at last, and told the flunkey he had the apples as'd cure the princess if she cared to eat them. Well, the king was only deloighted and he summoned Paddy to his presence, but be-dad! when he had the basket open, what d'yez tink was in it but frags' legs and they still twitchin, not apples at all. And the king was in a moighty rage and had him owt on his ear.

Well, when he got home he went and told his da what had happened to him, so his da sent his second son, a lad be the name of Mick; but didn't the very same ting happen to him as happened to Paddy. He loikewise met the little leprechaun all in oirn as asked him what he had in his basket. 'Sure, it's pigs' brestles,' says he. 'Roight yez are,' says the leprechaun. When he came to the pallis and told yer man the flunkey that he had the apples that'd be curin the princess, sure they wouldn't let

him in at all and told him another feller had been already and
made a roight fooal owt of the lot of them. But Mick insisted that
he had the apples and they should be lettin him in, and in the
end they took him at his word and brought him into the king's
presence. And when he opened his basket, yez can be sure
there were pigs' brestles in it. So the king was only livid and had
him whepped out of the pallis.

Well, when he got himself home, he told them what had
happened to him. Then the youngest lad, that they'd only ever
called Soft Seamus, ups and asks his da if he'd let him go and
take apples too. 'Be the hokey,' said his da, 'and a foine feller
yez'd be to troy it. If the brainy boys can't do it, d'yez tink you
can?' But the lad wouldn't give up. 'Honest, da, oi want to go.'
'Give over, ye stupit gaum, wait till yez've a few more brains on
yez,' said his da, and turned his back on him. But Seamus gave
a pull at the tail of his coat and said: 'Honest, da, oi want to go.'
'Al roight then,' said his da impatiently. 'Off wit yez, yez'll be
back before long, oi bet.' And the lad was only deloighted and
leppin for joy. 'There yez go, actin the giddy goat,' said his da.
'Sure, yez grow into a bigger eejit daily.' But Seamus didn't give
a damn and was as happy as Larry in spoite of it all. But it bein
nearly dark, he tought he'd wait at home till morning as he
couldn't have gone to the pallis today. And all noight, loyin in
his bed, he couldn't sleep for the loife of him, and if he did drop
off for a moment, he was dreamin of handsome colleens and
foine cassles and gold and silver and what have yez.

Early next marnin he set off owt on his wey, and shortly after
who d'yez tink he met but the dirty little leprechaun in his oirn
coat as asks him what he has in his basket there. So Seamus
answers: 'Sure, isn't it apples to cure the princess.' 'Foine,' says
the leprechaun, 'roight yez are,' sez he. But when he got to the
caert, they wouldn't let him in at all, for, said they, two fellers
had already been there sayin they had apples, and didn't one of
them have frags' legs and the other pigs' brestles. But Seamus
stuck to his guns al roight and said it wasn't frags' legs he was
after carryin but the foinest apples in all the kingdom. Well, the
gatekeeper tought he couldn't be a loiar and him so well
spoken and he let him in, and it's roight he was to do so, for

when Seamus took the lid off his basket nothin but golden
apples appeared. The king was only deloighted and had some
brought to his darter roight away, and waited his heart in his
gob to see what the effect moight be. And before very long
someone came and brought the news, and who d'yez tink
brought it? Who but his very own darter! The minute itself she
tasted the apples she lept owt of her bed in the very best of
health. Oi could never tell yez how overjoyed the king was. But
he wouldn't give Seamus the princess to marry yet; no wey,
first he must build a boat that'd travel faster on dry land than on
wather. So Seamus agreed to that and went off to his home and
told them what had happened.

Well, their da sent Paddy off into the forest to build that kind
of a boat. He worked hard and whestled all the whoile. At
midday, the sun bein roight overhead, the same oirnclad leprechaun comes along as asks him what he moight be doin there.
'Sure, oi'm makin wooden spoouns,' said Paddy. Said the
leprechaun: 'Roight yez are.' When evenin came, there was
Paddy tinking he'd built a boat, but when he tried to sit in it,
sure it was nothin but a lot of old wooden spoouns. The next
day Micky went into the forest, and didn't the very same thing
happen to him as happened to Paddy. So on the third day off
goes Soft Seamus. He worked powerful hard, the forest was
ringin wit his moighty blows, and all the whoile he was merrily
whestlin and singin away. And once again along comes the
little leprechaun at midday, the sun bein at its hottest, and asks
him what he moight be doin there? 'Amn't oi buildin a boat
that'll travel faster on dry land than on wather,' says he, and
when he'd have it finished, he'd get the princess for his wife, so
he would. 'Well now,' says the leprechaun, 'roight yez are.' In
the evenin when the sun turned golden, Seamus had his boat
finished, oars, riggin and all, so he sat himself in it and rowed
off to the pallis, and the boat went loike the clappers. The king
watched it comin from moiles away, but still he wouldn't give
Seamus his darter to marry, not at all; before he'd do that, he
requoired Seamus to herd a hundred hares from dawn till dark,
and if a single one of them craytures got away, he'd not get his
darter. 'Al roight,' said Seamus, and first thing in the mornin he

was off into the meadow with his herd and guardin them so that
nivver a one would get away. Before many hours had passed
there came a maid from the pallis as says to Seamus that he
must give her a hare and be nifty abowt it, for company had
come. But didn't Seamus see through the trick, and he said the
king could wait till tamarrer to serve the company hare stew.
But the maid would have none of that and foinally began arguin
the toss wit him. 'Very well,' said Seamus, 'if the princess
herself will come and ask, oi'll give her a hare.' The maid
reparted all this at the pallis, and then the princess came, her
very own self. But in the meantime the little leprechaun came to
Seamus and asked him what he moight be doin there? 'Oh,'
said he, 'oi'm herdin these hundred hares and seein to it that
nivver a one gets away, and then oi can marry the princess and
be king.' 'Roight yez are,' said the leprechaun. 'Here's a poipe
for yez; if one of yer hares runs away, just give a toot on it and
he'll be back in a jiffy.' So, when the princess came, Seamus put
a hare in her apron for her, but she hadn't gone more'n a
hundred yards when Seamus ups with his poipe and gives a
blow on it; out leps the hare out of the apron and whisht back
into the herd wit him. Well, when evening came the hareherd
blew on his poipe again and counted that they were all there
and drove them back to the pallis. And the king was utterly
bemused that Seamus had managed to herd a hundred hares
and nivver a one of them run away. But still he wouldn't give
him his darter, not till Seamus had brought him a fedder from
the Griffin's tail.

So Seamus set owt on his wey and came on at a great speed.
In the evenin he arroived at a cassle and asked for a bed for the
noight, for in those days there wasn't such a ting as an inn,
d'yez see. Well, the lord of the cassle was glad to agree and
asked him where he moight be makin for, and sez Seamus: 'To
the Griffin.' 'Is that roight, to the Griffin? Oi'm told that man is
powerful knowledgeable. Oi've lost the key to me treasure-
chest, yez moight koindly ask him where it moight be.' 'I'd be
only deloighted to,' sez Seamus. So airly next marnin he was off
again on his wey, and he comes to another cassle where he stays
the noight. When the men and women of the house heared he

was off to see the Griffin, they told him their darter was sick and they'd troied every cure, but divil a one that'd work, and would he koindly ask the Griffin what moight cure their darter, and Seamus said he'd be only deloighted and out on his wey wit him. Then he came to a river, and there was no ferry at it at all, but a great strappin feller that had to carry yez over. Well, didn't this feller ask Seamus where he moight be makin for, and Seamus told him: 'The Griffin.' 'Well now, when yez foind him,' sez the feller, 'ask him whoy it is oi have to be carrying everyone over this here river.' And sez Seamus: 'Begob, oi'll do that all roight.' And the feller took him up on his shoulders and carried him over.

Well, Seamus came at last to the Griffin's house, but only the woife was at home, himself bein out. The woife asked him what he wanted, and Seamus told his tale, how he wanted a fedder from the Griffin's tail, and then the people in the cassle had lost the key to their treasure-chest and he was to ask where it'd be, and in the other cassle they had a sick darter and he was to ask what moight cure her. Then there was a river nearby and a feller that had to carry yez over it and he was to ask why that moight be. 'Well now, me boy,' sez the Griffin's woife, 'there's not a Christian soul that can spake to the Griffin, for he eats every last one of them. But if yez loike, yez can hoide yerself under his bed and when he's fast asleep be noight put up yer hand and pull owt a fedder from his tail; and oi'll ask him the things yez're wantin to know.' So Seamus agreed and hid himself under the bed.

So in the evenin the Griffin came home, and the minute itself he came into the room didn't he say: 'Woife, oi smell a Christian.' 'Sure yez do,' sez his woife, 'wasn't one here today, but he's gone again,' and the Griffin no more on the matter. In the middle of the noight as the Griffin lay snaarin, Seamus ups wit his hand and whips a fedder from the Griffin's tail. The Griffin jerked awake and said: 'Woife, oi smell a Christian and oi think somebody's been at me tail.' Sez his woife: 'Sure yez've been dreamin, didn't oi tell yez that there was a Christian here and he's gone off again? He told me all sarts of tings. There's a cassle where they've lost the key to their treasure-chest and can't foind it anywhere.' 'Ah, the eejits,' sez the Griffin, 'the key's loying there in the woodshed behoind the door under a log.' 'And he told me there's a cassle where the darter's sick and they can't foind a cure for her.' 'Ah, the eejits,' sez the Griffin, 'below the cellar stairs there's a toad has made a nest out of her hair; she'll get well when she takes the hair back.' 'And he told me that there's a river wit a feller by it that has to carry everyone over.' 'Ah, the eejit,' sez the Griffin, 'all he needs to do is drap someone half-way over and then he needn't carry anyone ever again.'

Airly next marnin the Griffin ups owt of bed and laves the house. Seamus came owt from under the bed, and now he had his foine fedder and had heared what the Griffin had said abowt the key and the darter and the feller by the river. The Griffin's woife told him the whole story again so he wouldn't go and farget it, and then he was off on his wey home. Fairst he came to the feller by the river who asked him roight away what the Griffin had said. 'Fairst, carry me across,' sez Seamus, 'and then oi'll tell yez.' When the man had carried him across, Seamus told him that all he had to do was drap someone in the middle of the river and then he'd nivver have to carry anyone ever again. The feller was altogether deloighted and offered to carry Seamus there and back again by way of thanks, but Seamus said no, he wouldn't trouble him, thank yez very much, and he went off on his wey. Next he came to the cassle with the poorly darter; he took her on his back, for she couldn't walk a step, d'yez see, and carried her down the cellar stairs, took the toad's nest from under the last step and put it in her hand, and she jumped off his back and ran up the stairs parfectly recovered. And her ma and her da were altogether overjoyed and presented Seamus with gifts of silver and gold; whatever he cared to have they gave it him. Then when Seamus reached the other cassle he went straight to the woodshed, and sure enough, there was the key under a log behoind the door, and he brought it to the lord of the cassle. And he was only deloighted, and he gave Seamus a good share of the gold from the chest as a reward and a lot more besoides, cattle and sheep and goats.

Well, when Seamus came to yer man the king wit all that stuff
– money and gold and silver and cattle and sheep and goats –
the king asked him where he'd got it all from, and Seamus said
wouldn't the Griffin give yez anything yez asked for. And sez
the king to himself: Now that would be a great help. And off he
went to foind the Griffin. But when he came to the river, be the
hokey, wasn't he the fairst man there since Seamus, and the
feller dumped him half-way over, and the king was drowned
dead. So Seamus married the princess and was made the king.

28

THE THREE SNAKE-LEAVES

Once upon a time there was a poor man who could no longer afford to keep his only son. So his son said: 'Dear father, you have fallen on very hard times and I'm a burden to you; it will be better if I go away and try to earn my living.' His father gave him his blessing and took leave of him with great sadness. At this time the king of a powerful kingdom was engaged in a war; the young man took service with him and joined the fighting. And when they met the enemy a battle took place, and there was great peril and a great hail of bullets, with his comrades falling all round him. And when even the commander was killed the rest wanted to take to their heels, but the young man stepped forward and rallied them, crying: 'We must not let our father-land perish.' At this the others followed him, and he pressed forward and defeated the enemy. When the king heard that he owed the victory to him alone, he raised him above all the others, gave him great wealth and made him the first man in his kingdom.

The king had a daughter who was very beautiful, but there was also something very strange about her. She had made a vow to take no man for her lord and husband unless he promised to let himself be buried alive with her if she died before him. 'If he truly loves me,' she said, 'why would he want to go on living?' In return she was prepared to do the same for him and go down into the grave with him if he died first. This strange vow had hitherto deterred all suitors, but the young man was so entranced by her beauty that he was heedless of everything, and asked her father for her hand. 'But do you know what promise you will have to make?' said the king. 'I shall have to go to her grave with her if I outlive her,' he replied, 'but my love is so great that I care not for this danger.' Then the king consented and the marriage was celebrated with great magnificence.

They now lived happily and contentedly for a time, and then it happened that the young queen fell seriously ill and no doctor could help her. And when she lay there dead, the young king remembered what he had had to promise, and he was filled with horror at the thought of being buried alive, but there was no help for it: the king had ordered all the gates to be watched, and there was no way of escaping his fate. When the day came for the queen's dead body to be laid to rest in the royal vault, he was taken down into it with her, and then the door was locked and bolted.

Beside the coffin stood a table on which there were four candles, four loaves of bread and four bottles of wine. As soon as these provisions gave out he would have to die of hunger. So there he sat full of grief and sorrow, eating only a morsel of bread each day and drinking only a mouthful of wine, and yet he realized that his death was coming closer and closer. Now as he sat there staring in front of him, he saw a snake crawl out of one corner of the vault and approach the coffin. Thinking it was going to gnaw at the dead body, he drew his sword and exclaimed: 'You shan't touch her so long as I am alive!' And he hacked the snake into three pieces. A few moments later a second snake came crawling out of the corner, but when it saw the other one lying dead and dismembered it turned back, and presently approached again carrying three green leaves in its mouth. Then it took the three pieces of the snake, put them together the way they belonged, and laid one of the leaves on each of the wounds. At once the dismembered parts joined, the snake stirred and came to life again, and both snakes crawled quickly away leaving the leaves behind them. The unfortunate prince had watched all this, and he now began to wonder whether the miraculous power of the leaves which had restored the snake to life might also help a human being. So he picked up the leaves and laid one of them on the dead woman's mouth and the other two on her eyes. And scarcely had he done so when her blood stirred in her veins, rose into her pallid countenance and gave it the flush of life again. She drew breath, opened her eyes and said: 'Alas, where am I?' 'You are with me, my dear wife,' he answered and told her all that had happened and how he had revived her. Then he gave her some wine and bread and when she had recovered her strength she stood up, and they went to the door and knocked on it and shouted so loudly that the guards heard them and reported it to the king. The king himself came down and opened the door; he found both of them in full health and vigour, and rejoiced with them that now all their troubles were over. But the young king took the three snake-leaves with him, gave them to a servant and said: 'Keep them carefully for me, and carry them on you wherever you go; who knows what trouble they may yet help us out of.'

But since being brought back to life his wife had undergone a change: it was as if all her love for her husband had been drained out of her heart. Some time later he decided to make a voyage across the sea to visit his old father, and after they had boarded the ship she forgot the great love and loyalty he had shown her and how he had saved her from death, and conceived a guilty passion for the ship's captain. One day when the young king was lying there asleep, she called the captain and seized her sleeping husband by the head and made the captain take him by the feet, and thus they threw him into the sea. When this shameful deed had been done she said to the captain: 'Now let's go home, and we'll say he died at sea. You can leave it to me to keep singing your praises to my father till he marries me to you and makes you heir to his crown.' But the faithful servant, who had witnessed the whole thing, secretly lowered a small boat from the ship and set out in it, following his master and letting the traitors sail away. He fished up the drowned man, and by putting the three snake-leaves, which he had with him, on the young king's eyes and mouth, he successfully restored him to life.

Then they both rowed day and night with might and main, and their boat sped along so quickly that they got home to the old king before the others. He was astonished to see them arriving alone, and asked what had happened to them. When he heard of his daughter's wickedness he said: 'I can't believe that she did so evil a thing, but the truth will soon come to light.' He told them both to go into a secret room and let no one know of their presence. Soon after this the big ship came sailing in, and the prince's godless wife appeared before her father with a sorrowful air. He said: 'Why have you returned alone? Where is your husband?' 'Oh, dear father,' she replied, 'I have come home in great grief: during the voyage my husband suddenly fell sick and died, and if the kind ship's captain had not helped me it would have gone ill with me. But he was present at my husband's death and can tell you all that happened.' The king said: 'I will bring this dead man back to life,' and he opened the door of the room and told the two men to come out. When the woman saw her husband she stood as if thunderstruck, then fell to her knees and begged for mercy. The king said: 'There can be no mercy for you: he was ready to die with you, and he gave you your life back again, but you murdered him in his sleep and you shall have your just reward.' Then she and her accomplice were put on board a ship full of holes and sent out to sea, where they soon perished in the waves.

29

FAITHFUL JOHN

Once upon a time there was an old king who was ill and thought to himself: I am probably lying on my deathbed. So he said: 'Send Faithful John to me.' Faithful John was his favourite servant, who had been loyal to him all his life, which was how he had got his name. When he came to the bedside the king said to him: 'My dear Faithful John, I feel that my end is near, and the only thing that troubles me is the thought of my son. He is still young and not always able to make wise decisions, and unless you promise me to teach him all he needs to know and be a foster-father to him, I shall not be able to close my eyes in peace.' And Faithful John answered: 'I will not forsake him and will serve him faithfully, even if it should cost my life.' Then the old king said: 'Now I can die with my mind at rest.' And then he went on: 'After my death you must show him the whole palace, all the rooms large and small, and the vaults and the treasures that are in them: but you must not show him the last room on the long corridor, the room where the portrait of the Princess of the Golden Roof is hidden. If he sees that portrait, he will fall violently in love with her and collapse in a faint, and for her sake will expose himself to great dangers; from this you must protect him.' And when Faithful John had again given his word that he would do so, the king fell silent and laid his head on his pillow and died.

After the old king had been laid in his grave, Faithful John told the young king what he had promised his father on his deathbed, and said: 'This promise I will most surely keep, and will be faithful to you as I have been to him, even if it should cost me my life.' The period of mourning passed, and Faithful John said to him: 'It is time now for you to see your inheritance; I will show you the palace of your fathers.' So he took him all over it, upstairs and downstairs and everywhere, and let him see all the treasures and magnificent rooms; there was only one room he didn't open, the room where the dangerous portrait was. The portrait was placed in such a way that when the door opened it was the first thing one saw, and it was so splendidly painted that you would have thought it lived and breathed and was the most beautiful and lovely thing in the whole world. But the young king did not fail to notice that Faithful John always passed one door by, and he said: 'Why do you never unlock this one?' 'There is something in there that would frighten you,' he answered. But the king replied: 'I've seen the whole palace, so now I want to know what's in that room,' and he went and tried to open the door by force. Faithful John held him back, saying: 'I promised your father before his death not to let you see what is in that room: it could bring great misfortune to both of us.' 'Ah, no,' answered the young king, 'if I can't get into that room it will certainly be the end of me: I should have no peace day and night till I have seen it with my own eyes. And now I shall not budge from here till you have unlocked the door.'

Then Faithful John realized that now there was no help for it, and with a heavy heart and a deep sigh he took his great bunch of keys and sought out the one that opened the door. When he had opened it, he entered the room first and tried to block the king's view of the portrait: but what was the use! The king stood on tiptoe and looked over his shoulder; and at the sight of the maiden's portrait, so magnificent and glittering with gold and precious stones, he fell down in a dead faint. Faithful John lifted him from the ground and carried him to his bed, thinking very apprehensively: The misfortune has happened, dear heavens, what will come of this! Then he gave the young king wine to strengthen him, and the first words he spoke when he came to himself were: 'Alas! whose is that beautiful portrait?' 'It is the Princess of the Golden Roof,' answered Faithful John. Then the king said: 'My love for her is so great that if all the leaves on the trees were tongues they could not declare it; I will risk my life to win her. You are my dearest Faithful John, and you must help me.'

The faithful servant pondered for a long time how to set about this business; for it was difficult even to gain admission to the presence of the princess. At last he thought of a way and said to the king: 'Everything she has around her is of gold: the tables, the chairs, the dishes, the cups, the bowls and every other article. In your treasury there are five barrelfuls of gold: give orders for one of them to be fashioned by the goldsmiths of your kingdom into all sorts of vessels and household things, and into birds and game and wonderful animals of all kinds. That will please her, and we shall take them and travel to her country and try our luck.' The king sent for all the goldsmiths, and they had to work day and night until finally all the marvellous things were ready. When they had all been loaded on board a ship, Faithful John disguised himself as a merchant, and the king had to do the same, so that he would be quite unrecognizable. Then they sailed over the sea and sailed on and on until they came to the city where the Princess of the Golden Roof lived.

Faithful John told the king to stay on the ship and wait for him. 'Perhaps I shall bring the princess back with me,' he said, 'so see that everything is made ready, have the golden vessels put on view and the whole ship decorated with them.' Then he collected a number of the golden things and put them in his apron, and he went ashore and walked straight to the royal palace. When he entered the courtyard there was a beautiful girl standing by the well, holding two golden pails and drawing water with them. And when she turned round to carry off the clear shining water, she saw the stranger and asked who he was. He answered: 'I am a merchant,' and opened his apron and let her look in. Then she exclaimed: 'Oh, what lovely golden things!' And she put down the pails and gazed at one article after another. Then she said: 'The princess must see these; she loves golden things so much that she will buy it all from you.' She took him by the hand and led him upstairs, for she was the princess's maid-in-waiting. When the princess saw the merchandise she was delighted, and said: 'These are so beautifully made that I will buy the lot from you.' But Faithful John said: 'I am only the servant of a rich merchant: what I have here with me is nothing by comparison with what my master has on his ship, for there he has the most exquisite and precious things that have ever been made in gold.' She wanted it all brought up to the palace, but he said: 'Madam, that would take many days, there is so much to bring, and it needs so many rooms to exhibit it that there is not space enough for it in your house.' At this her curiosity and desire grew even stronger, so that in the end she said: 'Take me to the ship, I will go there myself and look at your master's treasures.'

Then Faithful John took her to the ship, delighted at his success, and when the king caught sight of her he saw that her beauty was even greater than it had appeared in the portrait; and he felt that his heart was going to burst. Then she came aboard, and the king took her below; but Faithful John stayed behind with the steersman and gave orders for the ship to put to sea. 'Hoist full sail,' he said, 'and let the ship speed like a bird on the wing.' Meanwhile the king was below with the princess, showing her the golden vessels one by one, the dishes and cups and bowls, and the birds and the game and the strange animals. Many hours passed as she examined everything, and in her excitement she didn't notice that the ship was moving. After she had looked at the last of the things, she thanked the merchant and wanted to return to her palace: but when she came on deck she saw that the ship was on the high seas, far away from land and speeding along under full sail. 'Alas!' she exclaimed in terror, 'I have been deceived, I have been abducted and fallen into the power of a merchant; I would rather die!' But the king took her by the hand and said: 'I am no merchant, I am a king and no less nobly born than yourself; but I abducted you by this trick because of the excess of my love for you. The first time I saw your portrait I fell to the ground in a faint.' When the Princess of the Golden Roof heard this she was consoled, and her heart was drawn to him, so that she gladly consented to be his wife.

But it happened, as they were sailing along over the high seas, that Faithful John, as he sat in the bows playing on a pipe, noticed three ravens flying through the air towards him. At this he stopped playing and listened to what they were saying to each other, for he well understood bird-speech. One of them cried: 'Why, he is going to marry the Princess of the Golden

Roof.' 'Well,' answered the second, 'he hasn't got her yet.' The
third said: 'Yes he has, she's sitting beside him in the ship.'
Then the first began again and cried: 'Much good that'll do him!
When they land, a chestnut horse will come galloping up to
him; he'll want to mount it, and if he does so it'll gallop away
with him into the sky, and he'll never see his bride again.' The
second said: 'Is there no way of saving him?' 'Oh yes, if another
man mounts the horse at once, seizes the gun it will be carrying
in its harness and shoots it dead, then the young king will be
saved. But which of them knows that! And anyone who knows
it and tells him will be turned to stone from his toes to his
knees.' Then the second said: 'I know another thing: even if the
horse is killed the young king will still lose his bride. When they
enter the palace together, the bridal tunic will be lying there
ready for him in a shallow vessel, looking as if it were woven out
of silver and gold: but it's only pitch and sulphur, and if any
man wears it it'll burn him to the bare bones.' The third said: 'Is
there no way of saving him from that?' 'Oh yes,' answered the
second. 'If someone wearing gloves seizes the tunic and throws
it into the fire and burns it, then the young king will be saved.
But what's the use! Anyone who knows that and tells him will
be half turned to stone, from his knees to his heart.' Then the
third said: 'I know another thing: even if the bridal tunic is
burnt, the young king will still not have his bride. For when the
dance begins after the wedding feast and the young queen is
dancing, she will suddenly turn pale and fall down as if she were
dead; and unless someone raises her up and sucks three drops
of blood from her right breast and spits them out again, she will
die. But if any man knows that secret and reveals it, his whole
body will turn to stone from his toes to the top of his head.'
When the ravens had said all this to each other they flew on,
and Faithful John had understood everything clearly; but after
this he was sad and silent, for unless he told his master what he
had heard, his master would suffer great misfortune; and if he
did tell him, he must forfeit his own life. But finally he said to
himself: 'I will save my master, even if I myself must perish in
doing so.'

When they landed, everything happened as the ravens had

predicted. A splendid chestnut horse came galloping up, and the king said: 'Good, he shall carry me to my palace.' And he was just about to mount when Faithful John anticipated him, leapt quickly into the saddle, pulled the gun out of the harness and shot the animal dead. At this the king's other servants, who in fact envied Faithful John, exclaimed: 'How shameful to kill that beautiful animal when the king was going to ride it to his palace!' But the king said: 'Be silent and let him be, he is my dearest Faithful John; who knows what good reason he may have had?' So they went to the palace, and there in the hall stood a vessel, and in it the bridal tunic lay ready, looking just as if it were woven of silver and gold. The young king approached it and was about to pick it up, but Faithful John pushed him aside, seized it with his gloved hands, quickly carried it to the fire and burnt it. The other servants again began to murmur and said: 'Look, now he's even burning the king's bridal tunic.' But the young king said: 'Who knows what good reason he may have for this? Let him be, he is my dearest Faithful John.' Now the wedding was celebrated; the dance began and the bride took part, and Faithful John watched her face carefully; suddenly she turned pale and fell to the floor as if dead. Then he rushed up to her, lifted her in his arms and carried her to a bedchamber where he laid her on the bed, knelt down and sucked three drops of blood from her right breast and spat them out. Instantly she breathed again and recovered; but the young king had seen what Faithful John had done and didn't know why he had done it, so he was angry and cried out: 'Throw him into prison!' Next morning Faithful John was condemned to death and led out to the gallows, and as he stood up there on the scaffold and the sentence was about to be carried out, he said: 'Every condemned man is allowed to speak once more before he dies; shall I too have that right?' 'Yes,' replied the king, 'it shall be granted to you.' Then Faithful John said: 'I am unjustly condemned and have always been loyal to you,' and he told how he had heard the ravens talking when they were at sea, and how he had had to do all these things in order to save his master. Then the king cried: 'Oh my dear Faithful John! Mercy and pardon! Bring him down.' But Faithful John, as he uttered his last word, had collapsed lifeless and lay there turned to stone.

At this the king and the queen were grief-stricken, and the king said: 'Alas, how ill I have rewarded such great loyalty!' And he had the stone image raised up and placed in his bed-chamber beside his bed. Every time he looked at it he wept, saying: 'Alas, if only I could bring you back to life, my dearest Faithful John!' Some time passed, and the queen gave birth to twins, two little sons, and they grew and gave her great joy. One day when the queen was in church and the two children were sitting by their father playing, he again very sorrowfully looked at the stone image and sighed and exclaimed: 'Alas, if only I could bring you back to life, my dearest Faithful John!' Then the stone began to speak and said: 'Yes, you can bring me back to life, if you will sacrifice what you love most.' The king exclaimed: 'I will give everything for you, everything I have in the world.' The stone then said: 'If with your own hand you strike both your children's heads off and smear me with their blood, my life will be given back to me.' The king was appalled to hear that he himself would have to kill his beloved children; but he remembered the great loyalty of Faithful John and how he had died for him, so he drew his sword and with his own hand struck off the children's heads. And when he had smeared the stone with their blood, life came back to it, and Faithful John stood before him again alive and well. He said to the king: 'Your loyalty shall not go unrewarded.' And he took the children's heads, put them back on their necks and smeared the wound with their blood: this healed them instantly, and they went on jumping around and playing as if nothing had happened to them. Now the king was overjoyed, and when he saw the queen coming he hid Faithful John and the two children in a big cupboard. When she entered he said to her: 'Did you say your prayers in the church?' 'Yes,' she answered, 'but I kept on thinking of Faithful John and the great misfortune he suffered because of us.' Then he said: 'My dear wife, we can give his life back to him, but it will cost us our two little sons: we shall have to sacrifice them.' The queen turned pale and her heart was stricken, but she said: 'We owe it to him for his great loyalty.' Then he was glad that she felt the same way as he had done. He went and opened the cupboard, fetched out the children and Faithful John and said: 'God be praised, he is saved; and we have our little sons again as well.' And he told her all that had happened. After that they lived happily together till the end of their lives.

30

ONE-EYE, TWO-EYES AND
THREE-EYES

There was once a woman who had three daughters, of whom the eldest was called 'One-Eye' because she had only a single eye in the middle of her forehead, and the second 'Two-Eyes', because she had two eyes like other people, and the youngest 'Three-Eyes', because she had three eyes, with one of them also in the middle of her forehead. But because Two-Eyes didn't look different from other folk, her sisters and her mother hated her. They said to her: 'You with your two eyes are no better than the common people, you aren't one of us.' They pushed her about and threw her dirty rags to wear, and gave her nothing to eat but their leavings, and tormented her in every way they could think of.

It happened that Two-Eyes had to go out into the field and mind the goat, but was still very hungry because her sisters had given her so little to eat. And she sat down at the edge of a field and began to cry, and cried so hard that the tears ran from her eyes like two little streams. And looking up as she wept, she suddenly saw a woman standing beside her who asked: 'Two-Eyes, why are you crying?' Two-Eyes answered: 'How can I help crying! Because I have two eyes like other people, my sisters and my mother hate me, they drive me from corner to corner, throw me old clothes to wear and give me nothing to eat but their leavings. Today they've given me so little that I'm still ever so hungry.' The wise-woman said: 'Two-Eyes, dry your tears and listen to what I tell you, and you need never be hungry again. Just say to your goat:

> "Little goat, bleat,
> Lay me a table
> With lots to eat,"

and a neatly laid little table will appear in front of you with a delicious meal on it, for you to eat as much as you like. And when you've had enough and don't need the table any longer, just say:

> "Little goat, bleat,
> Take the table away
> I've had all I can eat,"

and it will disappear again.' When she had said this the wise-woman left her. But Two-Eyes thought: I must try it at once, to see if what she told me is true, because I'm as hungry as anything. And she said:

> 'Little goat, bleat,
> Lay me a table
> With lots to eat,'

and no sooner had she uttered the words than a little table stood before her, covered with a white cloth. On it was a plate, knife and fork and a silver spoon, surrounded by the most delicious food, all steaming hot as if it had just been brought from the kitchen. Then Two-Eyes said the shortest prayer she knew: 'Lord God, always be our guest, Amen,' and set to and ate to her heart's content. And when she had done she said, as the wise-woman had taught her:

> 'Little goat, bleat,
> Take the table away
> I've had all I can eat.'

At once the table vanished with everything that was on it. This is a good way to keep house, thought Two-Eyes, and she felt ever so happy.

In the evening, when she got home with her goat, she found a little earthenware dish with some food which her sisters had left for her, but she didn't touch any of it. Next day she went out with her goat again and left the few scraps that were handed to her. Her sisters paid no attention to this the first time or two, but when it happened every day they began to notice it and said to each other: 'There's something funny going on; Two-Eyes keeps leaving her food untouched, and before she always used to swallow everything that was given to her – she must be

getting it some other way.' But to get at the truth they agreed
that next time Two-Eyes took the goat out to graze, One-
Eye should go with her and watch what she was up to and
whether anyone was bringing her anything to eat or drink.

So when Two-Eyes was setting out again, One-Eye went up
to her and said: 'I'd like to come with you and see whether you
are really looking after the goat and grazing it properly.' But
Two-Eyes guessed One-Eye's purpose, and she drove the goat
out into the thick grass and said: 'Come, One-Eye, let's sit
down, and I'll recite something to you.' One-Eye sat down; she
wasn't used to walking and the sun was hot, so she felt tired,
and Two-Eyes sang over and over again:

> 'One-Eye, are you awake?
> One-Eye, are you asleep?'

And One-Eye closed her one eye and fell asleep. And when
Two-Eyes saw that One-Eye was fast asleep and couldn't tell on
her, she said:

> 'Little goat, bleat,
> Lay me a table
> With lots to eat,'

and sat down at her table and ate and drank her fill; then she
called out again:

> 'Little goat, bleat,
> Take the table away
> I've had all I can eat,'

and in a trice everything had vanished. Then Two-Eyes
wakened One-Eye and said: 'One-Eye, you try to watch the
goat and you fall asleep! It could have run a long way away.
Come, let's go home.' So they went home, and again Two-Eyes
didn't touch her dish, and One-Eye couldn't tell their mother
why she was not eating; she excused herself by saying: 'I fell
asleep out there.'

Next day their mother said to Three-Eyes: 'This time you
must go out with Two-Eyes and watch whether she eats anything there and whether anyone brings her food and drink,

because she must be secretly eating and drinking.' So Three-Eyes went up to Two-Eyes and said: 'I'd like to come with you and make sure the goat is being looked after and grazed properly.' But Two-Eyes guessed Three-Eyes's purpose, and drove the goat out into the thick grass and said: 'Let's sit down, Three-Eyes, I'll sing something to you.' Three-Eyes sat down, and the walk and the heat of the sun had made her tired, and Two-Eyes began her little song again as before:

> 'Three-Eyes, are you awake?'

But then, instead of singing as she should have done:

> 'Three-Eyes, are you asleep?'

she was careless and sang:

> 'Two-Eyes, are you asleep?'

and she kept on singing:

> 'Three-Eyes, are you awake?
> Two-Eyes, are you asleep?'

So two of her sister's eyes closed and slept, but the spell was not being sung to the third of them, so it stayed awake. Three-Eyes shut it of course, but this was only a trick; she pretended it was asleep, but it was peeping between its lids and could see quite well what was going on. And when Two-Eyes thought Three-Eyes was fast asleep, she said her spell:

> 'Little goat, bleat,
> Lay me a table
> With lots to eat,'

and ate and drank to her heart's content and then dismissed the table again:

> 'Little goat, bleat,
> Take the table away
> I've had all I can eat.'

And Three-Eyes had seen everything. Two-Eyes came up to her, wakened her and said: 'Why, Three-Eyes, have you been asleep? You're good at watching goats! Come, let's go home.'

And when they got home Two-Eyes again ate nothing, and Three-Eyes said to their mother: 'I've found out now why that proud slut doesn't eat. Out there, when she says to the goat:

> "Little goat, bleat,
> Lay me a table
> With lots to eat,"

a table appears before her with all sorts of fine food on it, much better than what we have here; and when she's eaten her fill she says:

> "Little goat, bleat,
> Take the table away
> I've had all I can eat,"

and everything vanishes again; I watched the whole thing from beginning to end. She had put two of my eyes to sleep with a spell, but luckily the one on my forehead had stayed awake.' Then their envious mother exclaimed: 'So you want to live better than we do, do you? I'll put an end to that!' She seized a butcher's knife, stabbed the goat to the heart and it fell down dead.

When Two-Eyes saw this she was grief-stricken, went out and sat down at the edge of her field and wept bitter tears. Suddenly the wise-woman was standing beside her again, and said: 'Two-Eyes, why are you crying?' 'How can I help crying!' she answered. 'My mother has slaughtered the goat that brought me that lovely table every day when I said your little spell to it; and now I shall have to be hungry and miserable again.' The wise-woman said: 'Two-Eyes, I'll give you a piece of good advice: ask your sisters to give you the innards of the dead goat and bury them just outside the front door, and it'll bring you luck.' So saying she vanished, and Two-Eyes went home and said to her sisters: 'Dear sisters, won't you give me some little bit of my goat? It doesn't need to be a good part, just let me have the innards.' Then they laughed and said: 'You can have those if that's all you want.' And Two-Eyes took the innards and buried them quietly that evening outside the front door as the wise-woman had advised her.

Next morning, when they all woke up and went outside the house, there was a wonderful magnificent tree growing there with silver leaves, and golden fruit hanging among them; there had surely never been anything more beautiful or precious seen in the whole wide world. But they had no idea how the tree had got there in the night; only Two-Eyes noticed that it had grown up out of the goat's entrails, for it stood on the exact spot where she had buried them. Then their mother said to One-Eye: 'Climb up the tree, my dear, and pick some of that fruit for us.' One-Eye climbed up, but when she tried to seize one of the golden apples, the branch jumped back out of her grasp; and this happened every time, so that she couldn't pick a single apple, try as she would. So their mother said: 'Three-Eyes, you climb up; you with your three eyes can look about you better than your sister.' One-Eye slid down and Three-Eyes climbed up. But Three-Eyes was no better at it, she could look about her as much as she liked, the golden apples still slipped out of her grasp. Finally their mother got impatient and climbed the tree herself, but she had no more success in reaching the fruit than One-Eye and Three-Eyes; she just snatched at the empty air. Then Two-Eyes said: 'I'll climb up, perhaps I'll be able to pick it.' And although her sisters exclaimed: 'You with your two eyes, what good'll you be!' she climbed the tree, and the golden apples didn't draw back from her but dropped into her hand of their own accord, so that she was able to pick one after another and brought down a whole apronful. Her mother took them from her; and as for One-Eye and Three-Eyes, so far from treating poor Two-Eyes better, as a result they just envied her for being the only one who could pick the fruit, and they behaved even more harshly to her than before.

One day, when they were all standing by the tree together, it happened that a young knight rode up. 'Quick, Two-Eyes,' cried the two sisters, 'crawl under this, you'll disgrace us if you're seen,' and they hastily took an empty barrel that happened to be standing by the tree and turned it upside down over poor Two-Eyes, pushing the golden apples she had picked under it as well. Now when the knight approached, and a handsome gentleman he was, he stopped and admired the magnificent gold and silver tree and said to the two sisters: 'Whose is this beautiful tree? Anyone who gave me one of its branches could ask any price for it.' And One-Eye and Three-Eyes said that the tree was theirs, and that they would break off a branch of it for him if he liked. And they both made great efforts to do so but they both failed, for the branches and the fruit evaded their grasp every time. Then the knight said: 'That's a strange thing, that the tree belongs to you and yet you're not able to pick anything from it.' They insisted that the tree was their property. But as they were talking, Two-Eyes rolled a couple of golden apples out from under the barrel towards the knight's feet, because she was angry with One-Eye and Three-Eyes for not telling the truth. When the knight saw the apples he was astonished, and asked where they had come from. One-Eye and Three-Eyes answered that they had another sister, but that she was not fit to be seen because she had only two eyes like other common people. But the knight demanded to see her and called out: 'Two-Eyes, come out.' So Two-Eyes came boldly out from under the barrel, and the knight was amazed by her great beauty and said: 'I'm sure you, Two-Eyes, can break a branch off the tree for me.' 'Yes,' answered Two-Eyes, 'I think I can, because it's my tree.' And she climbed up and very easily broke off a branch with lovely silver leaves and golden fruit and handed it to the knight. Then he said: 'What shall I give you for this, Two-Eyes?' 'Oh,' answered Two-Eyes, 'I'm hungry and thirsty and miserable from early every morning until late at night – if you could take me with you and save me from this place, I'd be happy.' Then the knight seated Two-Eyes on his horse and rode home with her to his father's castle. There he gave her beautiful clothes, and food and drink to her heart's content, and because he loved her so much he had himself betrothed to her with God's blessing, and the wedding was celebrated with great joy.

Now, when Two-Eyes was carried off like this by the handsome knight, her two sisters envied her good fortune all the more bitterly. But we shall still have the magic tree, they thought, and even if we can't pick its fruit someone will be bound to stop and buy it on his way past, and visit us and say what a fine tree it is; who knows what luck may yet be ours! Next morning, however, the tree had disappeared and their hope was dashed. And when Two-Eyes looked out of her bedroom window she was overjoyed to see the tree growing just outside; so it had followed her.

Two-Eyes lived for many happy years. One day two poor women visited her at the castle and begged for alms. And when Two-Eyes looked at their faces she recognized her sisters One-Eye and Three-Eyes, who had become so poor that they had to wander round begging for their bread from door to door. But Two-Eyes bade them welcome and was kind to them and looked after them, so that they both repented from their hearts of having been so cruel to their sister when they were young.

31

ASHIEPATTLE

There was a rich man, and his wife fell ill, and when she felt that her end was near she called her little only daughter to her bedside and said: 'My dear child, always say your prayers and be good, as you are now, and God will always stand by you, and I shall look down at you from heaven and protect you.' So saying, she closed her eyes and died. The little girl would go out every day to weep at her mother's grave, and she went on saying her prayers and being good. When winter came, the snow put a white coverlet on the grave, and when the sun had taken it off again in spring, her father remarried.

His new wife had brought two daughters into the household with her, who had beautiful lily-white faces but ugly black hearts. This was the beginning of a bad time for the poor stepdaughter. 'Is this stupid goose to sit with us in the parlour?' they said. 'Those who want to eat bread must earn it. Away with you to the kitchen, kitchen maid!' They took away her pretty dresses, put her into an old grey smock and gave her wooden shoes. 'Just look at the proud princess, how smart she looks!' they exclaimed; and they laughed at her and put her into the kitchen. So she had to do the rough work from morning till night, get up early before daybreak, fetch water, make the fire and do the cooking and washing. In addition her sisters tormented her and poured peas and lentils into the ashes, forcing her to sit there and pick them out again. At night when she had worked herself weary, she got no bed to sleep in but had to lie down in the ashes by the hearth. And because this made her always so dusty and dirty they called her 'Ashiepattle'.

It happened one day that their father was about to go to the fair; so he asked his two stepdaughters what they would like him to bring back for them. 'Fine dresses,' said one. 'Pearls and precious stones,' said the second. 'But what about you,

Ashiepattle,' he said, 'what would you like to have?' 'Father, break off the first twig that brushes against your hat on the way home and bring it to me.' So he bought fine dresses and pearls and precious stones for the two stepsisters, and on his way back, as he was riding through a wood, a hazel twig brushed against him and knocked his hat off. So he broke off the twig and took it with him. When he got home he gave his stepdaughters what they had asked for, and to Ashiepattle he gave the twig from the hazel bush. Ashiepattle thanked him, went out to her mother's grave and planted the twig on it, and cried so much that her tears watered it as they fell. But it grew into a beautiful tree. Every day Ashiepattle went three times and stood under it and cried and said her prayers, and every time a little white bird came and perched on the tree, and when she uttered a wish the bird would drop whatever she had wished for at her feet.

Now it came about that the king decided to give a feast which would last for three days and to which all the good-looking young ladies in the country were invited, because he wanted his son to choose a bride. When the two stepsisters heard that they were to be there too, they were mightily pleased and called Ashiepattle and said: 'Comb our hair, brush our shoes and fasten our buckles; we're going to the wedding feast at the royal palace.' Ashiepattle obeyed, but she cried because she would very much have liked to have gone to the dance as well, and she begged her stepmother to allow her to go. 'You kitchen slut,' exclaimed her stepmother, 'you want to go to the wedding, all dusty and grimy as you are? You haven't any dresses or shoes and want to go dancing?' But when her stepdaughter begged and begged she finally said: 'Look, I've poured this bowlful of lentils into the ashes: if you can sort out the lentils again in two hours, you shall come with us.' The girl went out into the garden by the back door and called: 'Oh, you gentle doves, you turtle doves, all you birds of the sky, come and help me do my sorting –

>   Into the pot if they're good to eat,
>   And swallow the bad ones, nice and neat.'

Then two white doves flew in at the kitchen window, and after them the turtle doves, and finally all the birds of the sky came swirling and swarming in and settled on the floor round the ashes. And the doves nodded their little heads and began, peck peck peck peck, and then the others began too, peck peck peck peck, and sorted all the good grains into the bowl. In scarcely an hour they had finished and out they all flew again. Then the girl took the bowl to her stepmother, overjoyed at the thought that she would be allowed to go to the wedding feast now. But her stepmother said: 'No, Ashiepattle, you've got no clothes and can't dance, they'll only laugh at you.' Then when Ashiepattle burst into tears she said: 'If you can sort two bowlfuls of lentils for me out of the ashes in one hour, you shall come with us.' She'll never do it, of course, thought the stepmother to herself, and shook out two bowlfuls of lentils into the ashes. The girl went out into the garden by the back door and called: 'Oh, you gentle doves, you turtle doves, all you birds of the sky, come and help me do my sorting –

> Into the pot if they're good to eat,
> And swallow the bad ones, nice and neat.'

Then two white doves flew in at the kitchen window, and after them the turtle doves, and finally all the birds of the sky came swirling and swarming in and settled on the floor round the ashes. And the doves nodded their little heads and began, peck peck peck peck, and then the others began too, peck peck peck peck, and sorted all the good grains into the bowls. And before even half an hour had passed they had already finished, and out they all flew again. Then the girl took the bowls to her stepmother, overjoyed at the thought that she would be allowed to go to the wedding feast now. But her stepmother said: 'It's no good, you can't come because you've no clothes and can't dance, and we should be ashamed of you.' And so saying, she turned her back on her and hurried off with her two proud daughters.

So when everybody had left the house, Ashiepattle went to her mother's grave under the hazel tree and called out:

'Shake your branches and leaves, my little tree,
Drop gold and silver down on me.'

And the bird threw down for her a golden and silver dress and a
pair of slippers embroidered in silk and silver. As fast as she
could she put on the dress and went to the feast. But her sisters
and her stepmother didn't recognize her and thought she must
be a princess from a foreign land, she looked so beautiful in
the golden dress. They never dreamt it could be Ashiepattle,
they thought she was sitting at home in the dirt picking lentils
out of the ashes. The prince came to meet her, took her by
the hand and danced with her. And he would dance with
no one else, and never let go of her hand, and if another man
approached to ask her for a dance he would say: 'She is my
partner.'

She danced till it was evening, and then she wanted to go
home. But the prince said: 'I'll come with you, I'll accompany
you.' For he wanted to see whose daughter this beautiful
girl was. But she gave him the slip and jumped up into the
dovecot. So the prince waited until her father came, and told
him that the unknown girl had jumped up into the dovecot. The
old man thought; Could this possibly be Ashiepattle? And he
sent for an axe and a pick to break into the dovecot – but there
was no one there. And when they went indoors Ashiepattle
was lying among the ashes in her dirty clothes, and a dim little
oil lamp was burning at the fireplace, for Ashiepattle had jumped
down from the far side of the dovecot and run to the little hazel
tree; there she had taken off her beautiful clothes and laid them
on the grave, and the bird had taken them away again. Then she
had sat down in the kitchen among the ashes in her old grey
smock.

Next day, when the festivities began again and her parents
and stepsisters had left, Ashiepattle went to the hazel tree and
said:

'Shake your branches and leaves, my little tree,
Drop gold and silver down on me.'

And the bird threw down a still more magnificent dress than on

the day before. And when she arrived at the feast wearing this
dress, everyone wondered at her beauty. But the prince had
waited till she came, and at once he took her by the hand and
danced only with her and no one else. If other men approached
and asked her for a dance, he would say: 'She is my partner.'
Then when evening came she wanted to leave, and the prince
followed her and tried to see what house she would go to, but
she eluded him and ran into the garden behind the house,
where there was a beautiful big tree with fine pears growing on
it. She climbed up among its branches as nimbly as a squirrel
and the prince had no idea where she had gone. But he waited
till her father came and said to him: 'That strange girl has given
me the slip; I think she jumped up into the pear tree.' Her father
thought: Could it possibly be Ashiepattle? And he sent for the
axe and chopped the tree down, but there was no one in it. And
when they went into the kitchen, Ashiepattle was lying there in
the ashes as usual, for she had jumped down from the tree on
the far side, given back her beautiful clothes to the bird that
perched on the hazel, and put on her old grey smock again.

On the third day, when her parents and sisters had left,
Ashiepattle went again to her mother's grave and said to the
little tree:

> 'Shake your branches and leaves, my little tree,
> Drop gold and silver down on me.'

And now the bird threw down a dress that was so splendid and
shining that she had never had one like it in her life, and the
slippers were golden all over. When she appeared at the wedding feast in that dress, everyone was speechless with wonder.
The prince danced with her and with no one else, and if anyone
asked her for a dance he said: 'She is my partner.'

Then when evening came Ashiepattle wanted to leave, and
the prince wanted to accompany her, but she leapt away from
him so quickly that he couldn't follow. But the prince had
thought of a trick: he had had the whole staircase smeared with
pitch, and as she sped down it the girl's left slipper had stuck
there. The prince picked it up, and it was small and dainty and
golden all over. Next morning he went with it to Ashiepattle's

father and said to him: 'I will marry no woman but the one
whose foot this golden shoe fits.' Then the two sisters were
delighted, for they had beautiful feet. The older one took the
shoe to her bedroom to try it on, and her mother stood beside
her. But she couldn't get her big toe into it, the shoe was too
small; so her mother handed her a knife and said: 'Chop off
your toe – when you're queen you won't need to do any more
walking.' The girl chopped her toe off, forced her foot into the
shoe, gritted her teeth against the pain and went back to the
prince. So he took her as his bride and set her on his horse and
rode off with her. But their way took them past the grave, and
there the two doves were perching on the hazel tree, and they
called out:

> 'Rookity-coo, rookity-coo!
> Her foot is bleeding in the shoe,
> Her foot's too long or her foot's too wide:
> He's left her behind, the rightful bride.'

Then he looked at her foot and saw the blood oozing out. He
turned his horse round, took the false bride back home, and
said she was not the right one and the other sister must try on
the shoe. So the second sister went to her bedroom and managed to get her toes into it, but her heel was too big. So her
mother handed her a knife and said: 'Chop a slice off your heel –
when you're queen you won't need to do any more walking.'
The girl chopped a slice off her heel, forced her foot into the
shoe, gritted her teeth against the pain and went back to the
prince. So he took her as his bride and set her on his horse and
rode off with her. As they passed the hazel tree, the two doves
were perching on it and they called out:

> 'Rookity-coo, rookity-coo!
> Her foot is bleeding in the shoe,
> Her foot's too long or her foot's too wide:
> He's left her behind, the rightful bride.'

He looked down at her foot and saw that the blood was oozing
out of her shoe and making a red stain all over her white
stocking. So he turned his horse round and took the false bride

back home. 'She's not the right one either,' he said. 'Have you
not got another daughter?' 'No,' said the man, 'the only other
person is a dirty little kitchen girl my former wife left with me –
she can't possibly be the bride.' The prince told him to send her
up, and the stepmother answered: 'Oh no, she's much too
dirty, she's not fit to be seen.' But he insisted, and Ashiepattle
had to be sent for. So first she washed her hands and face clean,
then went up and curtsied to the ground before the prince, who
handed her the golden shoe. Then she sat down on a stool,
drew her foot out of the heavy wooden clog and put on the
slipper, which fitted as if it had been made to measure. And
when she stood up and the prince looked into her face, he
recognized the beautiful girl who had danced with him, and
cried out: 'This is my rightful bride!' The stepmother and the
two sisters trembled and turned pale with rage; but he set
Ashiepattle on his horse and rode off with her. As they passed
the hazel tree, the two white doves called out:

> 'Rookity-coo, rookity-coo!
> Her foot's not bleeding, it fits the shoe,
> It's not too long and it's not too wide:
> He has found her now, the rightful bride.'

And when they had sung this they both came flying down and
settled on Ashiepattle's shoulders, one on the right and the
other on the left, and there they remained.

When her wedding with the prince was about to be celebrated, the two false sisters came and tried to ingratiate themselves and have a share in her good fortune. So when the bridal
pair were entering the church, the elder sister was on their right
and the younger to their left – and the two doves flew at each of
them and pecked out one of her eyes. Afterwards, as they were
coming out of the church, the elder one was on the left and the
younger on the right – and the doves flew at each of them and
pecked out her other eye. And thus, for their malice and deceit-
fulness, they were punished with blindness for the rest of their
days.

32

MANYPELTS

Once upon a time there was a king who had a wife with golden hair, and she was so beautiful that there was no one like her left in the world. It came about that she fell ill, and when she felt that she was going to die she called the king and said: 'If you want to marry again after I am dead, then marry no one who is not as beautiful as I am and who does not have golden hair like mine; you must promise me this.' And when the king had made her this promise, she closed her eyes and died.

The king was inconsolable for a long time, and had no wish to take a second wife. Finally his councillors said: 'This can't go on, the king must marry again so that we may have a queen.' So messengers were sent out in all directions to look for a bride for him who would be just as beautiful as the late queen. But in the whole world there was none to be found, and even if they had found one there was still none who had golden hair like the queen's. So the messengers came back empty-handed.

Now the king had a daughter who was just as beautiful as her late mother and had golden hair like her as well. When she had grown up, the king looked at her one day and saw that she resembled his late wife in every respect, and all at once he fell violently in love with her. So he said to his councillors: 'I intend to marry my daughter, for she is the living image of my late wife and I can find no other bride who so resembles her.' When his councillors heard this they were alarmed, and said: 'It is against God's law for a father to marry his daughter. Nothing good can come of sin, and the kingdom and all of us will fall into ruin.' The princess was even more alarmed when she heard of her father's decision, but she still hoped she might be able to make him change his mind. So she said to him: 'Sir, before I consent to your wish I must first have three dresses, one as golden as the sun, one as silver as the moon and one that shines as brightly as the stars; I also want a cloak made up of a thousand different kinds of animal furs and pelts, and every beast in your kingdom must give a piece of its hide towards it.' For she thought: It's quite impossible to have such a thing made, and so my father will give up his evil thoughts. But the king didn't give up, and the most highly skilled maidens in his kingdom were ordered to weave the three dresses, one as golden as the sun, one as silver as the moon and one that shone as brightly as the stars; and his huntsmen had to capture all the beasts in his whole kingdom and skin a piece of hide off each, and in this way the cloak of a thousand pelts was made. When everything was at last ready, the king had the cloak brought, spread it out before his daughter and said: 'Tomorrow shall be our wedding day.'

So when the princess saw that there was no more hope of getting her father to change his mind, she decided to run away. That night when everyone was asleep, she got up and took three pieces of her jewellery: a golden ring, a little golden spinning-wheel and a golden clasp. She took the three dresses that were like the sun and the moon and the stars and hid them in a nutshell, then put on the cloak of many pelts and blackened her face and hands with soot. Then she commended herself to God and left, and walked all night until she found herself in a great forest. And being tired she sat down in a hollow tree and went to sleep.

The sun rose, but she slept on and was still sleeping long after daybreak. Now it happened that the king to whom the forest belonged was hunting in it, and when his hounds came to the tree they started sniffing and running round it and barking. The king said to his huntsmen: 'Go and see what sort of animal's hiding in there.' The huntsmen did as he commanded, and when they came back they said: 'There's a strange animal lying in the hollow tree, we've never seen one like it before: its skin's covered with a thousand different kinds of fur, and it's lying there asleep.' The king said: 'See if you can catch it alive, then tie it to the cart and take it with you.' When the huntsmen seized the girl, she woke up in terror and cried out to them: 'I'm a poor child abandoned by my father and mother; have pity on me and take me with you.' And they said: 'Well, Manypelts, you'll do as a kitchen maid; come along with us and you can

sweep up the ashes.' So they put her in the cart and drove back
to the royal palace. There they took her to a little cubbyhole
under the stairs, a place that never got any daylight, and said:
'Here you are, furry beast, you can live and sleep here.' Then
she was sent to the kitchen, where she fetched wood and
carried water, made up the fire, plucked the poultry, picked the
vegetables, swept up the ashes and did all the dirty work.

So here Manypelts lived for a long time, and a hard time it
was for her. Alas, poor beautiful princess, what's to become of
you now! But one day there was to be a grand feast at the palace,
and she said to the cook: 'May I go up and watch for a little? I'll
stand just outside the door.' The cook answered: 'Yes, go along
with you, but mind you're back here in half an hour to do the
ashes.' So she got her oil lamp and went to her cubbyhole, took
off her furry cloak and washed the soot from her face and
hands, so that her full beauty was revealed again. Then she
opened the nut and took out her dress that shone like the sun.
And when she had done that she went upstairs to the feast, and
everyone made way for her, for no one recognized her and they
all thought she must be a princess. But the king came to meet
her, and took her by the hand and danced with her, thinking in
his heart: I've never yet seen such a beautiful girl. When the
dance was over she bowed low, and the king had no sooner
glanced about him than she had vanished, and no one knew
where she had gone. The sentries outside the palace were
summoned and questioned, but no one had seen her.

But she had run back to her cubbyhole and quickly taken off
her dress and blackened her face and hands and put on her
furry cloak and become Manypelts again. When she got to the
kitchen and was going to set about her work and sweep up the
ashes, the cook said: 'That can wait till tomorrow: you just cook
this soup for the king, I want to go upstairs too and have a bit of
a look; but mind you don't drop a hair into the soup, or you'll
get no more to eat from now on.' So off the cook went, and
Manypelts cooked the soup for the king. She cooked him the
best bread soup she knew how, and when it was done she
fetched her golden ring from the cubbyhole and put it in the
soup-tureen. When the dance was over the king sent for the

soup and ate it, and it was so good he thought he had never tasted a better soup in his life. But when he got to the bottom of the dish he saw a golden ring lying in it, and couldn't understand how it had got there. So he had the cook summoned. The cook took fright when he heard the order, and said to Manypelts: 'You've let a hair fall into that soup, I'll be bound; and if you have I'll beat you black and blue.' When he appeared before the king, the king asked him who had cooked the soup. The cook answered that he had cooked it himself, but the king replied: 'That's not true, because it was cooked a different way and much better than usual.' The cook answered: 'I must confess I didn't cook it, the furry-beast girl did.' The king said: 'Go and send her to me.'

When Manypelts appeared the king asked: 'Who are you?' 'I'm a poor child and I've no father or mother now.' Then he asked: 'Why are you in my palace?' And she answered: 'I'm good for nothing but to have boots thrown at my head.' He asked her: 'Where did you get that ring that was in the soup?' She answered: 'I don't know anything about the ring.' So the king couldn't get any sense out of her and had to send her away again.

Some time later there was another feast, and again Manypelts asked the cook for permission to go and watch. He answered: 'Yes, but come back in half an hour and cook that bread soup for the king that he likes so much.' So she ran to her cubbyhole, washed herself quickly, opened the nut and took out the dress that was silver like the moon, and put it on. Then she went upstairs, looking like a princess; the king came to meet her and was delighted to see her again, and the dance was just beginning, so they danced together. But when it ended she vanished again so quickly that the king couldn't see where she'd gone. She rushed back to her cubbyhole and turned herself into Manypelts again, and went to the kitchen to cook the bread soup. When the cook was upstairs she fetched the little golden spinning-wheel and put it into the tureen, so that the soup was poured on top of it. Then the soup was taken to the king and he ate it, and it tasted just as good as before, and he sent for the cook who again had to confess that Manypelts had cooked the soup. Manypelts appeared again before the king, but all she would answer was that she was in the palace to have boots thrown at her head and that she knew nothing about the golden spinning-wheel.

When the king gave a feast for the third time, everything happened as before. The cook did say: 'You're a witch, Furry Beast, and you always put something in the soup that makes it so good, and makes the king like it better than anything I cook.' But because she pleaded with him so, he let her go upstairs at the agreed time. And now she put on a dress that shone as brightly as the stars, and went into the hall wearing it. Again the king danced with this beautiful maiden, thinking she had never looked so beautiful before. And as he danced he slipped a golden ring on to her finger without her noticing, and he had given orders that it was to be an extra long dance. When it was over he tried to hold on to her by her hands, but she broke free and leapt away into the crowd so quickly that she vanished before his very eyes. She ran as fast as she could back to her cubbyhole under the stairs, but because she had stayed too long and been away for more than half an hour she hadn't time to take off the beautiful dress, but just threw the fur cloak over it, and in her haste she didn't blacken herself completely either, but left one finger white. Then Manypelts rushed to the kitchen, cooked the bread soup for the king, and put the golden clasp into it when the cook was out of the room. When the king found the clasp at the bottom of the dish he sent for Manypelts; and he noticed her white finger and saw the ring he had slipped on to it during the dance. Then he seized her by the hand and held her fast, and when she tried to break free and run away the fur cloak opened a little, and there was the starry dress gleaming from inside it. The king took hold of the cloak and pulled it off; and then they could see her golden hair, and there she stood in all her splendour and could no longer conceal herself. And when she had wiped the soot and ashes from her face, she was more beautiful than anyone yet seen on earth. But the king said: 'You are my beloved bride, and we shall never part again.' Then the wedding was celebrated, and they lived happily for the rest of their lives.

33

THE RIGHTFUL BRIDE

Once upon a time there was a girl who was young and beautiful, but her mother had died long ago and her stepmother did everything she could to make her wretched. Whenever she gave her a task to do, however difficult it was, the little girl would work at it bravely and do her best; but whatever she did the wicked woman's heart was not touched, she was still not satisfied, it was still not enough. The harder the child worked the more she was given to do, and all her stepmother ever thought about was how she might burden her still further and make her life a real torment.

One day she said to her: 'Here are twelve pounds of feathers for you to strip, and if they're not ready by this evening you'll get a good thrashing. Do you expect to be able to sit idle all day?' The poor girl began her task, but the tears ran down her cheeks as she worked, for she saw clearly enough that it was impossible to finish it in one day. Whenever she had a little pile of feathers in front of her and heaved a sigh or struck her hands together in anxiety, the feathers would scatter and she would have to pick them up and begin again. Suddenly she put her elbows on the table, buried her face in both hands and cried out: 'Is there no one on God's earth who will take pity on me?' And at that moment she heard a gentle voice saying: 'Be comforted, my child, I have come to help you.' The young girl looked up and saw an old woman standing beside her, who took her kindly by the hand and said: 'Just trust me and tell me what's the matter.' And because she spoke so comfortingly the young girl told her all about her unhappy life, and how one task after another was imposed on her and she couldn't finish the things she was given to do. 'If I haven't done these feathers by this evening, my stepmother will beat me; she's threatened to, and I know she means it.' Her tears began to flow again, but the kind old woman said: 'Don't worry, my child, lie down and rest, and

meanwhile I'll do your work for you.' The young girl lay down
on her bed and soon fell asleep. The old woman sat down at the
table where the feathers were and, my goodness, how they
flew! She scarcely touched the quills with her skinny hands, but
the twelve pounds were soon done. When the young girl woke
up she found them piled in big snow-white heaps, and the
room was all neatly swept, but the old woman had disappeared. She gave thanks to God, and sat quietly until evening. Then her stepmother came in, and was amazed to find the
work finished. 'Well, you slut,' she said, 'look what a bit of hard
work will do! Couldn't you have got started on something else?
Just look at you, sitting with your hands in your lap!' As she left
the room she said to herself: This creature's good for more than
just filling her belly; I'll have to find some more difficult work
for her.

Next morning she called the young girl and said: 'Here's a
spoon; take it and go to the pond outside the garden and scoop
the water out of it for me. If you've not got that done by tonight,
you know what'll happen to you.' The young girl took the
spoon and saw that it was full of holes, and even if it hadn't
been she could never have scooped the pond empty with it. She
started the work at once, kneeling on the bank and scooping,
and her tears fell into the water. But the kind old woman
appeared again, and when she heard the cause of her grief she
said: 'Never mind, my child. Go and lie down among the
bushes and sleep. I'll do your work for you.' When the old
woman was alone she merely touched the pond: the water rose
from it like a mist and mingled with the clouds. Gradually the
pond emptied, and when the young girl woke up not long
before sunset and came back to look, there was nothing left of
the pond except fishes wriggling in the mud. She went to her
stepmother and reported that the work was done. 'You should
have finished it long ago,' said her stepmother, turning pale
with rage. But then she thought of another plan. On the third
morning she said to the girl: 'Over there on the plain you're to
build me a grand castle, and it's to be ready by this evening.'
The girl answered in great alarm: 'How can I possibly do such a
thing!' 'I won't have you contradict me!' screamed her step-

mother. 'If you can empty a pond with a spoon full of holes, then you can build a castle too. I'll move into it this very day, and if there's anything missing, even the least thing missing from the kitchen or the cellar, then you know what to expect.' She drove her out of doors; and there in the valley, when the girl reached it, were rocks lying piled on top of each other, and with all her strength she couldn't even move the smallest of them. She sat down and wept, but she hoped the kind old woman would come and help her. And sure enough she soon came, and spoke comfortingly to her. 'Just lie down over there in the shade and go to sleep,' she said. 'I'll soon build the castle for you. If you like it, you can live in it yourself.' When the girl had gone away the old woman touched the grey rocks. At once they began to stir and moved into place beside each other, and there they stood like a wall built by giants. Then the whole building rose from the ground, and it was as if innumerable hands were working invisibly, putting stone upon stone. The earth groaned, great columns rose from it of their own accord and placed themselves in order side by side. The tiles fitted themselves to the roof, and by midday the great weathervane in the form of a golden maiden in flowing robes was spinning round at the top of the tower. By evening the inside of the castle was finished. I don't know how the old woman managed it, but the walls were covered with silk and velvet, and in the rooms stood embroidered chairs of many colours and richly decorated armchairs beside marble tables; crystal chandeliers hung down from the ceilings and were mirrored in the polished floors; green parrots and sweet singing birds from foreign lands sat in golden cages. All over the castle there was such magnificence that it was fit for the arrival of a king. It was nearly sunset when the girl woke up, and there before her she saw a thousand glittering lights. She hurried towards them and passed through the open gate into the castle. The stairway was laid with red carpet and all along the golden bannisters stood flowering trees. When she saw how magnificent the rooms were, she stood as if rooted to the spot. Who knows how long she would have stood there if she hadn't remembered her stepmother. 'Oh dear,' she said to herself, 'if only she would be satisfied

now and stop making my life a misery!' She went and reported
to her that the castle was ready. 'I shall move in at once,' said
her stepmother, and rose from her chair. When she entered the
castle she had to hold her hand in front of her eyes, she was so
dazzled by the splendour. 'You see,' she said to the girl, 'how
easy it was for you! I ought to have given you something more
difficult to do.' She walked through all the rooms and inspected
every corner to see whether anything was missing or not quite
right, but she could find nothing. 'We'll go downstairs now,'
she said, glaring furiously at the girl. 'I've still to examine the
kitchen and cellar, and if you've forgotten anything you'll still
get what's coming to you.' But the fire was burning on the
hearth, the food was cooking in the pots, the tongs and the
shovel were standing where they belonged and the gleaming
brass utensils were arranged along the walls. Nothing was
missing, not even the coal scuttle or the water buckets.
'Where's the entrance to the cellar?' shouted the stepmother. 'If
it's not plentifully stocked with barrels of wine, it'll be the worse
for you.' She lifted the trap-door herself and began to climb
down, but she had hardly taken two steps when the heavy
trap-door, which wasn't fastened, crashed down on top of her.
The girl heard a scream and quickly lifted the trap-door again to
go to her help. But her stepmother had fallen to the bottom and
she found her lying dead on the floor.

The girl was now the sole owner of the magnificent castle. At
first she could scarcely get used to her good fortune: beautiful
dresses were hanging in the cupboard, the chests were filled
with gold and silver or pearls and precious stones, and her
every wish could be satisfied. Soon the fame of her beauty and
wealth spread far and wide. Suitors presented themselves
every day, but she cared for none of them. Finally a prince came
too, and he succeeded in touching her heart and they became
betrothed. In the castle garden stood a green linden tree, and
one day when they were sitting under it lovingly together he
said to her: 'I'll go home and get my father's consent to our
marriage. Please wait for me here under this linden tree; in a
few hours I shall be back.' The girl kissed him on the left cheek
and said: 'Be true to me, and let no other woman kiss you on

this cheek. I shall wait here under the linden tree until you return.'

The girl sat on under the linden tree until the sun had set, but he didn't return. She sat for three days from morning till evening waiting for him, but in vain. When he had not yet come on the fourth day she said: 'I'm sure something has happened to him. I'll go out and look for him, and not return till I've found him.' She packed three of her most beautiful dresses, one embroidered with glittering stars, the second with silver moons and the third with golden suns; then she tied up a handful of precious stones in her kerchief and set out. She asked for her bridegroom everywhere, but no one had seen him or knew anything about him. She wandered through the world far and wide, but couldn't find him. Finally she hired herself to a farmer as a herdsmaid, and buried her dresses and jewels under a stone.

So now she lived the life of a herdsmaid, minding her cattle, and her heart was heavy with longing for her beloved. She had a little calf that she made a pet of, feeding it out of her hand, and when she said:

> 'Little calf, kneel down to greet me,
> My little calf, do not forget me,
> As the prince has forgotten his bride
> Who sat under the linden at his side,'

then the little calf would kneel down and she would stroke it.

When she had lived for a few years in loneliness and sorrow, she heard it rumoured in the land that the king's daughter was going to celebrate her wedding. The road into the city went past the village where the girl was living, and one day it happened that as she was driving her herd to pasture the bridegroom rode by. He sat proudly on his horse and didn't look at her, but when she looked at him she recognized her beloved. She felt as if a sharp knife were cutting her to the heart. 'Alas,' she said, 'I thought he was true to me, but he has forgotten me.'

Next day he came riding the same way again. When he was close to her she said to her little calf:

'Little calf, kneel down to greet me,
My little calf, do not forget me,
As the prince has forgotten his bride
Who sat under the linden at his side.'

When he heard her voice he looked down at her and reined his horse in; he gazed into the herdsmaid's face, then pressed his hand against his eyes as if he were trying to remember something, but then he rode on quickly and soon disappeared. 'Alas,' she said, 'he no longer knows me,' and she grew more and more sorrowful.

Soon after this there was to be a great feast at the royal palace lasting three days, and everyone in the kingdom was invited. Now I will try my last chance, thought the girl, and when evening fell she went to the stone under which she had hidden her treasures. She fetched out the dress with the golden suns, put it on and adorned herself with the jewels. She undid her hair, which she had hidden under a kerchief, and it fell down about her in long tresses. Then she walked to the city and no one noticed her in the dark. When she entered the brightly lit hall everyone stepped back from her in amazement, but no one knew who she was. The prince came to meet her but didn't recognize her. He invited her to dance with him and was so enchanted by her beauty that he forgot all about his other bride. When the feast was over she vanished in the crowd and hurried back before daybreak to the village, where she put on her herdsmaid's clothes again.

On the following evening she took out the dress with the silver moons and put a crescent of precious stones in her hair. When she arrived at the feast everyone turned to gaze at her, but the prince hurried towards her, quite entranced with love, and danced only with her and didn't even look at any other girl. Before she left he made her promise to come to the feast again on the last night.

When she appeared for the third time she was wearing the dress covered with stars, which glittered with every step she took, and her headband and girdle were stars of precious stones. The prince had been waiting some time for her already and pushed his way to her through the crowd. 'Please tell me who you are!' he said. 'I feel as if I had met you already long ago.' She answered: 'Don't you remember what I did when you left me?' Then she stepped up to him and kissed him on the left cheek: and at that moment scales seemed to fall from his eyes, and he recognized his rightful bride. 'Come,' he said to her, 'I will stay here no longer.' And he gave her his hand and led her down to his carriage. As if it were harnessed to the wind, the horses sped with it to the magic castle. Its brightly lit windows shone from far off. Countless fireflies swarmed in the linden tree as they passed it, and its branches shook and scattered fragrance. The trees were blossoming on the stairs, the birds from foreign lands could be heard singing in the rooms, but in the hall their own court was assembled and the priest was waiting to marry the bridegroom to his rightful bride.

34

THE IRON STOVE

In the days when wishing still worked, a prince was put under a spell by an old witch and made to sit in the forest inside a big iron stove. He spent many years there and nobody could set him free. One day a princess came into the forest. She was lost and couldn't find her way back to her father's kingdom: she had wandered about like this for nine days, and finally she found herself standing in front of this iron box. A voice from inside it asked her: 'Where have you come from and where are you going?' She answered: 'I've lost my way to my father's kingdom and can't get home again.' Then the voice from the stove said: 'I'll help you back home again and get you there in no time if you will sign an agreement to do what I shall ask of you. I am a prince, and my father is a greater king than yours, and I want to marry you.' She was alarmed and thought: Heaven save me, how can I marry an iron stove! But because she was very anxious to get home to her father, she nevertheless signed the agreement to do as he asked. And he said: 'You are to come back here bringing a knife with you, and scrape a hole in the iron.' Then he gave her a companion who walked beside her and didn't speak, but got her home in two hours. There was great rejoicing in the palace that the princess was back, and the old king fell on her neck and kissed her. But her mind was very troubled and she said: 'Dear father, if you knew what had happened to me! I would never have got home again out of that great wild forest if I hadn't met an iron stove, and in return I had to sign a promise that I would go back to it and set it free and marry it.' This alarmed the old king so much that he nearly fainted, for she was his only child. So they thought up a plan and decided to get the miller's daughter, who was a beautiful girl, to stand in for the princess. They took her out there, gave her a knife and told her to scrape the iron stove. And she whittled away at it for twenty-four hours, but couldn't make

even the slightest scratch. Then as day was breaking the voice
inside the stove said: 'I think it is day out there.' And she
answered: 'So do I, I think I hear my father's mill going
clickety-clack.' 'So you're a miller's daughter. Then leave the
forest at once and tell them to send the princess here.' So she
went back and told the old king that the person in the forest
didn't want her, he wanted the king's daughter. Then the old
king took fright, and his daughter wept. But they also had a
swineherd's daughter who was even more beautiful than the
miller's daughter, and they decided to pay her to take the
princess's place and go out to the iron stove. So she was taken
out, and she too had to scrape away for twenty-four hours, but
she couldn't get any of the iron to come off it. Then as day was
breaking the voice inside the stove said: 'I think it is day out
there.' And she answered: 'So do I, I think I hear my father
blowing his horn.' 'So you're a swineherd's daughter. Go away
at once and tell them to send the princess: and tell her that it
shall be as I promised her, and that if she fails to come every
building in the entire kingdom shall fall apart and collapse and
not one stone shall be left standing on another.' When the
princess heard this she burst into tears; but now there was no
more to be done, she had to keep her promise. So she said
goodbye to her father, took a knife with her and went out to the
iron stove in the forest. When she got there she began to scrape,
and the iron gave way, and after two hours she'd already dug
out a little hole. Then she took a look through it, and, oh my
goodness, she saw such a beautiful young man, all glittering
with gold and precious stones, that she lost her heart to him
completely. So then she carried on scraping till she had made
the hole big enough for him to come out. And he said: 'You
belong to me, and I to you: you are my bride and have released
me from the spell.' He wanted to take her with him to his
kingdom, but she asked him as a favour to let her go and see her
father once more, and the prince let her do this, but on condition that she was not to speak more than three words to her
father, after which she must return. So she went home, but she
spoke more than three words: and immediately the iron stove
disappeared and was carried far away over glass mountains and

razor-edged swords; but the prince had been released and was
no longer imprisoned in it. Then she said goodbye to her father
and took some money with her but not very much, and went
back into the great forest and looked for the iron stove; but it
was nowhere to be found. For nine days she searched; and then
she became so hungry that she was at her wits' end, for she had
nothing more to live on. And when evening fell she climbed a
small tree, thinking she would spend the night sitting on it, for
fear of the wild beasts. When midnight came she saw a faint
light in the distance and thought: Oh, perhaps that's where I'll
find help. And she climbed down from the tree and walked
towards the light, praying as she went. She came to a little old
house with lots of grass growing round it and a little pile of
wood in front of it. She thought: Oh, wherever have I come to!
And when she looked through the window she couldn't see
anything inside but a lot of puddocks*, fat ones and little ones,
but there was a table there too, beautifully laid with wine and
roast meat and silver plates and cups. So she plucked up courage and knocked at the door. At once the fattest puddock called
out:

> 'Little Miss Greenlegs,
> House hop-goblin,
> Watchdog goblin,
> Hop along, go and see,
> Who's at the door, who can it be?'

At this a little puddock came hopping up and opened the door
for her. When she went in they all bade her welcome, told her to
sit down and asked: 'Where have you come from, my lady, and
where are you going?' Then she told them everything that had
happened to her and that because she had disobeyed the command not to speak more than three words the stove and the
prince had disappeared, and that now she intended to go on
wandering over hill and dale and searching for him till she
found him. Then the old fat one said:

* toads.

'Little Miss Greenlegs,
House hop-goblin,
Fetch-and-carry goblin,
Hop along, quick sticks,
Fetch me the box of tricks.'

So off the little one went and brought her the box. After this they gave her food and drink and took her to a lovely bed all made up and ready and as soft as silk and velvet; so she lay down on it and commended herself to God and went to sleep. At daybreak she got up, and the old puddock took three needles out of the big box and gave them to her for her journey, saying she would need them, for she would have to climb over a high glass mountain and pass over three razor-edged swords and cross a great river; if she succeeded in all this she would get her lover back again. So the puddock gave her three things that she must take great care of, namely three big needles, a plough wheel and three nuts. Then the princess set off, and when she came to the slippery glass mountain she stuck the three needles into it, first behind her feet and then in front of them, and thus managed to get over; and at the other side she hid them away in a place which she noted well. Then she came to the three razor-edged swords, so she stood on her plough wheel and rolled over them. Finally she came to a great river, and when she had crossed it she reached a beautiful big castle. She went in and asked if they had any work for her, saying she was a poor maidservant who would be glad to be hired; but she knew that in this castle was the prince whom she had freed from the iron stove in the great forest. So she was taken on as a kitchen maid for a low wage. Now the prince, who thought she was long since dead, already had another girl at his side and intended to marry her. That evening, when the kitchen maid had washed up and finished her work she felt in her pocket and found the three nuts the old puddock had given her. She cracked one open with her teeth to eat the kernel, but lo and behold, in it was a magnificent royal dress. When the bride heard about this she came and offered to buy the dress from her, saying it was no dress for a serving-wench. She said no, it wasn't for sale, but that the bride might have it if she would allow her one favour, namely to sleep for one night in her bridegroom's bedchamber. The bride gave her leave to do this because the dress was so beautiful and none of her own was like it. So that night she said to her bridegroom: 'The silly maid wants to sleep in your bedroom.' 'If you don't mind, neither do I,' he replied. But she also gave him a glass of wine into which she had put a sleeping potion. So he and the maid went into the bedchamber and he slept so soundly that she couldn't wake him. She wept all night and cried out: 'I set you free from the wild forest and from an iron stove, and I sought you and climbed a glass mountain and passed over three razor-edged swords and crossed a great river before I found you, and yet you will not hear me.' The servants were sitting outside the door and heard her weeping like this all night, and they told their master about it in the morning. And on the second evening, when she had washed up, she cracked open the second nut, and in it was a still more beautiful dress, and when the bride saw it she wanted to buy it too. But the girl refused money and asked leave to sleep once more in the bridegroom's bedchamber. But the bride gave him a sleeping potion and he slept so soundly that he could hear nothing. The kitchen maid wept all night and cried out: 'I set you free from a forest and from an iron stove, I sought you and climbed a glass mountain and passed over three razor-edged swords and crossed a great river before I found you, and yet you will not hear me.' The servants were sitting outside the door and heard her weeping like this all night, and they told their master about it in the morning. When she had washed up on the third evening she cracked open the third nut, and inside was a still more beautiful dress with pure gold all over it. When the bride saw this she wanted to have it, but the girl would only part with it if she were allowed to sleep a third time in the bridegroom's bedchamber. But the prince was heedful, and he poured the sleeping potion past his lips. So when she began to weep and cry out: 'Dearest love, I set you free from the cruel wild forest and from an iron stove,' the prince jumped out of bed and said: 'You are my true love, you belong to me and I to you.' And he got into a carriage with her that very night, and they took the false bride's dresses away so that she couldn't get up. When they came to the great river they crossed it in a boat, and when they came to the three razor-edged swords they rode over them on the plough wheel, and when they came to the glass mountain they stuck the three needles into it. Thus they finally reached the little old house, but as soon as they stepped in, it was a great castle: the puddocks had been released from their spell and were all princes and princesses, and they were all rejoicing. Then the wedding took place, and they stayed on in the castle, which was much bigger than her father's castle. But the old man complained about being left alone. So they drove off and fetched him to live with them, and thus they had two kingdoms and lived in married bliss.

> My tale is done,
> See that mouse run!

THE TWA ROYAL BAIRNIES

Eence there wiz a king that haed a saen, an the signs at the loonie's birth tellt that a staig waed kell im fan he wiz saxteen year auld. Fan he cam tae be saxteen the huntsmen gaed huntin wi im. In the waed the king's saen wiz pairtet fae the huntsmen, an aa at eence he saa a muckle staig an try't tae shot im but he couldnae hit im; an bi the en o't the staig ran an ran till he wiz oot o the waed, an suddent-like it wisnae a staig that steed there but a muckle lang chiel that said: 'So, I've teen ye at last! I've run throu sax pair o gless skatchers seekin ye an couldnae tak ye.' Syne he took im wi im an gart im plouter throu a great stretch o watter, till they cam tae a muckle royal pailace, an there he made im sit doon at a table an ait mait. Fan they haed aitten thegither the king said: 'I haev three dothers; ye maun watch the nicht throu in the auldest een's chaumber fae nine at nicht tae sax in the mornin, an ilka time the clock rings I'll come my ainsèl an cry tae ye, an gin ye dinnae gie me an answer ye'll be kellt the morn, but if ye gie me an answer ilka time ye'll get er for a wife.' Fan the young couple cam intae the chaumber, there steed a steen effigy o Sanct Christopher, an the king's dother spak till't an said: 'My daddie will come at nine an ilka oor till it streck three o the clock; fan he spiers, ye answer im for the prince here.' Thereat the steen Christopher noddit his heid as fast as onything at first, syne slower an slower till at last he stoppit.

The next mornin the king said till him: 'Ye've deen weel, but I cannae gie ye my dother until ye watch a nicht throu in my secant dother's chaumber, an syne I'll consider gin I can gie ye my auldest dother for a wife; but I'll come ilka oor my ainsèl, an fan I cry tae ye, answer me, an gin I cry an ye dinnae answer, yer bleed will flou for me.' Sae the twasome gaed up tae the chaumber, an there steed anither bigger steen effigy o Sanct Christopher, an the king's dother spak till't an said: 'Fan my daddie spiers, ye answer.' An the muckle steen Christopher noddit he heid again as fast as onything at first, syne slower an slower till he stoppit at last. An the king's saen lay doon on the door-sill wi his haan ablò his heid an gaed tae sleep.

The next mornin the king said till im: 'Ye've deen weel, I wyte, but I cannae gie ye my dother till ye watch a nicht throu in the youngest princess's chaumber, an syne I'll tak thocht whether I can gie ye my secant dother for a wife. But I'll come ilka oor my ainsèl, an fan I cry tae ye, answer me, an gin I cry an ye dinnae answer, yer bleed will flou for me.' Sae they gaed up thegither till er chaumber, an there steed a steen Christopher far bigger an langer nor the first twa. Tae him the princess said: 'Fan my daddie cries, ye answer.' An the muckle lang Christopher noddit a gweed half-oor lang till his heid stoppit at last. Sae the king's saen lay doon on the door-sill an gaed tae sleep.

The next mornin the king said: 'Weel, ye keepit yer watch weel, but I cannae gie ye my dother yet. I aicht a muckle waed, an gin ye can hyow't doon for me the morn atween sax in the mornin an sax in the forenicht, I'll tak thocht aboot it.' An he furnisht im wi a gless aix, a gless wadge an a gless chapper. Fan he gat tae the waed, he set tee tae hyow, an the aix it brook; sae he took the wadge an duntit it wi the chapper, an it brook in bitties as smaa as saan. An he wiz sair-made an sure that he maun dee, an he sat an grat. Syne dennertime cam an the king said: 'Een o you quines micht bring im something tae ait.' 'Na,' said the twa auldest quines, 'we'll bring im naething, the last een that he baid the nicht wi can dee that.' Sae the youngest she haed tae tak his mait till im. Fan she gat tae the waed she spiert at im foo things steed. 'Oh,' said he, 'gey ill.' An she socht im tae sit doon first an ait his mait. Na, said he, that he couldnae dee, he wiz like tae loss his life an he waednae ait. Sae she priggit wi im tae try a bittie, an he ait some mait; an fan he haed feeneesht she said: 'Noo I'll straik yer hair tae ye tae tak oot the lice, that'll gie ye ither thochts.' An as she straikit im he gat drowsy an fell tae sleep, an she took her kerchie an ty't a knot in't an struck the grun' thrice wi't an said: 'Warkers, come oot!' An stracht awà dizzens o dwarfies cam oot an spiert fit er orders war. An said she: 'In three oors the hale waed maun be hyown doon an aa the waed laid in piles.' An the dwarfies they gaed an summonst their hale kinàbrach tae help them wi the wark; an they set tee an bi the en' o three oors the wark wiz aa deen, an they cam back tae the princess an tellt her. Syne she took up her fite kerchie again an said: 'Warkers, gae hame!' an they aa vanisht again. Fan the king's saen waukent he wiz kinechtit; an she said: 'Fan it's strucken sax, come hame again.' That he daed, an the king spiert: 'Haev ye teen the waed doon?' 'Aye,' said the king's saen. Syne as they sat at the table the king said: 'I cannae gie ye my dother for a wife yet,' an he maun dee ae thing mair for her. 'An fit micht that be?' said the king's saen. 'I aicht a muckle dam,' said the king. 'The morn ye maun gyang oot till't an clean't till it's as clear as a looking-gless an full o aa kyn' o fesh.' The next mornin the king gied im a gless shuffél an said: 'The dam maun be clear bi sax o'clock.' Sae aff he set, an fan he gat tae the dam, he caa't his shuffel intae the mairsh an the hannel brook aff, an he caa't his chapper intae the mairsh an it wiz eeseless tee. Sae he wiz gey sair-made. At dennertime the youngest princess brocht im is mait an spiert foo things steed; gey ill, said the king's saen, he wiz like tae loss his life. 'My tools is aa broken again,' said he. 'Oh,' said she, 'first come an ait yer mait, that'll gie ye ither thochts.' Na, said he, he couldnae ait a bite, he wiz ower sair-made; but she priggit wi im till he ait a bittie. Syne she straikit the lice fae his hair again an he gaed tae sleep: an eence again she took a kerchie, ty't a knot in't an struck the grun' three times wi the knot, sayin: 'Warkers, come oot!' An stracht awà dizzens o dwarfies cam oot an spiert fit she wiz seekin. In three oors they maun clean the hale dam till it wiz that clear ye could see yer face in't an full o aa kyn' o fesh, said she. Sae the dwarfies gaed an summonst their hale kinàbrach tae help them; an I wyte the wark wiz aa deen in twa oors. Back cam the dwarfies an said: 'We haev deen yer biddin,' an the princess took her kerchie again, struck the grun' wi't thrice an said: 'Warkers, gae hame!' an they vanisht again. Fan the king's saen waukent, the dam wiz feeneesht; an the princess she gaed awà tee, tellin him tae come hame again fan it struck sax o'clock. An fan he cam hame the king spiert at im: 'Haev ye deen the dam?' 'Aye,' said the king's saen. An that wiz fine.

An noo as they sat at the table again, the king said: 'I wyte ye've deen the dam, but I cannae gie ye my dother till ye've deen ae thing mair.' 'An fit micht that be?' spiert the king's saen. Weel, said the king, he aichtet a great hill covert wi thorn-busses, that maun be hyown doon, an the king's saen maun bigg a great castle on the tap o't as grand as ony man ever saa an plenisht wi aathing needfae. Fan he raize up the next mornin, the king gaed im a gless aix an a gless borin-braess, an said: 'See that it's feeneesht bi sax o'clock.' But as seen as he startit tae hyow at the first thorn-buss his aix brook in smithers that smaa that they flew aawey, an his borin-braess wiz eeeseless an aa. An he wiz sair-made an wytit for his lass tae come an help im oot o the snorl he wiz in. At dennertime she cam wi his mait, an he ran till er an tellt er aa an lat er straik im till he gaed tae sleep. An again she took the knottit kerchie an struck the grun' wi't an said: 'Warkers, come oot!' An again dizzens o dwarfies cam oot an spiert fit she wiz seekin; an she said: 'In three oors ye maun clear aa the thorn-busses an bigg a castle on the tap o the hill, as grand as ever a man saa an plenisht wi aathing needfae.' An the dwarfies they gaed an summonst their hale kinàbrach tae help them, an bi the en' o the time the wark wiz deen. Sae they cam tae the princess an tellt er that, an the princess took er kerchie an struck the grun' wi't thrice an said: 'Warkers, gae hame!' an at that they vanisht. An fan the king's saen waukent an saa't aa, he wiz as happy as a larkie, an fan it strack sax they gaed hame thegither. 'Weel, is the castle feeneesht?' said the king. 'Aye,' said the king's saen.

As they sat at the table the king said: 'I cannae gie my youngest dother awà or the twa auldest eens is mairrit.' Oh, than the twa royal bairns war sorrafae, an the king's saen didnae ken far tae turn. Sae he cam bi nicht tae the princess and ran awà wi er. Aifter they haed traivelt a bittie, the princess lookit roon an saa her father ahin er. 'Oh,' said she, 'fit'll we dee? My father's ahin's an he'll owertak's. I'll turn you intae a thorn-buss an mysèl intae a rose an hide in the hairt o the buss.' Sae fan the father cam up, there steed a thorn-buss wi a rose on't. He wiz jist gyan tae pick the rose, but the thorn prickit im in the finger an he haed tae gyang hame again. His wife spiert

fit-wey he haednae brocht them back, an he said he'd nearly
been on them but aa at eence haed lost sicht o them and a
thorn-buss an a rose haed steed there instead. An the queen
said: 'Gin only ye haed pickit the rose, the buss waed hae come
an aa.' Sae awà he gaed again tae fess the rose; but meantime
the twasome wiz hine awà an the king he gaed rinnin aifter
them. Again his dother lookit roon an saa her father comin an
said: 'Oh, fit will we dee noo? I'll turn you intae a kirk an mysèl
intae the minister an I'll stan' in the pulpit an preach.' Sae fan
the king gat that far, there steed a kirk wi a minister stannin in
the pulpit preachin; an he harkent tae the sermon an gaed hame
again. Fan the queen spiert fit-wey he haednae brocht them
back, he said: 'No, I ran aifter them lang aneuch, an fan I thocht
I'd gotten them, there steed a kirk wi a minister preachin in the
pulpit.' 'Ye shaed hae brocht the minister,' said the queen, 'an
the kirk waed hae come an aa. It's nae eese sennin you oot, I'll
hae tae gyang mysèl.' Fan she haed traivelt a bittie an could see
them hine awà, the princess lookit roon an saa her mither comin
an said: 'Oh alais, yonder's my mither ersèl com aifter's; I'll
turn you intae a dam an mysèl intae a fesh.' An fan her mither
cam up, there lay a braid dam, an in the middle o't a fishie
loupin aboot an bobbin its heid oot o the watter, a shortsome
sicht. An she try't tae tak the fishie but she couldnae; an she
gaed fair wid an drank doon the hale dam tae get the fishie, but
she grue't an haed tae spew an spewt the hale dam back up
again. Sae syne she said: 'I can see there's nae remeìd,' an socht
them back. Sae they gaed till er, an the queen gied her dother
three walnuts an said: 'They'll help ye fan ye need them
sairest.'

Sae the young fowk set aff thegither, an they walkit forty mile
afore they cam tae the castle far the king's saen cam fae, an a
toonie aside it. Fan they gat till't, the king's saen said: 'Ye bide
here, my dearie, an I'll gyang up tae the castle an syne come
back wi a cairrage an sairvints tae convye ye.' Sae he cam tae the
castle, an oh but they war glaed tae hae the king's saen back
again. An he tellt them he haed a bride wytin in the toonie, an
they waed gyang wi the cairrage an convye her. Sae they hetcht
up the horses an a quorn flunkies loupit ontae the cairrage. But

the verra meenit the king's saen wiz boordin the cairrage, his mither gied im a kiss; an he forgot aathing that haed happint an fit he wiz gyan tae dee. His mither gart them lowse the horses an they aa gaed inside again.

But the quine she sat in the toonie an wytit an wytit for him tae convye her, but back cam niver. Sae the princess fee't ersèl as a sairvint at the mull that belangt tae the castle, an ilka aifterneen she haed tae sit bi the watter an scoor the pans. Ae day the queen cam doon fae the castle an gaed walkin bi the watter an saa the bonny lass sittin there an said: 'My, but that's a bonny lass, I like the look o her,' an aa the mengie lookit at her but neen o them kent her. An the quine warkit in the mull for mony a year an day an wiz a true an faithfae sairvint.

Meantime, the queen she socht a wife till er saen, an the wife cam fae hine awà. Fan the bride cam, they war tae be mairrit stracht awà. Thoosans o fowk cam fae aa roon tae see't, an the lassie she socht leave fae the muller tae gyang till't, an he said: 'Aye, an willintly.' Jist as she wiz ready tae gyang she opint een o the walnuts, an inside wiz a braa goun that she dresst ersèl in an awà she gaed tae the kirk an steed anent the altar. Ben cam the bride an bridegroom an sat themsells doon afore the altar, an jist as the minister wiz gyan tae jine them in wedlock, the bride she keest a look sideweys an saa her stannin there. Up she steed an said she waednae be mairrit until shé haed a goun as fine as the leddy haed. Sae back hame they gaed an sent tae spier at the leddy gin she waed sell the goun. No, she waednae sell't, but maybe they micht earn't, said she. Sae they spiert fit they maun dee; an she said, gin they waed lat er sleep the nicht throu afore the prince's door, she'd gie them't; an they said aye, an willintly. But the flunkies they haed tae cairry in a sleepin-draucht tae the prince; an she laid ersèl doon on the door-sill an girnt an grat the hale hadden nicht throu, sayin foo she'd gotten the waed hyown doon for im an cleant the dam for im an biggit the castle for im an turnt im intae a thorn-buss, an he'd forgotten her sae fast. The prince heert naething o aa thes, but the flunkies waukent an harkent but kenntnae fit it meant.

The next mornin fan they raize, the bride pat on er goun an awà wi the bridegroom tae the kirk. Meantime the braa lass opint her secant walnut, an inside wiz an even bonnier goun that she pat on an awà she gaed tae the kirk an steed anent the altar. An the same thing happint as the day afore. An again the lass lay on the door-sill tae the bridegroom's chaumber, an again the flunkies wiz suppos't tae cairry in a sleepin-draucht till im. But they cam an gied im something tae keep im waukin instead, an he took that tae his bed. An again the muller's sairvint-lass girnt an grat on the door-sill an tellt aa that she haed deen. An the prince heert it aa an wiz aafa come-at. Aathing past cam back till im, an he try't tae get till er, but his mither haed barrt the door. But the next mornin he gaed stracht tae his dearie an tellt her aa that haed happint an socht her tae nae mislike im for forgettin her sae lang. Syne she opint the third walnut, an inside o't lay a braa goun, bonnier bi far nor the ithers. She dresst ersèl in't an drave tae the kirk wi er bride-groom. An dizzens o bairnies cam an gied them flooers an held colort ribbands at their feet; an they gat mairrit, an merry wiz the bridal-feast they held. But the fauss mither and bride war banisht.

An the een that last tellt this tale is still livin tae tell't.

36

THE GOOSEGIRL

There once lived an old queen whose husband had died many years ago, and she had a beautiful daughter. When the girl grew up she was promised in marriage to a prince who lived over the hills and far away. So when the time came for them to be married and the girl had to set off on her journey to the other kingdom, her mother packed up a great many precious articles and ornaments for her to take with her, gold and silver, goblets and jewels, in fact everything that was needful for a royal dowry; for she loved her daughter very dearly. She also gave her a maid-in-waiting who was to ride with her and deliver the bride to the bridegroom, and each of them was given a horse for the journey; but the princess's horse was called Falada and could speak. When the hour of parting came the old queen went to her bedroom, took a little knife and cut her fingers with it so that they bled; then she held out a piece of white cloth and let three drops of blood fall on it. These she gave to her daughter, saying: 'My dear child, keep these safely, you will need them on your way.'

So they took leave of each other sadly; the princess hid the piece of cloth in her bosom, mounted her horse and set off to travel to her bridegroom. When they had ridden for an hour she felt a burning thirst and said to her maid-in-waiting: 'Take my goblet which you have brought for me, and dismount and fetch some water from the stream for me to drink.' 'If madam is thirsty,' replied the maid, 'she can dismount herself. Lie by the stream and drink, I'll not be your maid.' The princess was so thirsty that she dismounted and stooped over the stream and drank the water straight from it, since she mightn't drink from her golden goblet. 'Dear God!' she exclaimed, and the three drops of blood answered: 'If the queen your mother knew, grief would break her heart in two.' But the royal bride was humble and said nothing and mounted her horse again. So they rode a few miles further, but the day was hot and the sun beat down and she was soon thirsty again. So when they came to a stream of water she called out again to her maid: 'Take my golden goblet and dismount and bring me water' – for she had forgotten all about the girl's wicked words. But the maid answered still more haughtily: 'If you want water, fetch it for yourself. I'll not be your maid.' So the princess dismounted because she was so thirsty, and lay right over the running water, and wept and exclaimed: 'Dear God!' And the drops of blood answered again: 'If the queen your mother knew, grief would break her heart in two.' And as she drank and leant right out over the stream, the piece of cloth with the three drops of blood on it fell from her bosom and floated away on the water, and her mind was so troubled that she didn't notice it. But the maid had been watching and saw with delight that she would now have power over the bride: for by losing the drops of blood the princess had become weak and helpless. So as she was about to mount her horse again, the one called Falada, the maid said: 'I'll ride Falada, he's for me; my nag's good enough for you.' And the princess had to accept this. Then the maid ordered her harshly to take off her royal garments and exchange them for her own rough clothes; and finally she made her swear under the open sky that when they arrived at the royal court she would not breathe a word of all this to anyone, threatening to kill her on the spot if she refused to take this oath. But Falada watched it all and took good note of it.

So the maid now mounted Falada and the rightful bride mounted the ordinary horse, and so they rode on till at last they came to the royal palace. There was great rejoicing at their arrival, and the prince ran to meet them and lifted the maid down from her horse, thinking she was his wife. She was escorted up the stair, but the rightful princess was left standing down in the courtyard. Then the old king looked out of his window and saw her waiting down there, and saw how graceful and delicate and beautiful she was. And he went at once to the royal bedchamber and wanted to know about the bride's companion who had been left standing in the courtyard. 'Who is she?' he asked. 'Oh, I brought her with me to keep me company; give her some work to do, a maid shouldn't stand idle.' But the old king hadn't any work to give her, and all he could think of was to say: 'Well, I've that little lad who minds the geese, she can help him.' So the rightful bride was told to help the gooseboy, whose name was Conrad, or Curdie for short.

But soon after this the false bride said to the young king: 'My dearest husband, I should like to ask you a favour.' He answered: 'I'll gladly do it.' 'Then have the knacker sent for and have him cut off the head of that horse I rode here on; it annoyed me during the journey.' But her real reason was that she was afraid the horse might speak and tell people how she had treated the princess. Now when this thing was about to be done and the faithful Falada was to die, the true princess also heard of it, and she secretly promised the knacker some money, saying she would pay him if he did her a small service. In the town wall there was a big dark gateway through which she had to pass morning and evening with her geese; and she asked him to nail up Falada's head under this dark gateway, so that she might see him more than once again. So the knacker promised to do this, and after cutting off the horse's head he nailed it fast under the dark gateway.

Early in the morning when she and Curdie were driving the geese out through the gate, she said as she passed:

'Oh poor Falada, hanging there,'

and the head answered:

'Why, there you go, my lady fair.
If the queen your mother knew,
Grief would break her heart in two.'

After this she walked on in silence, and they drove the geese out into the country. And when she reached the meadow she sat down and undid her hair, and it was like pure gold. Curdie saw it and loved the way it glittered in the sun, and he wanted to snatch a little of it and pull it out. But she said:

> 'Little wind, blow today,
> Blow Curdie's hat away:
> Make it fly and make him run,
> Till my hair is combed and done.'

And at this such a strong wind started blowing that it blew Curdie's hat all over the place, and he had to run after it. Before he got back she had finished combing and doing up her hair, so he couldn't pull out any of it. This made Curdie angry and he wouldn't speak to her. So they went on minding the geese till evening, and then they went home.

Next morning as they were driving the geese through the dark gateway, the princess said:

> 'Oh, poor Falada, hanging there,'

and Falada answered:

> 'Why, there you go, my lady fair.
> If the queen your mother knew,
> Grief would break her heart in two.'

And outside the town she sat down again in the meadow and began to comb out her hair and Curdie ran up and tried to snatch at it, but quickly she said:

> 'Little wind, blow today,
> Blow Curdie's hat away:
> Make it fly and make him run,
> Till my hair is combed and done.'

And the wind blew and whirled his hat right off his head, so that he had to run after it; and long before he got back she had finished braiding up her hair, and he couldn't get at any of it. So they minded the geese till evening.

But that evening after they got home Curdie went to the old king and said: 'I'm not going to mind geese any more with that girl.' 'Why ever not?' asked the old king. 'Oh, she annoys me all day.' Then the old king ordered him to tell what happened between them, and Curdie said: 'Every morning as we are driving the flock through that dark gateway, there's an old nag's head nailed to the wall, and she says to it:

> "Poor Falada, hanging there,"

and the head answers:

> "There you go, my lady fair.
> If the queen your mother knew,
> Grief would break her heart in two." '

And Curdie went on to tell the king what happened in the meadow where they took the geese, and how he had to chase after his hat in the wind.

The old king ordered him to drive the geese out again next day, and in the morning he himself sat down behind the dark gateway and heard the goosegirl's conversation with Falada's head; and then he followed her out into the country as well and hid behind a bush in the meadow. There he soon saw with his own eyes how she and the boy brought the flock of geese here and how presently she sat down and unwound her glittering golden hair. And soon she was repeating:

> 'Little wind, blow today,
> Blow Curdie's hat away:
> Make it fly and make him run,
> Till my hair is combed and done.'

Whereupon a gust of wind came and carried off Curdie's hat so that he had to run far and wide, and the goosegirl went on quietly combing and braiding her tresses; and all this the old king observed. Then he went back without letting them see him, and when the goosegirl came home that evening he called her and asked her privately what her reason was for doing all this. 'Sir,' she said, 'I am not allowed to tell you, and I am not allowed to tell my sorrows to anyone, for I swore under the open sky not to do so, and I had to swear or I would have lost my life.' He urged her to tell him and gave her no peace, but couldn't get a word out of her. So he said: 'If you won't tell me anything, you can tell your sorrows to that iron stove,' and he left her alone. Then she crawled into the iron stove and began to weep and lament and poured out her heart, saying: 'Here I sit, forsaken by everyone, and yet I am a king's daughter. And my maid-in-waiting has betrayed me, forcing me to take off my royal clothes and taking my place beside my bridegroom, so that I must do common service as a goosegirl; and if the queen my mother knew, grief would break her heart in two.' But the old king was standing outside with his ear to the stove-pipe, and he heard what she said. So he came in again and told her to come out of the stove. Then royal clothes were put on her, and it seemed a miracle how beautiful she was. The old king called his son and explained to him that he had got the wrong bride: she was merely a maid-in-waiting, but the former goosegirl was the rightful princess and here she stood. The young king rejoiced when he saw her beauty and virtue, and a great feast was prepared, to which all the courtiers and good friends were invited. At the head of the table sat the bridegroom, with the princess on one side of him and the maid-in-waiting on the other, and the maid's eyes were bedazzled and she didn't recognize the princess in her splendid jewels. When they had eaten and drunk and were in high spirits, the old king asked the maid-in-waiting a riddle. He asked her what a woman would deserve who had deceived her master thus and thus – and he told the whole story, ending with the question: 'What sentence does such a woman deserve?' And the false bride answered: 'She deserves nothing better than to be stripped stark naked and pushed into a barrel that has sharp nails driven into it so that they stick out all over the inside, and then two white horses must be harnessed to it and drag her up and down the streets till she is dead.' 'The culprit is you,' said the old king, 'and you have invented your own punishment; for that is what shall be done to you.' And when the sentence had been carried out the young king married his rightful wife, and the two of them ruled over their kingdom in peace and happiness.

37

JACK OF IRON

Once upon a time there was a king who had a great forest beside his castle, and game of all kinds running around in it. One day he sent out a huntsman to shoot a deer, but the huntsman didn't come back. 'Perhaps he's had an accident,' said the king, and next day he sent out two more huntsmen to look for the first; but they didn't come back either. So on the third day he summoned all his huntsmen and said to them: 'Search the entire forest, and don't stop searching till you have found all three of them.' But none of these huntsmen came home either, and not one of the pack of hounds they had taken with them was ever seen again. From that time on no one dared enter the forest, and there it lay in deep silence and solitude, and all that could be seen from time to time was an eagle or a hawk flying over it. This lasted for many years; then a huntsman from another country came before the king, asked leave to stay at his court and offered to go into the dangerous forest. But the king was unwilling to give his consent, saying: 'That forest is unlucky, I fear you'll fare no better in it than the others and never get out of it again.' The huntsman answered: 'Sir, I will do it at my own risk; I am afraid of nothing.'

So the huntsman went into the forest with his dog. Before long the dog picked up a scent and began following it: but it had hardly run a few steps when it found itself standing in front of a deep pool which it couldn't cross; and here a naked arm rose out of the water, seized it and dragged it under. When the huntsman saw this, he went back and fetched three men who had to come with buckets and bale the water out of the pool. When they had got deep enough to see the bottom, they found a wild man lying there: his skin was as brown as rusty iron and his hair hung down over his face right to his knees. They tied him up with ropes and carried him off to the palace. There everyone was amazed to see this wild man, but the king had

him locked up in an iron cage which was placed in the courtyard; he forbade anyone to open the cage door on pain of death,
and the queen had to take charge of the key herself. From now
on anyone could go safely into the forest.

The king had an eight-year-old son who was playing in the
yard one day, and as he was playing his golden ball fell into the
cage. He ran up to it and said: 'Give me my ball.' 'No,'
answered the man, 'not till you have opened this door.' 'No,'
said the boy, 'I won't do that, the king said we mustn't,' and he
ran away. On the next day he came again and asked for his ball,
and the wild man said: 'Open my door,' but the little boy
refused. On the third day the king had gone hunting, and the
boy came back again and said: 'I can't open your door even if I
wanted to, because I haven't got the key.' The wild man replied:
'It's under your mother's pillow, you can go there and fetch it.'
The little boy wanted to have his ball back, so he threw all
scruple to the winds and fetched the key. The door was hard to
open and he nipped his finger in it. When it was open the wild
man came out, gave him the golden ball and ran away. The little
boy was scared now, and ran after him crying out: 'Oh, wild
man, don't go away, or I'll get a beating!' The wild man turned
round, picked him up, hoisted him on to his shoulders and
went striding off into the forest. When the king got home he
noticed the empty cage and asked the queen how this had
happened. She knew nothing about it and looked for the key,
but it was gone. She called her son but no one answered. The
king sent out servants to search the countryside for him, but
they didn't find him. It could easily be guessed what had
happened and the whole court was grief-stricken.

When the wild man had got back into the dark forest, he put
the boy down and said to him: 'You will not see your father or
mother again; but you may stay with me, because you freed me
and I feel sorry for you. If you do everything I tell you, it shall go
well with you. I have plenty of gold and other treasures, in fact
more than anyone in the world.' The boy went to sleep on a bed
of moss the man made for him and next morning the man took
him to a spring and said: 'You see, this golden spring is as clear
and transparent as crystal. I want you to sit beside it and make

sure nothing falls into it, because then it would be defiled. Every evening I will come and see whether you have obeyed my orders.' The boy sat down at the edge of the spring; sometimes he saw a golden fish in the water and sometimes a golden snake, and he took care to let nothing drop into it. As he was sitting there his finger suddenly began hurting so much that he dipped it into the water without thinking what he was doing; he quickly drew it out again, but saw that it had turned golden all over, and however hard he tried to wipe the gold off, it was all in vain. That evening Jack of Iron came back, looked at the boy and asked: 'What has happened to the spring?' 'Nothing, nothing,' he answered, keeping his finger behind his back so that it wouldn't be seen. But the man said: 'You dipped your finger in the water. This time it doesn't matter, but take care not to let anything drop in again.' Early next morning he was already sitting by the spring keeping watch over it. His finger hurt him again and he rubbed it on his head, and unluckily one of his hairs fell into the spring. He pulled it out again quickly but it was all golden already. Jack of Iron came back and knew at once what had happened. 'You dropped a hair into the spring,' he said. 'I will let it pass once more, but if it happens a third time, then the spring will be defiled and you can no longer stay with me.' On the third day the boy sat by the spring and didn't move his finger however much it hurt. But he grew bored and began gazing at the reflection of his own face in the water. And as he leant down further and further, trying to look right into his own eyes, his long hair fell from his shoulders into the water. He straightened himself up again quickly, but all the hair on his head was golden already and shining like sunlight. You may imagine how scared the poor boy was. He took his hand-kerchief and tied it round his head so that the man wouldn't see it. But when he returned he knew everything at once, and said: 'Untie the cloth.' Then the golden hair came rolling out from under it, and try as he would to excuse himself, it was no good. 'You have failed the test and can remain here no longer. Go out into the world, you will learn there what poverty is like. But because you have a good heart and I mean well by you, I will allow you one thing: if you are ever in trouble, go to the forest and call out "Jack of Iron!" and then I will come and help you. My power is great, greater than you imagine, and I have more gold and silver than I need.'

So the prince left the forest and travelled on along highways and byways, till at last he reached a great city. There he looked for work but couldn't find any; he had learnt no skill or trade he could have lived by. Finally he went to the palace and asked if they would keep him. The courtiers had no idea how they were to employ him, but they liked him and told him he could stay. In the end the cook gave him work, telling him to fetch wood and water and sweep out the ashes. One day, when there happened to be no one else available, the cook told him to carry the food to the royal table; but because he didn't want his golden hair seen, he kept on his hat. The king had never seen this happen before, and he said: 'When you come to serve at the royal table, you must take your hat off.' 'Oh, sir,' he answered, 'I can't do that, I've got terrible scurf on my head.' At this the king sent for the cook and scolded him, asking how he could ever have given employment to such a boy, and telling him to get rid of him at once. But the cook was sorry for him and exchanged him for the gardener's boy.

So now the young lad had to work in the garden in all weathers, planting and watering and digging and hoeing. One summer day when he was alone there, it was so hot that he took his hat off to get some fresh air on his head. When the sun shone on his hair it glistened and flashed, and the glitter of it came through the princess's window. She jumped up to see what this was, caught sight of the boy and called out to him: 'Boy, bring me a bunch of flowers!' He quickly put on his hat, picked some wild flowers and tied them together. As he was carrying them up the steps the gardener met him and said: 'How can you take the princess a bunch of common flowers like that? Go at once and fetch different ones, the finest and rarest you can find.' 'Oh no,' answered the boy, 'wild flowers have a stronger fragrance and she'll like them better.' When he got to her room the princess said: 'Take off your hat, it's improper for you to keep your head covered in my presence.' And again he answered: 'I can't, I have scurf all over my head.' But she snatched at his hat and pulled it off; and out tumbled his golden hair, right down to his shoulders, looking very splendid. He tried to run away, but she caught hold of his arm and gave him a handful of ducats. He went off with them, but since he cared nothing for gold he took them to the gardener and said: 'Here's a present for your children, they can play with these.' Next day the princess called out to him again, asking him to bring her a bunch of wild flowers, and when he came in with them she snatched at his hat straight away and tried to take it off, but he held on to it with both hands. She gave him another handful of ducats, but he had no wish to keep them and gave them to the gardener as toys for his children. On the third day the same thing happened; she couldn't pull off his hat, and he wouldn't take her gold.

Not long after this the whole country was at war. The king assembled his troops, not knowing whether he would be able to resist the enemy army, which far outnumbered his own. Then the gardener's boy said: 'I'm grown up now and want to fight in the war, so give me a horse.' The others laughed and said: 'Look for one when we've left; we'll leave one behind for you in the stable.' When they had set out he went to the stable and fetched the horse; it was lame in one foot and went hobbledy-clop, hobbledy-clop. But he mounted it and rode off towards the dark forest. When he had reached the edge of it he called out: 'Jack of Iron!' three times, shouting so loudly that his voice echoed through the trees. After a moment the wild man appeared and said: 'What is your request?' 'I request a strong steed, for I want to go to war.' 'You shall have it, and you shall have more than you have asked for.' Then the wild man went back into the forest, and before very long a groom came out leading a charger that snorted and neighed and was almost untameable, and behind him followed a great host of fighting men, all in armour, and their swords flashed in the sun. The young man gave the groom his three-legged nag, mounted the warhorse and rode off at the head of his army. By the time he got near the battlefield, many of the king's men had already fallen and the rest were on the point of being routed. Then the young man galloped up with his iron-clad troops, charged in among the enemy like a thunderstorm and struck down everyone who resisted him. They took to flight, but the young man pressed hard behind them and fought on till not one of them was left alive. But instead of going back to the king, he led his troops by a round-about way back to the forest and called Jack of Iron. 'What is your request?' asked the wild man. 'Take back your warhorse and your fighting men and give me my three-legged nag.' Everything was done as he requested, and he took his three-legged nag and rode home. When the king returned to his palace, his daughter came to meet him and congratulated him on his victory. 'It wasn't I who won the victory,' he said, 'but a strange knight who came with his army to help me.' His daughter wanted to know who the strange knight was, but the king had no idea and said: 'He went in pursuit of the enemy, and I didn't see him again.' She asked the gardener where his boy was, but he laughed and said: 'He's just arrived back on his three-legged nag; the others have been making fun of him and calling out: "Here comes old hobbledy-clop." And they asked him: "Where have you been all this time? Sleeping under some hedge, no doubt." But he said: "I did better than anyone else, and things would have gone badly but for me." And they laughed at him all the more for that.'

The king said to his daughter: 'I will have a great feast announced, a feast lasting three days, and you shall toss a golden apple; perhaps the stranger will turn up.' When the feast had been announced, the young man went out to the forest and called Jack of Iron. 'What is your request?' he asked. 'I want to catch the princess's golden apple.' 'You as good as have it already,' said Jack of Iron, 'and you shall have red armour as well and ride on a fine chestnut horse.' On the appointed day the young man galloped up and joined the other knights, and no one recognized him. The princess came out and tossed a golden apple to the knights, but he was the only one who caught it; and yet as soon as he had it he galloped away. On the second day Jack of Iron had fitted him out as a knight in white armour and given him a grey horse to ride. Again he was the only one to catch the apple, but he didn't stop an instant and galloped away with it. The king was angry and said: 'He can't behave like this, he is to present himself to me and tell me his name.' He gave orders that if the knight who caught the apple rode away again he was to be pursued, and if he didn't come back willingly they were to attack him with their swords. On the third day he got from Jack of Iron a suit of black armour and a black mount, and sure enough he caught the apple again. But as he was galloping away with it the king's servants pursued him, and one of them got close enough to wound him in the leg with the point of his sword. He escaped them nevertheless, but his horse reared so mightily that his helmet fell from his head, and they could see that he had golden hair. They rode back and reported everything to the king.

On the following day the princess asked the gardener where his boy was. 'He's working in the garden; what a strange fellow he is! He went to the feast, too, and only got back last night; he even showed my children three golden apples he had won.' The king had him summoned to his presence, and he appeared, with his hat still on his head. But the princess went up to him and took it off, and then his golden hair fell over his shoulders, and everyone wondered at his beauty. 'Are you the knight who came to the feast every day wearing different colours and caught the three golden apples?' asked the king. 'Yes,' he answered, 'and here are the apples.' And he took them out of his pocket and handed them to the king. 'If you desire further proof, sir, you can see the wound I got from your men when they were pursuing me. But I am also the knight who helped you to defeat your enemies.' 'If you can do deeds like these, then you are no gardener's boy: tell me, who is your father?' 'My father is a powerful king, and I have gold in abundance and as much of it as I want.' 'I can very well see that I have much to thank you for,' said the king. 'Is there anything I can do for you?' 'Yes,' he answered, 'there is indeed, sir: give me your daughter in marriage.' At this the maiden laughed, and said: 'He doesn't waste words, does he! But I saw from his golden hair, anyway, that he was no gardener's boy.' And she went to him and kissed him. His father and mother came to the wedding and were overjoyed, for they had already given up all hope of seeing their beloved son again. And as they were sitting at the wedding banquet, the music suddenly stopped, the door swung open and a proud king entered with a great retinue. He went up to the young man, embraced him and said: 'I am Jack of Iron. I was under a spell that changed me into a wild man, but you have released me from it. All the treasures I possess shall be yours.'

38

THE FROG KING, OR IRON HARRY

In the old days, when wishing still worked, there lived a king, and his daughters were all beautiful; but the youngest was so beautiful that the sun itself, although it had seen so many things, wondered whenever it shone into her face. Near the king's palace was a big dark forest, and in the forest under an old linden tree was a well; so when it was a very hot day the princess used to go out into the forest and sit down at the edge of the cool well – and when she was bored she would take a golden ball and throw it into the air and catch it again; and this was her favourite toy.

Now it happened one day that when the princess held out her little hand to catch her golden ball, it did not fall into it but bounced past it onto the ground and rolled right into the water. The princess stared after it but the ball vanished, and the well was deep, so deep that no one could see the bottom. At this she began to cry and cried louder and louder and was quite inconsolable. And as she wailed she heard a voice call out to her: 'Now, princess, what are you howling about? It's enough to make a stone take pity on you.' She looked round to see where the voice was coming from and saw a frog sticking its fat ugly head out of the water. 'Oh, it's you, old puddlefoot,' she said. 'I'm crying for my golden ball, it's fallen down into the well.' 'Be quiet and don't cry,' answered the frog, 'I think I can do something about it; but what will you give me if I fetch up your toy for you again?' 'Whatever you want, dear frog,' she said, 'my dresses, my pearls and jewels, even the golden crown I wear.' The frog answered: 'I don't want your dresses, your pearls and jewels and your golden crown – but if you will love me and let me be your companion and playmate, sitting by you at your table, eating from your golden plate, drinking from your cup, sleeping in your bed; if you will promise me that, then I will go down and fetch up your golden ball for you again.' 'Oh yes,' she said, 'I'll promise you anything you like if only you'll bring me back the ball.' But she thought: What nonsense this silly frog is talking! It sits in the water and croaks with the other frogs, how can it ever have a human companion?

As soon as the frog had her promise he stuck his head in the water and dived down, and before long he came swimming up again with the ball in his mouth and threw it onto the grass. The princess was overjoyed when she saw her beautiful toy again, and she picked it up and ran away with it. 'Whoa, whoa!' cried the frog. 'Take me with you, I can't run so fast as you!' But he might shout his quaw, quaw as loud as he could, much good it did him. She paid no attention, hurried back home and had soon forgotten the poor frog, who had to go back down into his well.

Next day, when she had seated herself at table with the king and all the courtiers and was eating from her little golden plate, something came plish-plash plish-plash crawling up the marble stairs, and when it had got to the top it knocked at the door and called out: 'Princess, youngest daughter, let me in!' She ran to see who was there, but when she opened the door there sat the frog. She slammed it shut and sat down again at the table feeling very frightened. The king saw clearly enough that her heart was beating fast, and said: 'Why are you scared, child, is there a giant or something at the door who has come to fetch you?' 'Oh no,' she answered, 'it's not a giant but a horrid frog.' 'What does the frog want of you?' 'Oh, father dear, yesterday when I was sitting playing beside the well in the wood, my golden ball fell into the water. And because I cried so, the frog fetched it up again, and because it absolutely insisted I promised it to let it be my companion; but I never thought it would be able to leave the water where it lives. Now it's out there and wants me to let it in.' And already there was a second knock and the voice said:

> 'Princess, youngest daughter,
> Let me in!
> Have you forgotten
> Your promise of yesterday

By the well's cool water?
Princess, youngest daughter,
Let me in!'

Then the king said: 'When you have made a promise, you must keep it; so go and let him in.' She went and opened the door, and the frog hopped in and followed her close at her heels and up to her chair. There he squatted and called out: 'Pick me up and put me beside you.' She hesitated, till finally the king ordered her to do it. Once the frog was on the chair he wanted to be on the table, and when he was on it he said: 'Now push your golden plate nearer, so we can eat together.' And although she did it, you could see that she didn't like to. The frog ate heartily, but she could hardly swallow a morsel. Finally he said: 'I've eaten my fill and I'm tired; now carry me to your bedroom and make your little silk bed, and then we shall lie down and sleep.' The princess began to cry; she was afraid of the cold frog which she didn't even dare touch, and now it was to sleep in her lovely clean bed. But the king grew angry and said: 'When someone has helped you out of trouble, you must not despise him afterwards.' So she took the frog between her finger and thumb, carried him upstairs and put him in a corner. But when she was in bed he came crawling up and said: 'I'm tired, I want to sleep as well as you – lift me up, or I'll tell your father.' At this she really got furious, picked him up and hurled him against the wall as hard as she could, saying: 'Now you'll sleep, you horrid frog.'

But when he dropped to the floor he was no longer a frog, but a prince with beautiful soft eyes; and he, at her father's wish, became her dear companion and husband. He told her that a wicked witch had put a spell on him, and that no one had been able to save him from the well until she came, and tomorrow they would travel together to his kingdom. Then they went to sleep, and when the sun woke them next morning a carriage came driving up: it had eight white horses in harness, with white ostrich plumes and golden chains, and behind them stood the young king's servant, who was known as Faithful Harry. Faithful Harry had been so sad when his master had been turned into a frog that he had had three iron bands put round his heart to stop it bursting with grief and sorrow. But the carriage had come to fetch the young king home; Faithful Harry lifted both of them into it, stood up again in his place and was full of joy that his master had been saved. And when they had driven a little way, the prince heard a crack behind him as of something breaking. He turned round and called out:

> 'Harry, the carriage
> Is falling apart.'
> 'No, sir, from my heart
> An iron band fell;
> For my heart grieved sore
> When you were a puddock
> And sat in a well.'

A second time and a third time there was a crack as they drove along, and each time the prince thought the carriage was breaking, yet it was only the bands bursting round Faithful Harry's heart because his master was saved and happy.

39

THE YOUNG DONKEY

Once upon a time there was a king and a queen who were rich
and had all they wanted except that they had no children. The
queen bewailed this day and night, saying: 'I am like a field on
which nothing grows.' At last God granted her wish, but when
the baby was born it didn't look like a human child: it was a little
donkey foal. When its mother saw this she began to weep and
wail all the more, saying she would rather have had no child at
all than a donkey, and telling the servants to throw it in the river
for the fish to eat. But the king said: 'No; since God has given it
to us it shall be my son and heir, and he shall sit on the royal
throne after my death and wear the royal crown.' So the baby
donkey was reared and grew up, and his ears grew up nice and
straight too. But he was a merry little creature, jumping about
and playing, and in particular he was very fond of music; so he
went to a famous minstrel and said: 'Teach me your skill and
make me able to play the lute as well as you.' 'Oh, my dear little
sir,' answered the minstrel, 'I think you would find that difficult: after all, sir, your fingers are not the right shape, they are
much too big, and I'm afraid they'd break the strings.' But the
donkey wouldn't take no for an answer – play the lute he would
and he must; he was patient and worked hard, and learnt in the
end to play as well as his master. One day the young gentleman
was pensively taking a walk and came to a spring, and looking
into its clear bright water he saw he was shaped like a donkey.
This upset him so much that he set off into the world, taking
only one faithful companion with him. They wandered hither
and thither: finally they reached a kingdom ruled by an old king
who had only one daughter, but she was of great beauty. 'We'll
stay here,' said the donkey. So he knocked at the gate and called
out: 'A guest has come; open up and let him in.' But when they
didn't open the gate he sat down, took his lute and played
enchanting music on it with his two forefeet. At this the

gatekeeper opened his eyes very wide, and ran to the king and said: 'There's a young donkey sitting outside the gate, playing the lute like a past master.' 'Well, bring the musician in to see me,' said the king. But when the minstrel donkey trotted in, they all burst out laughing at him. They were going to put him downstairs to eat with the servants, but this angered him and he said: 'I'm no ordinary ass from any old stable, I'm of noble birth.' So they said: 'If that's so, then you can sit among the soldiers.' 'No,' he said, 'I want to sit beside the king.' The king laughed and said good-humouredly: 'Very well, it shall be as you wish, my young donkey; come and sit beside me.' Then he asked: 'My good young ass, how do you like my daughter?' The donkey turned his head and looked at her, then nodded and said: 'Very well indeed, she is more beautiful than any girl I have seen.' 'Well, then you shall sit next to her,' said the king. 'That suits me,' said the donkey, and he sat by her side and ate and drank and showed very good clean table-manners. When the noble little beast had spent some time at the king's court, he thought: What's the use, I must just go home again. And he hung his head sadly, went to the king and asked to take his leave. But the king had become fond of him and said: 'My dear donkey, what's the matter? You look as sour as a jar of vinegar. Stay with me and I'll give you whatever you want. Do you want gold?' 'No,' said the donkey and shook his head. 'Do you want jewellery and precious things?' 'No.' 'Do you want half of my kingdom?' 'Oh no.' Then the king said: 'If only I knew what would content you! Would you like to marry my beautiful daughter?' 'Oh yes,' said the donkey, 'that indeed I would like.' And suddenly he was merry and in good spirits, for this was exactly what he had been longing for. So a great wedding feast was held. That evening, when the bride and bridegroom were in their bedchamber, the king wanted to find out whether the donkey would behave in a gentle and well-bred manner and he ordered a servant to hide in the room. So when they had both entered the bridegroom bolted the door, looked about him and, thinking that they were all by themselves, suddenly cast off his donkey skin, and there he stood in the form of a handsome young prince. 'Now you see who I am,' he said to his bride, 'and as you see, I was not unworthy of you.' Then she was glad and kissed him and loved him with all her heart. But when morning came he jumped out of bed, put on his animal skin again, and no one would ever have guessed what its real wearer looked like. And presently along came the old king. 'My word, the donkey's up and about already!' he exclaimed, and said to his daughter: 'I suppose you're very sad not to have married a proper man?' 'Oh no, father dear, I love him as if he were the handsomest of men, and I want to live with him all my life.' The king was astonished, but the servant who had hidden in the bedroom came and told him everything. The king said: 'That can't possibly be true.' 'Then keep watch tomorrow night yourself, sir, you will see it with your own eyes. And, my lord, let me tell you something: take away his skin and throw it into the fire, and then I think he will have to show himself in his true shape.' 'Your advice is good,' said the king. And that night, when they were asleep, he crept into the room, went over to the bed, and there in the moonlight lay a fine young man, with the cast-off skin on the floor beside him. So he took it away and had a blazing fire lit and the skin thrown into it, and stayed there himself until it was completely burnt to ashes. But he wanted to see what the young man would do now that he had lost his skin, so he stayed awake for the rest of the night and listened at the door. At daybreak, when the young man had slept his fill, he got up and was going to put on his donkey skin, but it was nowhere to be found. At this he took fright and said in great sorrow and alarm: 'Now I must make good my escape.' But when he opened the door the king was standing there and said to him: 'My son, what are you thinking of, where are you off to in such a hurry? Stay here! You are such a fine-looking man that I won't let you leave me again. I'll give you half my kingdom now, and after my death you'll get the whole of it.' 'Then I wish,' said the young prince, 'that all may end as well as it has begun; I will stay with you, sir.' So the old man gave him half the kingdom and when he died a year later the prince got the rest, and another one in addition after the death of his own father; and so he lived happy and glorious.

40

JACK MY HEDGEHOG

Once upon a time there was a farmer who had plenty of money and property, but rich as he was he still lacked one thing to be happy: he and his wife had no children. Often enough when he was travelling into town with the other country folk, they would make fun of him and ask him why he was childless. In the end this made him angry, and when he got home he said: 'I'll have a child, even if it's only a hedgehog.' After this his wife did have a child, and the top half of it was a hedgehog and the bottom half a boy; and when she saw this child she was frightened and said: 'Look what you've done, you've bewitched us!' 'Well,' said her husband, 'it can't be helped, and the boy must be christened, though we can't ask anyone to be his godfather.' His wife said: 'There's only one name we can give him, too, and that's Jack my Hedgehog.' When he had christened him the priest said: 'You won't be able to put this prickly fellow in a proper bed.' So they arranged some straw behind the stove and put Jack my Hedgehog there. He couldn't drink his mother's milk either, because he'd have pricked her with his quills. So there he lay behind the stove for eight years, and his father was sick of him and wished he would just die: but he didn't die, he just went on lying there. Now one day it happened to be market day in the town and the farmer wanted to go to market, so he asked his wife what she would like him to bring her. 'A little meat and some bread,' she said, 'something for the house-keeping.' Then he asked the maid, and she wanted a pair of slippers and clock-stockings. And lastly he asked: 'Well, Jack my Hedgehog, what would you like?' 'Father dear,' he replied, 'please bring me a set of bagpipes.' So when the farmer came home again he gave his wife what he had bought for her, meat and bread-rolls, then he gave the maid her slippers and clock-stockings, and lastly he went behind the stove and gave Jack my Hedgehog his bagpipes. And when Jack my Hedgehog had the bagpipes he said: 'Father dear, please go to the blacksmith and get him to put shoes on my cock-horse; then I'll ride off on it and never come back.' His father was glad to hear he would be rid of him and had the rooster shod. When it was ready Jack my Hedgehog mounted it and rode off, taking some pigs and donkeys with him to look after them out in the forest. When he got to the forest, he made the rooster fly him up to the top of a tall tree; there he sat looking after the donkeys and pigs, and he sat there for many years until his herd had grown quite big, and never a word his father had of him. But as he sat on the tree he played his bagpipes, and very fine music it was. One day a king who had lost his way came riding by and heard the music. In astonishment he sent his servant to look round and find out where it was coming from. The servant looked round, but all he saw was a small animal sitting at the top of the tree: it looked like a cock with a hedgehog on its back, and this was what was making the music. So the king told his servant to ask it why it was sitting there and whether it could tell him the way to his kingdom. So Jack my Hedgehog came down from the tree and said he would show the king the way if he would write out a contract promising to give him the first living creature he met when he set foot again in the palace courtyard. The king thought: I may as well do so; after all, Jack my Hedgehog won't understand a word of it and I can write what I like. So he took pen and ink and scribbled something down, after which Jack my Hedgehog showed him the way and he reached home safely. But his daughter saw him when he was still some way off and was so overjoyed that she ran out to meet him and kissed him. Then the king remembered Jack my Hedgehog and told her what had happened: how he had had to make a contract with a strange animal to give it whoever he would first meet when he got home, and how the animal had been mounted on a cock as if it were a horse, playing beautiful music. But actually he had written down that the creature was not to have what it wanted, for after all Jack my Hedgehog couldn't read. The princess was glad to hear this and said it was a good thing he had done so, because she would never have gone to the creature anyway.

But Jack my Hedgehog went on looking after his donkeys and pigs, and remained in a good humour, sitting there on the tree and playing his bagpipes. Now it happened that another king came riding by with his servants and footmen, and he too had lost his way and didn't know how to get home again because the forest was so big. So he too heard the fine music from some way off, and said to one of his footmen: 'I wonder what that is; go and have a look.' The footman went to the tree and saw the rooster perched at the top with Jack my Hedgehog on its back, and asked him what he was doing up there. 'I'm looking after my donkeys and pigs; but what might you be wanting, sir?' The footman explained that they were lost and couldn't get back to their kingdom; perhaps he would kindly show them the way. So Jack my Hedgehog came down from the tree with his cock and told the old king that he would show him the way if he would hand over to him the first living thing he met outside his palace. The king agreed, and signed a contract with Jack my Hedgehog promising him this. Then Jack my Hedgehog rode ahead on his cock-horse and showed him the way, and the king got safely back to his kingdom. As he arrived at the palace there was great rejoicing. Now he had an only daughter who was very beautiful, and she came running to meet him, fell on his neck and kissed him, overjoyed that her old father had come home. She also asked him where in the world he had been for so long, and he told her he had lost his way and might never have got home at all; but that as he had been riding through a great forest there had been a fellow, half like a hedgehog and half like a man, sitting astride a cock on a tall tree and playing beautiful music. This creature had helped him on his way and set him right, but in return he had promised it the first living thing he would meet on reaching the palace, and that meant her, and now he was very sorry about it. But she promised him that for her old father's sake she would gladly go with the creature when it came to claim her.

But Jack my Hedgehog went on keeping his pigs, and the pigs had more pigs, till there were so many of them they filled the entire forest. Then Jack my Hedgehog decided he had lived in the forest long enough, and sent word to his father that all the

pig-sties in the village must be cleared out, because he was
coming with so big a herd that everyone who wanted to slaughter could start slaughtering. His father was dismayed to hear
this, for he thought Jack my Hedgehog had died long ago. But
Jack my Hedgehog mounted his cock, drove the pigs into the
village and had them slaughtered; wow, what a hacking and a
cutting of throats there was! You could hear it two leagues
away. When it was finished Jack my Hedgehog said: 'Father
dear, get the blacksmith to shoe my cock-horse once more and
I'll ride away and never come back again in my life.' So his
father had the rooster shod, and was glad that Jack my Hedgehog would be gone for good.

Jack my Hedgehog rode off to the first kingdom. Here the
king had given orders that if anyone turned up carrying bagpipes and riding on a cock, they were all to shoot and hack and
stab at him and stop him entering the palace. So when Jack my
Hedgehog came riding up they attacked him with their
bayonets, but he dug his spurs into the cock and flew right up
over the gate on to the king's window sill. There he perched and
called out to the king to give him what he had promised;
otherwise he would kill both him and his daughter. So the king
begged his daughter to go out to Jack my Hedgehog and save
his life and her own. So she dressed all in white, and her father
gave her a coach and six and a fine retinue of servants and a lot
of money and treasures. She stepped into the coach, and Jack
my Hedgehog with his cock and his bagpipes sat beside her,
and they said goodbye and off they drove. The king thought he
would never see her again, but here he was wrong: for when
they were a little way out of the town, Jack my Hedgehog took
off her fine clothes and rolled on her with his prickles till she
was all bloody. Then he said: 'That's to pay you out for your
treachery; off you go, I don't want you.' So saying, he chased
her back home, and she was disgraced for the rest of her life.

But Jack my Hedgehog, with his cock and his bagpipes, rode
on to the second kingdom, the one whose king he had also
helped on his way. Now here the king's orders were that if
anyone like Jack my Hedgehog should turn up, the soldiers
were to present arms and he was to be cheered and escorted in

and brought to the royal palace. When the princess saw him she took fright, for he really was a strange-looking creature; but then she reflected that there was nothing to be done, for she had made her promise to her father. So she welcomed Jack my Hedgehog and he was married to her. He had to sit down at the royal table, and she sat beside him and they ate and drank together. At nightfall, when it was time for them to go to bed, she was terribly afraid because of his prickles, but he told her not to be afraid and said no harm would come to her. And he told the old king to order four men to keep watch outside the bedroom door and to light a big fire: when he entered the room to go to bed he would crawl out of his hedgehog's skin and leave it lying by the bedside, at which point the men must rush in, throw it into the fire and stay there till it was all burnt up. So when the clock struck eleven he entered the bedroom, pulled off his hedgehog's skin and dropped it at the bedside. The men rushed in, snatched it from the floor and threw it into the fire; and when the fire had burnt it up, he was released from the spell. There he lay on the bed, properly shaped like a man, but coal-black as if he had been burnt. The king sent for his doctor, who rubbed him clean with precious salves and ointment; so now his skin turned white and he was a handsome young gentleman. When the princess saw this she was delighted, and next morning they got up very happily and ate and drank together, and then they had a real wedding celebration and the old king gave his kingdom to Jack my Hedgehog.

When a few years had passed, he went with his wife to visit his father and told him he was his son. His father said he had no son, he had only had one child but it had been born with prickles like a hedgehog and had gone away. Then he explained the truth, and his old father was glad and went back with him to his kingdom.

> My tale is done;
> Go next door if you want a better one.

41

THE MAGIC TABLE, THE GOLD-DONKEY, AND THE CUDGEL IN THE SACK

Long ago there was a tailor who had three sons and only one goat. But the goat gave milk for all four of them, so it had to be well fed and taken out to graze every day. The sons did this turn about. One day the eldest son took her to the churchyard, where the best greenery grew, and let her graze and jump around there. In the evening, when it was time to go home, he asked her: 'Goat, have you had enough to eat?' And the goat answered:

> 'I've had enough,
> I'm full of the stuff, bah! bah!'

'Come along home then,' said the boy, and he took her by the halter, led her back to her shed and tied her up. 'Well,' said the old tailor, 'has the goat been properly fed?' 'Oh,' said his son, 'she's had enough, she's full of the stuff.' But his father wanted to make sure for himself, so he went down to the shed, stroked the precious animal and asked: 'Goat, are you sure you've had enough to eat?' The goat answered:

> 'What do you mean?
> I've been jumping around
> Over stones in the ground:
> Not a leaf or a blade to be seen, bah! bah!'

'What's this I hear!' cried the tailor, and he ran back up and said to the boy: 'Why, you liar, you tell me the goat's had enough to eat but you've let her starve!' And in his rage he took his yardstick from the wall and beat his son out of the house.

Next day it was the second son's turn: he chose a place by the garden hedge where there was nothing but good fresh greenery, and the goat cropped it right down to the ground. In the evening, before going home, he asked: 'Goat, have you had enough to eat?'

And the goat answered:

'I've had enough,
I'm full of the stuff, bah! bah!'

'Come along home then,' said the boy, and he led her home and tied her up in her shed. 'Well,' said the old tailor, 'has the goat been properly fed?' 'Oh,' said his son, 'she's had enough, she's full of the stuff.' That wasn't good enough for the tailor, who went down to the shed and asked: 'Goat, are you sure you've had enough to eat?' The goat answered:

'What do you mean?
I've been jumping around
Over stones in the ground:
Not a leaf or a blade to be seen, bah! bah!'

'The heartless wretch,' yelled the tailor, 'to let such a good gentle animal starve!' And he ran up and took his yardstick to the boy and drove him out of the house.

Now it was the third son's turn, and he was determined to do the thing properly: he chose a place with fine leafy bushes and let the goat nibble at them. In the evening, before going home, he asked: 'Goat, are you sure you've had enough?' The goat answered:

'I've had enough,
I'm full of the stuff, bah! bah!'

'Come along home then,' said the boy, and he took her to the shed and tied her up. 'Well?' asked the old tailor, 'has the goat been properly fed?' 'Oh,' said his son, 'she's had enough, she's full of the stuff.' The tailor didn't trust him, but went down and asked: 'Goat, are you sure you've had enough to eat?' And the wicked beast replied:

> 'What do you mean?
> I've been jumping around
> Over stones in the ground:
> Not a leaf or a blade to be seen, bah! bah!'

'Oh, you pack of liars!' shouted the tailor, 'every one of you godless and undutiful! You'll not make a fool of me any longer!' And quite beside himself with rage he rushed up and so mightily tanned the poor boy's back with the yardstick that he fled out of the house.

So now the old tailor was alone with his goat. Next morning he went down to the shed, caressed the goat and said: 'Come along, my little pet, I'll take you out to graze myself.' He took her by the halter and led her to where there were green hedges and milfoil and all the other things goats like eating. 'Look, here you can eat your fill for once,' he said to her and let her graze till evening. Then he asked: 'Goat, have you had enough to eat?' And she answered:

> 'I've had enough,
> I'm full of the stuff, bah! bah!'

'Come along home then,' said the tailor, and he led her to the shed and tied her up. As he was leaving her he turned round once more and said: 'Now for once you've really had enough to eat.' But he fared no better with the goat than his sons had done, for she bleated out:

> 'What do you mean?
> I've been jumping around
> Over stones in the ground:
> Not a leaf or a blade to be seen, bah! bah!'

When the tailor heard that, he was very much taken aback and realized that he'd turned out his three sons without just cause. 'Just you wait,' he shouted, 'you ungrateful creature! Being driven out of doors is too good for you; I'll make a mark on you that'll stop you showing your face again among respectable tailor-folk.' He rushed back upstairs, seized his razor, lathered the goat's head and shaved it as smooth as the palm of his hand. And as the yardstick would have been too honourable a weapon, he fetched his whip and so belaboured her with it that she went bounding away for dear life.

So the tailor was now all by himself in his house, and he fell into a great sadness and would gladly have had his sons back again, but no one knew where they had got to. The eldest had apprenticed himself to a joiner; he was hard-working and diligent, and when his apprenticeship ended and it was time for him to go on his travels, his master gave him a little table. It looked in no way unusual and was of ordinary wood, but there was one good thing about it. If one placed it in front of one and said: 'Table, be laid!' this excellent little table would at once cover itself with a clean tablecloth, and there would be a plate, with a knife and fork beside it, and as many dishes of roast and stewed meat as there was room for, and a fine big glass of red wine gleaming to warm your heart. The young journeyman thought to himself: Now you've got enough for a lifetime; and he travelled round the world in high spirits, not bothering whether any inn he came to was good or bad or whether you could get a decent meal there or not. Sometimes, if he felt like it, he didn't stop at an inn at all, but out in the open, in the woods, on a field or wherever he pleased, he would take the table from his back, put it down in front of him and say: 'Be laid!' and at once he had all the food he could want. Finally it occurred to him to go back home to his father, thinking: He'll not still be angry with me after all this time, and with my magic table he's sure to give me a good welcome. It happened that on his way home one evening he came to an inn that was full of guests: they welcomed him and invited him to sit down and eat with them, saying that otherwise there wasn't likely to be any food left for him. 'No,' answered the joiner, 'I won't take from you the few morsels you've got; you shall be my guests instead.' They laughed and thought he was playing a joke on them. But he put down his little wooden table in the middle of the room and said: 'Table, be laid!' Immediately it was covered with better food than the landlord could ever have provided, and the smell of it fairly tickled the guests' nostrils. 'Help yourselves, my friends,' said the joiner to the guests, and when they saw how things were they didn't wait for a second invitation, but moved up their chairs, pulled out their knives and set to with a will. And the thing that amazed them most was that as soon as one dish was empty another full one took its place at once. The landlord stood in a corner and watched what was happening; he didn't know what to say, but he thought: I could do with a cook like that in my inn. The joiner and his party made merry until late into the night, then finally they went to bed, and the young journeyman lay down to sleep as well, placing his wish-table against the wall. But the landlord's thoughts gave him no peace. He remembered that in his attic he had an old table that looked exactly like this one, so very quietly he fetched it and substituted it for the wish-table. Next morning the joiner paid for his night's lodging, hoisted the table on to his back, never thinking for a moment that he had the wrong one, and went on his way. At midday he arrived home, and his father was over-joyed to see him. 'Well, my dear son, what have you learnt?' he asked him. 'Father, I've become a joiner.' 'That's a good trade,' replied the old man, 'but what have you brought back from your travels with you?' 'Father, the best thing I've brought with me is this little table.' The tailor examined it from all sides and said: 'Well, you've made no masterpiece there, it's just a shabby old table.' 'But it's a magic table,' replied his son. 'When I put it down in front of me and tell it to lay itself, the finest dishes appear on it at once and a wine to go with them and gladden your heart. Just invite all our friends and relations and let's give them a real treat: on that table they can eat and drink their fill.' When the guests had all come, he put his little table in the middle of the room and said: 'Table, be laid!' But the table did nothing and stayed just as bare as any other table that doesn't understand when it's spoken to. At this the poor journeyman realized that another table had been substituted for his, and there he stood, ashamed that everyone should be thinking him a liar. His relations had a good laugh at his expense and had to go home again as hungry and thirsty as before. His father fetched out his pieces of cloth again and went on tailoring, and the young man himself went to work for a master joiner.

The second son had arrived at a mill and apprenticed himself to the miller. When he had finished his time his master said to him: 'Because you've worked so well, I'm going to give you a donkey, and he's rather special; he doesn't draw a cart and he won't carry sacks either.' 'What use is he then?' asked the young journeyman. 'He spits out gold,' replied the miller. 'If you stand him on a cloth and say to him "Shitsyspitsy," this admirable creature will spew out gold coins for you from both ends.' 'That's an excellent thing,' said the journeyman, and he thanked his master and set off into the world. When he needed gold all he had to do was to say 'Shitsyspitsy' to his donkey, and out would come a shower of gold pieces, and he then merely had to give himself the trouble of picking them up. Wherever he went the best was good enough for him, and the dearer the better, for his purse was always full. When he had travelled around in the world for a time, he thought: I must go and visit my father; when I come home with the gold-donkey he'll have forgotten his anger and make me welcome. It so happened that he stopped on his way at the very same inn at which his brother had had his table exchanged. He was leading his donkey, and the landlord was about to take it from him and tie it up, but the young journeyman said: 'Don't trouble yourself, landlord, I'll take this grey beast of mine to the stable myself and tie him up myself too, because I have to know where he is.' This struck the landlord as odd, and he thought that a man who had to look after his own donkey wasn't likely to have much money to spend. But when the stranger put his hand in his pocket, fetched out two gold pieces and just told him to go and buy him something good, the landlord opened his eyes very wide, and off he went and bought the best food and drink he could find. After dinner his guest asked what he owed him; the landlord thought he might as well chalk up double the price, and said he must pay another two gold pieces. The journeyman put his hand in his pocket and found that he happened to have run short of gold. 'Wait a moment, landlord, I'll just go and get some gold,' he said; but he took the tablecloth with him. The landlord couldn't think what to make of this, and was filled with curiosity; he crept along behind, and finding that his guest had bolted the stable door, peered in through a chink in the wood. The stranger spread the tablecloth under the donkey, called out 'Shitsyspitsy' and immediately the animal began to spew out gold from both ends, fairly showering it on to the ground. 'Well, bless my soul!' said the landlord. 'That's a quick way to coin ducats! I could do with a moneybag like that.' The guest paid for his dinner and went to bed, but the landlord crept down to the stable during the night, led the master coiner away and tied up another donkey in its place. Early next morning the journeyman set off with his donkey, thinking it was his own gold-donkey. At midday he reached home, and his father was very glad to see him again and welcomed him warmly. 'Well, my boy, and what have you become?' asked the old man. 'A miller, father dear,' he answered. 'What have you brought back with you from your travels?' 'Only a donkey.' 'There are plenty of donkeys here,' said his father. 'I'd have been better pleased if you'd brought a decent goat.' 'Yes,' replied his son, 'but this is no ordinary donkey, it's a gold-donkey. When I say "Shitsy-spitsy" the admirable creature lets fly a whole tableclothful of gold coins. Just you have all our relations invited round and I'll make them all rich men.' 'That would suit me,' said the tailor, 'I won't need to toil away any longer with this needle then.' And he ran round himself and invited his relations. As soon as they were all there the miller told them to make room, spread out his cloth and led in the donkey. 'Now watch this,' he said, and called out 'Shitsyspitsy!' But what fell down on the cloth wasn't a shower of gold, and it turned out that this animal didn't have that particular talent, for making money isn't something any old ass can do. At this the poor miller pulled a long face, realized that he had been tricked, and apologized to his relatives, who had to go home as poor as they had come. There was nothing to be done but for the old man to take up his needle again and for the boy to get a job with a miller.

The third brother had apprenticed himself to a turner, and because this is a skilled trade he took longest to learn it. But his brothers wrote him a letter telling him how badly they had fared and how they had both been cheated out of their fine magic gifts by the landlord on the night before they got home. So when the turner had finished his apprenticeship and was setting out to travel, his master rewarded him for his good work with a sack, telling him: 'It's got a cudgel inside it.' 'I can sling this sack over my shoulder,' said the young man, 'and it'll be very useful; but why the cudgel? It will only make it heavy to carry.' 'I'll tell you why,' answered his master. 'If anyone ever does you wrong, just say "Cudgel, come out of the sack," and the cudgel will jump out among whoever's there and dance such a merry dance on their backs that they'll not be able to stir hand or foot for a week; and it won't stop till you say "Cudgel, get back in the sack."' The journeyman thanked him, slung the sack over his shoulder, and after that if anyone didn't treat him with proper respect or tried anything on, he would say: 'Cudgel, come out of the sack.' And at once the cudgel would jump out and give their coats or their doublets a fine old dusting then and there, without waiting till they had taken them off, and it went to work so quickly that before the next man knew what was going on it was his turn already. The young turner arrived in the evening at the inn where his brothers had been tricked. He put his luggage down in front of him on the table and began to talk about all the curious things he had seen in the world. 'Yes,' he said, 'you come across things like magic tables, gold-donkeys and so on; all these are excellent and I've nothing against them, but they're not to be compared to the treasure I've found and that I've got there in my sack.' The landlord pricked up his ears and thought: What in the world can that be? That sack must be filled with precious stones. By rights I should get it as well: twice is nice but thrice is nicer. When it was time to go to bed, his guest lay down on the bench and put his sack under his head as a pillow. When the landlord thought the young man was fast asleep, he came slinking up and began shifting and tugging at the sack very gently and carefully, to try if he could pull it out and put another one in its place. But this was exactly what the turner had been waiting for, and just as the landlord was about to give a good big tug he cried: 'Cudgel, come out of the sack!' and in an instant the cudgel was out of the sack and went for the landlord and gave him a fine old dusting down. The landlord howled piteously, but the louder he howled the harder the cudgel beat time on his back, till finally he collapsed on the ground in exhaustion. Then the turner said: 'If you don't hand over the magic table and the gold-donkey, the dance will begin again.' 'Oh, no!' cried the landlord, and he was talking very meekly now. 'I'll hand over the whole lot again willingly, sir, just make that devilish thing get back into its sack.' 'I'll temper justice with mercy,' said the journeyman, 'but beware what may come to you!' Then he called out: 'Cudgel, get back in the sack!' and the cudgel had a rest.

Next morning the turner went home to his father with the magic table and the gold-donkey. The tailor was very glad to see him again, and asked him too what he had learnt while he had been away. 'Father dear,' he replied, 'I've become a turner.' 'That's a skilful trade,' said his father. 'And what have you brought back with you from your travels?' 'Something very valuable, father dear,' answered his son, 'I've brought a cudgel in a sack.' 'What!' cried his father, 'a cudgel! That's a fine reward for labour! You can hack one off the nearest tree.' 'But not one like this, father dear. When I say "Cudgel, come out of the sack," the cudgel jumps out and does a pretty effective dance on anyone who's trying to play games with me, and it doesn't stop until he's flat on the ground begging for mercy. Look, father, with this cudgel I've got back the magic table and the gold-donkey which that thief of a landlord took from my brothers. Now send for both of them and invite all our relations; I'll give them food and drink and fill their pockets with gold as well.' The old tailor was a bit doubtful, but he did get his relations to come. Then the turner put a cloth down on the floor, led in the gold-donkey and said to his brother: 'Now, my dear brother, you speak to him.' The miller said 'Shitsyspitsy,' and at once the gold pieces came raining down on the cloth like a shower-burst, and the donkey didn't stop till they all had so much that they couldn't carry any more (you look as if you wouldn't have minded being there too). Then the turner fetched the little table and said: 'Now speak to it, my dear brother.' And hardly had the joiner said: 'Table, be laid!' than it was laid and loaded with the finest dishes. And then such a feast was had as the poor tailor had never known in his house before, and the whole family were together till late at night making merry and enjoying themselves. The tailor locked away his needle and thread and yardstick and smoothing-iron in a cupboard, and lived happy and prosperous with his three sons.

But what about the goat whose fault it was that the tailor had turned his three sons out of the house? I'll tell you where she got to. She was ashamed of having a bald head, so she ran to a fox's earth and crawled into it to hide. When the fox came home he saw a great pair of eyes glowering at him out of the darkness, and he was scared and ran back out again. The bear met him, and seeing the fox looking so frantic he asked: 'What's the matter, brother fox, why are you making such faces?' 'Oh,' answered the redskin, 'there's a dreadful beast sitting in my earth, glaring at me with fiery eyes.' 'We'll soon see him out,' said the bear, and he went back to the fox's hole with him and looked in. But when he saw the fiery eyes he was scared too, decided to have nothing to do with so savage a beast and ran away. The bee met him, and when she saw that he was put out about something she said: 'Bear, that's a mightily bad-tempered face you're making, what can have upset you?' 'You may well talk,' answered the bear. 'Out there's a savage beast with glowering eyes sitting in brother fox's house, and we can't drive it out.' The bee replied: 'Poor old bear! I'm only a weak little creature you don't even bother to look at as you go by, but in fact I think I can help you.' She flew into the fox's earth, settled on the goat's smooth shorn head and gave her such a ferocious sting that she jumped up bleating: 'Bah! Bah!' and ran out into the wide world as if she were demented; and no one knows to this day where she ran to.

42

THE KNAPSACK, THE HAT AND
THE HORN

Once upon a time there were three brothers who had grown
poorer and poorer, till finally things got so bad that they were
starving and hadn't a bite or a scrap left. So they said: 'We can't
go on like this. We'd better go out into the world and seek our
fortunes.' They set out, but when they had already gone a long
way and walked over many blades of grass they still hadn't
found their fortunes. Then one day they came to a great forest,
and in the middle of it was a mountain, and when they got
closer they saw that it was a mountain entirely of silver. Then
the eldest brother said: 'Now I've found the fortune I wanted,
and I ask for no more than this.' So he took as much of the silver
as he could carry, then turned back and went home again. But
the other two said: 'We expect our fortunes to be something
more than mere silver,' and they went on without touching it.
After they had walked for another few days they came to a
mountain that was entirely of gold. The second brother stood
still and pondered and hesitated. 'What shall I do?' he said.
'Shall I take as much of this gold as I need for the rest of my life,
or shall I go on?' Finally he made up his mind, crammed as
much into his pockets as they would hold, said goodbye to his
brother and went home. But the third brother said: 'Silver and
gold mean nothing to me: I'll go on trying my luck, perhaps
there's something better in store for me.' He travelled on, and
when he had walked for three days he got to a forest that was
even bigger than the others. There seemed to be no end to it,
and as he could find nothing to eat or to drink he was nearly on
the point of starvation. Then he climbed up a tall tree to try and
get a sight of the forest's end from the top of it: but as far as his
eye could reach he saw nothing but tree-tops. So he started
climbing down the tree again, but his hunger plagued him and
he thought: If only I could just fill my stomach once more!

When he got down he saw to his astonishment a table standing under the tree, all ready laid with dishes of food that steamed in his nostrils. 'This time I've had a wish granted at the right moment,' he said, and without stopping to ask who had brought the meal and who had cooked it he went up to the table and ate with a hearty appetite till he was satisfied. When he had done he thought: It would really be a shame to leave this pretty tablecloth to get ruined in the forest. So he folded it up neatly and put it in his pocket. Then he walked on, and in the evening, when hunger began to stir again, he decided he would put his tablecloth to the test, so he spread it out and said: 'Be set with good food again.' And no sooner had the wish passed his lips than there were as many dishes sitting on it as it had room for, all filled with delicious food. 'Well,' he said, 'now I see what kitchen my food is cooked in; you'll be a greater treasure to me than mountains of silver or gold.' For he had realized that it was a magic tablecloth. But he wasn't content just to take it and sit at home with it in retirement: he preferred to go on wandering around in the world and try his luck further. One evening in a lonely forest he came across a charcoal burner, all black and dusty, burning his charcoal and with some potatoes baking on his fire, which he was going to eat for supper. 'Good evening, blackbird,' said the young man, 'how do you like being here all by yourself?' 'One day's just like the next,' replied the charcoal burner, 'and it's potatoes every evening; if you'd like some you can be my guest.' 'Thank you very much,' replied the traveller. 'I'd rather not take your supper from you; you weren't reckoning with a guest. But if you don't mind taking pot luck with me, you can be my guest instead.' 'Who's to cook for you?' asked the charcoal burner. 'I can see you've got nothing with you, and there's no one anywhere round here within two hours' walk who could give you food.' 'And yet,' answered the young man, 'you shall have as fine a dinner as you've ever tasted in your life.' So saying, he fetched out his tablecloth, spread it on the ground and said: 'Tablecloth, be laid.' And in an instant there stood dishes of roast meat and stewed meat, steaming hot as if they had just left the kitchen. The charcoal burner was amazed, but needed no second invitation: he just fell to and began shovelling bigger and bigger pieces into his black mouth. When they had done eating, the charcoal burner gave a chuckle and said: 'You know, I like that tablecloth of yours, I could do with a thing like that here in the forest where no one ever cooks anything decent for me. I'll make you a proposition. There's a soldier's knapsack hanging in the corner there: it's old of course and nothing much to look at, and yet it possesses miraculous powers. But since I don't need it any longer, I'll exchange it with you for the tablecloth.' 'First you must tell me what those miraculous powers are,' replied the young man. 'I'll tell you,' answered the charcoal burner. 'Every time you give it a slap with your hand, a corporal and six men will appear, all fully armed and equipped, and they'll do whatever you order them to do.' 'All right,' said the young man, 'if you insist, let's make that exchange.' And he gave the charcoal burner the tablecloth, took the knapsack from its hook, hung it over his back and took his leave. Before he had walked far he thought he would test his knapsack's miraculous powers, and he gave it a slap. Instantly the seven warriors presented themselves, and the corporal said: 'Reporting for duty and to ask for your orders, sir.' 'Off with you to that charcoal burner at the double, and get my tablecloth back from him.' They made a left-about turn and in a matter of minutes they brought him the cloth, having relieved the charcoal burner of it with little ceremony. He dismissed them again and walked on, full of hopes that fortune would shine on him even more kindly. At sunset he came to another charcoal burner who was preparing his evening meal by the fire. 'Sit down if you'd care to have supper with me,' said the sooty fellow. 'It'll just be potatoes, with salt and no sauce.' 'No,' he replied, 'this time you shall be my guest.' And he spread out his tablecloth, which was laid at once with the finest dishes. They ate and drank together in high spirits. After dinner the charcoal burner said: 'Up there on the shelf there's a little shabby old hat that has strange qualities: if anyone puts it on and turns it round on his head, whole batteries of cannon start firing, twelve at a time, and shoot everything down, so that no one has a chance against them. That hat's no use to me, and I'll give it to you for your tablecloth if you like.' 'That's all right by me,' replied the young man, and he took the hat, put it on and left his tablecloth behind. But no sooner had he gone a little way than he slapped his knapsack, and his soldiers were ordered to fetch the cloth back for him. 'This is just one good thing after another,' he thought, 'and I feel I haven't reached the end of my luck yet.' Nor did his hopes deceive him. After he had travelled on for another day he came to a third charcoal burner, who invited him to a meal of plain baked potatoes just as the other two had done. But he gave him a meal off his magic cloth which the charcoal burner found so tasty that in the end he offered in exchange for it a little horn, which had qualities even more remarkable than those of the hat. When it was sounded, all walls and fortifications, and finally every town and village for miles around, would collapse in ruins. He gave the charcoal burner his tablecloth for it of course, but afterwards sent his troops to demand it back, so that altogether he now had the knapsack, the hat and the horn. 'Now at last,' he said, 'I've made my fortune, and it's time for me to go home and see how my brothers are getting on.'

When he reached home, he found that his brothers had used their silver and gold to build a fine house and were living in riotous style. He went in to see them; but because he was wearing a ragged coat and had the shabby little hat on his head and the old knapsack on his back, they refused to recognize him as their brother. They made fun of him and said: 'You pretend to be our brother, the one who despised silver and gold and wanted a better fortune for himself! We don't doubt he'll have become a powerful king, and he'll drive up here in a magnificent carriage, not come like a beggar.' And they turned him out of the house. At this he was angry, and went on slapping his knapsack until a hundred and fifty men were drawn up in ranks before him. He made them surround the house, and two of them were ordered to arm themselves with hazel rods and soften his two haughty brothers' hides with a good tanning till they knew who he was. They set up a tremendous clamour, and all the neighbours rushed up and tried to help them, but they were powerless against the soldiers. Finally the matter was reported to the king, who was angry and sent out a company of

men under a captain, with orders to drive the trouble-maker
out of town: but the man with the knapsack had soon drummed
up enough reinforcements to beat back the captain and his
troops, who had to retreat with bloody noses. The king said: 'I'll
soon put this fellow from nowhere back in his place,' and next
day he sent out a still larger force against him, but it had even less
success. The young man called up more and more troops, and
to bring the matter to a still quicker conclusion he turned the hat
round on his head a few times: at this the heavy artillery went
into action, and the king's men were completely routed. 'I'll not
make peace now,' he said, 'until the king gives me his daughter
in marriage and appoints me to govern the whole kingdom in
his name.' He had this message sent to the king, and the king
said to his daughter: 'Force and might are hard nuts to bite:
what choice have I but to do as he says? If I'm to have peace and
keep the crown on my head, I must hand you over to him.'

So the wedding was celebrated, but the princess was
annoyed that her husband was a common man wearing a
shabby hat and carrying an old knapsack. She longed to get rid
of him again, and pondered day and night to find some way of
managing this. Then she thought: Perhaps it's his knapsack
that contains his miraculous powers. So she pretended great
affection and caressed him, and when his heart had grown soft
she said: 'If only you'd take off that dirty old knapsack! It looks
so unbecoming that it makes me feel ashamed of you.' 'My
dear girl,' he answered, 'this knapsack is my greatest treasure:
so long as I have it I need fear no power in the world.' And he
told her the secret of its miraculous qualities. At this she threw
her arms round his neck as if she were going to kiss him, but
instead she skilfully snatched the knapsack from his shoulders
and ran away with it. As soon as she was alone she slapped on it
and ordered the troops to arrest their former commander and
remove him from the royal palace. They obeyed, and his false
wife sent still more troops after him with orders to drive him
right out of the country. And that would have been the end of
him had he not been wearing his hat. But no sooner were his
hands freed than he swung it round a few times: and in an
instant the artillery began to thunder and shot down all his

enemies, and the princess herself had to come and beg for mercy. She pleaded so movingly, promising to be a better wife to him, that he let himself be persuaded and made peace with her. She behaved lovingly towards him, pretended to be very fond of him, and after a time she managed so to beguile him that he confided in her and said: 'Even if someone gets hold of my knapsack, he's still powerless against me so long as I still have this old hat.' Once she knew the secret, she waited till he was asleep, then snatched the hat from his head and had him thrown out into the street. But he still had the horn left, and in a great rage he sounded it as hard as he could. In an instant everything collapsed, the walls and fortifications, the towns and the villages, and the king and the princess were both killed. And if he hadn't put down the horn but blown it for a bit longer, everything else would have come crashing to the ground and not a stone been left standing on another. After that he met no further resistance, and made himself king over the whole country.

43

THE BLUE LAMP

Once upon a time there was a soldier who had served the king faithfully: but when the war was finished and he couldn't serve any longer because of his many wounds, the king said to him: 'You can go home, I need you no longer; you'll get no more money, because I only pay wages to people who are serving me.' The soldier didn't know how he was to make a living; he went away very downcast and walked all day till in the evening he came to a forest. When darkness fell, he saw a light and approached it and came to a house where a witch lived. 'Give me a bed for the night, please,' he said to her, 'and a little to eat and drink, for I'll starve otherwise.' 'Oho!' she answered, 'why should one give anything to a runaway soldier? But I'll have pity on you and take you in, if you'll do what I ask.' 'What do you want me to do?' asked the soldier. 'I want you to dig over my garden tomorrow.' The soldier consented, and worked all next day with might and main, but couldn't get it finished before evening. 'I see that you can't get any further today,' said the witch, 'and I'll let you stay a second night, but in return you shall chop up a whole load of wood for me tomorrow into small pieces.' That took the soldier the whole of the next day, and in the evening the witch proposed he should stay one more night. 'Tomorrow,' she said, 'you shall do me only a small service: behind my house there's an old dry well and my lamp has fallen into it; it burns blue and never goes out. I want you to fetch it up for me again.' Next day the old woman took him to the well and let him down in a basket. He found the blue lamp and signalled to her to pull him up again. And so she did, but when he was nearly at the top she reached down with her hand and tried to take the blue lamp from him. 'Oh no,' he said, reading her evil thoughts, 'I'll not give you the lamp till I've got both feet safely on the ground.' At this the witch flew into a rage, let him fall down again into the well and went away.

The poor soldier fell down on to the damp earth at the bottom without injuring himself, and the blue lamp went on burning, but what use was that to him? He saw clearly that he would not escape death. He sat for a while very downhearted; then by chance he put his hand in his pocket and found his pipe, which was still half full of tobacco. 'This'll be my last pleasure,' he thought; and he pulled it out, lit it from the blue lamp and began to smoke. When the smoke had drifted round the well shaft, he suddenly saw a little black man standing in front of him, who asked: 'Master, what are your orders?' 'Why should I give you orders?' asked the soldier in surprise. 'I have to do everything you tell me to do,' said the little man. 'Good,' said the soldier, 'then first get me out of this well.' The little man took him by the hand and led him along an underground passage, not forgetting to take the blue lamp as well. On the way he showed him all the treasures the witch had collected and hidden down here, and the soldier took away as much gold as he could carry. When he got back above ground he said to the little man: 'Now go and tie up that old witch and take her before the court.' Presently she came riding by on a wild cat, as fast as the wind and shrieking horribly; and shortly after that the little man reappeared. 'It has all been done,' he said, 'and the witch is hanging from the gallows already. What are your further orders, master?' 'Nothing at the moment,' replied the soldier. 'You can go home; but be sure to be ready to come when I call you.' 'All you need do,' said the little man, 'is to light your pipe from the blue lamp, and I'll be standing before you immediately.' So saying, he disappeared.

The soldier went back to the town he had come from. He went to the best inn and had fine clothes made for him, then he ordered the landlord to furnish a room for him as magnificently as possible. When it was ready and the soldier had moved into it, he summoned the little black man and said: 'I served the king faithfully, and he dismissed me and left me to starve, so now I want my revenge on him for this.' 'What am I to do?' asked the little man. 'Late at night, when the princess is in bed, you are to bring her here to me without waking her up and I'll make her work for me as my maidservant.' The little man said: 'For me that is an easy matter, but for you it is dangerous: if you are found out, things will go badly with you.' When midnight had struck, his door flew open and the little man carried in the princess. 'Aha, you've come, have you?' cried the soldier. 'Then get to work! Go and fetch the broom and sweep my room out.' When she had done that he called her over to his chair, stuck out his legs at her and said: 'Now pull off my boots.' Then he threw them in her face and she had to pick them up, clean them and polish them. But she did everything he ordered her to do, without resistance, in silence and with half-closed eyes. At first cockcrow the little man carried her back to the royal palace and put her into her bed.

When the princess got up next morning, she went to her father and told him she had had a strange dream. 'I was carried through the streets as quick as lightning and taken to a room where there was a soldier: I had to serve him and wait on him as his maid and do all the dirty work, sweeping the room and polishing his boots. It was only a dream and yet I feel as tired as if I'd really done it all.' 'Maybe your dream did actually happen,' said the king. 'I'll tell you what to do: fill your pockets with peas and make a small hole, and then if you're carried off again they'll fall out into the street and leave a trail.' As the king was saying this the little man was standing by him invisibly and listening. That night as he was carrying the sleeping princess through the streets again, some peas did fall out of her pocket, but they couldn't make a trail, because before fetching her the cunning little man had scattered peas along every street in the town. And the princess again had to work like a maidservant till cockcrow.

Next morning the king sent out his servants to find the trail, but it was impossible, because in every street the poor children were sitting picking up peas and saying: 'It rained peas last night.' 'We must think of something else,' said the king. 'Keep your shoes on when you go to bed, and before you come back from where you're taken to, hide one of them; I'll find it all right.' The little black man overheard this scheme, and that evening when the soldier asked for the princess to be brought again he advised him against it, saying that he knew no answer to that trick and that if the shoe were to be found in the soldier's room things could go badly with him. 'Do as I tell you,' replied the soldier, and the princess had to work like a maidservant on the third night too; but before she was carried back she hid one of her shoes under the bed.

In the morning the king had the whole town searched for his daughter's shoe: it was found in the soldier's room, and the soldier himself, who had left the town because the little man begged him to do so, was soon overtaken and thrown into prison. In the hurry of escaping he had forgotten his most precious possessions, the blue lamp and the gold, and all he had left in his pocket was one ducat. So as he was standing loaded with chains at the window of his prison, he saw an old comrade passing. He knocked on the window-pane, and when his comrade approached he said: 'Do me a favour and fetch me the little bundle I left behind at the inn; I'll give you a ducat.' The man hurried off to the inn and brought him back what he wanted. As soon as the soldier was alone again he lit his pipe and summoned the little black man, who said to his master: 'Don't be afraid, just go where they lead you and submit to everything, but be sure to take the blue lamp with you.' Next day the soldier was put on trial, and although he had committed no crime the judge nevertheless condemned him to death. As he was being led out to the place of execution, he asked the king to grant him a last wish. 'What wish?' asked the king. 'To smoke one more pipe on my way.' 'You can smoke three for all I care,' answered the king, 'but you needn't think I'll spare your life.' So the soldier took out his pipe and lit it at the blue lamp, and when a few rings of smoke had drifted up the little man was already standing there with a small cudgel in his hand. 'What are my master's orders?' he asked. 'I want those false judges and their officers knocked flat, and don't spare the king either, considering how badly he's treated me.' At this the little man started zigzagging to and fro like lightning, and anyone he so much as touched with his cudgel fell to the ground at once and didn't dare stir. The king was terrified, he started begging for mercy, and simply in order to have his life spared he gave the soldier his kingdom and his daughter in marriage.

44

THE SALAD-DONKEY

Once upon a time there was a young huntsman who went into
the forest to shoot. He had a merry and lively nature, and as he
was sauntering along whistling his lure-call on a leaf, an ugly
old woman met him, and she said: 'Good day to you, my dear
huntsman, I see you are happy and contented, but I am hungry
and thirsty: won't you spare me a coin or two?' And the huntsman felt sorry for the poor old woman, put his hand in his
pocket and gave her what he could afford. Then he was going to
walk on, but the old woman held him back and said: 'Dear
huntsman, listen to me. I want to reward you for your kind
heart. Just continue on your way, and presently you'll come to a
tree with nine birds perching on it: they're holding a cloak in
their talons and quarrelling over it. So take aim with your gun
and fire a shot in among them: they'll drop the cloak for you,
but one of the birds will be hit too and drop down dead. Take
the cloak with you, for it's a wishing-cloak: when you throw it
round your shoulders you need only wish yourself at such and
such a place and in an instant you will be there. But take the
heart out of the dead bird and swallow it whole. And then early
every morning when you get up you'll find a gold coin under
your pillow.'
  The huntsman thanked the wise-woman and thought to
himself: These are fine promises she's made me; it would be
nice if they were to come true. But when he had gone about
another hundred paces he heard a screeching and twittering in
the branches above him that made him look up, and there he
saw a number of birds tearing at a piece of cloth with their beaks
and claws, shrieking and tugging and fighting, as if each of
them wanted it for himself. 'Well,' said the huntsman, 'that's
strange, things are happening just as the old lady said.' He took
his gun from his shoulder, aimed and fired his shot in among
them, making the feathers fly. At once the creatures fled with

piercing squawks, but one of them fell down dead, and the cloak dropped to the ground too. Then the huntsman did as the old woman had told him: he cut open the bird, found its heart, swallowed it, and took the cloak home with him.

Next morning when he woke up, he remembered her promise and lifted his pillow to see if it had come true as well: and there before his eyes lay a gleaming gold piece, and next morning he found another, and so on every time he got up. He collected a pile of gold, but in the end he thought: What's the use of all my gold if I just stay at home? I'll go out into the world and look around.

So he took leave of his parents, slung his hunting-bag and gun over his back and went out into the world. It happened that one day he passed through a thick forest, and when he came to the end of it, there in the plain before him stood an imposing castle. An old woman with a very beautiful maiden beside her was standing in one of its windows looking down. But this old woman was a witch, and she said to the girl: 'There's a man coming out of the forest who has a miraculous treasure in his body, and you and I, my darling daughter, must get it from him by trickery: such a thing will become us better than him. He has a bird's heart in him, and that is why every morning there's a gold piece under his pillow.' She told her the secret and how she was to act in order to gain possession of the treasure, and finally she glared at her and said threateningly: 'If you don't obey me it'll be the worse for you.' So when the huntsman came nearer he saw the girl and said to himself: 'I've been wandering round for so long, now I'd like to rest and stay in this beautiful castle; after all, I have money enough.' But the real reason was that he had cast an eye on the girl's pretty face.

He entered the house and was kindly received and courteously entertained. It was not long before he was so much in love with the witch's daughter that he could think of nothing else and looked nowhere but into her eyes, and he willingly did everything she asked. Then the old woman said: 'Now we must get the bird's heart out of him, he won't notice when it's missing.' She prepared a drink, and when it was brewed she poured it into a goblet and handed it to the girl to offer to the huntsman.

The girl said: 'Now, my dearest, drink to me.' So he took the cup, and as soon as he had swallowed the drink he vomited out the bird's heart. The girl had to remove it stealthily and then swallow it herself, for this was what the old woman wanted. From now on the huntsman found no more gold under his pillow, it lay under the girl's pillow instead, and from there the old woman fetched it every morning; but he was so infatuated with love that he could think of nothing else but whiling away the time with the girl.

Then the old witch said: 'We've got the bird's heart, but we must take the wishing-cloak from him as well.' The girl replied: 'Let's let him keep it; after all, he's lost all his wealth.' At this the old woman was angry and said: 'A cloak like that is a miraculous thing, there are hardly any in the world to be found, and I must and shall have it.' She gave the girl instructions and told her that if she didn't obey her it would be the worse for her. So the girl did as the old woman told her, and one day she stood at the window gazing out into the surrounding countryside and looking very sad. The huntsman asked: 'Why are you standing there so sadly?' 'Oh, my darling,' she replied, 'over there is the Garnet Mountain where the precious stones grow. I have such a longing for them that whenever I think of them I grow sad; but how are they ever to be fetched! Only the birds that fly can reach that mountain, no human being can get to it.' 'If that's all that's troubling you,' said the huntsman, 'I'll soon take that sorrow from your heart.' So saying, he put his arm round her so that she was covered by his cloak, and wished himself on the Garnet Mountain, and sure enough they were both there in a trice. The precious stones glittered at them from every side, a joy to behold, and they collected the most beautiful and valuable pieces they could find. Now the old woman, by her witch's arts, had put a spell on the huntsman to make him feel drowsy. He said to the girl: 'Let's sit down and rest for a little; I'm so tired that I can't stay on my feet any longer.' So they sat down, and he laid his head in her lap and went to sleep. When he was asleep the girl unfastened the cloak from his shoulders and put it on herself; then she took all their garnets and other stones and wished herself back home.

But when the huntsman had slept his fill and woke up, he saw that his beloved had deceived him and left him alone on this wild mountain. 'Alas,' he said, 'what faithlessness there is in the world!' And he sat there in grief and anguish and didn't know what to do. Now the mountain belonged to savage and monstrous giants who lived and went about their business there, and he hadn't been sitting for long before he saw three of them approaching. So he lay down and pretended to be very fast asleep. The giants came up to him, and the first gave him a kick and said: 'What earthworm is this lying here gazing at his own guts?' The second said: 'Trample him to death.' But the third said contemptuously: 'Why waste the effort! Just let him live; he can't stay here, and if he climbs up to the summit the clouds will catch him and carry him off.' With that they passed him by, but the huntsman had listened to their conversation, and as soon as they had gone he got to his feet and climbed to the summit of the mountain. When he had been sitting there for a few minutes a cloud came floating along, picked him up and carried him away. For a time it drifted across the sky, then it came down and settled over a big walled vegetable garden, and he dropped gently to the ground among cabbages and lettuces.

Here the huntsman looked around and said to himself: 'If only I had something to eat! I'm so hungry that I don't know how I'm to travel further; but I can't see so much as an apple here or a pear, there's no fruit at all, just all these vegetables.' Finally he thought: I suppose as a last resort I can eat some salad; it hasn't much of a taste but it'll be refreshing. So he chose a fine head of lettuce and ate some of it, but hardly had he swallowed a couple of mouthfuls than he began to feel very odd and found that his shape was changing. Four legs were growing on him, and a big thick head and two long ears, and he saw with horror that he had been turned into a donkey. But because he was still very hungry and in his present form found the juicy lettuce delicious, he went on eating more and more of it. Finally he came across a different sort of lettuce, but no sooner had he devoured some of this than he felt another change coming over him and his human shape returned.

Then the huntsman lay down and had a good long sleep.

When he woke up next morning he picked a head of the bad lettuce and a head of the good, thinking to himself: This shall help me to regain my possessions and to punish treachery. So he put the two lettuce heads in his bag, climbed over the wall, and set out to look for his sweetheart's castle. And by good fortune, after wandering about for a few days, he found it. At once he dyed his face dark brown so that his own mother wouldn't have known him, then went into the castle and asked for a night's shelter. 'I'm so tired,' he said, 'I can't go any further.' The witch asked: 'And who may you be, sir, and what is your business?' He replied: 'I am one of the king's messengers and I was sent out to look for the most delicious lettuce that grows under the sun. I've been lucky enough to find it, too, and I have it with me, but the weather is really so hot I'm afraid the tender leaves won't stay fresh, and I don't know whether I'll be able to carry it any further.'

When the old woman heard about the delicious salad she grew greedy, and said: 'My dear sir, won't you let me taste some of that wonderful salad?' 'Why not?' he answered. 'I've brought two heads of lettuce with me, and you, madam, may have one of them.' And he opened his bag and gave her the bad one. The witch suspected nothing, and her mouth was watering so much at the thought of this new dish that she went into the kitchen herself and prepared it. When it was ready she couldn't even wait till it was on the table, but pulled off a couple of leaves straight away and put them in her mouth: but hardly had they gone down than her human shape went as well, and she trotted out into the yard as a donkey. Presently the maid came into the kitchen, saw the bowl of lettuce standing ready, picked it up and was going to serve it. But on the way, as usual, she thought she would just have a bit of a nibble, and she ate a leaf or two. At once the magic worked: she too became a donkey and trotted out to where the old woman was, and the bowl of lettuce fell to the floor. Meanwhile the supposed messenger was sitting with the beautiful girl; she too was eager to taste the salad, and when no one brought it she said: 'I can't think what's happening to that salad.' Then the huntsman thought: Those leaves must have done their work already, and he said: 'I'll go to the kitchen and find out.' When he got downstairs he saw the two donkeys trotting about in the yard and the salad lying on the floor. 'Good,' he said. 'Those two have already got what was coming to them.' And he picked up the remaining lettuce leaves, put them in the bowl and took them to the girl. 'I'm bringing you this exquisite dish myself, madam,' he said, 'so that you won't be kept waiting any longer.' So she began eating it, and immediately lost her human form like the others and ran down into the yard as a donkey.

After the huntsman had washed his face clean so that he would be recognized again by the three donkey women, he went down into the yard and said: 'Now you shall be repaid for your treachery.' He tied all three of them to a rope and drove them along till he came to a mill. He knocked on the window; the miller stuck his head out and asked what he wanted. 'I've got three ill-natured beasts here, miller,' he answered, 'and I want to be rid of them. If you'll take them in and give them their feed and somewhere to sleep, and treat them in the way I tell you, I'll pay you whatever you like.' The miller said: 'Well, why not? But how am I to treat them?' So the huntsman told him that the treatment of the old she-ass, the one that was the witch, was to be three beatings and one feed daily; the younger one, the maid, was to get one beating and three feeds; and the youngest, who was the girl, was to get no beatings and three feeds – for after all he hadn't the heart to have the girl beaten. Then he went back to the castle and found everything there that he needed.

A few days later the miller came and said he had to report that the old she-ass, who had only had beatings and one meal daily, had died. 'The other two,' he went on, 'have been getting their three feeds, but although they're still alive they look so downhearted that they probably won't last much longer.' At this the huntsman relented, forgot his anger and told the miller to bring the two donkeys back to the castle. And when they arrived, he gave them some of the good lettuce to eat, and they got back their human form. The beautiful girl fell on her knees before him and said: 'Oh, my darling, forgive the wicked things I did to you! My mother forced me to do them, but it was against my

will, for I love you dearly. Your magic cloak is hanging in a
cupboard, and as for the bird's heart I'll drink something to
make me bring it up again.' But then he changed his mind and
said: 'Just keep it; after all, it doesn't matter, for I'm going to
marry you and you shall be my loyal wife.' So now the wedding
was celebrated, and they lived happily together for the rest of
their days.

45

THE THREE BROTHERS

There was once a man who had three sons and no fortune other than the house he lived in. Now each of the sons would have liked to inherit the house after his death, but he loved them all equally and could think of no way to avoid hurting the feelings of any of them. He didn't want to sell the house either, because it had belonged to his ancestors; otherwise he would have divided the money among the three. At last he thought of a plan, and said to his sons: 'Go out into the world and try what you can do and let each of you learn a trade; then when you come back, whichever one of you gives the best demonstration of skill shall have the house.'

His sons were well content with this, and the eldest decided to become a farrier, the second a barber and the third a swordsman. They agreed on a date on which they would all return home together, and then they parted. And it so happened that each of them found an excellent master from whom he learned his trade well. The farrier was appointed to shoe the king's horses, and he thought: I'm a made man now, I'll get the house. The barber shaved only rich and noble clients, and he too felt sure that the house was as good as his. The swordsman got quite a few slashes, but he gritted his teeth and persisted, telling himself that if he was afraid of a wound or two he would never own the house. So when the appointed day came they met again at home; but they couldn't think how to find the best opportunity of showing their skills, and sat discussing this together. And as they sat, a hare suddenly came bounding across the field. 'Why,' said the barber, 'he's just what I wanted.' And taking his bowl and his soap, he prepared a good lather as the hare approached, then lathered its face as it ran by and trimmed its beard for it too while it was still running at full tilt, and all without cutting it or hurting it in the slightest. 'I like that,' said their father. 'If the other two don't work very hard

indeed to rival it, the house will be yours.' Before very long a
gentleman came racing towards them in a carriage, driving at
full tilt. 'Now, father, you shall see what I can do,' said the
farrier; and he dashed after the carriage, snatched all four shoes
off the horse as it galloped and hammered four new ones on as it
was still galloping. 'You're a proper fellow,' said his father,
'and as handy as your brother; I don't know which of you I
should give the house to.' Then the third son said: 'Father, give
me a chance as well.' And as it was beginning to rain just then,
he drew his sword and brandished it above his head, thrusting
and parrying, so that not a drop fell on him; and as the rain got
heavier, until finally it was simply pouring down in bucketfuls,
he swung the sword faster and faster and stayed as dry as if he
had been safely indoors. When his father saw that, he was
amazed and said: 'Your demonstration is the most masterly of
all, and the house is yours.'

The other two brothers were content with his decision, which
they had all promised to accept, and because they were all so
fond of each other all three of them lived in the house together.
They plied their trades, and they had all learnt them so
thoroughly and become so skilful that they earned a lot of
money. And so they lived happily together until they were old
men, and when one of them fell ill and died the other two were
so grief-stricken that they fell ill as well and died soon after.
And then, because they had been so clever and so fond of each
other, they were all three buried together in the same grave.

46

THE FOUR SKILFUL BROTHERS

There was once a poor man who had four sons, and when they grew up he said to them: 'My dear boys, you must go out into the world now, for I have nothing to give you; make ready and travel abroad, and let each of you learn some trade, and see how you manage.' So the four brothers said goodbye to their father, left home and set off together through the town gate. When they had walked for a while they came to a crossing, with roads leading in four different directions; and the eldest said: 'Here we must separate, but let's meet again at this spot four years from today, and meanwhile we'll try our luck.'

So now each of them went his way, and the eldest met a man who asked him where he was going and what he meant to do. 'I want to learn a trade,' he answered. The man said: 'Come with me and learn how to be a thief.' 'No,' he answered, 'it's no longer considered an honest occupation, and the way that song ends is with a dance on the air.' 'Oh, you needn't fear the gallows,' said the man. 'I'll only teach you how to get your hands on things that no one else in the world can touch, and in such a way that you can never be traced.' So he let himself be persuaded, and under this man's instruction he became a master thief and so skilful that nothing was safe from him if he once set his heart on having it. The second brother met a man who asked him the same question: what was he going out into the world to learn? 'I haven't decided yet,' he answered. 'Then come along with me and I'll teach you to be a star-gazer: it's the best thing to be, one's eyes never miss anything.' This was agreeable to him, and he became so skilful a star-gazer that when he had finished learning and was about to set off again his master gave him a spyglass and told him: 'With this you'll be able to see everything that's happening in heaven and earth, and nothing will be able to hide from you.' The third brother was taken on as an apprentice by a huntsman, who taught him so well that he ended up knowing everything there was to know about hunting and there was nothing more for him to learn. When he left, his master gave him a gun and said: 'This gun never misses: take aim at anything you like and you'll be certain to hit it.' The youngest brother also met a man who spoke to him and asked what his plans were. 'Wouldn't you like to become a tailor?' 'You must be joking,' said the boy. 'Sitting bent up double from morning till evening, and pushing a needle or a flat-iron to and fro! That's not the life for me.' 'Come now,' answered the man, 'you're talking nonsense. I'll teach you quite a different sort of tailoring, very respectable and proper and sometimes highly honoured.' So he let himself be persuaded, went with the man and learnt his skill inside and out. When he left, his master gave him a needle and said: 'With this you'll be able to mend anything you like, whether it's as soft as an egg or as hard as steel, and it'll become one complete piece with no join to be seen.'

When the appointed four years were at an end, the four brothers all met at the crossroads, embraced and kissed each other and went home to their father. 'Well!' he said, delighted to see them again, 'so the wind has blown you back to me, has it?' They told him all that had happened to them and how each of them had learned his trade. They were sitting outside the house under a big tree; and their father said to them: 'Now I'll put you to the test and see what you can do.' He glanced upwards and then said to the second son: 'At the top of this tree, in the fork of two branches, there's a chaffinch's nest: can you tell me how many eggs there are in it?' The star-gazer took his spyglass, looked up through it and said: 'There are five.' The father said to the eldest son: 'Now you go and fetch down the eggs without disturbing the mother bird that's sitting on them.' The ingenious thief climbed up and removed the five eggs from under the mother bird, who sat on quietly without noticing a thing, and brought them down to his father. His father took them and laid them out on the table, one at each corner and the fifth in the centre, then he said to the huntsman: 'Now I want you to shoot at these eggs and break them all with a single shot.' The huntsman took aim with his gun and smashed all five eggs with a single shot, just as his father had said. I dare say he had the kind of gunpowder that shoots round corners. 'Now it's your turn,' said the father to the fourth son. 'You're to sew the eggs together again, and the chicks inside them too, in such a way that the shot will have done them no harm.' The tailor fetched out his needle and sewed them all up just as his father had said When he had finished, the thief had to take the eggs back up the tree to the nest and put them back under the mother bird without her noticing. The little creature finished hatching them, and a few days later the chicks crawled out of their shells, and each of them had a little red line round its neck where the tailor had sewn it together.

'Well,' said the old man to his sons, 'I certainly must congratulate you. You've made good use of your time and really learnt something. I can't judge which of you has done best; but no doubt that'll soon be seen if you have an opportunity to use your skills.' Not long after this, a great cry went up that the king's daughter had been carried off by a dragon. The king worried about her day and night and had it announced that whoever brought her back to him should have her for his wife. The four brothers said to each other: 'This would be a chance for us to show what we can do,' and they decided to set out together and rescue the princess. 'I'll soon find out where she is,' said the star-gazer, and he looked through his spyglass and said: 'I see her already, she's a long way from here, sitting on a rock in the middle of the sea, and the dragon's beside her guarding her.' So he went to the king and asked for a ship for himself and his brothers and sailed with them over the sea till they came to the rock. On it sat the princess, but the dragon was lying asleep with its head on her lap. The huntsman said: 'I can't shoot, it would kill the pretty maiden as well.' 'Then I'll try my luck,' said the thief, and he crept near her and stole her from under the dragon, and he did it so nimbly and deftly that the monster noticed nothing and went on snoring. Overjoyed, they hurried back with her to the ship and put out to sea; but when the dragon woke up and found the princess gone, it came hurtling through the air in pursuit of them, roaring furiously. Just as it was hovering over the ship and about to dive down, the huntsman took aim with his gun and shot it right through the heart. The monster fell down dead, but its body was so huge and heavy that as it fell it smashed the whole ship to pieces. They managed to cling to a few planks and floated about on the open sea. So now they were again in dire peril, but the tailor lost no time, took out his magic needle, quickly sewed the planks together with a few long stitches, sat down on them and collected all the pieces of the ship. Then he sewed these together too, so skilfully that in no time the ship was seaworthy again and they were able to sail safely home.

When the king saw his daughter again, there was great rejoicing. He said to the four brothers: 'One of you shall have her for his wife, but as to which of you it shall be, that you must settle among yourselves.' Then there was a heated dispute between the four, for each of them claimed her. The star-gazer said: 'If I hadn't seen where the princess was, all your skills would have been useless, so she's mine.' The thief said: 'What would have been the use of your seeing where she was if I hadn't got her out from under the dragon? So she's mine.' The huntsman said: 'All of you, and the princess as well, would have been torn to pieces by the monster if my bullet hadn't killed it, so she's mine.' The tailor said: 'And if I hadn't had the skill to mend the ship for you again, you'd all have drowned miserably, so she's mine.' So the king decided the matter by saying: 'Each of you has an equal right, and because you can't all have the princess none of you shall have her, but I shall give each of you half a kingdom as your reward.' The brothers were pleased by this decision and said: 'It's better that way than that we should quarrel.' So they each got half a kingdom and they lived on with their father in great happiness for as long as it pleased God.

47

THE YOUNG GIANT

A peasant had a son who was the size of a thumb and never got any bigger; years passed and he didn't grow by a hair's breadth. One day the peasant was about to go out and plough his fields, and the little fellow said: 'Father, I want to go out with you.' 'You want to come out with me? You stay here,' said his father. 'You'll be no use at all out there, and anyway you might get lost.' At this the thumbkin began to cry, and for peace and quiet's sake his father put him in his pocket and took him with him. When he got to the fields he took him out again and put him down in a newly ploughed furrow. As he sat there a huge giant came striding over the hill. 'Do you see that big bogey man there?' said his father, thinking to frighten the little fellow so that he would be good. 'He's coming to fetch you.' But the giant had scarcely taken another two steps with his great legs when he reached the furrow. He picked up the little thumbkin carefully with two fingers, took a look at him and carried him off without saying a word. His father stood there speechless with fright, thinking that his child was lost and that he would never set eyes on him again.

But the giant took the child home and let him suck at his breast, and the thumbkin grew and became tall and strong the way giants are. After two years he took him into the forest to try him out, and said: 'Pull yourself a stick.' And the boy was already strong enough to tear a young tree out of the ground, roots and all. But the giant said: 'We must do better than that,' and took him home again and suckled him for another two years. When he next tried him out, he had already got so much stronger that he could pull an old tree out of the ground. The giant was still not satisfied, but suckled him for two more years, and then when he went with him into the forest and said: 'Now pull yourself a proper stick,' the boy went to the thickest oak tree he could see and tore it out with a great crash, thinking nothing of it. 'Good,' said the giant, 'that's the end of your schooling.' And he took him back to the field where he had fetched him. His father was standing there behind his plough, and the young giant approached him and said: 'Well, father, look what a fine man your son's grown into!' The peasant took fright and answered: 'No, you're not my son, I don't want you, get away from me.' 'Of course I'm your son! Let me do the work, I can plough as well as you, in fact better.' 'No, no, you're not my son, and you can't plough either, get away from me.' But because he was scared of the huge fellow he let go his plough, stepped aside and sat down. Then the boy took the plough and just pushed it with one hand, but it was such a powerful push that the ploughshare dug deep into the ground. The peasant couldn't bear to see this and shouted to him: 'If you want to do the ploughing you mustn't push so hard, that's not the way to go to work.' But the boy unharnessed the horses and started pulling the plough himself, saying: 'You just go home, father, and get mother to cook a big dish of something for my dinner; meanwhile I'll soon turn over this field.' So the peasant went home and told his wife to prepare the dinner. But the boy ploughed the two-acre field all by himself, then he harnessed himself to the harrows as well and harrowed it all, using two harrows at once. When he had finished he went into the forest and pulled up two oak trees: he laid these over his shoulders and put both harrows on them, one at the back and one in front, and both the horses as well, back and front, and carried the whole lot to his parents' house as if it had been a bundle of straw. When he got to the yard his mother didn't recognize him and asked: 'Who is that terrible great man?' And the peasant said: 'That's our son.' 'No!' she said, 'that can't possibly be our son, we never had one as big as that, ours was a tiny little thing.' And she shouted at him: 'Go away, we don't want you!' The boy said nothing, led his horses to the stable and gave them oats and hay, all properly and in order. When that was done he came into the parlour, sat down on the bench and said: 'Mother, now I'd like some dinner, will you have it ready soon?' So she said: 'Yes,' and brought in two huge dishes full of food, enough to have kept herself and her husband going for a week. But the boy ate the whole lot up by himself and asked her if she couldn't bring him some more. 'No,' she said, 'that's all we've got.' 'But that was only a titbit, I must have some more.' She didn't dare refuse, so she filled an enormous pig-swill cauldron full of meat and put it on the fire, and when it was cooked she brought it in. 'Here's another bite or two at last,' he said, and devoured the lot; but it still wasn't enough to satisfy his hunger. So he said: 'Father, it's clear that you'll never be able to give me enough to eat; if you'll have an iron cudgel made for me, a good strong one that I can't break across my knees, I'll go out into the world.' The peasant was glad to hear this. He harnessed two horses to his cart, drove to the blacksmith's and brought back such a great thick cudgel that the pair of horses could hardly move it. The boy put it across his knee, and snap! he broke it in two as if it had been a beanpole, and threw it away. His father harnessed four horses and fetched such a great thick cudgel that the four horses could hardly move it. His son snapped this one across his knee too, threw it down and said: 'Father, that's no use to me, you must harness a better team and bring me a stronger cudgel.' So his father harnessed eight horses and fetched such a great thick cudgel that the eight horses could hardly drag it to the house. As soon as his son took this one in his hand, a piece broke off the top of it. 'Father,' he said, 'it's clear that you can't get me the kind of cudgel I need, so I'll be off and not trouble you any longer.'

So he went on his way, passing himself off as a journeyman blacksmith. He came to a village where a very miserly smith lived, a man who begrudged everyone everything and wanted to keep it all for himself. The boy entered his smithy and asked if he needed a journeyman. 'Yes,' said the blacksmith, looking him up and down and thinking: This is a stout fellow, he'll wield the hammer well and earn his bread. He asked: 'What wages do you want?' 'I don't want any at all,' he replied, 'except that every fourteen days, when the other journeymen get their pay, you must let me give you two little smacks.' The miser was happy to agree to this, thinking it would save him a lot of money. Next morning the new journeyman was to be the first to swing the hammer, and his master brought him a red hot bar of iron. But when he struck the first blow, the iron was smashed into smithereens and the anvil was driven so deep into the ground that they couldn't get it out again. This angered the miser and he said: 'What are you playing at, hitting it so hard? You're no use to me. What extra pay do you want for a blow like that?' The young man replied: 'I'll just give your backside a little tap, that's all.' And he lifted his foot and gave him such a kick that he went sailing through the air over four cartloads of hay. Then he took the thickest iron bar he could find in the smithy and went on his way using it as a walking stick.

After travelling for a while he came to a farm and asked the bailiff if he needed a foreman. 'Yes,' said the bailiff, 'I could do with one. You look like a stout fellow who knows a thing or two already: what pay do you want for a year?' The boy again answered that he didn't want any wages, but that once a year the bailiff must let him give him three smacks. That suited the bailiff, for he was a miserly fellow too. Next morning the farm-hands had all been told to go out into the forest and cut wood, and the others were all ready, but the foreman was still in bed. One of them shouted to him: 'Get up, it's time, we're going into the woods and you're to come with us.' 'Oh, be off with you,' he answered very ill-temperedly. 'You go ahead, I'll be back here before the lot of you anyway.' The others went to the bailiff and told him that the new foreman was still in bed and refused to come with them. The bailiff told them to wake him again and get him to harness the horses. But he answered the same as before: 'Be off with you and go ahead, I'll be back here before the lot of you anyway.' So he stayed in bed for another two hours, then he finally got up, but first he fetched two bushels of peas down from the loft, cooked them into a porridge and took his time about eating it. Then, when he had done all this, he went and harnessed the horses and drove off. Not far from the forest he had to pass through a narrow ravine, so he first drove the cart through and halted the horses, then he went back, gathered trees and brushwood and made a great barricade that would stop any horse. Then just as he got to the edge of the forest he met the others, driving homewards with their carts fully loaded. So he said to them: 'Drive on, I'll still get home before you anyway.' When he had gone only a little way into the forest, he just tore up two of the biggest trees he could find, tossed them on to the cart and turned round. When he got to the barricade, he found the others still standing there, unable to get through. 'You see,' he said, 'if you'd stayed with me you could have got home just as quickly as well as having another hour's sleep.' Then he tried to drive on but his horses couldn't make any headway, so he unharnessed them, lifted them on to the cart, grabbed the shaft himself, and hey presto! he pulled the whole lot through as easily as if it had been a load of feathers. When he got to the far side he called back to the others: 'You see, I got through quicker than you did!' And off he drove, leaving them stuck. When he arrived back at the farm, he picked up one of the trees, showed it to the bailiff and said: 'How's this for a fine piece of timber?' And the bailiff said to his wife: 'That's a good servant we've got; he may sleep longer than the others, but he gets back before they do.'

So he served the bailiff for a year; and when the year was over and the other farmhands got their wages, he said it was time for him to take his too. But the bailiff was scared at the thought of the smacks he was to get, and implored the young giant to let him off, offering to be foreman himself instead and to let him be bailiff. 'No,' said the giant, 'a foreman I am and a foreman I'll stay, but you're to get what we agreed.' The bailiff said he would pay him whatever sum he liked to name, but it was no good, the foreman refused everything. The bailiff was at his wits' end and asked to be reprieved for a fortnight to think the matter over. The foreman agreed to give him a fortnight. The bailiff summoned all his clerks and told them to think hard and come up with some advice. The clerks racked their brains and finally said that this foreman was a public danger, he would strike any man dead as easily as killing a fly. The bailiff should tell him to climb down into the well and clean it out; when he was down there they would roll up one of the millstones that lay nearby and drop it on to his head, and then they'd have seen the last of him. The bailiff liked this idea, and the foreman consented to climb down into the well. When he was at the bottom they rolled the biggest of the millstones down after him and thought it had bashed his skull in, but he shouted: 'Will you shift the chickens away from round the well, they're scratching about and throwing grains of sand down into my eyes, and I can't see.' So the bailiff went 'shoo, shoo!' and pretended to be shooing away the chickens. When the foreman had finished his work, he came up out of the well and said: 'Just look what a fine necklace I'm wearing!' and there was the millstone round his neck. He now wanted to claim his wages, but again the bailiff asked for a fortnight's grace. His clerks met and advised him to send his foreman to grind corn at night in the haunted mill: this was a place, they said, from which no man had ever come out alive the next morning. This suggestion appealed to the bailiff; he sent for the foreman that very evening and ordered him to drive a hundred bushels of grain to the mill and grind it into flour that night, telling him they needed it urgently. So the foreman went up to the loft and put twenty-five bushels in his right pocket and twenty-five in his left, and fifty in a sack which he slung across his shoulders; and with this load he set off for the haunted mill. The miller told him that it was all right grinding flour there by day, but not at night: the mill was bewitched at that time, and everyone who had gone into it had been found dead next morning. The young man said: 'I'll be all right, just you go away and go to bed.' With that he entered the mill and poured the grain into the hopper. At about eleven o'clock he went into the miller's room and sat down on the bench. When he had been sitting there for a while, the door suddenly opened and an enormous table came in, which was immediately laid with goblets of wine and dishes of roast meat and other good food in abundance, but it seemed to lay itself, because there was no one there to do so. And presently the chairs moved up to the table, but no one came to sit on them; suddenly, however, he saw fingers handling the knives and forks and putting food on to the plates, but that was all he could see. The food was there, however, and he felt hungry, so he sat down and tucked into it as well, and very tasty it was. When he had had enough and the others had emptied their plates too, the candles were suddenly all snuffed out – he could hear this happening quite clearly. And when it was pitch dark he got something that felt like a slap in

the face. At this he said: 'If that happens again, I'll slap back.'
And when his ears were boxed a second time he struck out too.
And so it went on all night: he repaid every blow in good
measure and laid about him with a will. But at daybreak it all
stopped. When the miller got up, he came to look for him and
was amazed to find him still alive. The young man said: 'I've
had plenty to eat, and I got a few slaps, but I gave back as good
as I got.' The miller was glad: he told him that the spell on the
mill was now broken and offered him a lot of money as a
reward, but he answered: 'I don't want money, I've got plenty.'
Then he slung his sack of flour over his shoulders, went home
and told the bailiff that he had done what he had been asked to
do and would now like to have his wages as agreed. When the
bailiff heard this he was more scared than ever: he paced up and
down the room in desperation, and the sweat trickled down his
forehead. Then he opened the window to get some fresh air,
but before he knew what had happened the foreman had given
him such a kick that it sent him sailing through the window, up
into the air and on and on until everyone lost sight of him. Then
the foreman said to the bailiff's wife: 'If he doesn't reappear, it'll
have to be you that gets the second one.' 'No, no!' she cried, 'I
can't bear it,' and she opened the other window, because the
sweat was trickling down her forehead too. Then he gave her a
kick and sent her sailing up through the air just like her husband, but much higher because she was lighter. 'Come to me,
come here!' shouted her husband, but she shouted: 'You come
here, I can't come to you!' And they flew round and round in
the air and neither could reach the other, and for all I know
they're still there flying round and round. But the young giant
took his iron cudgel and went on his way.

48

THICKASATHUMB

There was once a poor peasant who sat at his hearth all evening poking the fire while his wife sat spinning. And he said: 'It's so sad that we don't have any children! Our house is so silent, and the others are full of noise and fun.' 'Yes,' answered his wife with a sigh, 'even if we had only one, even just a tiny little one the size of a thumb, I'd be content; we'd love him just the same.' Then it came about that the wife was poorly, and seven months later she bore a child; and though all its limbs were perfectly formed, it was no bigger than a thumb. So they said: 'It's what we wished for, and he shall be our own dear child.' And because he was so tiny they called him Thickasathumb. Though they gave him plenty to eat, he never grew any bigger but stayed the same size as he had been when he was born. All the same, he had an intelligent face and soon showed himself to be a clever and nimble little creature, successful in everything he undertook.

One day as the peasant was getting ready to go out into the forest and fell some timber, he muttered to himself: 'I wish I had someone who could follow me there and bring me the cart.' 'Oh, father,' exclaimed Thickasathumb, 'I'll bring you the cart, you can count on me, it shall be there in the forest at whatever time you say.' The man laughed and said: 'How will you manage that? You're much too tiny to hold a horse by the reins.' 'That's all right, father; if mother will just harness him, I'll sit in his ear and call out to him which way to go.' 'Well,' answered his father, 'we'll try it for once.' When the time came, Thickasathumb's mother harnessed the cart and put him into the horse's ear, and then the little fellow shouted his orders to the horse, 'Ho–whoa! Hoy – gee-up!' and off they went in as orderly a fashion as if a mastercarter had been driving, and the cart took the right road to the forest. It happened that just as it was turning a corner and the little fellow was shouting 'Hoy,

hoy!' that two strangers came walking along. 'Goodness me,' said one of them, 'what's this? Here's a cart being driven and a carter calling out to the horse, and yet there's no sign of him.' 'There's something queer about it,' said the other. 'Let's follow the cart and see where it stops.' But the cart went right into the forest to the very place where the timber was being felled. When Thickasathumb saw his father, he called out to him: 'You see, father, here I am with the cart! Now fetch me down.' His father held the horse with his left hand, and with his right he took his little son out of its ear, and Thickasathumb sat down very merrily on a blade of straw. When the two strangers caught sight of him, they were speechless with astonishment. Then one of them took the other aside and said: 'Do you know, that little fellow could make our fortune if we exhibited him for money in a big city: let's buy him.' They went to the peasant and said: 'Sell us the little man, we'll treat him well.' 'No,' answered the father, 'he's the apple of my eye and I won't part with him for all the gold in the world.' But Thickasathumb, when he heard what was afoot, had crept up a fold in his father's coat, and now he stood on his shoulder and whispered into his ear: 'Father, just hand me over, I'll get back again all right.' So his father handed him over to the two men for a tidy sum of money. 'Where do you want to sit?' they asked him. 'Oh, just put me on the brim of your hat, sir, I'll be able to walk up and down there and look at the countryside and not fall off.' They did as he asked, and when Thickasathumb had said goodbye to his father they set off with him. They walked on till evening began to fall, and then the little fellow said: 'Lift me down for a minute, I have to do something.' 'Just stay where you are,' said the man whose head he was sitting on, 'it won't worry me; the birds often drop things on me anyway.' 'No,' said Thickasathumb, 'I know what's right and proper: just you lift me down quickly.' The man took off his hat and put the little fellow down in a field by the roadside, where he hopped and crawled about for a while among the clods and then suddenly vanished into a mouse-hole which he had been looking for. 'Good evening, gentlemen!' he called to them. 'Now you can just go home without me.' And he laughed his head off at them. They rushed up and poked sticks into the mouse-hole, but it was all in vain: Thickasathumb crawled further and further in, and as it soon became quite dark they just had to set off for home with their noses out of joint and their purses empty.

When Thickasathumb saw they had gone, he crawled out of his underground passage again. 'It's dangerous walking on this field in the dark,' he said, 'one can easily break one's leg or one's neck!' Luckily he came across an empty snail-shell. 'God be praised,' he said, 'here I can pass the night in safety.' And he settled down in it. Presently, just as he was falling asleep, he heard two men passing, and one of them said: 'How are we to get hold of that rich priest's money and silver?' 'I could tell you how!' cried Thickasathumb. 'What was that?' said one of the thieves in alarm. 'I heard someone speak.' They stood still and listened, and Thickasathumb spoke again: 'Take me with you,' he said, 'and I'll help you.' 'But where are you?' 'Just search the ground, and listen where my voice is coming from,' he replied. Eventually the thieves found him and picked him up. 'You little midget,' they said, 'how will you help us?' 'Well, don't you see,' he replied, 'I'll crawl between the iron bars into the priest's room and hand you out whatever you want.' 'Very well,' they said, 'let's see what you can do.' When they got to the presbytery Thickasathumb crawled into the room, but at once began yelling for all he was worth: 'D'you want to take everything there is here?' The thieves took fright and said: 'For heaven's sake speak quietly, or someone'll wake up.' But Thickasathumb pretended he hadn't heard them properly and yelled again: 'What'll you have? D'you want everything that's here?' The cook, who slept in the next room, heard this and sat up in her bed to listen. The thieves had got such a fright that they had run back part of the way they had come; but finally they plucked up their courage again, thinking: The little fellow's making fun of us. They came back and whispered to him: 'Now stop playing the fool and hand us out something.' At this Thickasathumb yelled out again as loud as he could: 'I'll give you anything you like, just put your hands in through the bars.' The listening maidservant heard this quite clearly; she jumped out of bed and stumbled in through the door. The thieves ran away as if they had the Wild Huntsman at their heels: but the maid, finding there was nothing to be seen, went to light a candle. When she came back with it, Thickasathumb slipped out unnoticed into the barn. But when the maid had searched in every corner and found nothing she finally went back to bed, thinking she must just after all have been dreaming with her eyes and ears wide open.

Thickasathumb had been climbing around in the hay and found himself a nice place to sleep; he decided he would stay here till daybreak and then go home to his parents. But his adventures were not over yet! Ah yes, the world is full of trouble and sorrow. By daybreak the maid had already got up to feed the cattle. The first place she went to was the barn, where she took up an armful of hay, and it happened to be the very hay poor Thickasathumb was lying asleep in. But he was sleeping so soundly that he noticed nothing, and he didn't wake up till he was in the jaws of the cow, who had picked him up with her hay. 'Oh, good Lord!' he exclaimed, 'how did I get into this washing-machine?' But he soon realized where he was. So he had to take good care not to get between the cow's teeth and be crushed, and presently he had to slide down into her stomach all the same. 'They've forgotten to put windows in this little room,' he said, 'so it doesn't get any sunlight, and I can't see anyone bringing a lamp either.' In short he found it pretty poor accommodation, and the worst of it was that more and more new hay kept piling in through the door, leaving less and less room for him. In the end he was so scared that he shouted as loud as he could: 'Stop feeding me, stop feeding me!' The maid was just milking the cow, and when she heard a voice speaking and couldn't see the speaker, and it was the same voice as she had heard in the night too, she got such a fright that she fell off her stool and spilt the milk. She ran as fast as she could to her master and cried out: 'Oh, God bless us, father, the cow's started talking!' 'You're crazy,' answered the priest, but all the same he came to the cowshed himself to see what was going on. But scarcely had he set foot in it when Thickasathumb shouted again: 'Stop feeding me, stop feeding me!' This scared the priest too; he thought an evil spirit had got into the cow, and ordered it to be killed. So the cow was slaughtered and its stomach, with Thickasathumb still inside, was thrown on the dungheap. Thickasathumb had a lot of trouble working his way through its contents, but eventually he managed to clear himself some space, and was just about to push his head out when a new misfortune overtook him. A hungry wolf ran up and swallowed the whole stomach at one gulp. Thickasathumb wasn't downhearted; perhaps I can come to an agreement with this wolf, he thought. And he called out to the wolf from inside its belly: 'Dear wolf, I know a place where you can get a fine meal.' 'Where's that?' asked the wolf. 'In such and such a house; you must crawl in through the drain, and then you'll find as many cakes and hams and sausages as you'll ever want to eat.' And he gave him an exact description of his father's house. The wolf didn't need a second telling; that night he squeezed in through the drain and plundered the larder to his heart's content. When he had eaten his fill he tried to leave, but he was so fat now that he couldn't get back the way he had come. Thickasathumb had foreseen this, and he now began to make a tremendous noise inside the wolf, raging and screaming as hard as he could. 'Will you stop that noise!' said the wolf, 'you'll waken everybody.' 'Come now,' answered the little man, 'you've had a good meal, and I want to cheer myself up too,' and he began to scream his head off again. In the end it woke his father and his mother, and they ran to the larder, opened the door slightly and peered in. When they saw there was a wolf inside they hurried off, and the man fetched the axe and his wife the scythe. 'Stay behind me,' said the man as they went in. 'I'll give him a bash, but if that doesn't kill him you have a go with the scythe and cut him in half.' Thickasathumb heard his father's voice and called out: 'Father dear, it's me, I'm in the wolf's belly.' His father was overjoyed and said: 'God be praised, we've found our dear child again,' and told his wife to put away the scythe in case Thickasathumb should get injured. Then he swung the axe and struck the wolf such a blow on the head that it fell dead, and after that they fetched a knife and scissors and cut open its body and pulled out their little son. 'Oh,' said his father, 'we've been worried to death about you!' 'Yes, father, I've had quite a lot of adventures; thank goodness I can breathe freely again!' 'But wherever have you been?' 'Oh, father, I've been in a mouse-hole, in a cow's stomach and in a wolf's belly; now I'm going to stay at home with you.' 'And we'll never sell you again for all the riches in the world,' said his parents, and they hugged and kissed their dear Thickasathumb. They gave him something to eat and drink and had new clothes made for him, because the ones he had on had got spoilt during his travels.

49

BEARSKIN

Once upon a time there was a young fellow who enlisted as a soldier. He was a brave fighter and always the foremost man when it was hailing bullets. All went well with him while the war lasted, but when peace was made he got his discharge and the captain sent him packing. His parents were dead and he had no home to go to, so he went to his brothers and begged them to take him in till the war started again. But his brothers were hard-hearted and said: 'What good would that do us? We don't want you, be off and make your own way in the world.' All the soldier had left was his gun, so he slung it over his shoulder and set out into the world. Presently he came to a great moor with nothing to be seen on it but a circle of trees, and here he sat down in great dejection to ponder his fate. I've no money, he thought; the only trade I know is soldiering, and now that peace has been made they don't need me any more; I can see there's nothing left for me but to starve. Suddenly he heard a rushing noise, and when he looked round there was a stranger standing there, a man in a green coat, quite handsome-looking but with an ugly cloven hoof. He said to the soldier: 'I know what your trouble is. I can give you more money and wealth than you'll know what to do with, but first I have to know that you're not afraid, because I don't want to spend my money to no purpose.' 'Afraid!' he replied, 'what sort of soldier do you think I am? You can put me to the test.' 'Very well,' answered the man, 'look behind you.' The soldier turned round and saw a huge growling bear trotting towards him. 'Oho!' cried the soldier, 'I'll give your nose a tickle that'll stop you growling.' And he took aim and shot the bear in the muzzle. The bear dropped to the ground and lay motionless, and the stranger said: 'I see that you're not lacking in courage. But I've got another condition to make, and you'll have to observe it.' 'So long as it doesn't put my soul in danger,' answered the soldier, who knew very well

who he was dealing with, 'otherwise I'll agree to nothing.'
'That you must judge for yourself,' replied the fellow in the
green coat. 'For the next seven years you must neither wash nor
comb your beard and hair nor cut your nails, nor say one single
Our Father. I'll now give you a coat and a cloak which you must
wear till the end of that time. If you die within these seven years
you'll be mine, but if you survive them you'll be free, and rich
till the end of your days into the bargain.' The soldier remembered the desperate straits he was in, and having so often
braved death before he decided to do so again, and agreed to
the terms. The Devil took off his green coat, handed it to the
soldier and said: 'If you wear this coat and put your hand in
your pocket, you'll find that it's always full of money.' Then he
skinned the bear and said: 'This is to be your cloak and your bed
too, for you must sleep on it and in no other. And because of
this you shall be called Bearskin.' Having said this the Devil
disappeared. The soldier put on the coat, felt in his pocket at
once and found that he had not been misinformed. Then he
threw the bearskin round his shoulders, went out into the
world and lived merrily, doing everything he could think of to
gladden his heart and grieve his pocket. For the first year things
went not too badly, but in the second he was already a monstrous sight. His hair almost completely covered his face,
his beard was matted like an old piece of felt, his fingernails
were long claws, and his face was so thick with dirt that
you could have sown watercress on it and it would have
sprouted. Everyone who saw him ran away from him, but
because everywhere he went he gave money to the poor for
them to pray that he would not die within the seven years, and
because he always paid well, he could still always find a lodging.
In the fourth year the landlord of an inn he came to wouldn't
take him under his roof or even let him sleep in the stable,
fearing that his horses would shy. But when Bearskin fetched
a handful of ducats out of his pocket, he relented and gave
him a room at the back of the building, on condition that he
promised not to give the house a bad name by letting anyone
see him.

One evening, when Bearskin was sitting by himself and

heartily wishing the seven years were over, he heard someone weeping and wailing in the next room. Being a kind-hearted fellow, he opened the door and saw an old man weeping out loud and wringing his hands above his head. Bearskin approached him, but the man jumped up and tried to run away. Finally, hearing a human voice, he let himself be reassured, and by kindly persuasion Bearskin got him to tell him the cause of his grief, which was that he had gradually spent his whole fortune and he and his daughters were on the verge of starvation: he was so poor that he couldn't even pay the landlord, and they were going to put him in prison. 'If your trouble is nothing more than that, sir,' said Bearskin, 'I have plenty of money.' He sent for the landlord, paid the debt and gave the unfortunate man a purse full of gold as well.

When the old man saw that his troubles were at an end, he couldn't think how to show his gratitude. 'Come home with me,' he said. 'My daughters are miracles of beauty: choose one of them as your wife. When she hears what you have done for me she won't refuse. It's true that you look a bit strange, but she'll soon set that to rights.' This proposition appealed to Bearskin, and he went home with the old man. When the eldest daughter saw him, she was so scared by his appearance that she screamed and ran away. The second daughter didn't run away, and she had a good look at him, but then she said: 'How can I marry a man who no longer looks human? I'd almost rather have that shaved bear they showed here once, pretending to be a man: it did at least wear a hussar's uniform and white gloves. If he were just ugly I could get used to him.' But the youngest daughter said: 'Dear father, he must be a good man if he helped you when you were in need; you promised him a bride as his reward, and your promise must be kept.' It was a pity that Bearskin's face was covered with hair and dirt, or one could have seen how his heart leapt for joy at those words. He took a ring from his finger, broke it in two and gave her one half, keeping the other for himself. But on her half he wrote his name and on his half he wrote hers, and he asked her to keep her part of the ring carefully. Then he took his leave and said: 'I must travel for another three years, but if I don't come back then you will be released from your promise, because I shall be dead. But pray to God to preserve my life.'

The poor bride dressed all in black, and when she thought of her bridegroom the tears came to her eyes. From her sisters she got nothing but mockery and derision. 'You'd better watch out,' said the eldest. 'When you give him your hand, he'll grab at it with his paw.' 'Be careful,' said the second. 'Bears like sweet things, and if he likes you he'll eat you.' 'You'll have to do just as he tells you,' said the eldest again, 'or he'll start growling.' And the second added: 'But the wedding will be fun, bears are such good dancers.' The bride was silent and took no notice. But Bearskin travelled round in the world from one place to another, helping people whenever he could, and giving generously to the poor so that they would pray for him. Finally, when the last day of the seven years dawned, he went out to the moor again and sat down in the circle of trees. Before long there was the sound of rushing wind and the Devil stood before him. He glared at him in annoyance, threw him his old coat and demanded his own green coat back. 'Not so fast,' said Bearskin, 'you must clean me up first.' And the Devil, willy-nilly, had to fetch water and wash the dirt off Bearskin, and comb his hair and cut his nails. When this had been done, he looked like a gallant soldier and was much more handsome than he had been before.

When he was safely rid of the Devil, Bearskin felt relieved and his spirits rose. He went into the town, put on a fine velvet coat, then drove to his bride's house in a coach and four. No one recognized him; the old man took him for a high-ranking officer and gentleman, and showed him into the room where his daughters were sitting. He was put between the two eldest, who poured out wine for him, offered him the daintiest food and reckoned they had never seen a more handsome man in all the world. But the bride sat opposite him in her black dress, with downcast eyes and not speaking a word. When he finally asked their father if he would give him one of the girls as his wife, the two eldest sisters jumped up and ran to their room and began putting on their best clothes, for each of them imagined that she was the one he had chosen. As soon as the stranger was alone with his bride, he took out the half-ring and dropped it into a glass of wine which he handed to her across the table. She took it and drank it, but when she found the half-ring at the bottom her heart beat fast. She took the other half, which she wore on a ribbon round her neck, held the two together, and lo and behold, they fitted perfectly. Then he said: 'I am your betrothed bridegroom, whom you saw when I was Bearskin; but by God's grace my human shape has been restored to me and I am clean again.' He went over to her, took her in his arms and kissed her. Just then her two sisters entered in their full finery, and when they saw that the youngest had won this handsome husband and heard that he was Bearskin, they rushed out of the house in a terrible rage: one of them drowned herself in the well, and the other hanged herself from a tree. That evening there was a knock at the door, and when the bridegroom opened it there was the Devil in his green coat, and he said: 'There you are, you see, I've got two souls now instead of just yours.'

50

THE DEVIL AND HIS GRANDMOTHER

Once there was a great war being fought and the king had a great many soldiers, but the pay he gave them was so bad that they couldn't live on it. So three of them got together and decided to desert. One of them said: 'If we're caught they'll string us up on the gallows; how shall we go about it?' Another replied: 'You see that big cornfield there? If we hide in that no one'll find us. The army's not allowed into it, and they've got to move on tomorrow.' So they crawled in among the corn. But the army didn't move on, it stayed encamped right round the field. They squatted there among the corn for two days and two nights till they were nearly dying of hunger, but it would have meant certain death if they'd come out. And they said: 'What was the use of deserting! We're going to die here miserably anyway.' At that moment a fiery dragon came flying through the air, dived down towards them and asked them why they were hiding. They answered: 'We're three soldiers and we've deserted because our pay was so bad; and now we'll either starve if we stay here or swing on the gallows if we come out.' 'Will you serve me for seven years,' said the dragon, 'if I carry you right over the army so that no one will catch you?' 'We've no choice but to accept,' they answered. So the dragon seized them in his claws, carried them off through the air right above the army and brought them down to earth again a long way from it. Now the dragon was of course the Devil. He gave them a small whip and said: 'If you crack this whip, it'll set as much money as you want dancing about on the ground in front of you; then you can live like lords, keep horses and ride in carriages. But when the seven years are up you will belong to me.' Then he held out a book to them, and all three had to sign their names in it. 'However,' he added, 'before I take you I'll set you a riddle, and if you can guess the answer you shall be free and released from my power.' Then the dragon flew away, and off they went with their whip. They were never short of money, bought themselves fine clothes and travelled around in the world. Wherever they went they made merry and lived in style, riding on horses and driving in carriages and eating and drinking; but they never did anything wicked. The time passed quickly for them, and when the seven years were coming to an end two of them became sick with fear, but the third took it lightly and said: 'Don't worry, brothers, I'm no fool and I'll guess the riddle.' They went out into the fields, and as they sat there, two of them looking very gloomy, an old woman approached them and asked why they were so sad. 'Oh, why should you ask, old lady? You won't be able to help us.' 'Who knows,' she replied. 'Just tell me what the trouble is.' So they told her that they had been the Devil's servants for almost seven years, and that he had given them any amount of money, but that they had had to sign themselves over to him and would fall into his power unless they could solve a riddle when the seven years were up. 'If you want to save yourselves,' said the old woman, 'one of you must go into the forest, where he will find a rocky cliff that has caved in and looks like a hut; he must go inside and then he'll find help.' The two dejected ones thought: What good will that do us? and stayed where they were; but the third, the light-hearted one, got up and went into the forest and walked on and on till he found the rocky hut. And in it sat a woman as old as the hills: she was the Devil's grandmother, and she asked him where he came from and what he wanted here. He told her everything that had happened, and because she liked the look of him she took pity on him and promised to help him. She lifted a big stone under which there was a cellar, and said: 'Hide down there: you'll be able to hear everything that's said up here, so just sit still and don't move. When the dragon comes I'll ask him about the riddle, because he tells me everything. Then you must listen carefully to his answer.' At midnight the dragon came flying in and asked for his dinner. His grandmother laid the table and served food and drink, putting him into a good mood, and they ate and drank together. Then as they talked she asked him what sort of a day he'd had and how many souls he'd caught. 'I didn't have all that much luck today,' he replied, 'but I've got three soldiers in my clutches, at least they'll not escape me.' 'Well, well! three soldiers!' she said. 'They'll know a thing or two, you may lose them yet.' The Devil answered scornfully: 'I've got them all right. I've still to ask them a riddle, but they'll never guess the answer.' 'What riddle is that?' she asked. 'I'll tell you: at the bottom of the great North Sea there's a dead baboon, and that's the meat we'll roast for them; and a whale's rib, that's the silver spoon they'll use; and an old hollow horse's hoof, that's the wine-glass they'll drink from.' When the Devil had gone to bed, his old grandmother raised the stone and let the soldier out. 'Well, did you take good note of all that?' 'Yes,' he said, 'I've heard enough and I'll know what to do.' Then he had to leave secretly another way, through the window, and hurry back to his companions. He told them how the Devil had been tricked by his old grandmother and how he had heard him give the answer to his riddle. So now they were all in very high spirits, and cracked their whip and whipped up lots of money, making it dance about on the ground. When the last moment of the seven years had gone by, the Devil came with his book, showed them their signatures and said: 'I'm going to take you with me to hell, and when you get there you'll be given a meal. If you can guess what roast meat we'll serve to you, I'll let you go free, and you can keep the whip as well.' So the first soldier began the answer: 'At the bottom of the great North Sea there's a dead baboon, and that's the meat you'll roast for us.' The Devil was angry and went 'Hm! hm! hm!' Then he asked the second of them: 'But what will be the spoon you'll use?' 'A whale's rib, that's the silver spoon we'll use.' The Devil made a face and growled again three times 'Hm! hm! hm!' Then he asked the third of them: 'And do you know what wine-glass you'll drink from?' 'An old horse's hoof, that's the wine-glass we'll drink from.' At this the Devil flew away with a loud shriek and had no more power over them; but the three of them kept the whip, and whipped up as much money as they wanted, and lived happily till the end of their lives.

51

THE KING OF THE GOLDEN
MOUNTAIN

A merchant had two children, a boy and a girl, who were still so small that they couldn't walk. Now two of his ships were sailing across the sea carrying his entire fortune in rich cargoes, which he was hoping to sell for a lot of money; but then the news reached him that they had both been lost. So now instead of being a rich man he was poor, and all he owned was one field outside the town. To take his mind off his misfortune for a little he went out to his field, and as he was walking up and down on it he suddenly saw beside him a little black mannikin, who asked him why he was so sad and what had so stricken him with grief. The merchant said: 'If you could help me I'd tell you soon enough.' 'Who knows,' answered the little black man, 'perhaps I'll help you.' Then the merchant told him how he had lost his entire fortune at sea and had nothing left but this field. 'Don't worry,' said the little man. 'If you promise to bring to me here on this spot in twelve years' time whatever living creature first touches your legs when you get home, then you shall have as much money as you wish.' The merchant thought: That will surely only be my dog, but he didn't think of his little boy. He consented, signed and sealed the agreement with the black man and went back home.

When he got there his little boy was so glad to see him that, clinging to benches to keep himself upright, he came toddling over and hugged his legs. At this his father took fright, remembering his promise and realizing now what he had signed away. But he could still find no money in his chests and coffers, so he thought that the little man must just have been joking. A month later he went up to his attic to look for some more tin to sell, and up there he saw a great pile of coins lying on the floor. This put him in a good humour again, and he replenished his stocks, became a more prosperous merchant than before and blessed his luck. Meanwhile his son was growing up and becoming a very intelligent and sensible little boy. But the nearer he got to the age of twelve the more worried the merchant became, and you could read his anxiety in his face. One day his son asked him what was the matter: his father wouldn't tell him, but the little boy went on asking and asking until finally he said that without knowing what he was doing he had pledged him to a little black man in return for a lot of money. He had signed and sealed the agreement, he said, and now he would have to hand the boy over at the end of twelve years. But his son said: 'Oh, father, don't worry, it'll be all right, the black fiend has no power over me.'

The boy got the priest to bless him, and when the appointed time came he and his father went out together to the field. The son drew a circle and they both stood inside it. Presently the little black man appeared and said to the merchant: 'Have you brought me what you promised?' The father was silent but his son asked: 'What do you want here?' The little black man said: 'I'm talking to your father and not to you.' The boy replied: 'You tempted and deceived my father. Give back the contract.' 'No,' said the little black man, 'I'll not give up what is mine by right.' They went on arguing for some time, till finally they agreed that because the boy belonged neither to the Evil One nor to his father he should get into a boat on the river, and his father should push it off downstream with his own foot and let him take his chance in the water. So he said goodbye to his father, got into a boat, and his father had to push it off with his own foot. The boat capsized, so that its keel was uppermost and its deck underwater; his father thought his son was drowned, and went home and mourned for him.

But the boat didn't sink, it floated gently downstream and the boy sat safely inside it; and thus it floated for a long time, until finally it ran ashore in an unknown country. So he climbed onto the bank, and seeing a magnificent castle standing ahead of him he approached it. But when he entered it he found that it was bewitched: he walked from room to room and they were all empty until he reached the last, where he found a snake coiling on the floor. The snake was a bewitched maiden, and she was delighted to see him and said: 'Have you come at last, my rescuer? I have waited for you twelve years already; this kingdom is bewitched, and you must break the spell.' 'How can I do that?' he asked. 'Tonight twelve black men loaded with chains will come, and they will ask you what you are doing here; but you must be silent and give them no answer and let them do what they like with you. They will torment you and beat you and stick things into you, but just submit to everything and don't speak; at midnight they must leave again. And on the second night another twelve will come, and twenty-four on the third night, and they will chop off your head; but at midnight their power will cease, and if you have endured it all without uttering a word I shall be freed from the spell. I shall come to you with a flask containing the Water of Life and sprinkle some of it on you, and then you will be alive and well as before.' So he said: 'I will gladly free you from the spell.' Then everything happened as she had said: the black men couldn't force him to utter a word, and on the third night the snake turned into a beautiful princess who came to him with the Water of Life and made him alive again. And then she fell on his neck and kissed him, and there was joy and rejoicing in the whole castle. Then their wedding was celebrated, and he became King of the Golden Mountain.

So they lived happily together, and the queen gave birth to a beautiful little son. Eight years had passed and now he remembered his father: his heart was touched and he felt a desire to go home and visit him. But the queen didn't want him to leave and said: 'I know that it will bring misfortune on me.' But he left her no peace till she consented. When they parted she also gave him a magic ring, saying: 'Take this ring, and when you put it on your finger you will instantly be carried to whatever place you wish; but you must promise me that you will not use it to wish me away from here to your father's house.' He promised her this, put the ring on his finger and wished himself at home outside the city where his father lived. And in an instant he was there; but when he approached the city gate and tried to enter, the sentries wouldn't let him pass because he was wearing strange-looking clothes, although they were very rich and magnificent. So he went to a hill where there was a man keeping sheep, changed clothes with him and put on his old shepherd's cloak, and thus entered the city unhindered. When he got to his father's house he told him he was his son, but his father wouldn't believe this, saying that he had indeed had a son but he had been dead for many years. He added, however, that he could see he was a poor needy shepherd, so he would give him something to eat. But the shepherd said to his parents: 'I really am your son: don't you know of any birthmark you'd recognize me by?' 'Yes,' said his mother, 'our son had a strawberry-mark under his right arm.' So he pulled back his shirt and they saw the strawberry-mark under his right arm and no longer doubted that he was their son. Then he told them that he was King of the Golden Mountain and had married a princess and that they had a beautiful seven-year-old son. His father said: 'That's a fine story! Do you expect me to believe that a king would walk about in a ragged shepherd's cloak?' At this his son was angry, and forgetting his promise he turned the ring round on his finger and wished both his wife and his child into his presence. And in an instant they were there, but the queen wept and lamented, telling him he had broken his word and made her unhappy. He spoke soothingly to her, saying he had done it thoughtlessly and not meaning any harm; and indeed she pretended to forgive him, but secretly she planned revenge.

Then he took her to the field outside the town and showed her the river where he had been set adrift in the boat, and after that he said to her: 'I'm tired; sit down and let me sleep for a little on your lap.' So he laid his head on her lap and she groomed the lice from his hair for a little till he fell asleep. As he slept, she first took the ring from his finger and then drew her foot out from under him, leaving only her slipper behind; then she took her child in her arms and wished herself back in her kingdom. When he woke up he found himself lying there all alone, and his wife and his child had gone and so had the ring on his finger; only the slipper was still there as proof of it all. Well, he thought, I can't go back home to my parents, because they would say I'm a sorcerer; I'd better clear out and get back to my kingdom. So he walked on and finally came to a mountain, and at the foot of it were three giants quarrelling about how to divide their father's inheritance. When they saw him passing, they called out to him and said: 'Little people have clever brains, tell us how to divide this inheritance.' Now the inheritance consisted firstly of a sword, and when anyone grasped it and said: 'All heads off except mine!' everyone's head rolled to the ground. Secondly there was a cloak that made anyone who put it on invisible. Thirdly there was a pair of boots, and when you put them on and wished yourself anywhere, you were there in a trice. So he said: 'Give me the three things, for me to try whether they're still working properly.' So they gave him the cloak and as soon as he put it on he was invisible and had turned into a fly. Then he resumed his proper shape and said: 'The cloak's all right, now give me the sword.' They said: 'No, we won't give you that! If you were to say: "All heads off except mine!" our heads would all roll and only you would keep yours.' But they gave it to him on condition that he would try it out on the tree. This he did, and the sword cut through the trunk of the tree as if it had been a straw. Now he wanted to have the boots as well, but they said: 'No, we won't part with those; if you were to put them on and wish yourself to the top of this mountain, we'd be left standing down here with nothing.' 'No,' he said, 'I won't do that.' So they gave him the boots as well. But now that he had all three things his only thought was for his wife and child, and he said to himself: 'Oh, if only I were on the Golden Mountain!' And instantly he vanished from the sight of the giants, and that was how their inheritance was divided. When he got near his palace, he heard sounds of rejoicing and flutes and violins being played, and he was told that his wife was celebrating her wedding with another man. At this he was angry and said: 'That false-hearted woman deceived me, and abandoned me when I was asleep.' So he put on his cloak and went invisibly into the palace. When he entered the hall, he saw a great table laid with magnificent dishes, and the guests eating and drinking and laughing and making merry. And among them all his wife was sitting on a throne, wearing royal clothes and with the crown on her head.

He went and stood right behind her and no one saw him. When a piece of meat was put on her plate, he would snatch the plate from her and eat the meat; and when a glass of wine was poured out for her, he would snatch it from her and drain it dry; they kept giving her things and yet she still got nothing, for her plate and her glass kept vanishing immediately. At this she was astonished and ashamed, and got up and went to her room and wept, but he walked close behind her. And she said: 'Am I in the Devil's power then, or did my rescuer never come?' Then he struck her in the face and said: 'Did your rescuer never come? You treacherous woman, you are in your rescuer's power. Have I deserved this of you?' So saying, he made himself visible and went back into the hall and called out: 'The wedding is over, the rightful king has come!' The whole gathering of kings and princes and councillors mocked him and laughed at him, but he wasted no words and cried: 'Will you or won't you get out of here?' So they tried to arrest him and pressed in on him, but he drew his sword and said: 'All heads off except mine!' At this all their heads rolled to the ground, and now he alone was master and King of the Golden Mountain again.

52

THE PRINCE AFRAID OF NOTHING

Once upon a time there was a prince who had got tired of living at home in his father's house, and as he was afraid of nothing he thought: I'll go out into the wide world, I won't be bored there, and I'll see plenty of strange sights. So he took leave of his parents and set out on his journey. He travelled on and on, from morning till evening, not caring where his way led him. It so happened that he came to a giant's house, and as he was tired he sat down outside it to rest. And as he looked about him, his eyes fell on the giant's playthings lying in the yard – a set of enormous bowls, and skittles as tall as a man. Presently he felt like playing with them, set up the skittles and rolled the bowls at them, crying out merrily when the skittles fell and having a fine time. The giant heard the noise, stuck his head out of the window and saw a man who was no bigger than other men but was playing with his skittles. 'Little worm,' he shouted, 'why are you skittling with my skittles? Who gave you strength enough to do that?' The prince raised his eyes, took a look at the giant and said: 'You great clod, I suppose you think you're the only one with strong arms? I can do anything I feel like doing.' The giant came down, watched in great surprise as the prince went on with his game, and said: 'Man-child, if that's the kind of fellow you are, then go and fetch me an apple from the Tree of Life.' 'What do you want it for?' asked the prince. 'I don't want the apple for myself,' answered the giant, 'but I've got a girl I'm going to marry who keeps asking for it; I've gone round about in the world, far and wide, and I can't find the tree.' 'I'll find it all right,' said the prince, 'and I'd like to see what will stop me picking the apple off it.' The giant said: 'Do you think it's as easy a matter as all that? The garden where the tree is has an iron fence round it, and outside the fence are wild beasts lying side by side keeping watch, and they'll let no one through.' 'They'll let me through all right,' said the prince. 'Yes, but even if you get into the garden and see the apple hanging on the tree, i still won't be yours: there's a ring hanging in front of it, and anyone wanting to reach the apple and pick it has to put his hand through that ring, and no one's managed that yet.' 'I'll manage it all right,' said the prince.

With that he took his leave of the giant, and off he went over hill and dale, through fields and forests, till at last he found the magic garden. Round about it lay the beasts, but they had their heads down and were asleep. And they didn't wake up when he approached either, but let him step over them, and he climbed the fence and got successfully into the garden. There in the middle stood the Tree of Life with red apples glistening on its branches. He scrambled up the trunk, and as he was reaching out for an apple he saw a ring hanging in front of it. But he stuck his hand through without difficulty and picked the apple. The ring closed tightly round his arm, and he suddenly felt tremendous strength running through his veins. When he had got down again from the tree with the apple, he didn't want to climb back over the fence but seized hold of the great gate, and just had to give it one shake to make it open with a crash. So out he went, and the lion that had been lying in front of the gate had woken up and came leaping after him: but it wasn't savage and roaring, it followed him tamely as its master.

The prince took the promised apple to the giant and said: 'There you are, I hadn't any problem fetching it.' The giant was glad that his wish had been fulfilled so quickly, and he hurried off to his betrothed and gave her the apple she had asked for. She was wise as well as beautiful, and when she saw he didn't have the ring round his arm she said: 'I'll not believe you fetched the apple till I see the ring round your arm.' The giant said: 'I must just go home and get it,' for he thought it would be a simple matter to take something by force from a weak human being if he wouldn't hand it over willingly. So he went to him and demanded the ring, but the prince refused. 'The ring belongs with the apple,' said the giant, 'and if you won't give it to me willingly, you must fight with me for it.'

They wrestled with each other for a long time, but the giant couldn't overcome the prince, who was strengthened by the magic power of the ring. Then the giant thought of a trick and said: 'I've got all hot fighting and so have you; let's take a bathe in the river and cool off before we begin again.' The prince, who knew nothing of treachery, went with him to the water's edge and then took his clothes off and slid the ring off his arm as well and dived into the river. At once the giant snatched the ring and ran away with it; but the lion, who had seen him steal it, bounded after the giant, tore the ring out of his hand and took it back to his master. Then the giant hid behind an oak tree, and when the prince was busy putting on his clothes again he suddenly attacked him and poked out both his eyes.

So now the poor prince stood there blinded and didn't know what to do. Then the giant came up to him again, took him by the hand as if he were someone offering to guide him, and led him up to the top of a high cliff. Then he let go of him and thought: He just needs to take another step or two and he'll fall and kill himself, and then I can pull the ring off him. But the faithful lion hadn't abandoned his master, and took hold of him by his tunic and gradually pulled him back. When the giant came back to rob the dead man, he saw that his trick had not worked. 'Why can I not make an end of this feeble human creature!' he said to himself angrily. And he took hold of the prince and led him back to the precipice by another way; but the lion, noticing his evil plan, helped his master out of danger here too. When they had nearly reached the edge, the giant let go of the blind man's hand and was going to leave him there by himself, but the lion gave the giant a push, so that he fell over and was dashed to pieces at the bottom.

The faithful beast again drew his master back from the precipice and led him to a tree with a clear stream running beside it. There the prince sat down, but the lion lay down beside him and splashed the water into his face with its paw. Scarcely had a few drops touched the hollows of his eyes than he was able to see a little again. He noticed a little bird flying past quite close to him, but it knocked itself against a tree trunk: at this it went down into the water and bathed in it, then it flew up and darted among the trees without knocking into any of them, as if it had regained its sight. Then the prince understood this sign God had given him, and he stooped down to the water and washed and bathed his face in it. And when he raised his head there were his eyes again, brighter and clearer than they had ever been.

The prince thanked God for this great mercy and went on his way, wandering about the world with his lion. Now it so happened that he came to a castle that was bewitched. In the gateway·stood a maiden, beautifully shaped and with delicate features, but she was completely black. She spoke to him and said: 'Oh, if only you could release me from the evil spell that has been cast on me!' 'What am I to do?' asked the prince. The maiden answered: 'You must spend three nights in the great hall of the enchanted castle, but no fear must enter your heart. They will torment you in the most cruel fashion, but if you bear it without uttering a sound, then I shall be saved; they are not allowed to take your life.' Then the prince said: 'I'm not afraid, and with God's help I'll attempt it.' So he went gladly into the castle, and when it grew dark he sat down in the great hall and waited. But everything was silent until midnight; then suddenly a great noise started, and little devils came running out of every nook and corner. They pretended not to see him, sat down in the middle of the room, lit a fire and began to play a game. When one of them lost he would say: 'There's something wrong, there's someone here who isn't one of us, it's his fault that I'm losing.' Another said: 'Wait till I come for you, you there behind the stove.' The shrieking got louder and louder, fit to terrify anyone who heard it. The prince sat on quite calmly and felt no fear. But finally the devils jumped to their feet and went for him, and there were so many of them that he couldn't fight them off. They dragged him round on the floor, pinched him and pricked him and beat him and tormented him, but he didn't make a sound. Towards morning they vanished, and he was so exhausted that he could hardly move his limbs; but at daybreak the black maiden came in to see him. She was carrying a little flask containing the Water of Life, and as soon as she washed him with it he felt all his pain disappear and new strength run through his veins. She said: 'You have held out successfully for one night, but you still have two more to come.'

Then she left him again, and as she walked away he noticed that her feet had turned white. On the following night the devils came and began their game again: they attacked the prince and beat him much harder than on the previous night, so that there were wounds all over his body. But as he bore it all in silence they had to let him be, and at dawn the maiden came and healed him with the Water of Life. And when she left him, he was overjoyed to see that she had already turned white all over but for her fingertips. Now he had only one more night to endure, but it was the worst of them all. The devils that haunted the place came back and shrieked: 'Are you still here? We'll torture you till you choke.' They pricked him and beat him and threw him about and pulled at his arms and legs as if to tear him to pieces, but he bore it all and didn't utter a sound. Finally the devils vanished, but he lay there senseless and couldn't move; he couldn't even raise his eyes to see the maiden when she came in and sprinkled him and bathed him with the Water of Life. But suddenly he was relieved of all his pain and felt fresh and well as if he had wakened from a long sleep; and as he opened his eyes he saw the maiden standing beside him, snow-white and beautiful as the bright day. 'Rise up,' she said, 'and brandish your sword three times over the stairway, then we shall all be set free.' And when he had done this the whole castle was released from the magic spell, and the maiden turned out to be a rich princess. The servants came and announced that the table was already laid in the big hall and dinner already served. So they sat down and ate and drank together, and that night the wedding was celebrated with great joy.

53

THE CRYSTAL BALL

Once upon a time there was a sorceress who had three sons, and they loved each other like brothers; but the old woman didn't trust them and thought they wanted to steal her magic power. So she turned the eldest into an eagle, and he had to live on a mountain crag and would often be seen circling and swooping up and down in the sky. The second son she turned into a whale, and he lived deep under the sea, where from time to time he spouted up a mighty jet of water, and that was all that could be seen of him. They were both allowed their human form for only two hours each day. The third son was afraid she might turn him too into a bear or a wolf or some other wild animal, so he left home secretly. But he had heard that in the Castle of the Golden Sun there lived a princess who was under a spell and waiting to be released from it. He had been told that anyone trying to rescue her had to risk his life, and that twenty-three young men had already perished miserably and that only one more attempt was to be allowed. But since his heart was fearless he resolved to set out for the Castle of the Golden Sun. When he had travelled around for a long time and had still not found it, he wandered into a great forest and had no idea how to get out of it again. Suddenly he saw two giants in the distance beckoning to him, and when he got to them they said: 'We're quarrelling over a hat and can't decide which of us is to have it; we're both equally strong, so neither of us can overpower the other. Little people are cleverer than we are, so we want to leave the decision to you.' 'How can you be quarrelling over an old hat?' asked the young man. 'You don't know what's special about it,' they said. 'It's a wishing hat, and anyone who puts it on can wish himself to any place he likes and he'll be there in an instant.' 'Give the hat to me,' said the young man. 'I'll go on ahead a bit, then when I call you you must race towards me, and whichever of you reaches me first shall have it.' He put the hat on his head and walked on, but all he could think of was the princess and he forgot the giants and walked further and further. All at once he heaved a deep sigh and exclaimed: 'Oh, if only I were at the Castle of the Golden Sun!' and no sooner had he uttered the words than he found himself standing on a high mountain right outside the gate of the castle.

He went in and passed through all the rooms, till in the last of them he found the princess. But he was very startled when he saw her, for she had an ashy-grey wrinkled face, bleary eyes and red hair. 'Are you the princess so famous for her beauty?' he exclaimed. 'Alas,' she answered, 'this is not my true self, though human eyes can only see me in this ugly shape. But so that you may know what I am like, look into this mirror, for it cannot be deceived and will show you my image as it really is.' She handed him the mirror, and in it he saw the image of the most beautiful maiden in the world, and saw too that tears of sorrow were rolling down her cheeks. So he said: 'How can you be freed from the spell? I will shrink from no danger.' She replied: 'He who wins the crystal ball and shows it to the enchanter will destroy his power, and I shall return to my true shape. But alas,' she added, 'many men have already died in this attempt, and you are so young, I feel sorry for you, you are venturing into great peril.' 'Nothing can stop me from trying,' he said. 'But tell me what I must do.' 'I will tell you everything,' said the princess. 'At the foot of the mountain on which this castle stands you will find a wild bull standing by a spring, and you must fight with it. If you succeed in killing it, a fiery bird will rise up out of its body, and inside the bird there is a red-hot egg, and the yolk of that egg is the crystal ball. The bird will not let the egg drop till it is forced to; but if the egg drops on the earth, it will burn and destroy everything near it, and the egg itself will melt and so will the crystal ball, and all your efforts will have been in vain.'

The young man went down to the spring, where the bull stood snorting and bellowing at him. After a long fight he ran it through with his sword and it fell dead. At once the fiery bird rose up out of its body and tried to fly away, but the eagle, the young man's brother, who was soaring among the clouds, swooped down on it and drove it out to sea, harrying it with its beak until it was forced to drop the egg. But instead of falling into the sea the egg fell on a fisherman's hut by the shore, and at once the hut began to smoke and was about to burst into flames. But just then waves as big as houses rose in the sea and poured over the fire and put it out: the other brother, the whale, had come swimming in and stirred up the water. When the fire was out, the young man looked for the egg and luckily found it; it hadn't melted yet, but being suddenly plunged into cold water had made the hot shell crack, and he was able to remove the crystal ball undamaged.

When the young man took it to the enchanter and showed it to him, the enchanter said: 'My power is destroyed, and you are now king in the Castle of the Golden Sun. And you can give your brothers their human shapes back with it too.' So the young man hastened to the princess, and when he entered her room she was standing there in the full splendour of her beauty; and they exchanged rings with each other in great joy.

54

AULD RINKIE

Eence there wiz a king and he haed ae dother; an he gart bigg a gless mountain an said that fa'iver could rin up it an nae tummle should hae his dother for his wife. An there wiz een that loo't the king's dother gey sairly, and he spiert at the king gin he could get his dother. 'Aye,' said the king, 'if sae be he can rin up the mountain an nae tummle.' An the king's dother said that she waed rin up it wi im an haud im up if he tummelt. Sae they ran up the mountain thegither, an fan they wiz half-wey ower't, the king's dother she slippit an fell, an the gless mountain it gantit open an she tummelt doon intill't; an her lad he cudnae see far she haed faan throuw, for the mountain close't up again stracht awà. An he roart an grat somethin aafa, an the king wiz richt sair-made; an he gart them brak intae the mountain tae see gin he could get her oot again, but they couldnae fin' the place far she fell in.

Meantime the king's dother she haed faan deep doon intae a muckle great cave at the boddam; an there an auld carl wi a muckle lang grey baird cam till her an tellt er that if she wid be his sairvint an dee aa his biddin she could keep er life, an if nae, he wid kell er. Sae she did his biddin. Ilka mornin he oot wi his ledder oot o his pootch an set it up against the mountain waa an up he clomb oot o the mountain; an than he yarkit the ledder up efter im. An syne she maun mak his maet an mak his bed an tyaav for him, an syne fan he cam hame he aye brocht a heep o gowd an siller wi im. An fan she haed bidden wi im mony a year, he cam tae caa er Mistress Manreid an gart er caa him Auld Rinkie.

Weel, eence he wiz awà oot an she wiz makin his bed an washin his dishes, an fit did she dee but steek aa the doors an the windaes ticht tee, aa but ae windaekie that she left open. An fan Auld Rinkie cam hame, he chappit at the door an cryet: 'Mistress Manreid, open the door tae me.' 'Na,' said she, 'Auld Rinkie, I'll nae open the door tae ye.' An says he:

'Peer Auld Rinkie stannin, fegs,
Stannin on his saiventeen legs,
Stannin on his ae gowd faet,
Mistress Manreid, wash my dishes for me.'

'I've washen yer dishes already,' said she. An says he again:

'Peer Auld Rinkie stannin, fegs,
Stannin on his saiventeen legs,
Stannin on his ae gowd faet,
Mistress Manreid, mak my bed for me.'

'I've made yer bed already,' said she. An says he again:

'Peer Auld Rinkie stannin, fegs,
Stannin on his saiventeen legs,
Stannin on his ae gowd faet,
Mistress Manreid, open the door tae me.'

An he gaed loupin aa roon the ootside o his hoose, an fan he saw the windaekie open, thinks he till imsèl: I'll tak a lookie in tae see fit she's daen an fit-wey she winna open the door tae me. An fan he tried tae look in, he couldnae get his heid throuw for his baird, sae he pat his baird throuw the windaekie first; an as seen as he did that, up cam Mistress Manreid an yarkit the windaekie tee wi a tow that she'd fastent till't, an there wiz he, stuck fast bi the baird. Sae he began tae yammer an roar, it wiz that sair, an he priggit wi er tae lat im oot. 'Na,' said she, 'nae till ye gie me the ledder that ye clim' oot on.' An will he nill he, he maun tell her far the ledder wiz. Sae she tyet the hale length o his baird tae the windaekie, pat the ledder against the waa and clomb oot o the mountain; an as seen as she wiz oot she opint the windaekie. Syne hame she gaed tae her father an tellt him aa her throuwcome. An the king he wiz kinechtit, an her lad he wiz still there; an they gaed an diggit up the hale mountain an fund Auld Rinkie wi his heaps o siller an gowd. An the king gart kell Auld Rinkie an took aa his siller an gowd; an the king's dother got her auld lad for a man, an they livt weel contentit an canty an grand.

55

JORINDA AND JORINGLE

Once upon a time there was an old castle in the depths of a great dense forest: in it an old woman lived all by herself, and she was a most powerful sorceress. By day she would turn herself into a cat or a screech-owl, but at night she would take on proper human shape again. She knew how to entice animals and birds, which she would then slaughter and cook and roast. If anyone came within a hundred paces of her castle, he was rooted to the spot and couldn't move till she lifted the spell; but if an innocent girl happened to enter this magic circle, she would turn her into a bird and then shut her up in a wicker cage and take the cage to one of the rooms in her castle. She had about seven thousand cages, all containing these rare birds.

Now there was once a maiden called Jorinda, and she was more beautiful than any of the others. She was betrothed to a very handsome young man called Joringle; they were soon to be married, and to be in each other's company was their greatest joy. One day, wanting to talk to each other alone, they went for a walk in the forest. 'Take care not to get too close to the castle,' said Joringle. It was a beautiful evening, the bright rays of the sun shone through the tree trunks into the dark green of the forest, and the turtle-doves sang plaintively in the old beech trees.

Sometimes Jorinda wept; she just sat down in the sunshine and cried, and Joringle cried too. They felt as sad as if they had been going to die. They looked round and realized they were lost, and had no idea how to get home. The sun was still half above the hill and half of it was below. Looking through the bushes, Joringle saw the old wall of the castle close by them and started in terror. Jorinda was singing:

> 'My little bird that's ringed with red
> Sings lackaday and lackaday,

The little turtle-dove is dead,
Sing lacka – tirroo, tirroo, tirroo.'

Joringle looked round towards Jorinda. She had been turned
into a nightingale and was singing: 'Tirroo, tirroo, tirroo.' A
screech-owl with fiery eyes flew three times round her and
screeched three times: 'Shoo, hoohoohoo.' Joringle found that
he couldn't move: he stood there like a stone, unable to weep or
speak or stir hand or foot. The sun had set now; the owl flew
into a bush, and out of it a moment later came a crooked old
woman, yellow and skinny, with big red eyes and a crooked
pointed nose that touched her chin. She murmured some
words, caught the nightingale and carried it away on her
hand. Joringle couldn't say a thing and couldn't budge; the
nightingale was gone. Finally the old woman came back and said
in a hollow voice: 'Greetings, Zachiel! When the moon shines
into the cage, set him free, Zachiel, when it's time.' And
Joringle was released from the magic. He fell on his knees
before the old woman and begged her to give him back his
Jorinda, but she said he would never see her again, and went
away. He cried out and wept and lamented, but it was all in
vain. 'Oh! Oh! What's to become of me now!' Joringle wandered off and finally came to a strange village, where he stayed
for a long time minding sheep. He often walked round the
castle, but not too close to it. Then one night he dreamt that he
found a blood-red flower with a beautiful big pearl in the centre
of it, and that he picked this flower and took it to the castle;
everything he touched with the flower was freed from magic,
and he also dreamt that in this way he had recovered his Jorinda
again. When he woke up in the morning, he began to search
high and low to see if he could find such a flower, and early on
the morning of the ninth day of his search he found it: it was
blood-red and had a big drop of dew in the centre, as big as the
finest pearl. Then he travelled night and day and brought this
flower back to the castle. When he got within a hundred paces
of it, he wasn't held fast but was able to walk right on to the
castle gate. He was overjoyed. He touched the gate with the
flower, and it sprang open. He went in and through the court-

yard and stopped to listen for the sound of all the birds: at last
he heard where they were. On he went and found the room,
and in it was the sorceress feeding the birds in their seven
thousand cages. When she saw him she was very very angry
and scolded him and spat poison and gall at him, but she
couldn't come nearer him than two paces. He took no notice of
her and went and looked at the birdcages; but there were
hundreds and hundreds of nightingales, so how was he to pick
out his Jorinda? As he looked, he noticed that the old woman
had secretly picked up one birdcage and was creeping towards
the door with it. At once he leapt across the room and touched
the cage with the flower and the old woman as well: after that
she could work no more magic, and Jorinda was standing there
with her arms round his neck, as beautiful as she had ever been.
So then he turned all the other birds back into girls too, and
went home with his Jorinda, and they lived happily together for
many years.

56

THE NIXIE IN THE POND

Once upon a time there was a miller, who lived contentedly with his wife, for they had money and property and their prosperity increased from year to year. But ill luck comes like a thief in the night: just as their wealth had grown, so now from year to year it diminished, until at last the miller could scarcely call the mill he lived in his own. He was burdened with care, and when he lay down on his bed after the day's work he could find no rest, but tossed from side to side in anxiety. One morning he got up before daybreak and went for a walk out of doors, thinking it might lighten his heart. He walked along the mill-dam, and just as the rising sun was shedding its first rays he heard the sound of something moving in the pond. He turned round and saw a beautiful woman rising slowly out of the water. With her delicate hands she was holding her long hair, which fell down over her shoulders on both sides and covered her white body. He realized that she was the nixie of the pond, and was so frightened that he didn't know whether to walk on or stand still. But the nixie began speaking to him in a soft voice, called him by name and asked him why he was so sad. At first the miller was speechless; but when he heard her talk to him so kindly, he plucked up courage and told her that he had once been rich and fortunate, but was now so poor that he was at his wits' end. 'Have no fear,' said the nixie. 'I will make you richer and more fortunate than you have ever been, but you must promise that you will give me whatever has just been born in your house.' What can she mean, said the miller to himself, but a puppy or a kitten? And he consented to give her what she asked. The nixie disappeared again into the water, and he hurried back to his mill comforted and full of hope. When he was nearly there, the maid opened the front door and called out to him that there was good news: his wife had just given birth to a little boy. The miller stood thunderstruck: he realized that the sly nixie had known this all along and had tricked him. He approached his wife's bed with his head bowed, and when she asked him why he was not glad at the birth of their beautiful little boy, he told her what had happened and the promise he had had to make to the nixie. 'What good is wealth and fortune to me,' he added, 'if I am to lose my child? But what can I do?' And the relations who had called to congratulate him couldn't think what advice to give him either.

Meanwhile good fortune again returned to the miller's house. All his undertakings prospered, his chests and coffers seemed to fill of their own accord and the money in his strongbox seemed to multiply overnight. Before long his wealth was greater than it had ever been. But he could not enjoy it with an easy mind, for the promise he had made to the nixie tormented his heart. Each time he passed the pond he feared she might rise from the water and remind him of his unpaid debt. As for the boy himself, he never let him go near it. 'Be careful,' he would say to him, 'if you touch that water a hand will come out of it and take hold of you and drag you under.' But as year after year passed and no more was seen of the nixie, the miller began to feel reassured.

As the boy grew up he was apprenticed to a hunstman. When he had finished learning and become a fine huntsman himself, the lord of the village took him into his service. In the village there lived a beautiful and faithful girl with whom the huntsman fell in love, and when his master noticed this he gave him a small house; the two young people were married and lived quietly and happily together, loving each other dearly.

One day the young man was hunting a stag. When the animal broke out of the forest into open ground, he followed it and finally shot it dead. He didn't notice that he had come close to the dangerous pond, and after gutting the animal he went to the water's edge to wash his bloodstained hands. But hardly had he dipped them in when the nixie rose above the surface, laughingly flung her wet arms round him and quickly dragged him into the depths, making the water ripple and close over his head.

When evening came and the huntsman didn't return home,

his wife became alarmed. She went out to look for him, and as
he had often told her about how he must beware of the nixie's
attempts to entrap him and must never venture near the pond,
she had a foreboding of what had happened. She hastened to
the water's edge, and when she found his game-bag lying there
she could no longer doubt what misfortune had befallen him.
Wringing her hands and lamenting, she called her beloved, but
it was all in vain. Hurrying to the other side of the pond, she
called to him again and cried out to the nixie in bitter
reproaches, but there was no answer. The watery surface did
not stir; only the face of the half-moon looked up at her motion-
lessly.

The poor woman did not leave the pond. She went restlessly
round it again and again, half walking and half running, sometimes in silence, sometimes crying out in anguish or moaning
softly. At last her strength failed her: she sank to the ground
and fell into a deep sleep. Presently she had a dream.

She was climbing up and up, cold with fear, amid great rocky
boulders; thorns and creepers caught at her feet, the rain beat
into her face and the wind blew her long hair about. When she
reached the top the whole scene changed, the sky was blue and
the air mild, the ground sloped gently downwards, and on a
green meadow covered with all sorts of flowers stood a neat
little hut. She went up to it and opened the door, and there sat
an old woman with white hair who beckoned to her kindly. At
that moment the poor woman woke up. Day had already
dawned, and she decided to act on the dream at once. She toiled
up the mountainside and found everything just as she had seen
it the night before. The old woman received her kindly and
invited her to sit down. 'You must have suffered a misfortune,'
she said, 'since you visit my lonely hut.' Tearfully the huntsman's wife told her what had happened. 'Be comforted,' said
the old woman, 'I will help you. Take this golden comb: wait
until the full moon has risen, then go to the pond, sit down at
the water's edge and comb your long black hair with it. But
when you have finished, lay the comb down on the shore, and
you will see what happens.'

The young woman returned home, but she could hardly wait

for the full moon. At last its shining circle rose above the horizon; at once she went out to the pond, sat down and combed her long black hair with the golden comb, and when she had finished she laid it at the water's edge. Soon there was a rushing sound in the water, a wave rose, rolled in over the shore and carried off the comb. No sooner had the comb had time to sink to the bottom than the surface broke and the huntsman's head appeared above it. He did not speak, but gazed sadly at his wife. A moment later a second wave came rushing up and closed over his head. Everything had vanished, the pond lay motionless again, and only the face of the full moon gleamed from its surface.

The young wife went home grief-stricken, but in her dream she saw the old woman's hut. She set out for it again next morning and told her troubles to the wise-woman, who gave her a golden flute and said: 'Wait till it is full moon again, then take this flute, sit down on the shore, play a beautiful song on it, and when you have done that lay the flute on the sand; you will see what happens.'

The young wife did as the old woman had told her. Scarcely had she put the flute down on the sand when there was a rushing sound from the water: a wave rose, rolled towards her and carried off the flute. Presently the surface broke and not only the head but half the body of her husband rose above it. He held out his arms to her longingly, but a second wave rose and washed over him and drew him under again.

'Alas,' cried his unhappy wife, 'what good is it to me to see my darling only for a moment and then lose him again!' Grief filled her heart once more, but her dream took her for a third time to the old woman's house. She set off, and the wise-woman gave her a golden spinning-wheel, comforted her and said: 'All has not yet been accomplished. Wait till full moon, then taking the spinning-wheel, sit down on the shore and spin till the spindle is full; when you have done that, put the spinning-wheel near the water's edge, and you will see what happens.'

The young wife carefully followed this advice. As soon as the full moon rose, she carried the golden spinning-wheel to the shore and spun busily till there was no more flax and the spindle was full of thread. But scarcely had she put the wheel down on the shore when there was an even louder rushing sound than usual from the depths of the water; a mighty wave swept up and carried off the wheel. At once her husband's head and whole body rose up in a jet of water: quickly he leapt onto the shore, seized his wife's hand and fled. But they had not run more than a short distance when with a hideous roar the whole pond overflowed its banks and poured all over the fields in a swirling flood. The fugitives thought their last hour had come; then the wife in her terror called out to the old woman for help, and in an instant they were transformed, she into a toad and her husband into a frog. The flood overtook them, and although it could not drown them it snatched them apart and carried both of them far away.

When the water had subsided and they were both on dry ground again, they recovered their human shapes. But neither knew where the other had gone; they found that they were among strangers who had no idea where their home was. High mountains and deep valleys separated them. To make a living they both had to mind sheep. For many years they drove their flocks through the fields and woods and were filled with sorrow and longing.

Once, when spring had broken out again over the earth, they both set off on the same day with their flocks, and by chance they both drove them towards the same place. He saw a flock on a distant hillside and drove his own sheep in that direction. They met in a valley and did not recognize each other, though they were glad to be no longer alone. After that they drove their flocks side by side every day; they spoke little, but felt comforted. One evening, when the full moon had risen and the sheep were lying down, the shepherd took the flute from his pocket and played a beautiful but mournful song. As he finished playing, he noticed that the shepherdess was weeping bitterly. 'Why are you crying?' he asked. 'Alas,' she answered, 'the full moon was shining just like this when I last played that song on the flute and my darling's head rose above the water.' He looked at her, and a veil seemed to fall from his eyes: he recognized his dear wife, and when she looked at him and the moon shone on his face, she recognized him too. They embraced and kissed each other, and we need not ask whether they were happy.

57

FETCHER'S FOWL

Once upon a time there was a wizard who used to take on the shape of a poor man and go from house to house begging and snatch beautiful girls away. No one knew where he took them, because no one ever saw them again. One day he turned up at the house of a man who had three beautiful daughters; he looked like a poor, frail beggarman, and had a basket slung over his back, as if for collecting alms. He asked for a bite to eat, and when the eldest daughter came out and was going to hand him a piece of bread, he just touched her and she had to jump into his basket. Then he strode quickly away and carried her to his house, which stood in the middle of a dark forest. The house was magnificently furnished and he gave her everything she wanted, saying: 'My precious, you'll enjoy living with me; here you have everything your heart desires.' This lasted for a few days, then he said: 'I must go on a journey and leave you alone here for a short time; here are the keys of the house, you may go anywhere you like and look at everything, except the room which is unlocked by this little key: that room I forbid you to enter on pain of death.' He also gave her an egg and said: 'See that you keep this egg, and indeed carry it with you always, for if it were lost terrible things would happen.' She took the keys and the egg and promised to do all that he had told her. When he had gone she explored the house from top to bottom and looked at everything: the rooms were shining with silver and gold, and she thought she had never seen such splendour in her life. And finally she also came to the forbidden door. She tried to walk past it, but curiosity left her no peace. She examined the key, it looked just like any other key, she put it in the lock and turned it a little, and the door sprang open. But what did she see when she went in? A huge basin full of blood stood in the middle of the room, full of chopped-up dead people, and beside it stood a wooden block on which lay a gleaming axe.

She was so scared that the egg, which she was holding in her hand, went plopping into the basin. She fetched it out again and wiped the blood off it, but it was no good, the blood appeared again at once; she wiped it and scraped it, but she couldn't get it off.

Shortly after this the man came back from his journey, and the first thing he did was to ask for the key and the egg. She handed them to him, but she was trembling with fear, and as soon as he saw the red stains he knew that she had been in the Room of Blood. 'Since you have entered that room against my will,' he said, 'you shall enter it again against yours. Your life is forfeit.' He cast her to the ground, dragged her to the place by her hair, struck off her head on the block and chopped her to pieces, so that her blood ran all over the floor. Then he threw her into the basin with the others.

'Now I'll fetch the second of them,' said the wizard, and taking the shape of a poor man again he went back to the house and begged. The second sister brought him a piece of bread, and he captured her like the first by merely touching her, and carried her off. She fared no better than her sister had done, let herself be tempted by curiosity, opened the Room of Blood and looked in, and had to pay for it with her life when her captor returned. Then he went and fetched the third sister, but she was clever and crafty. After he had given her the keys and the egg and gone away, she first carefully put the egg in a safe place, then she explored the house and finally entered the forbidden room. Alas, what did she see! There lay her two dear sisters in the basin, horribly murdered and chopped up. But she set to and fished out the pieces and put them all together correctly, heads and trunks and arms and legs. And when they were all complete, the limbs began to stir and joined themselves up, and the two girls opened their eyes and came alive again. Then they were all glad, and kissed and hugged each other. When the man came home he at once demanded the key and the egg, and when he could find no trace of blood he said: 'You have passed the test, and you shall be my bride.' He now no longer had power over her and had to do as she told him. 'Very well,' she replied, 'then first you shall take a basket of gold to my father and mother, carrying it yourself on your back; meanwhile I shall prepare the wedding.' Then she ran to her sisters, whom she had hidden in a little room, and said: 'The time has come and now I can save you; that villain shall carry you back home himself. But as soon as you get there you must send help to me.' She put both of them in a basket and covered them up completely with gold so that nothing could be seen of them, then she called in the wizard and said: 'Now take this basket and be off with you; but mind you don't stop to rest on the way, I shall be looking from my little window and watching you.'

The wizard lifted the basket on to his back and set off with it; but it weighed so heavily on him that the sweat poured down his face. So he sat down to rest for a little, but at once one of the girls in the basket called out to him: 'I'm looking from my window and I can see you resting: get a move on at once!' He thought it was his bride calling out to him and set off again. Then he tried to sit down a second time, but at once a voice called out: 'I'm looking from my window and I can see you resting: get a move on at once!' And every time he stopped, the voice called out and he had to carry on, until finally he arrived groaning and breathless, with the basket containing the gold and the two girls, at their parents' house. But back at his own house his bride was arranging the wedding feast and she had the wizard's friends invited to it. Then she took a skull with grinning teeth, decorated it with jewellery and a wreath of flowers, and carried it upstairs and put it in an attic window to look out. When everything was ready she plunged herself into a barrel full of honey, cut open the feather bed and rolled around in it till she looked like a strange bird and no one could recognize her. Then she left the house, and on her way she met some of the wedding guests who asked her:

'Fetcher's Fowl, Fetcher's Fowl, where have you been?'
'Fitzy the Fetcher's house I've seen.'
'What is the young bride finding to do?'
'She has swept the house, she has swept it clean:
From her attic window she's looking for you.'

Finally she met the bridegroom walking slowly back home. He asked her as the others had done:

'Fetcher's Fowl, Fetcher's Fowl, where have you been?'
'Fitzy the Fetcher's house I've seen.'
'What is my young bride finding to do?'
'She has swept the house, she has swept it clean:
From her attic window she's looking for you.'

The bridegroom looked up and saw the skull with the flowers round it; thinking it was his bride, he nodded and waved to her. But when he and his guests were all in the house, the bride's brothers and relations who had been sent to rescue her arrived. They locked all the doors so that no one could get out, then they set fire to the house and burnt the wizard and all his crew to death.

58

THE ROBBER BRIDEGROOM

Once upon a time there was a miller who had a beautiful daughter, and when she grew up he was anxious to see her well married and provided for. He thought: If a proper suitor comes along and asks for her hand, he shall have her. Before long a suitor turned up who seemed to be very rich, and since the miller could find nothing against him he promised him his daughter. But the girl didn't really take to him as a girl should to her betrothed bridegroom: she didn't trust him, and her heart contracted with horror every time she looked at him or thought of him. One day he said to her: 'You're my betrothed bride and yet you never even come to visit me.' The girl replied: 'I don't know, sir, where your house is.' And the bridegroom said: 'My house is out there in the dark forest.' She tried to think of excuses and said she wouldn't be able to find the way there. The bridegroom said: 'Next Sunday you must come out to visit me. I've invited the guests already, and to help you find your way through the forest I'll put down a trail of ashes for you.' When Sunday came and she had to set out, she felt afraid without really knowing why, and filled both her pockets with peas and lentils to mark the path. When she came to the edge of the forest, she found that ashes had been scattered and she followed the trail, but at every step, left and right, she threw a few peas on the ground. She walked nearly all day till she came to the middle of the forest, where it was darkest of all, and here she found an isolated house. She didn't like the look of it, it seemed gloomy and sinister. She went in, but there was no one there and everything was very silent. Suddenly a voice called out:

> 'Go home, go home, my lady bride,
> This is a house where murderers hide.'

Looking up, she saw that the voice was that of a bird hanging in a cage on the wall. It called out again:

> 'Go home, go home, my lady bride,
> This is a house where murderers hide.'

Then the fair bride walked on from room to room and explored the whole house, but it was all empty and not a soul was to be seen. Finally she reached the cellar, and there a very old woman was sitting wagging her head. 'Can you not tell me, good woman,' asked the girl, 'whether my bridegroom lives here?' 'Oh, you poor child,' answered the old woman, 'what a place you have strayed to! This is a den of murderers. You think you're a bride soon to be wedded, but it's death you're going to wed. Look, I've had to fill that great cauldron with water and put it on the fire; once they have you in their power, they'll chop you up without mercy and cook you and eat you, for they're eaters of human flesh. If I don't take pity on you and save you, you're lost.'

So saying, the old woman hid the girl behind a huge barrel where she couldn't be seen. 'Be as quiet as a mouse,' she said, 'don't move and don't stir, or it'll be the end of you. In the night, when the robbers are asleep, we'll escape; I've waited long enough for a chance myself.' Scarcely had she said this when the godless crew returned home. They were dragging another young maiden with them; they were drunk, and paid no heed to her screams and lamentations. They gave her some wine to drink, three glasses full, one of white and one of red and one of yellow, and that made her heart burst. Then they tore off her pretty clothes, laid her out on a table, hacked her fair body to pieces and sprinkled them with salt. The poor bride hidden behind the barrel trembled and shuddered, for she saw clearly what a fate the robbers had had in store for her. One of them noticed a gold ring on the murdered girl's little finger, and as it didn't come off at once when he pulled, he took an axe and chopped the finger off. But the finger jumped up into the air and jumped right over the barrel and fell straight into the bride's lap. The robber took a candle and began looking for it, but he couldn't find it. Then another of them said: 'Did you look behind the big barrel as well?' But the old woman exclaimed: 'Come along and eat, and leave searching till tomorrow; the finger won't run away.'

The robbers said: 'The old woman's right,' and stopped looking for it and sat down to their supper; and the old woman poured a sleeping draught into their wine, so that they were soon lying down in the cellar asleep and snoring. When the bride heard this, she came out from behind the barrel. She had to step over the sleeping men, who were lying on the ground in rows, and she was terrified that she might wake one up. But God helped her and she got past them safely. The old woman came upstairs with her and opened the door, and they hurried away from that murderers' den as fast as they could. The wind had blown away the ash trail, but the peas and lentils had sprouted up and showed them the way in the moonlight. They walked all night and reached the mill in the morning, and the girl told her father everything that had happened.

When the day came on which the wedding was to take place the bridegroom appeared, and the miller had had all his friends and relatives invited. As they sat at dinner, everyone in turn was asked to tell a story. The bride sat silent and didn't speak a word. Then the bridegroom said to her: 'Well, my love, can you think of nothing? Why don't you tell us a story too?' She answered: 'I will tell you a dream I had. I was walking alone through a forest and finally came to a house with not a living soul in it, but on a wall there was a bird in a cage that called out:

"Go home, go home, my lady bride,
This is a house where murderers hide."

It said these words to me twice. My dear, it was only a dream. Then I explored all the rooms, and they were all empty and it was all so uncanny; finally I went down to the cellar and found a very old woman sitting there wagging her head. I asked her: "Does my bridegroom live in this house?" She answered: "Oh, you poor child, you have come to a den of murderers; your bridegroom lives here, but he intends to chop you up and kill you and then cook you and eat you." My dear, it was only a dream. But the old woman hid me behind a big barrel, and no

sooner was I hidden there than the robbers came home dragging a girl with them. They gave her three kinds of wine to
drink, white and red and yellow, and that made her heart burst.
My dear, it was only a dream. Then they pulled off her pretty
clothes, chopped her fair body in pieces on a table and sprinkled
them with salt. My dear, it was only a dream. And one of the
robbers saw that on her ring-finger there was still a gold ring,
and because it was hard to get off he took an axe and chopped it
off; but the finger jumped up into the air and jumped right over
the big barrel and fell into my lap. And here is the finger with
the ring on it.' So saying, she took it out and showed it to the
company.

The robber, who had turned white as a sheet as she told her
story, jumped up and tried to escape, but the guests seized him
and handed him over to the authorities. Then he and his whole
band were brought to justice for their foul deeds.

59

THE BREMEN TOWN BAND

A man had a donkey who had been patiently hauling sacks of grain to the mill for many a long year, but now his strength was failing and he was becoming less and less fit for work. His master was thinking of sparing his feed and getting rid of him; but the donkey sensed that there was trouble afoot, so he ran away and set out towards Bremen, reckoning that he might get a job there in the town band. When he'd been on his way for a little while, he came across a hound lying by the roadside and panting as if he'd been running very hard. 'Well now, Buster,' asked the donkey, 'what are you puffing and blowing like that for?' 'Oh,' said the dog, 'I'm old and getting weaker day by day, and I'm no good at hunting any more, so my master was going to kill me: and so I ran away, but how shall I earn my living now?' 'I'll tell you what,' said the donkey, 'I'm on my way to Bremen to join the town band: come with me and let them sign you up in it too. I'll play the lute and you can bang the drums.' The dog accepted this invitation, and on they went. Before long they found a cat sitting by the roadside making a face like three rainy days in a row. 'Now then, Mr Whiskerwiper, what's happened to make you look so sour?' asked the donkey. 'How do you expect me to look when my life's in danger?' answered the cat. 'Just because I'm not so young as I was and my teeth aren't as sharp as they used to be and I'd sooner sit by the fire and purr than chase about after mice, my mistress tried to drown me. I managed to escape of course, but now what's to be done and where am I to go?' 'Come with us to Bremen: you sing very good serenades, so they'll take you on in the town band.' The cat thought this a good idea and joined them. Next our three refugees passed a farm, and there was the cock sitting on the gate crowing its head off. 'What a horrible noise you're making,' said the donkey, 'what's it all about?' 'I've been fore-casting fine weather,' said the cock, 'because it's today Our

Lady does her washing and wants to hang the Christ Child's shirts out to dry; and yet, just because tomorrow's Sunday and guests are coming, my hard-hearted mistress has told the cook that she wants to have me in tomorrow's soup, so I'm to have my head cut off this evening. So now I'm having a good crow while I still can.' 'Nonsense, Redcrest,' said the donkey, 'come along with us instead: we're going to Bremen, and any place'll suit you better than a stewpot. You've got a great voice, and when we all make music together, let me tell you, it'll certainly sound like something.' The cock thought this a sensible proposal, and all four of them went on their way together.

But they couldn't reach Bremen in one day, and in the evening they came to a forest and decided to spend the night there. The donkey and the dog lay down under a big tree, and the cat and the cock took to its branches, but the cock flew right to the top where he would be safest. Before going to sleep, he took one more look round in all directions and thought he saw a spark of light in the distance, so he called out to his companions that there must be a house not far away because he could see a light burning. The donkey said: 'Then we must get on our feet and go to it, because we've got a pretty poor lodging here.' The dog said he wouldn't mind either if he could have a bone or two, with some meat on them. So they set off in the direction of the light, and soon enough it was getting brighter, and it got bigger and bigger till they came to a well-lit house where a band of robbers lived. The donkey, being the tallest, went up to the window and looked in. 'What do you see, Greyskin?' asked the cock. 'What do I see?' exclaimed the donkey. 'I see a table laid with fine food and drink, and a pack of robbers sitting round it enjoying themselves.' 'That would be something for us,' said the cock. 'Yes, yes, my goodness, I wish we were there!' said the donkey. So the animals put their heads together to decide what would be the best way of driving the robbers out of the house, and at last they thought of a plan. The donkey had to stand with its front feet against the window, the dog had to jump onto the donkey's back and the cat climb onto the dog, and finally the cock flew up and perched on the cat's head. When they had done that, one of them gave a signal, and all together they began making their music: the donkey brayed, the dog barked, the cat mewed and the cock crowed, and then they all crashed into the room through the window, smashing the panes to smithereens. At this bloodcurdling din the robbers started to their feet, thinking some hobgoblin had broken into the house, and rushed out into the wood in a panic. Whereupon our four friends sat down at the table, made the best of what was left, and ate as if they had a month's fast ahead of them.

When our four minstrels had finished their meal, they put out the light and looked for sleeping quarters, each according to his natural needs and preferences. The donkey lay down on the dung-heap, the dog behind the door and the cat near the warm ashes on the hearth, while the cock went to its roost among the rafters; and being tired after their long journey, they soon fell asleep. When midnight was past and the robbers, watching from a safe distance, noticed that the house was now dark and that all seemed quiet, their captain said: 'Well now, we shouldn't have let ourselves be frightened off like that,' and he ordered one of his men to go back to the house and investigate. The man found the whole place lying silent, went into the kitchen to fetch a light, mistook the cat's fiery red eyes for live coals and tried to light a match at them. But the cat wasn't to be trifled with like this, and leapt at his face spitting and scratching. At this he panicked, took to his heels and tried to leave by the back door, but the dog was lying there and jumped up and bit him in the leg. He ran for his life across the yard, and just as he was passing the dung-heap he got a mighty kick in the backside from the donkey; meanwhile the cock, perching on its roost and wakened by the noise, began screeching: 'Kikiriki-kee! Kikiriki-kee!' The robber ran back as fast as he could to his captain and said: 'Oh my God, there's some horrible witch sitting in the house who hissed at me and scratched my face with her long nails, and there's a man with a knife standing by the door who stabbed me in the leg, and a black monster in the yard who started beating me with a wooden club, and up in the roof there's the judge sitting, and he called out: "Bring the thief to me! Bring the thief to me!" So I got away while the going was good.' After that the robbers didn't dare enter the house again, but the four members of the Bremen town band so much enjoyed living there that they just stayed on.

And for many a year this tale has been told;
The last tongue to tell it's not yet cold.

60

CLEVER ELSIE

There was a man who had a daughter whom everyone called
Clever Elsie. And when she grew up her father said: 'Let's get
her married.' 'Yes, let's,' said her mother, 'if only we could find
a man who'd be willing to take her.' Finally a young fellow from
another part of the country came along; his name was Jack and
he asked for her hand in marriage, but he made it a condition
that Clever Elsie really was clever. 'Oh,' said her father, 'she's
as sharp as a needle and thread.' 'Bless you,' said her mother,
'she can see the wind blowing up the alley and hear flies
clearing their throats.' 'Well,' said Jack, 'if she's not really
bright, I'll not have her.' So when they were sitting at table and
had finished their meal, her mother said: 'Elsie, go down to the
cellar and fetch some beer.' So Clever Elsie took the jug from the
wall and went down to the cellar, not forgetting to go
clapperty-clap with the lid as she went, to keep herself amused.
When she got downstairs she fetched a stool and placed it in
front of the beer-barrel, to avoid having to stoop and so perhaps
hurt her back or injure herself in some way. Then she put the
jug down in front of her and opened the spigot; but while the
beer was running into the jug, she remembered to keep her eyes
busy, letting them wander up the wall and peer this way and
that, until finally she caught sight of a pickaxe right above her
head, which the masons had left there by mistake. At this,
Clever Elsie began to cry and said: 'If I marry Jack and we have a
child and he grows up and we send him down here to the cellar
to draw beer, that pickaxe'll fall on his head and kill him.' And
there she sat and wept and cried her heart out over this future
misfortune. The others were waiting upstairs for their drink,
but Clever Elsie didn't come back and didn't come back. So her
mother said to the maid: 'Go on down to the cellar and see what
Elsie's doing.' The maid went down and found her sitting in
front of the beer-barrel howling. 'Elsie!' asked the maid, 'what

are you crying for?' 'Oh,' she answered, 'isn't it enough to make anyone cry! If I marry Jack and we have a child and he grows up and gets sent down here to fetch drink, maybe that pickaxe'll fall on his head and kill him.' The maid said: 'What a clever girl our Elsie is!' and sat down beside her and began to weep about the accident too. After a while, when the maid didn't come back and the others upstairs were thirsty for their drink, Elsie's father said to the manservant: 'Go on down to the cellar and see what Elsie and the maid are doing.' The manservant went down, and there were Clever Elsie and the maid sitting side by side weeping. So he said: 'What are you crying about?' 'Oh,' said Elsie, 'isn't it enough to make anyone cry! If I marry Jack and we have a child and he grows up and gets sent down here to fetch drink, that pickaxe'll fall on his head and kill him.' The manservant said: 'What a clever girl our Elsie is!' and sat down beside her and began howling too. Upstairs they were waiting for the manservant to come back, but when he didn't, Elsie's father said to his wife: 'Go on down to the cellar and see what Elsie's doing.' His wife went down and found all three of them lamenting and asked them what the matter was, whereupon Elsie told her too about her future child who might perhaps be killed by the pickaxe when he grew up and was sent to draw beer and the pickaxe fell on his head. So her mother too said: 'My, what a clever girl our Elsie is!' and sat down and cried with the rest of them. Upstairs her husband waited for a little; but when his wife didn't come back and he got thirstier and thirstier, he said: 'I must just go down to the cellar myself and see what Elsie's doing.' But when he got to the cellar and saw them all sitting in a row crying their eyes out and was told the reason, namely that it was on account of the child Elsie might have one day and who might be killed by the pickaxe if he happened to be sitting under it drawing beer just when it fell off the wall, he exclaimed: 'What a clever girl she is!' and sat down and joined in the weeping. The intending bridegroom waited upstairs by himself for some time, but when no one came back he thought: They must be waiting for me, I must go down as well and see what they're up to. When he got downstairs, there sat the five of them howling and lamenting so piteously you couldn't tell who was crying loudest. 'What in the name of goodness has happened?' he asked. 'Oh, Jack my dear,' said Elsie, 'if we get married and have a child and he grows up and maybe we send him down here to fetch drink, that pickaxe that's been left up there might fall down and cut his head open, and he'll die; isn't that enough to make anyone cry?' 'Well,' said Jack, 'that's as much brains as I need in my household; since you're such a clever girl, Elsie, I'll marry you.' And he seized her by the hand and took her upstairs and she became his wedded wife.

When they'd been married for a while, Jack said to her: 'Wife, I'm going out to work and earn us some money; you go out to the field and cut the corn so that we can have some bread.' 'Yes, Jack dear, I'll do that.' When Jack had gone, she cooked up a good dish of porridge for herself and took it out to the field with her. When she got there she said to herself: 'What shall I do? Shall I cut the corn first or shall I eat first? Ee, I'll eat first.' So she ate the whole of her pot of porridge, and when she was well and truly fed she said again: 'What shall I do? Shall I cut corn first or sleep first? Ee, I'll sleep first.' So she lay down in the corn and went to sleep. When Jack had been home for some time, there was still no sign of Elsie, and he said: 'What a clever girl my Elsie is, she's such a hard worker that she doesn't even come home for dinner.' But when evening came and she still didn't reappear, Jack went out to see how much corn she'd cut; but she hadn't cut any at all, she was lying in the corn asleep. Then Jack hurried home and fetched a bird-net with little bells all over it, and came and threw it over her, and she just slept on. Then he went back home, locked the door and sat down to work. Finally, when it had got quite dark, Clever Elsie woke up, and when she got to her feet she heard a jingling and a jangling all round her and the bells jingled at every step she took. This got her all scared and confused: she didn't know whether she really was Clever Elsie or not, and asked herself: 'Am I, or amn't I?' But she didn't know how to answer the question, and stood there for quite a time wondering; finally she thought: I'll go home and ask whether it's me or not, they'll know for sure. She came running up to the door of her house, but it was locked; so she knocked at the window and called out: 'Jack, is Elsie in there?' 'Yes,' answered Jack, 'she's here.' At this she took fright and said: 'Oh my goodness, then I'm not me!' Then she went to someone else's front door, but when people heard the bells jingling they wouldn't let her in, and she couldn't find anywhere to sleep. So off she ran right out of the village, and no one has ever seen her since.

61

LAZY HARRY

Harry was so lazy that although he had nothing else to do but drive his goat out to graze every day, he still heaved many a sigh when he got back home in the evening after completing his day's labours. 'What a weary job it is,' he would say, 'what a terrible burden, year after year, driving that goat out into the fields every day till Michaelmas! If I could even lie down and take a nap while she feeds! But no, I've got to keep my eyes open or she'll damage the young trees, or squeeze through a hedge into someone's garden, or even run away altogether. What sort of a life is that? No peace of mind, no relaxation.' He sat down and collected his thoughts and tried to work out some way of getting this burden off his back. For a long time all his ponderings were in vain, then suddenly the scales seemed to fall from his eyes. 'I know what I'll do!' he exclaimed. 'I'll marry Fat Katie; she's got a goat as well, so she can take mine out with hers and I won't have to go on wearing myself to a shadow like this.'

So Harry got up, set his weary limbs in motion and walked right across the street, for it was no further than that to where Fat Katie's parents lived; and there he asked for the hand of their hard-working, virtuous daughter. Her parents didn't stop to think twice; 'Like to like makes a good match,' they remarked, and gave their consent. So now Fat Katie became Harry's wife and drove both the goats out to graze. Harry spent his days very pleasantly, with nothing more strenuous to recover from than his own idleness. He only went out with her now and then, saying: 'I'm just doing this so that I'll enjoy my bit of a rest afterwards all the more; you lose all your appreciation of it otherwise.'

But Fat Katie was no less idle than Harry. 'Harry dear,' she said one day, 'why should we needlessly make our lives a misery like this and spoil the best years of our youth? Those two goats wake us out of our best morning sleep anyway with their bleating: wouldn't it be better to give them both to our neighbour and get a beehive from him in exchange? We'll put up the beehive in a sunny place behind the house and just leave it to look after itself. Bees don't need to be minded and taken out to graze: they'll fly out and find their own way home and make honey, without our having to raise a finger.' 'You're a very sensible girl,' answered Harry, 'and we'll do as you suggest right away. What's more, honey's tastier than goat's milk and it does you more good and you can store it for longer.'

The neighbour willingly gave them a beehive in exchange for their two goats. The bees flew in and out tirelessly from early in the morning till late in the evening and filled the hive with the finest honey, so that in the autumn Harry was able to collect a whole jar of it.

They stood the jar on a shelf that was fixed to the wall above their bed; and fearing that someone might steal it or the mice might get at it, Katie fetched in a sturdy hazel rod and put it at the bedside, so that she wouldn't have to bestir herself unnecessarily but just reach for it and drive away any unwelcome visitors without having to get up.

Lazy Harry didn't like to rise before midday: 'Too soon out of bed and you'll soon be dead,' he would remark. So there he was one morning, still lolling among the feathers in broad daylight, having a good rest after his long sleep, and he said to his wife: 'Women have a sweet tooth, and you've been at that honey again; I think our best plan, before it all gets eaten up by you, would be to give it in exchange for a goose and a young gander.' 'But not till we have a child to mind them!' replied Fat Katie. 'You don't suppose I'd want to be bothered with young goslings, needlessly wearing out my strength?' 'And do you suppose,' said Harry, 'that the boy will look after geese? Nowadays children don't do what they're told any more, they do just as they please, because they think they're cleverer than their parents, just like that farmhand who was sent to fetch a cow and started chasing three blackbirds.' 'Well then,' answered Katie, 'this one had better look out if he doesn't do as I tell him. I'll take a stick to him and give his hide a real good tanning. Watch me,

Harry!' she exclaimed in her excitement, seizing the stick she kept to drive away the mice, 'watch me beat the backside off him!' She lifted the stick, but unfortunately struck the honey-jar above the bed. The jar was knocked against the wall and fell to smithereens, and all that fine honey went trickling over the floor. 'Well, so much for the goose and the young gander,' said Harry, 'we shan't have to mind them now. But it's a bit of luck that the jar didn't fall on my head; we've every cause to be content with our lot.' And seeing that some honey was still left in one of the fragments, he reached out and picked it up and said cheerfully: 'Wife, let's enjoy the little that's left over here, and then take a bit of a rest after the fright we've had. What does it matter if we get up a little later than usual, the day's still long enough.' 'Oh yes,' answered Katie, 'better late than never. You know the one about the snail that was invited to the wedding? It set out and got there in time for the christening. And just outside the house it fell from the top of a fence, and said to itself: "More haste, less speed."'

62

THE THREE ARMY-SURGEONS

There were once three army-surgeons who reckoned that they had nothing more to learn about the art of surgery. They were on their travels, and stopped for the night at an inn. The landlord asked them where they had come from and where they were going, and they answered: 'We're on our travels and living by our skill.' 'Well, just show me what you can do,' said the landlord. The first said he would cut off his hand and put it back on again next morning and make it heal; the second said he would tear out his heart and put it back in again next morning so that it would heal; the third said he would gouge out his eyes, and they too would heal when he replaced them next morning. 'If you can do that,' said the landlord, 'then you've nothing more to learn.' Now they had with them an ointment which was able to close and heal any wound they smeared it on, and they always carried the flask containing it wherever they went. So they cut from their bodies the hand and the heart and the eyes as they had said they would, put them all together on a plate and gave it to the landlord; and the landlord gave it to a maid-servant, telling her to put it aside in the larder and keep it carefully. But this maidservant secretly had a sweetheart who was a soldier. So when the landlord and the three surgeons and everyone else in the house were asleep, the soldier came and asked her for something to eat. So the girl opened the larder and brought in something from it, and she was so much in love with him that she forgot to close the larder door. She sat down with her sweetheart at the table and they had a good chat, but as she sat there without a care in the world the cat came creeping in, found the larder open, snatched the hand and the heart and the eyes that belonged to the three surgeons and made off with them. So when the soldier had finished eating and the girl got up to clear away the dishes and lock the larder, she saw at once that the plate the landlord had given her to look after was empty. She took fright and said to her young man: 'Oh, heaven save me, what am I to do? The hand's gone, and the heart and the eyes are gone, whatever will happen to me tomorrow morning!' 'Stop crying,' he said. 'I'll get you out of this. There's a thief hanging on the gallows out there, and I'll cut his hand off: which hand was it?' 'The right hand.' So the girl gave him a sharp knife and he went outside, cut the poor sinner's right hand off and brought it in. Then he seized the cat and gouged out its eyes; now all that was needed was the heart. 'Haven't you just slaughtered some pigs and put their carcases in the cellar?' 'Yes,' said the girl. 'Well, that's all right then,' said the soldier, and he went down to the cellar and came back with a pig's heart. The maid put all the things together on a plate and left it in the larder: then her sweetheart took his leave and she went to bed thinking all was well.

When the three surgeons got up next morning, they told the maid to fetch them the plate with the hand and the heart and the eyes. So she fetched it out of the cupboard, and the first surgeon held the thief's hand in place and smeared the join with his ointment, whereupon the hand at once grew back on to his arm. The second took the cat's eyes and fitted them into his head, and the third put the pig's heart in place. The landlord stood and watched their skill with admiration, saying that he had never seen such a thing in his life and that he would praise and recommend them to all and sundry. Then they paid their bill and travelled on.

As they were walking along, the one who had the pig's heart kept on leaving the others: every time they passed some corner he would trot over to it and root around in it like a pig. The other two tried to hold him back by the coat tails, but it was no good, he kept running off to wherever the filth was thickest on the ground. The second of them also began to behave strangely, rubbing his eyes and saying to the other: 'My dear fellow, what's the matter with me? These aren't my eyes, I can't see a thing, for heaven's sake one of you give me your arm or I'll fall.' And they struggled on till evening, when they came to another inn. They all went into the parlour, and there in one corner a rich gentleman was sitting at the table counting money. The surgeon with the thief's hand sidled round behind him, his arm twitched a few times and finally, when the gentleman had his back turned, he reached out and snatched a handful of coins from the pile. One of the others saw this and said: 'My dear fellow, what are you doing? It's wrong to steal, you ought to be ashamed.' 'Yes, but I can't stop myself,' said his friend. 'My hand keeps twitching and just has to help itself whether I want to or not.' Then they went to bed, and as they lay there it was so dark that you couldn't have seen your hand in front of your face. Suddenly the one with the cat's eyes woke up, wakened the others and said: 'My dear friends, look at this, do you see all these white mice running about?' The other two sat up in bed but couldn't see a thing. Then he said: 'There's something wrong with us: we didn't get back our own parts, that landlord cheated us and we must go back to him.' So next morning they set off back and told the landlord that their right organs hadn't been returned to them: one of them had a thief's hand, the second cat's eyes and the third a pig's heart. The landlord said that it must be the maid's fault and was going to call her, but when the girl had seen the three surgeons returning she had fled through the back door, and she didn't reappear. Then the three of them told the landlord that unless he paid them a great deal of money they'd make a bonfire of his house; so he gave them all he had and all he could raise, and off they went with it. It was enough to keep them for the rest of their lives, but they'd still rather have had their own organs back.

63

THE CLEVER LITTLE TAILOR

Once upon a time there was a princess who was ever so proud: if any man came to woo her she would set him a riddle, and if he couldn't guess it he was laughed to scorn and sent packing. She also had it made known that whoever did guess the answer to her riddle should marry her, no matter who he might be. And indeed, in the end it so happened that three tailors were making the attempt at the same time. The two eldest reckoned that as they had already successfully sewn many a delicate stitch, they could hardly go wrong and were bound to succeed here as well; the third was a feckless, giddy young fellow who didn't even know his trade properly but thought he was bound to have luck in this case, for if not, then what luck would he ever have in any other case. The two others said to him: 'You'd better just stay at home, you with your feather-brain won't get far.' But the young tailor wouldn't be put off, saying that he had set his heart on this enterprise and would manage all right; and off he went, sauntering along as if the whole world belonged to him.

So all three of them appeared before the princess and asked her to put her riddle to them: she would find, they said, that she had met her match this time, because their wits were so sharp that you could thread a needle with them. So the princess said: 'I have two kinds of hair on my head, what colours are they?' 'That's easy,' said the first, 'I think they're black and white, like the cloth they call pepper and salt.' The princess said: 'You've guessed wrong; let the second of you answer.' So the second said: 'If it's not black and white, then it's brown and red like my respected father's frock-coat.' 'Wrong again,' said the princess. 'Let the third of you answer, I can see he knows it for sure.' So the young tailor stepped forward boldly and said: 'The princess has silver and gold hair on her head, and those are the two colours.' When the princess heard that, she turned pale and nearly fainted away in alarm, for the young tailor had guessed right, and she had been convinced that no one in the world would be able to do so. When she had recovered herself she said: 'This still doesn't give you the right to marry me, there's something else you must do first. Down in the stable there's a bear, and you must spend the night with him. If you're still alive when I get up tomorrow morning, then you shall marry me.' But she thought that she would get rid of the young tailor in this way, because no one had ever got into this bear's clutches and lived to tell the tale. But the young tailor wasn't to be daunted: 'Nothing venture, nothing win,' he commented cheerfully.

So that evening our young friend was taken down to the bear's den. And sure enough, the bear at once advanced on the little fellow, meaning to welcome him with a good swipe of his paw. 'Not so fast, not so fast,' said the young tailor, 'I'll soon take the steam out of you.' And in a leisurely manner, as if he were quite unconcerned, he took some walnuts out of his pocket, cracked them open with his teeth and ate the kernels. When the bear saw this, his appetite was whetted and he wanted some nuts as well. The young tailor put his hand in his pocket and held out some to him: these, however, weren't nuts but pebbles. The bear stuck them in his mouth, but couldn't crack a single one of them, bite as he might. Goodness me, what a booby I am, thought the bear, I can't even crack nuts. And he said to the young tailor: 'Hey, crack these nuts for me!' 'There now, what a fellow you are!' said the tailor. 'A big muzzle like that and you can't even crack a little nut!' And he took the stones, but nimbly put a nut into his mouth instead, and crack! he bit open the shell. 'I must try that again,' said the bear. 'To look at you doing it, you'd think I'd find it easy.' So the young tailor gave him another lot of pebbles, and the bear worked away at them, biting for dear life. But as you may imagine, they were more than he could crack. After this, the young tailor pulled out a fiddle from under his coat and began playing a tune on it. When the bear heard the music, he couldn't help himself and began to dance, and when he'd danced for a little he found himself enjoying it so much that he said to the tailor: 'Tell me, is it difficult to play the fiddle?' 'It's child's play:

look, my left hand fingers the strings, my right hand scrapes away at them with the bow, and out comes a merry noise, tralala, fiddledidee!' 'I'd like to learn to fiddle like that,' said the bear, 'then I could dance whenever I liked. What do you say to that? Will you give me lessons?' 'I'll be delighted to,' said the tailor, 'if you have the skill for it. But let's have a look at your paws: they're a mighty length, I'll have to pare your nails down a bit.' So a vice was fetched, and the bear held out his paws, but the young tailor screwed them in tightly and said: 'Now wait till I get the scissors.' So saying, he left the bear to stand there and growl, lay down in the corner on a pile of straw and went to sleep.

The princess, hearing the bear growl so loudly that night, assumed that he must be growling with satisfaction, having made an end of the tailor. In the morning she got up feeling very pleased and not worried at all, but when she took a look at the stable there was the young tailor standing outside it cock-a-hoop and safe and sound. So then there was nothing more she could say, because she'd publicly promised to marry him; and the king sent for a carriage to take her and the tailor to church to be married. As they drove off, the other two tailors, who were false-hearted and envied him his good fortune, went into the stable and unscrewed the bear. The bear in a great rage charged off in pursuit of the carriage. The princess heard him growling and snorting and cried out in terror: 'Oh, the bear's after us, he's coming to get you!' With great presence of mind the young tailor stood on his head, stuck his legs out of the window and shouted: 'Do you see this vice? If you don't clear off I'll screw you back into it.' When the bear saw that, he turned round and ran away. Our young friend then drove on to the church as calm as you like, and the princess gave him her hand at the altar, and he lived with her as happy as a woodlark. There's a fine of three marks for anyone who doesn't believe this story.

64

BUMPKIN

There was once a village full of rich peasants; only one of them was poor and the others all called him Bumpkin. He didn't even have a cow, let alone the money to buy a cow, though he and his wife longed to have one. One day he said to her: 'Listen, I've had a good idea: the joiner's a good friend of ours, I'll get him to make us a wooden calf and paint it brown so it'll look just like any other calf, and maybe in time it'll grow up and then we'll have a cow.' His wife liked this idea too, and their friend the joiner worked away with his saw and his plane and finished the calf, all properly painted and with its head hanging down to the ground as if it were grazing.

Next morning when the cows were being driven out, Bumpkin called in the cowherd and said: 'Look, I've got a calf here, but he's still only little and has to be carried.' 'Right you are,' said the cowherd, and picked the calf up and carried it out to the pasture and stood it in the grass. The little calf went on standing there just like one that's grazing, and the cowherd said: 'He'll soon be able to walk on his own, just look how much he's eating already!' That evening when he was about to drive the herd home again, he said to the calf: 'If you can stand here and eat your bellyful, then you can walk on your own four legs, I'm not going to pick you up and haul you back home.' But Bumpkin was standing by his front door waiting for his calf, and when the cowherd came driving his animals through the village and the calf wasn't among them he asked where it was. The cowherd answered: 'It's still standing out there, eating, I couldn't get it to stop and come with me.' But Bumpkin said: 'That's not good enough, I want my animal back.' So they went back to the meadow together, but someone had stolen the calf and it was no longer there. The cowherd said: 'I dare say it ran away.' But Bumpkin said: 'You don't play that sort of game with me!' And he took the cowherd before the mayor, who found him guilty of negligence and ordered him to compensate Bumpkin for the lost calf by giving him a cow.

So now Bumpkin and his wife had the cow they had wanted for so long, and were delighted. But they had no fodder to give it, so it had to go hungry and they soon had to slaughter it. They salted and stored the meat, and Bumpkin went into town to sell the hide, planning to buy a new calf with the proceeds. On the way he passed a mill where he saw a raven sitting with broken wings, and feeling sorry for it he picked it up and wrapped it in the hide. But the weather had changed and became so wet and stormy that he couldn't go on, so he took shelter in the mill and asked for a bed for the night. The miller's wife was alone in the house; she told Bumpkin to lie down in the straw and gave him a piece of bread and cheese. Bumpkin ate it and lay down with his cowhide beside him, and the miller's wife thought: He's tired and fast asleep. Presently the priest arrived and mine hostess received him well, saying: 'My husband's out, let's have a little feast together.' Bumpkin pricked up his ears, and when he heard her talk of a feast he was angry to have been fobbed off with bread and cheese. The miller's wife came back into the room bringing four different things, roast meat and salad and cakes and wine.

Just as they were going to sit down and eat, there was a knock at the door, and the miller's wife said: 'Oh my God, that's my husband!' She quickly hid the roast in the oven, the wine under the pillow, the salad in the bed, the cake under the bed and the priest in the hall cupboard. Then she opened the door to her husband and said: 'Thank God you're back! I've never seen such weather, you'd think it was the end of the world!' The miller saw Bumpkin lying on the straw and asked: 'What's that fellow doing there?' 'Oh,' said his wife, 'the poor wretch turned up when it was pouring with rain and asked for shelter, so I gave him a piece of bread and cheese and told him to lie on the straw.' Her husband said: 'That's all right by me, but hurry up and get me something to eat.' His wife said: 'But I've only got bread and cheese.' 'That'll do well enough,' answered her husband, 'even bread and cheese will do.' And he looked at Bumpkin and called to him: 'Come and have some more to eat with us.' Bumpkin didn't wait for a second invitation, but got to his feet and ate with them. Then the miller noticed the cowhide lying on the ground with the raven wrapped up in it, and asked him: 'What have you got there?' Bumpkin answered: 'I've got a fortune-teller in here.' 'And could he tell my fortune?' asked the miller. 'Why not?' replied Bumpkin. 'But he'll only tell you four things, the fifth he'll keep to himself.' The miller was full of curiosity and said: 'Well, let's have him tell them.' So Bumpkin squeezed the raven's head, making it croak and go 'krr, krr'. The miller asked: 'What did he say?' Bumpkin answered: 'The first thing he says is that there's some wine hidden under your pillow.' 'The devil there is!' exclaimed the miller, and he went and found the wine. 'Well, what's next?' he asked. Bumpkin made the raven croak again and said: 'The second thing he says is that there's a roast in the oven.' 'The devil there is!' exclaimed the miller, and he went and found the roast. Bumpkin made the raven prophesy again and said: 'The third thing he says is that there's some salad in the bed.' 'The devil there is!' exclaimed the miller, and he went and found the salad. Finally Bumpkin squeezed the raven again to make it croak, and said: 'The fourth thing he says is that there's cake under the bed.' 'The devil there is!' exclaimed the miller, and he went and found the cake.

So now the two of them sat down together at table, but the miller's wife was scared to death and went to bed taking all the keys with her. The miller was very keen to hear about the fifth thing, but Bumpkin said: 'Let's eat the other four in peace first, because the fifth is a piece of bad news.' So they had dinner, and then they bargained over how much the miller would pay for the raven's fifth prophesy, till finally they agreed on a hundred ducats. So Bumpkin squeezed the raven's head once more and it gave a loud croak. The miller asked: 'What does he say?' Bumpkin replied: 'He says that the Devil's hiding in your hall cupboard.' The miller said: 'I'll turn the Devil out of my house,' and he unbolted the front door. But his wife had to surrender the key to the hall cupboard and Bumpkin unlocked it. The priest jumped out and ran for dear life, and the miller said: 'I saw the black villain with my own eyes: that bird was right.' But Bumpkin made off with his hundred ducats as soon as day dawned.

Back at home, Bumpkin gradually improved his status, and built himself a nice little house, and the other peasants said: 'Our Bumpkin must have been to the land where it snows gold and you can pick up money by the bushel.' And Bumpkin was summoned before the mayor and asked where his new-found wealth came from. He answered: 'I went into town and sold my cowhide for a hundred ducats.' When the peasants heard that, they wanted to cash in on this excellent deal themselves, so they hurried home and had all their cows slaughtered and skinned, hoping to sell them in town at the same high profit. The mayor said: 'My herdsmaid must be the first.' But when she got to town and went to the merchant, he paid her no more than one ducat for each hide, and when the others arrived he gave them even less, saying: 'What do you expect me to do with all these hides?'

The peasants were furious now with Bumpkin for tricking them: they decided to take revenge on him, and brought him before the mayor on a charge of fraud. The innocent Bumpkin was unanimously condemned to death and sentenced to be rolled into the lake in a barrel full of holes. He was led out to execution and a priest was brought to read a mass for his soul. The others had to leave them together for this to be done, and as soon as Bumpkin set eyes on the priest he recognized him as the one who had been visiting the miller's lady wife. So he said to him: 'Father, I got you out of that cupboard, so you get me out of this barrel.' Now it happened at that moment that a flock of sheep was being driven past by a shepherd who, as Bumpkin knew full well, had for a long time wanted to be elected mayor; so he shouted out as loud as he could: 'No, I won't do it! Even if the whole place goes down on its knees to me, I won't do it!' The shepherd, hearing this, came up to him and asked: 'What's all this about? What won't you do?' Bumpkin said: 'They want to make me mayor if I'll sit in that barrel; but I won't do it.' The shepherd said: 'Is that all there is to it! If they'll make me mayor, I'll willingly sit in the barrel right away.' 'If you're willing to sit in it,' said Bumpkin, 'then they'll make you mayor.' The shepherd agreed, sat down in the barrel, and Bumpkin nailed the lid on; then he took charge of the shepherd's flock and drove it away. But the priest went to the village council and told them that he had read the mass. So they came and rolled the barrel towards the water. When the barrel began to roll, the shepherd cried out: 'But you can make me mayor, I'd like to be mayor!' They thought it was Bumpkin yelling, and said: 'I dare say you would, but you must take a look at the bottom of the lake first,' and they rolled the barrel into the lake.

After this the peasants set off back home, and as they got to the village they met Bumpkin calmly driving in a herd of sheep and looking very pleased with himself. At this they were amazed and said: 'Bumpkin, where have you come from? Haven't you been in the lake?' 'Of course,' answered Bumpkin. 'I sank down and down till finally I got to the bottom. Then I kicked open the barrel and crawled out of it; and down there were the finest meadows you ever saw, with lots of lambs grazing on them, so I brought this flock of them back with me.' The peasants asked: 'Are there still some left?' 'Oh yes,' said Bumpkin, 'more than enough for all of you.' So the peasants agreed that they would all go and fetch up some sheep as well, a whole flock for each of them, and the mayor said: 'I must have the first choice.' So off they all went to the lake together, and just at that time it so happened that there were little fleecy clouds in the blue sky, the kind called lambkins, and they were reflected in the water. 'There are the sheep!' cried the peasants, 'we can see them at the bottom from here!' The mayor elbowed his way to the front and said: 'I'll go down first and take a look round, and if everything's all right I'll call you.' So in he jumped with a plop. The others thought this was the mayor calling out to them: 'Hop!' and they all hurled themselves into the water after him. In this way the whole village died by drowning, and Bumpkin as the sole survivor became a rich man.

65

OWLD PEADAIR

There was this culchee farmer and he had a woife, and the village priest was terrible keen on his woife and was only poinin to spend a whole day alone with her havin a grand toime. Well now, herself was agreeable, so one day he sez to her: 'Look it, oi've tought up a way that we can have a grand toime the two of us together. This is what yez must do: get into yer bed on Wednesday and tell yer husband yez're poorly; yez must mowan and yez must growan, and kape it up till Sunday when it'll be toime fer me saremon. Now, in me saremon oi'll say that anyone with a sick choild, a sick husband, a sick woife, a sick father, a sick mother, a sick sister, brother or whatever should make a pilgrimage to Croaghpatrick in County Mayo, where yez can buy a peck of larrel laves fer a penny, and then his sick choild, sick husband, sick woife, sick father, sick mother, sick sister, brother or whatever will be cured in a jiffy.'

'Roight yez are,' sez the woman. So on Wednesday she took to her bed. She mowaned and she growaned fer all she was wort, and her husband procured her every medicine he could tink of, but nothin availed. When Sunday came, the woman sez: 'Oi feel only terrible, like oi was about to doie any minute, but there's one ting oi want to do before oi pass on, and that's hear the father's Sunday saremon.' 'Ah, don't do that, me darlin,' sez the culchee farmer. 'Gettin up moight make yez worse. Oi'll tell yez what: oi'll go to Mass and listen carefully to the saremon, and tell yez every word the priest praiches.' 'Roight yez are,' sez the woman. 'Go yerself and listen carefully and tell me everythin yez hear.' So off went the culchee peasant to Mass, and the priest got up on his legs in the pulpit, and said that if anyone had a sick choild, a sick husband, a sick woife, a sick father, a sick mother, a sick sister, brother or whatever, he should make a pilgrimage to Croaghpatrick in County Mayo, where a peck of larrel laves costs only a penny, and the sick choild, sick husband, sick woife, sick father, sick mother, sick sister, brother or whatever would be cured in a jiffy. And he finished up be sayin: 'If there's anyone wantin to make the trip, he should come and see me after Mass, and oi'll give him the penny and a sack fer the larrel laves.' Well, the culchee farmer was only deloighted. He went to the priest roight after Mass, and didn't the priest give him the penny and the sack fer the larrel laves. Then he went on home, and before he had even got one foot insoide the house he was yellin out: 'Thanks be to God, me darlin woife, yez're as good as cured. The priest said in his saremon today that anyone with a sick choild, a sick husband, a sick woife, a sick father, a sick mother, a sick sister, brother or whatever, he should make a pilgrimage to Croaghpatrick in County Mayo, where a peck of larrel laves costs only a penny, and the sick choild, the sick husband, the sick woife, the sick father, the sick mother, the sick sister, brother or whatever will be cured in a jiffy. Well, look it, oi've got the penny and the sack fer the larrel laves from the priest, and oi'm startin owt this very minute, so yez'll be cured all the sooner.'

Off he went on his way and he was hardly owt of the house when the woman upped owt of her bed, and it wasn't long before the priest arroived. But why don't we lave them two to themselves and go along with the culchee farmer. He wanted to get himself to Croaghpatrick as soon as possible, so he kept up a good steady pace, and as he was walkin along the wey, didn't he meet his cousin the egg man, as had just come from the mairket after sellin his eggs. 'God be with yez, cousin,' sez the egg man. 'Where are yez goin in such a hurry?' 'Be the Blessed Virgin Mary, cousin,' sez the culchee farmer, 'sure me woife is poorly, and oi heard the priest praiche today, and didn't he say that if anyone had a sick choild, a sick husband, a sick woife, a sick father, a sick mother, a sick sister, brother or whatever, he should make a pilgrimage to Croaghpatrick in County Mayo, where a peck of larrel laves costs only a penny, and the sick choild, the sick husband, the sick woife, the sick father, the sick mother, the sick sister, brother or whatever will be cured in a jiffy. So oi got me penny and me sack for the larrel laves from the priest and now oi'm makin me pilgrimage.' 'Me darlin cousin,' sez the egg man, 'are yez really stupit enough to believe that? Listen here to me! Yer man the priest wanted a whole day to himself havin a grand toime with yer woife, so they tought up this trick to get rid of yez.' 'Bejasus!' sez the culchee farmer, 'it's only achin oi am to know if that's the trut'!' 'Roight yez are,' sez the egg man. 'Listen here to what we'll do. Get yerself into me egg basket and oi'll carry yez home and yez can see fer yerself.' Well, didn't they do just that: the egg man settled the culchee farmer into his egg basket and carried him home on his back. When they got back to the house, be the hokey, yez wouldn't believe the hooley they were havin! The woman was after killin and cookin practically everythin they had in the farmyard and she'd made pancakes, and the priest himself was already there with his fiddle and all. The egg man knocked at the door and the woman asked who it moight be. 'Isn't it me,' sez the egg man. 'Would yez ever put me up fer the noight? Oi haven't sold me eggs, so now oi've got to carry them home again, and bejase, they're so heavy, oi can't go another step and it's gettin terrible dark.' 'Cousin,' said the farmer's woife, 'yez've come at a bad toime. But yez can't help bein here, so come in and sit yerself down over there on the bench behoind the hob.' So the egg man settled himself down wit his basket on the bench behoind the hob. Well, sure enough, the priest and the woman were havin a mairvellous toime and after a whoile the priest sez: 'Yez've got such a foine voice. Would yez ever sing me a song?' 'Ah sure, oi couldn't,' sez she. 'Oi can't sing any more. Oi could when oi was a young lass, but that's a ting of the past.' 'Ah go on, please!' sez the priest. 'Just sing me a little somethin.' So the woman sings:

> 'To Croaghpatrick me husband oi've sent
> To say Masses and tings of that bent.'

And the priest reploies:

> 'He can kape the owld sack
> If he doesn't come back
> For morer'n a year since he went. Hallelujah!'

Then the egg man behoind the stove begins to sing (and here oi

have to tell yez that the name on the culchee farmer was
Peadair):

> 'Oh, Peadair, bejasus, begob!
> What're yez doin in there be the hob? Hallelujah!'

And the culchee farmer as was in the basket begins to sing:

> 'That's enough of yer song;
> It's gone on too long,
> And it's toime oi got in on the job!'

Whereupon he stepped owt of the basket, took a stick to yer
man the priest and drove him owt of the house.

NOTES

(The italicized numerals refer to the Grimms' own final numbering, the others to the numbering of this selection. The date after each title refers to the edition in which the Grimms first published the story.)

1 THE FISHER AN HIS GWEEDWÌFE (*No. 19, 'Von dem Fischer un syner Fru', 1812*). Contributed by Philipp Otto Runge (see Introduction, p. 25), originally in Pomeranian dialect; a later text, revised by Runge's brother to approximate to Hamburg dialect, was used in the final edition. The Grimms also knew a Hesse variant in which the husband's final wish is to be God, with his wife as Mother of God, whereupon the fish sends him back 'into his pisspot'. In the Russian version 'The Golden Fish' (in Afanasev's collection; adapted by Pushkin as a verse tale in 1833) the wife's final demand is to be ruler of the seas and all the fishes, whereupon the fish disappears and the couple are back in their ramshackle hut. In another Russian variant called 'The Greedy Old Woman' the wish-granter is an old tree and the final wish is 'to be gods', whereupon the tree turns them into a bear and a she-bear (or a dog and a bitch). In some French and Italian versions the husband climbs to heaven on, for example, a beanstalk, and addresses his demands to God directly. In an analogous Japanese tale a stonemason wants to be 'the most powerful thing in the world' and is turned successively into the sun, a cloud, and a cliff, but as a cliff he sees a stonemason hacking at him and decides to become one again. Particularly remarkable in the Runge version (and perhaps attributable to some editing by Runge) is the descriptive detail and the highly developed dramatic effect: the husband's increasingly terrified dissociation of himself from his wife's ever more outrageous demands, the sense of menace and gradual climax, the storm symbolically rising (Pushkin also uses this feature) as the laconic patience of the all-powerful flounder continues to seem inexhaustible.

2 RUMPLESTILTSKIN (*No. 55, 'Rumpelstilzchen', 1812*). The Helper is here a kind of devil-figure. In the original version there is no

mention of his 'taking pity' on the heroine; on the other hand, the ending is weaker (merely 'he ran away in a rage and was never seen again'). The motif of sacrificing a child in return for gold etc. recurs in Nos. 51 and 56. The taboo character of names, the importance of concealing one's name from an adversary, release from a bargain if his name is guessed (or his riddles answered, as in No. 50), are all ancient motifs; in connection with the third, the Grimms themselves in their note mention the story of the princess Turandot (see note to No. 24) in which the hero will renounce his rights over the heroine if she can discover his name.

3   HANSEL AND GRETEL (No. 15, 'Hänsel und Gretel', 1812). The children's German names (with the first slightly anglicized) are so widely associated with this famous story that to translate them as something like 'Jackie and Jillie' seems inappropriate. As mentioned in the Introduction, the 'stepmother' was in the original version the children's own mother. She is also their 'stepmother', however, in Basile's partly equivalent tale 'Nennillo e Nennella' (which has a similar opening but continues differently).

4   LITTLE REDCAPE (No. 26, 'Rotkäppchen', 1812). Strictly, Kappe in Modern High German means 'cap', but it is not quite clear whether the Grimms intended it to mean this or (as Von der Leyen suggests) a cape or mantle, perhaps with a hood going over the head. The latter would be consistent with Perrault's chaperon or 'riding hood' by which the story is so well known. A curious point in certain French versions earlier than Perrault is that the wolf, after devouring the grandmother, leaves over some of her flesh and blood, which the little girl then unwittingly eats and drinks, though warned not to by magic voices. The Grimm text includes a variant ending in which the girl and her grandmother trick the wolf into falling off the roof and drowning; I have omitted this.

5   RAPUNZEL (No. 12, 'Rapunzel', 1812). Strictly the English for Rapunzel is 'rampion' (a bell-flower with edible white tuberous roots), but again there seems to be no point in changing so well known a name and title. In Basile's broadly similar tale the heroine is called 'Petrosinella' (parsley). In the Grimms' 1812 version the 'fairy' discovers Rapunzel's affair with the prince when the girl innocently asks her why her dresses no longer fit; this impropriety was altered in the later editions, in which she gives herself away by a much less plausible question.

6 **BRIAR-ROSE** (*No. 50, 'Dornröschen'*, 1812). This version of the 'Sleeping Beauty' story is discussed in the Introduction and compared with Perrault's 'La Belle au bois dormant'. In Basile's variant 'Sole, Luna e Talia' the heroine is called Thalia and her children 'Sun' and 'Moon' (Perrault's 'Day' and 'Dawn'). The Grimms pointed out the analogy between their story and that of Brynhild: her father Odin (Wotan) has put her to sleep by pricking her with a magic thorn, and the hero Sigurd penetrates a surrounding wall of fire to reach her and wake her. The association of the 'unlucky' number thirteen with the female sex (thirteen lunar months – that is, menstrual cycles – in the twelve-month solar year) seems also to occur in 'The Twelve Brothers' (No. 13).

7 **SNOWWHITE** (*No. 53, 'Sneewittchen'*, 1812). In the original edition, as in the case of No. 3, the wicked stepmother is the real mother; otherwise the story is almost exactly the same, except that Snowwhite is carried back in her coffin to the prince's palace where he gazes at her constantly, until one day in his absence a servant, annoyed at having to look after a corpse, pulls her upright and strikes her, causing the ejection of the poisoned apple. Common to both versions is the sexless, fraternal role of the seven dwarfs, an impression reinforced by the analogy between them and the seven enchanted brothers of 'The Seven Ravens' (see note on No. 14).

8 **THE JENIPER TREE** (*No. 47, 'Von dem Machandelboom'*, 1812). Contributed by Runge (see note to No. 1 and Introduction, p. 25). There are pleasing variants of the bird's song in a number of languages, for example in a Scots version: 'Pew wew, pew wew, my minny [=mother] me slew ...' Goethe's Gretchen, imprisoned after being abandoned by Faust and drowning their child, sings a tragic adaptation: 'My mother's a whore, she killed me; my father's a rogue, he ate me; my sister she carried my bones and buried them in a cool place; see now what a fine little bird am I, and away I fly, away I fly!' (see Introduction, p. 21).

9 **LITTLE BROTHER AND LITTLE SISTER** (*No. 11, 'Brüderchen und Schwesterchen'*, 1812). This is linked to Nos. 7, 8, 10 and others by the cruel stepmother motif, and to Nos. 10, 36 and others by that of the false (usurping, substituted) bride. An example of Wilhelm's textual elaborations occurs at the beginning: in the 1812 version only one stream has been bewitched and only the transformation into a deer is threatened. In triplicating this, Wilhelm was of

course adopting one of the most characteristic and well-known *Märchen* features (three chances, three siblings, etc.).

10 **THE THREE LITTLE MEN IN THE FOREST** (*No. 13*, 'Die drei Männlein im Walde', 1812). This and the next story share the very common motif of two sisters (or brothers) of whom one is humble, kind, polite to the Helper(s), and the other haughty, unkind, rude, lazy, etc.; the former is duly rewarded and a curse is put on the latter. The siblings thus represent polarized good–evil qualities.

11 **MOTHER SNOWBED** (*No. 24*, 'Frau Holle', 1812). 'Holle' or 'Holde' is the name of a goddess in Germanic mythology; I have adapted it to her own description of one of her functions. The Basile analogue to Nos. 10 and 11 is called 'Le tre fate' ('The Three Fairies').

12 **THE THREE BIRDIES** (*No. 96*, 'De drei Vügelkens', 1815). The German text is in the dialect of the villages near the Köterberg or Teutoberg, a mountain in Westphalia; the story is unusual in naming its own place of origin. The thrice-repeated rhyme is obscure, and remains so when rendered more literally: 'Ready for death, till further dispensation, (ready) for the garland of lilies: my fine boy, is that you?' The Grimms took this to mean that the child survives death, by divine grace, in the form of a bird or a lily; they cite in comparison the bird in 'The Jeniper Tree' and the twelve white flowers in 'The Twelve Brothers'.

13 **THE TWELVE BROTHERS** (*No. 9*, 'Die zwölf Brüder', 1812). Nos. 13, 14 and 15 are variants of each other, all having the motifs of the transformation of the brothers into birds and the sister's quest. Basile's 'Le sette palommielle' ('The Seven Doves') has a limited similarity to them. In the 1812 opening of No. 13 the Grimms did not rationalize the king's attitude as a wish to have a sole heiress: he simply does not want a mixed family at all and would rather cut off the twelve boys' heads himself 'than see a girl among them'. The twelve coffins and the sentimental identification of the youngest son as 'Benjamin' are also later editorial developments.

14 **THE SEVEN RAVENS** (*No. 25*, 'Die sieben Raben', 1819; originally 'Die drei Raben', 1812). In the 1812 version, from a Hesse source, there are only three sons, who are cursed by their mother for playing cards on a Sunday; the variant later adopted was from an Austrian source. At the end, in both versions, their servant is a dwarf and

their discovery of the heroine's presence ('Who's been eating from my plate?' etc.) is exactly similar to the seven dwarfs' discovery of Snowwhite (No. 7).

15 THE SIX SWANS (*No. 49, 'Die sechs Schwäne',* 1812). A curious detail is the use of shirts (mentioned also in No. 13) as the means of enchantment and disenchantment. In the 1812 version the children are not 'brought out of hiding' at the end, but have presumably been killed by the mother-in-law.

16 THE TWO BROTHERS (*No. 60, 'Die zwei Brüder',* 1819). In their note on this complex tale the Grimms mention several different German sources and various analogues or partial analogues, including Basile's 'Lo mercante' ('The Merchant') and 'La cerva fatata' ('The Enchanted Deer'). It may be divided into six episodes (elements, motifs) which do not necessarily all belong together: (*a*) the two sons of a poor man accidentally acquire magic gold by eating part of a gold-bird belonging to a rich man; (*b*) two brothers learn hunting, acquire various animal companions and part, leaving a magic object by which each will have news of the other; (*c*) the first brother saves a princess from a dragon, is himself killed by an impostor, is magically revived by his animals, disproves the impostor's claims by producing the dragon's tongues and marries the princess; (*d*) he is turned to stone by a witch when out hunting; (*e*) the second brother learns of this, comes to his rescue, is mistaken for him by the princess, defeats the witch and disenchants him; (*f*) the first brother in a fit of jealousy kills the second, then magically revives him with the help of the animals. These motifs occur internationally in various combinations or in detachment; we encounter (*c*) again in No. 17. In their first edition the Grimms used (*a*) on its own as 'The Golden Bird', and the sequence (*b*) (*c*) (*d*) (*e*) as 'John Waterspring and Caspar Waterspring' (this variant having a different opening: a king keeps his daughter in isolation to prevent her marrying; she becomes pregnant by drinking magic water and bears the twins, etc.). The whole sequence (*a*) to (*f*) is first combined in the 1819 edition as 'The Two Brothers', with the opening (*a*) now varied to introduce the motif of contrasting brothers: the poor father of the twins is the brother of the rich goldsmith, who is evil and avenges himself for the loss of the gold-magic by making his good brother turn the children out into the forest. The rest of the story then develops the contrary motif of siblings who, instead of representing polarized opposite qualities,

love each other and are closely identified (this identity being emphasized by their acquisition of five successive pairs of different animals, their similar deaths and revivals, physical indistinguishability, etc.); they thus represent reconciliation and integration.

17   THE MASTER HUNTSMAN (*No. 111*, '*Der gelernte Jäger*', 1815). In the more logical variants known by the Grimms but not used, the huntsman makes the princess pregnant without waking her; she refuses to marry the servant who falsely claims responsibility, and the king tries to humiliate her with bizarre punishments; the second of these, at least in the variant in which the notice at the inn promises free meals to all comers willing to tell their life story, may be intended to serve the purpose of tracing the father. The Grimms also point out in their note that the impostor motif (occurring also in No. 16) is paralleled in the medieval Tristan story (episode of the seneschal who claims to have killed the dragon and is confounded when Tristan produces its tongue). The huntsman snipping off parts of the sleeping princess's clothing reminds them of Sigurd cutting through the sleeping Brynhild's armour.

18   THE WATER OF LIFE (*No. 97*, '*Das Wasser des Lebens*', 1815). In this and the next story the motifs and their combination are closely similar.

19   THE GOLDEN BIRD (*No. 57*, '*Der goldene Vogel*', 1812). In an older variant of the opening the king is sick and can be healed if a magic bird is found; this reinforces the analogy with No. 18. The sibling-contrast is associated in No. 19 with the Helper's injunction to make the humble and not the proud choice (inn, cage, harness), as in the wooer-test in Shakespeare's *Merchant of Venice* (the hero will choose the leaden casket, not the golden or silver one).

20   THE DWARFIE (*No. 91*, '*Dat Erdmänneken*', 1819). This dialect tale from Paderborn shares certain motifs with Nos. 18 and/or 19 but more closely resembles No. 21, which indeed is not much more than a weaker variant of it.

21   JACK THE STRONG MAN (*No. 166*, '*Der starke Hans*', 1837). From a Swiss source. Essentially the same story as No. 20, but including

the motif of the supernaturally strong hero and that of the companions with extraordinary powers (the latter being left undeveloped).

22   THE SIX WHO WENT FAR IN THE WORLD (*No. 71, 'Sechse kommen durch die ganze Welt', 1819*). Broadly similar to Basile's 'Lo gnorante' ('The Simpleton'). See also note to No. 23.

23   THE SIX SERVANTS (*No. 134, 'Die sechs Diener', 1815*). Nos. 22 and 23 are variants of each other, the two principal motifs combined in both being (*a*) that of the tasks or tests imposed on suitors (wooertest, Oenomaos motif, as in Nos. 24 to 27; commonly with those who fail being put to death, as in Nos. 24 and 25) and (*b*) that of the extraordinary companions. The latter should be (as in these two stories) a variant of the Helper motif; although it occurs in No. 21 as well, it is there illogically deflected into that of the treacherous rival(s) and impostor(s).

24   THE SEA-RABBIT (*No. 191, 'Das Meerhäschen', 1857*). The Grimms did not add this story until the final edition, having taken it from a collection of German folktales from Transylvania published by Joseph Haltrich in Berlin in 1856. The best-known and probably the oldest story of the proud princess who tests her wooers with riddles is that of the princess Turandot, a tale of Persian origin later included in the *Thousand and One Nights*; it was dramatized (1762) by the Italian poet Gozzi and became the basis of Puccini's well-known opera (1926). In the Transylvanian story and its variants the 'riddle' is, in effect, 'Where is the hiding-place in which I shall not find you?' In the variants the hero is finally successful when he turns into (for example) a flower which the princess picks and wears, an apple she puts in her bosom, a flea in her clothes, an ant on the wall behind her, a pin which pricks her when she sits down but which she is unable to find; or when he hides under her chair in an earth dug by the fox, etc. The meaning of *Meerhäschen* (literally 'little sea-hare') is obscure. The author of a German doctoral thesis on the story (1953) found that this word recurred in none of its variants, as well as being unexplained in any work of reference, and suggested that it is a Transylvanian-Saxon name for the standard German *Meerschweinchen* (guinea-pig); this indeed would fit the animal's role in the story and seems highly probable. The word *Meerhase* (-*häschen*), so far as I can ascertain, appears in dictionaries if at all only as meaning a kind of fish, which is

impossible in the present context. (Mr Ralph Manheim translates it as 'mongoose', for reasons which are not clear.)

25   THE WORN-OUT DANCING-SHOES (No. 133, 'Die zertanzten Schuhe', 1815). A rather curious version of the wooer-test, in which his chief function seems to be to detect the pre-marital activities of the daughter(s); it amounts to answering a riddle about them, and he is still to be put to death if he fails. The Grimms describe two German variants of the story. In one there are only three princesses, and the soldier is the thirteenth wooer after twelve have perished; on the three nights the underground castle is successively made of copper, silver and gold (this last motif has several parallels in Afanasev's Russian stories). In the other there is only one daughter, who wears out twelve pairs of shoes every night, which must be replaced next day by a cobbler with twelve apprentices; the youngest apprentice hides and discovers that she is the victim of a spell by which twelve older princesses force her to go dancing with them. The youngest girl is sad during the dance, having fallen in love with the young apprentice. Next day she tells the cobbler that she now wants only one pair of shoes, to be brought by his youngest boy; the boy thus disenchants her and she marries him. Common to all three versions is the exaltation of the lowly hero after he has discovered the secret of the underground castle and the princes (it has been suggested that this resembles the discovery of a forbidden spectacle such as the midnight dance of elves) and the strange emphasis on the significance of the shoes. In the cobbler-apprentice version there is no wooer-test imposed by the father, and the motif of unkind sisters or enchantresses seems to take its place.

26   THE DEVIL'S THREE GOLDEN HAIRS (No. 29, 'Der Teufel mit den drei goldenen Haaren', 1812). A variant of No. 27, the chief difference being in the opening. In a third variant mentioned by the Grimms the Devil is also identified with a mythical bird (the phoenix). In a fourth, the princess sees the lowly hero from her window (as in No. 37) and wishes to marry him, subject to the wooer-test about the Devil's hairs. The helpful grandmother (wife, etc.) of the Devil or other monster recurs commonly (for example, in No. 49 and in the English tale of 'Jack and the Beanstalk').

27   THE GRIFFIN (No. 165, 'Der Vogel Greif', 1837). The Grimms were sent this lively Swiss-German version (from the Aargau district) of

the story also told in No. 26. In the Irish dialect of the translation, the main features are the changes in some vowels and one or two consonants. A 'leprechaun' is a kind of goblin, a 'colleen' a girl, and 'Seamus' is pronounced 'shame-us'.

28 THE THREE SNAKE-LEAVES (No. 16, 'Die drei Schlangenblätter', 1819). The first part of the story (entombment and resuscitation) and the second (faithlessness of the resuscitated wife, her treachery foiled and punished) are motif-sequences which often appear separately. The entombment of the survivor may result from a pact or be ordered as a punishment; the pair may be man and wife, blood-brothers, etc. (the Grimms mention the Greek legend of Polyeidos and Glaukos, and the Norse legend of Asmund and Asvit). The motif of learning to revive the dead from the example of snakes or other animals (by a magic plant, water, etc.) is characteristic.

29 FAITHFUL JOHN (No. 6, 'Der treue Johannes', 1819). In another German variant summarized by the Grimms the faithful self-sacrificing friends are not king and servant but a king's son and godson, who have been brought up as brothers. Principal characteristic motifs are: one friend is enamoured by a portrait he discovers, the other helps him to abduct the princess by a ruse but hears warning voices on the return voyage; he must perform magic deeds to save the hero and his bride (killing a horse, beheading a dragon which looks through the bedroom window, etc.) and these are misunderstood as treachery; when he explains them he is turned to stone, but is disenchanted when the friend sacrifices his own child(ren).

30 ONE-EYE, TWO-EYES AND THREE-EYES (No. 130, 'Einäuglein, Zweiäuglein und Dreiäuglein', 1819). In the present selection this is the first of the 'Cinderella' group discussed in the Introduction. The Grimms, without changing in this case the mother and sisters of the heroine to stepmother and stepsisters, nevertheless suggest in their note that the 'wise-woman' is 'probably her own mother who has died'. The fruit of the silver and gold tree which only Two-Eyes can pick parallels the silver and gold dresses which are shaken down from Ashiepattle's magic tree in No. 31 or which are concealed in nuts in Nos. 32, 34 and 35.

31 ASHIEPATTLE (No. 21, 'Aschenputtel', 1812). Basile's 'La gatta cenerentola' ('The Cinder Cat'), Perrault's 'Cendrillon ou la petite

pantoufle de verre' ('Cinderella or the Little Glass Slipper'). This is, as it were, the 'Cinderella' story itself, best known to English readers under that title, but I thought it preferable to use something like the German name. The word *Aschenputtel* means a dirty neglected kitchen drudge who sleeps and works among the ashes, and 'ashie-pattle' exists as a Scots word meaning a child or animal of this description. In the 1812 version the heroine simply plants the magic tree on her dying mother's advice; the hazel twig brought by her father is a development of the later editions, as is also the punishment of the sisters by the two doves at the end, although in the 1812 text the role of the doves as Helpers is in general more prominent. It is interesting that the sex of the main character in this story-type does not seem to be essential: the Grimms mention a number of variants in which Aschenputtel (or 'Askepott', etc.) is a (kitchen-) *boy* mocked by his proud brothers (see also note to No. 37). 'Sitting among the ashes' is in any case, as they point out, a very ancient expression of humility or grief. Instances in Grimm of the old motif of identification by means of a shoe occur also in Nos. 17, 43 and 51.

32   MANYPELTS (*No. 65*, '*Allerleirauh*', 1812; the German name literally means 'all-sorts-furry' or 'all-sorts-hairy'). The Grimms noted the analogy between this tale and No. 31. In the 1812 version the heroine, when her father proposes marriage to her, seems already (though this is not further explained) to have a fiancé, who has given her the golden trinkets. The king who finds her in the forest is in fact this fiancé, who at first fails to recognize her and throws his boots at her when she removes them as part of her lowly duties; in the end he identifies her by the golden objects and her golden hair. In the revised version the previous betrothal to her employer is dropped, the boot-throwing theme mitigated and the narrative style elaborated. In Perrault's corresponding but ironic verse-tale, 'Peau d'âne', the debased 'dirty' heroine wears the skin of a gold-donkey belonging to her father which he killed at her request, and she is helped by a 'fairy godmother'. In the Russian variant called 'The Swineskin Cloak' (Afanasev), she gets advice from her dead mother, and at the end, asked to explain her piggish disguise, answers: 'Because I looked like my dead mother and my father wanted to marry me.' In some of the international variants, instead of animal-skins she wears a wooden covering, apparently to protect her chastity and enable her to pass as a man. In Basile's 'Ll'orza' ('The She-Bear') she evades her father by

turning into a bear; the prince takes her home in this form, but sees her once as a girl and falls in love with her; when the animal-bride kisses him, the disguise ends.

33 THE RIGHTFUL BRIDE (*No. 186*, '*Die wahre Braut*', 1843). Both this and No. 56 are from a literary source (a periodical published in 1842 by Moritz Haupt) of which they show some stylistic traces. In its content No. 33 is a fairly straightforward example of the Cinderella type, though also using (like Nos. 34 and 35 and the original version of No. 32) the related motif of the prince's forgetting his 'true bride' for a time.

34 THE IRON STOVE (*No. 127*, '*Der Eisenofen*', 1815). In this and No. 35 the motifs related to or belonging to the Cinderella complex are the forgotten bride, the lowly disguise and the magic display. As to the 'iron stove' in which the prince is so oddly imprisoned, the Grimms in their note associated it with the stove which may hear secrets (Nos. 20 and 36) and with hell or the underworld. The 'glass mountain' (to be climbed or opened) recurs in Nos. 14 and 54. A Scottish variant of the forgotten bride's pleas at the end of Nos. 34 and 35 appears in the tale called 'The Black Bull of Norroway':

> 'Seven lang years I served for thee,
> The glassy hill I clamb for thee', etc.

35 THE TWA ROYAL BAIRNIES (*No. 113*, '*Die beiden Künigeskinner*', 1815). From Paderborn. The word *Arweggers* with which the princess summons the dwarfs does not mean 'earwigs' (Manheim) but is Westphalian dialect for *Arbeiter* (workers). The Grimms (wrongly) thought it might be derived from a horse name (Arvakr) or dwarf name (Aurvangur) in the Norse Edda. The tale in general is a rather odd mixture of motifs: abduction of the hero, wooer-test and tasks, magic flight, then forgotten bride and the concluding Cinderella sequence. It is interesting that the hero forgets the heroine the moment his *mother* kisses him.

36 THE GOOSEGIRL (*No. 89*, '*Die Gänsemagd*', 1815). Although tangentially related to the Cinderella type (heroine debased but eventually recognized, treacherous companion analogous to cruel sister, usurping bride exposed – this last motif occurring also in Nos. 9 and 10), this famous tale has a character of its own. The motif of the talking horse is as old as Homer; particularly notable here, and also ancient, is that of the severed head of a person or animal

continuing to speak (sing, prophesy). The Grimms referred to old customs in various places of fixing up horses' heads or human heads for magical purposes. Here the head of Falada (the name is stressed on the first syllable) reveals the treachery practised against the heroine, whose glittering golden hair (silver in the first edition) also betokens her royal birth (compare No. 37). Interesting also are the princess's wind-spells, and the magic power attributed to the piece of linen stained with three drops of blood (like the snow at the beginning of No. 7), which hints at the theme of sexual maturation.

37 JACK OF IRON (*No. 136*, '*Der Eisenhans*'). The 1815 volume of the first edition contained a shorter version of this called '*Der wilde Mann*' (The Wild Man); this was later elaborated from other sources, and the finished story appeared as '*Der Eisenhans*' in the 1850 edition. Although both titles refer to the captor and protector of the young prince, it is really the latter who is the 'hero'; the Grimms were in their 1815 note already describing him as 'essentially a male Cinderella [*ganz eigentlich ein männlicher Aschenputtel*]' and suggesting that this represented an older variant of the Cinderella theme. Their revised version, evidently made with the Cinderella motifs in mind, still reads like a mixture of two stories, with an incongruous opening; but the role of the 'wild' adoptive father (who seems to correspond to the magically helpful mother figure in the Cinderella stories) has been made more dignified and interesting, as has the sequence about the hero's lowly service at the court. He now becomes kitchen boy ('ashes' are mentioned) as well as gardener's boy, and hides his golden hair on the pretence of being scurfy or scabby. The princess notices him, but he does not simply marry her secretly as in the 1815 version. The tournament sequence has been added, in which he makes (though the Grimms did not invent the motif) three appearances in different suits of armour, corresponding to the three magic dresses in which the 'true bride' displays herself, and disappears unaccountably after each victory, until finally identified by the golden hair and golden apples. In certain variants the story is called 'Goldhead' or 'Scabbyhead'. The English tale 'Roswal and Lillian', which the Grimms knew, resembles both No. 36 and No. 37 in some respects (usurping companion, tournament, etc.).

38 THE FROG KING, OR IRON HARRY (*No. 1*, '*Der Froschkönig oder der eiserne Heinrich*', 1812). See Introduction, pp. 14f., 30 and 34f. So

far as the main part of the story is concerned (the frog and the princess), the Grimms printed another German variant of it in their 1815 volume ('*Der Froschprinz*'), in which the frog dirties the well-water until the youngest princess makes her promise, and is disenchanted after she has patiently allowed it to sleep in her bed three times. They also knew and quoted the old sixteenth-century Scottish tale (republished with others by John Leyden, *The Complaynte of Scotlande*, 1801) about the lady sent to draw water from 'the well at the world's end'. When she arrives, 'a frog [to quote Leyden's summary] emerges from the well, and, before it suffers her to draw water, obliges her to betroth herself to the monster, under the penalty of being torn to pieces. The lady returns safe; but at midnight the frog-lover appears at the door, and demands entrance according to promise, to the great consternation of the lady and her nurse:

"Open the door, my hinny [honey], my heart,
Open the door, my ain wee thing;
And mind [remember] the words that you and I spak
Down in the meadow, at the well-spring!"

. . . The frog is finally disenchanted and appears as a prince in his original form.'

39 THE YOUNG DONKEY (*No. 144*, '*Das Eselein*', 1815). This tale has a literary source, namely a medieval Latin poem of the same title ('Asinarius'), of uncertain authorship, dating probably from the eleventh century; Jacob Grimm saw one of the surviving manuscripts of it in Strasbourg in 1814, and the brothers adapted the narrative skilfully to their folktale manner. Donkeys playing stringed instruments with their hooves occur as a motif in medieval decorative art, along with similar ironic drolleries such as wolves guarding sheep, mice putting cats to flight, etc. The lute-playing donkey recurs in No. 59.

40 JACK MY HEDGEHOG (*No. 108*, '*Hans mein Igel*', 1815). Similar to No. 39, but from a local oral source (Frau Viehmann in Zwehrn). The bizarre motif of the bagpipe-playing hedgehog riding on a cock is analogous to that of the donkey-musician, and a certain irony of tone is common to both stories, which roughly correspond to Straparola's 'Il re porco' ('The Pig King') and Basile's 'Lo serpe' ('The Snake'). The rhyming end-formula in No. 40 (literally 'my tale is done and goes to Gustchen's house') is of an internationally attested folktale type meaning that it is someone else's turn to tell a story.

41 THE MAGIC TABLE, THE GOLD-DONKEY, AND THE CUDGEL IN THE
SACK (*No. 36, 'Tischleindeckdich, Goldesel, und Knüppel aus dem Sack'*,
1812). This is essentially the same as Basile's 'Dell huerco' ('The
Wild Man'), in which the magic command to the donkey is '*arre
cacaure*'. The motif (analogous to that of persons with extraordinary powers) of magic objects or animals which supply
unlimited food or gold, effect transformations, raise armies,
command spirits etc., is very widespread, as are the variations on
how the hero acquires, loses and recovers such objects. Sometimes the hero's brothers (or his treacherous wife, etc.) steal the
object(s); here the brothers are allies. Nos. 42 to 44 are further
examples.

42 THE KNAPSACK, THE HAT AND THE HORN (*No. 54, 'Der Ranzen, das
Hütlein und das Hörnlein'*). Originally (1812) as told by the retired
sergeant of dragoons Friedrich Krause; slightly revised and elaborated for the 1819 edition. In this magic-object tale the brothers and
the princess are all hostile to the hero.

43 THE BLUE LAMP (*No. 116, 'Das blaue Licht'*, 1815). The famous story
of Aladdin in the *Thousand and One Nights* shares with this tale
(from a Mecklenburg source) the motif of the magic spirit-
summoning lamp and a feature of the opening (the magician or
witch sends the hero into an underground place for the talisman
and angrily abandons him with it there when he refuses to hand it
over before coming out himself); otherwise the events of the two
stories are not significantly close. The word 'blue' in the title is
thought to have the connotation of 'magical' or 'miraculous'. In
the 1815 version the soldier's final orders are to kill everyone and
hack the king into three pieces; this has been attenuated in the
later editions. The well-known later parallel tale by Hans
Andersen is 'The Tinder Box' (Andersen's version of the Helper is
a series of three terrifying dogs with eyes as big as saucers, millstones and the Round Tower of Copenhagen).

44 THE SALAD-DONKEY (*No. 122, 'Der Krautesel'*, 1819). The magic
object is acquired from its quarrelling holders as in Nos. 51 and 53
and commonly, and stolen from the hero as in No. 51 by the
treacherous beloved or wife. The other magic object, a gold-
making bird's heart, also occurs in No. 16.

45 THE THREE BROTHERS (*No. 124, 'Die drei Brüder'*, 1815). This and
No. 46 are akin to tales such as Nos. 22 and 23 about persons with

extraordinary or fantastic gifts, though here there is less of a magical emphasis and more of the character of what the Grimms called the '*Scherz- und Lügenmärchen*' – that is, the comic tale based on preposterous lies or boasts. Notions such as being able to parry raindrops with a sword or to shoe or saddle a galloping horse were centuries old.

46 THE FOUR SKILFUL BROTHERS (*No. 129*, '*Die vier kunstreichen Brüder*', 1819). As in No. 45, the amity between the rival brothers is again emphasized.

47 THE YOUNG GIANT (*No. 90*, '*Der junge Riese*', 1819). Akin to No. 21, but with a stronger comic colouring. As so often, the Grimms were reminded by this tale too of certain elements of the Sigurd story: the hero's demand for an adequate weapon, the miserly dwarf whose anvil he drives right into the ground at one blow and who tries to get rid of him by sending him to a place generally dreaded (dragon's lair, haunted mill).

48 THICKASATHUMB (*No. 37*, '*Daumesdick*', 1819). The story of the thumb-size midget has many variants internationally (this is one of two German ones used by the Grimms), including the well-known English tale which goes back at least as far as the early seventeenth century: 'The History of Tom Thumbe' (1621) and 'Tom Thumbe, His Life and Death' (1630) are two surviving printed versions. A characteristic motif is that the minute hero is accidentally swallowed by a cow and/or other animals. In the present case the second swallower is a wolf from whose stomach he is carefully excised, like Red Ridinghood; the route of his escape is not always so delicate. Perrault's 'Petit Poucet' is not swallowed, but this despite its title is not really a Tom Thumb story (see Introduction, p. 17).

49 BEARSKIN (*No. 101*, '*Der Bärenhäuter*'). This first appeared in the 1815 volume as '*Der Teufel Grünrock*' ('The Devil in his Green Coat'), then in the 1843 edition under the present title, in slightly expanded form, the bearskin cloak having been added for no particularly good reason from a literary source (a version of the tale by the seventeenth-century novelist Grimmelshausen). The word '*Bärenhäuter*' has connotations of idleness, as in the idiom '*sich auf die Bärenhaut legen*', literally 'to lie down on the bearskin'. The

Devil's stipulation that his protégé must not wash or trim his hair
or nails occurs in some old versions of the Doctor Faustus story.

50 THE DEVIL AND HIS GRANDMOTHER (*No. 125, 'Der Teufel und seine
Grossmutter'*, 1815). As in Nos. 26 and 27, the Devil's grandmother
or wife enables the hero to overhear the answers to three questions, and as in No. 2 the bargain is remitted if a riddling question
can be answered. The outwitting or foiling of the Devil is an old
medieval comic motif. In another German variant known to
the Grimms, the Devil and Lucifer take a walk together and sit
down under a tree from the branches of which one of the
soldiers happens to overhear them discussing the proposed
riddles.

51 THE KING OF THE GOLDEN MOUNTAIN (*No. 92, 'Der König vom
goldenen Berge'*, 1815). This and Nos. 52 and 53 (which were added
in later editions) may be regarded as three tales which have a
limited affinity in that in each of them the hero disenchants a
princess (who has become in some way ugly or monstrous) by
undergoing an ordeal or by recovering a talisman after combats
and dangers. In No. 51, however, the disenchantment sequence is
preceded by a Devil's bargain story which seems to have no logical
connection with it, and is followed by a development in which
(rather as in No. 28) the wife turns hostile and treacherous for
some reason not fully explained, unless we consider as analogous
the various stories in which a mortal wins the love of some elvish
being but breaks his vow to keep their union secret.

52 THE PRINCE AFRAID OF NOTHING (*No. 121, 'Der Königssohn, der
sich vor nichts fürchtet'*, 1819). This ends with the disenchantment
sequence (see previous note) but begins like No. 51 with an apparently quite independent story (the quest for the Tree of Life, the
treacherous giant and the helpful lion); the Grimms remarked in
their note that the tradition (in their Paderborn source) had evidently 'become confused or obscure'.

53 THE CRYSTAL BALL (*No. 197, 'Die Kristallkugel'*, 1850). From a
literary source, but containing much traditional material. The
motif of someone (often a monster or evil magician) whose soul or
life is external to his body, hidden in an egg or other container, is
very ancient. (The Russian folktale figure 'Koshchey the Death-
less' keeps his 'death' hidden in this way; that is, his external self

must be found if he is to be destroyed.) The opening motif of the mother who bewitches two of her sons does not seem to be fully developed, though the animal-brothers appear at the end to help the hero.

54   AULD RINKIE (*No. 196*, '*Oll Rinkrank*', 1850). An enigmatic dialect tale from Frisia, perhaps incompletely transmitted or confused. The rhymes, also found in Norwegian variants which call the princess's weird captor 'Ridder Ranke' (= something like 'Sir Ranke'), seem to suggest that he is lame or otherwise deformed.

55   JORINDA AND JORINGLE (*No. 69*, '*Jorinde und Joringel*', 1812). This is from a literary source, the autobiography (1777) of J. H. Jung-Stilling (1740–1817), who was a friend of Goethe's in their student days and interested in folklore.

56   THE NIXIE IN THE POND (*No. 181*, '*Die Nixe im Teich*', 1843). From the same literary source as No. 33, though the basic material is widespread and ancient. The motif of water-nymphs, mermaids, sirens, etc. who entice men to their destruction or hold them captive goes back at least as far as Homer (the Sirens, or Calypso's detention of Odysseus). In German literature the most remarkable treatment of it is Goethe's ballad 'Der Fischer'; the legendary Rhine-maidens and Loreley are points of comparison. The seductress is usually associated with water but sometimes appears in a forest, etc.; the victims of Keats's 'Belle Dame Sans Merci' are taken to an 'elfin grot'.

57   FETCHER'S FOWL (*No. 46*, '*Fitchers Vogel*', 1812). Both this and No. 58 are variants of the 'Bluebeard' story, best known in Perrault's version 'Barbe Bleue'. The Grimms heard a German version of the latter (the same but for one or two details) and included it as 'Blaubart' in their 1812 volume, but later dropped it. The 1812 volume also included 'Das Mordschloss' ('The Murder Castle'), a Dutch story of which the first half is closely akin to No. 57 and the second half to No. 58, this mixture again illustrating the basic affinity of these two stories. The expression 'Fitchers Vogel' is obscure; the Grimms thought it might be connected with the Icelandic word *fitfugl* meaning a water-bird, for example a swan. In a further variant which they knew, from the Hanover area, the girls are enticed to the cave of three murderous dwarfs, the bride finally putting on the bird-disguise with the help of the blood and

escaping unrecognized though challenged by foxes and bears on
their way to the cave.

58 THE ROBBER BRIDEGROOM (*No. 40*, '*Der Räuberbräutigam*', 1819).
See previous note. No. 58 is relatively non-magical. Variants of it
include the old English tale of 'Mr Fox', which was apparently
known in Shakespeare's time, since *Much Ado About Nothing* (Act
I, Scene I) contains the allusion, 'Like the old tale: It is not so, nor
'twas not so; but, indeed, God forbid it should be so', which are
the words Mr Fox repeatedly exclaims as the bride tells her
'dream'; Lady Mary finally retorts (producing the severed hand):
'But it is so, and it was so, and here the hand I have to show.' There
was another English version from Kent which identified the mur-
derer with Sir John Baker ('Bloody Baker'), chancellor to Queen
Mary I.

59 THE BREMEN TOWN BAND (*No. 27*, '*Die Bremer Stadtmusikanten*',
1819). An old and widely dispersed tale, of which the Grimms
knew several German variants. One had been turned into a verse
fable in the sixteenth century by Hans Sachs; in this the house in
the forest is inhabited not by robbers but by a pack of wolves, a
feature which the Grimms thought was probably characteristic of
the earlier versions.

60 CLEVER ELSIE (*No. 34*, '*Die kluge Else*', 1819). Nos. 60 and 61 are
examples of an immense international category of comic tales
about foolish or simple-minded people (foolish wife, foolish
young man, foolish couple, etc.). The Grimms heard No. 60 from
Frau Viehmann, but its opening motif of absurd anxiety about a
remote contingency takes a closely similar form in a German poem
of the sixteenth century (by Heinrich Götting): the fiancée, sent to
fetch beer, sits down and worries about how a knife might fall on
her future child, her parents follow her and do the same, and
when none of them returns from the cellar the suitor decides they
are all fools and clears off. Another 'foolish wife' story used by the
Grimms but not here included is their *No. 59*, 'Der Frieder und das
Katerlieschen' ('Fred and Lizzy-Kate'), in which the wife lets the
dog snatch her husband's dinner and leaves the beer-tap open in
the cellar while she chases it, then uses a sack of the best flour to
soak up the flood of beer, then hands over their whole fortune in
gold coins to some pedlars for worthless wares, then uses butter to
smooth out cart-ruts, drops a cheese she is carrying and rolls the

other cheeses down the hill after it to fetch it, etc., finally becoming confused like Clever Elsie about her own identity and knocking at her own front door to ask whether she is at home or not.

61 LAZY HARRY (*No. 164, 'Der faule Heinz'*, 1837). The Grimms used a literary source, a collection of Latin and German proverbs (*Proverbiorum copia*) with illustrative anecdotes, published by Eucharius Eyerling in 1601. One of the numerous parallels is the tale, current in Europe for many centuries, about the milkmaid carrying a pitcher of milk to market who becomes so excited about how she will spend the money that she drops and spills the milk. Another (closer to the Grimm variant) is an old tale from India which found its way to Germany in the fifteenth century and was retold by Hans Sachs: a hermit collects a potful of honey in the woods and speculates on how he will sell it, buy goats, sell these and gradually amass a fortune, marry a beautiful wife and take a stick to his disobedient son, then accidentally smashes the pot.

62 THE THREE ARMY-SURGEONS (*No. 118, 'Die drei Feldscherer'*, 1815). Here again an analogous tale was told by Hans Sachs (a doctor has removed a peasant's stomach to clean it, a raven steals it and a sow's stomach has to be substituted), and the motif of such organ-transplants (cat's eyes for human eyes, etc.) exists in numerous variants. In the 1815 volume the 'filth' which attracts the pig-eyed man is designated by a less polite German word than in the later editions.

63 THE CLEVER LITTLE TAILOR (*No. 114, 'Vom klugen Schneiderlein'*, 1815). A comic variant of the wooer-test motif in its 'Turandot' form (as found in No. 24). The 'young tailor' who makes his fortune by preposterous boasts and trickery seems to be a folktale figure particularly popular in Germany. A parallel Grimm story, their *No. 20*, 'Das tapfere Schneiderlein' ('The Valiant Little Tailor'; longer and better known and with more international variants, but not here included), also tells of this joke-hero's exploits: how he impresses everyone by claiming to have killed 'seven at one blow' (actually seven flies which settled on his bread and jam), outwits giants, captures wild animals and in the end obliges the king to let him marry his daughter, to her disgust and that of the young Goethe, who as a small boy heard this tale from his mother and protested: 'Surely the princess won't have to marry the damned tailor, will she?'

BUMPKIN (*No. 61*, *'Das Bürle'*, 1819). The title (a dialect form for *das Bäuerlein*, though the tale itself is in High German) literally means 'the little farmer' or 'little peasant'. Again the essential motif is that of the clever little man taking advantage of the credulity and cupidity of his would-be superiors, and this has countless worldwide variants. The Grimms, as well as hearing this tale from Frau Viehmann, knew a tenth- or eleventh-century Latin version of it, a poem which tells how 'Unibos' (as the hero is derisively called for having only one ox) performs most of the exploits here narrated and one or two others, such as pretending to bring his (not really dead) wife to life again with a magic flute (which he sells to the villagers, who then all kill their own wives) and selling his mare as a magic animal after stuffing gold pieces into its backside.

65 OWLD PEADAIR (*No. 95*, *'Der alte Hildebrand'*, 1819). In an Austrian dialect. Characteristic features of the international variants are the husband sent away on some absurd pretext, his return inside a basket or sack, and the rhyming dialogue. In a French version the wife sings:

'Mon bon mari, il est parti
Dessur la route de Paris,
Quérir des concombres et des melons,
Alléluia, alléluia, alléluia!'

In the present Irish translation a 'culchee farmer' means a bog peasant, a country yokel.

GLOSSARY OF SCOTS WORDS

The mid-north-Lowland Scots dialect into which six of the foregoing tales (Nos. 1, 8, 12, 20, 35 and 54) are translated is that of the former maermordom of Buchan, an area covering much of Aberdeenshire and part of Banffshire. This glossary is intended solely as an aid to the reading of these texts, and does not include words or meanings irrelevant to them. A glossary can never please all readers, to some of whom it will seem to gloss too few words, and to others ridiculously many. In the six tales in question, most of the words are near enough to standard English for their meaning to be obvious in the context to anyone who has some degree of acquaintance with Scots speech. In most cases it is merely a matter of pronunciation and spelling. A number of typical vowel and consonant differences between Scots and English are fairly widely known, at least in Britain. Many readers do not need to be told, for instance, that **hoose**, **noo** and **oot** are 'house', 'now' and 'out', or that **hame** and **mair** are 'home' and 'more', **heid** and **deid** 'head' and 'dead', **licht** and **thocht** 'light' and 'thought'. They will also know, or soon notice, that in Scots certain consonants and vowels tend to be dropped or elided, and will thus not have much difficulty with **an** for 'and', **-in** for '-ing', **stannin** for 'standing', **roon** for 'round', **is** and **er** for 'his' and 'her', **aa** and **waa** for 'all' and 'wall', **wi** for 'with', **o't** for 'of it', **gie's** for 'give us', etc., even without the help of an excessive infestation of apostrophes. Relatively familiar, too, is the typical change of '-ed' to **-it** or **-t** in past tenses and participles – for example, **lookit**, **powkit**, **opint**, **wannert** for 'looked', 'poked', 'opened', 'wandered'. There are, however, some less well-known peculiarities of the Buchan dialect and north-eastern Scots generally. One is the replacement of the initial aspirated 'wh' sound (and sometimes of initial 'h') by **f**. Thus 'when', 'who', 'what', 'where', 'how' become **fan**, **fa**, **fit**, **far**, **foo**. Another is the prevalence of the sound **ee**, in the place not only of the short English 'i' as is common in Scots (for example, **meenit** for 'minute') but also of the 'oo' and long 'o' sounds, so that, for example, 'moon' becomes **meen**, 'stood' **steed**, 'blood' not just **bluid** but **bleed**, and 'stone' not **stane** but **steen**. There are also the intrusions of the semi-consonants **w** and **y**, as in **gweed** for 'good' (instead of **guid** as elsewhere in Scotland) and **gyang** for **gang**. On the whole, the possibilities of confusion and at least momentary puzzlement are such as to justify what some will regard as a vexatiously full glossary, though for others it may still be incomplete; the former seemed to us to be the lesser evil. Those who will be baffled only by specific points of vocabulary such as **lagàmachy** and **kinàbrach** will need to look up only these.

As to pronunciation, those not already having some familiarity with it will have to use the spelling (though Scots spelling is not standardized) as a rough guide; it is not possible to give a proper phonetic description here, but the following points may be mentioned: **ae** is pronounced as the 'ay' in 'day', **ei** as in 'weir', **ey** as the 'i' in 'bite', **ou** (or **ouw**) as in 'out'; **ch** at the beginning of a word or after a consonant is generally as in 'church', otherwise as in 'loch'; **g** before 'e' and 'i' is hard (as in 'get' or 'girl') rather than soft (as in 'gentle' or 'gist'). We have sometimes, though quite seldom, used the accent (`) to indicate stress (**avà, awà**, etc.). Very occasionally, an asterisk (*) has been put in front of a word to indicate that confusion of meaning may be avoided if the Glossary is referred to.

aa, all
aabody, everyone
aafa, awful, awfully
aathing, everything
aawey, everywhere, in all directions
ablò, beneath, under
ae, one
aff, off
afore, before, in front of
ahin, behind
aicht, own, possess
ainsèl, own self; **my ainsèl**, myself in person
an, and
an aa, also, as well
anent, opposite
aneuch, enough
ashet, serving-dish
auld, old
avà, at all
awà, away

aweel, well now!
aye, always, still; yes

bairn, child
baith, both
bauchle, slipper
beens, beenies, bones
beery, bury
ben, inside
Benachìe, a mountain in Aberdeenshire
berry-buss, fruit-bush
bigg, build
bleed, blood
blent, dazzled
boddam, bottom
bonny, pretty, beautiful
boo't, bowed, stooped
braa, fine, pretty
braalies: dee us braalies, do us nicely
bricht, bright

bring-up, shock, fright
brocht, brought
bund, bound
buss, bush
but an ben, in and out
byde, live, stay (**baid,
    bidden**, lived, stayed)
byle, boil
byre, cowshed
byuird, board

caa, call
caa, drive, knock; **caain's line**,
    plying his line; **caa'd is heid
    aff**, knocked his head off;
    caa'd her till a jeelie,
    smashed her to pulp
cannel, candle
canty, lively
carl, fellow
chantiepot, chamber-pot
chappit, knocked
chaumber, room
chaumer, cottage
chiel, fellow
chyne, chain
claith, cloth
clook, claw
come-at, upset
conter, contradict
cranny, little finger
creel, basket
cry, call

dae, dee, do; **canna be deein
    wi't**, can't bear it
daft, crazy
daith, death
dam, pond
danner, walk
daurnae, dare not
dee, do; die (**deet**, died)

deen, done, broken
deid, dead
devaul, cease
dinna, dinnae, don't
doon, down
doup, backside
dowie, languid, sickly
dunt, whack
dwallt, dwelt, lived
dwam, swoon, faint

een, one; eyes
eence, once
eese, use
eeseless, useless
elback, elbow
ersèl, herself

fa, who
fae, from
faet, fit, foot
fa'iver, whoever
fan, when
far, where
feel, fool
fee(t), hire(d)
fegs, forsooth
fesh, fish
fess, fetch (**feess**, fetched)
fit, what
fite, white
fit-for, why
fit-wey, why
fleer, floor
fleetch, entreat
fleuk, flounder
foo, how
fowk, folk, people
fraise, speak cajolingly
freemt, strange
freen, friend
fulpit, whelped, given birth to

fuppit, whipped, snatched
fyle, fylie, while, little while
fyles, sometimes

gae, go
gaed, went
gang, go
gantit, yawned
gar, make, compel (**gart**, made)
Gaudie Watter, a river in Aberdeenshire
geet, brat, bastard
gey, very
gie, give
gin, if
girn, whine, moan
girse, grass
glamourt, enchanted, under a spell
gowd, gold
greet, weep (**grat, grutten**, wept)
grue, retch
gurly, angry, agitated
gweed (= **guid**), good
gweedmàn, husband
gweedsìster, sister-in-law
gweedwìfe, wife
gyan, going
gyang, go
gyte, furious

hadden: hale hadden nicht, whole night long
hae, have (**haed, haen**, had)
hairst, harvest
haiver, talk nonsense
hale, whole
hame, home
haud, hold; **haud on**, cease
heich, high

heicht, height; **gaed till an aafa heicht**, flew into a rage
hine (aff, awà, up), far (off, away, up)
hingin, hanging
hinmaist, hindmost, last
hoot awà!, nonsense!
hyow, hew
hyuik, hook

ilka, each, every
imsèl, himself

jaloùse, suspect, guess
jeniper, juniper

kail, green vegetables
keest, cast, threw
kell(t), kill(ed)
ken, know
kennan, ken, sight
kinàbrach, friends and relations
kinechtit, delighted
kist, chest
kitlin, kitten
kye, cows

laft, loft
lagàmachy, speech, story
lang, long; **I think lang**, I'm bored
lauch, laugh
ledder, ladder
leen: her (his, ma) leen, on her (his, my) own, all alone
lichent, lightened
licht, light
lick, beat, thrash
lift, sky
lint, flax
loo, love (**loo't**, loved)

loon, loonie, lad, boy
losh, good Lord!
loup, leap, dance
louwin, burning
lowse, loose, release
lug, ear

mair, more
mait, food (literally 'meat')
man, husband
maun, must
meen, moon
meenie mee, (nonsense
  words)
meenit, minute
mengie, household,
  retainers
micht, might
mine't, remembered
mintit, insinuated
mirk, dark
mony, many
morn: the morn, tomorrow
muckle, big
mull, mill
mutch, cap
myaut, mew, little squeak
mysèl, myself

nae, no, not; **nae but,** only
naithmaist, lowest
needfae, needful
neen, none
neuk, corner
noo, now
nor, than
notion: haed sic a notion,
  loved so much

ony, any
onywey, anyway
oot, out

or, before, until
ower, over, too

peer, poor
pick, (black as) pitch
pintin, pointing
pit, put (**pat**)
plouter, wade
pootch, pocket
powk, poke, push
prigg, plead (**priggit,**
  pleaded)

quaet, quiet
quine, quinie, lass, girl
quorn, number

raa, row (line)
rae deer, roe deer
reef, roof
reek, smoke
reid, red
remeid, remedy
richt, right
rieve, tore
riggin, roof
rin, run
roon, round
rouwin, rolling

saan, sand
saatin, salting
sae, so
saen, sun; son
sair, sore
sair-made, upset, downcast
sappit, soaked
sark, shirt, shift
scunner, disgust; **scunner a
  body,** make you sick
scunnersome, disgusting
secht, sighed

seek, want, ask for
seen, soon
sheen, shoes; shone
shilpit, sickly
shoogle, quiver
shortsome, amusing
sic, such
siller, silver
skatchers, skates
skirl, scream
skreich, screech
smaa, small
snorl, dilemma, fix
socht, sought, asked
sodgers, soldiers
soon', sound
sooter, shoemaker
spier, ask, inquire
stannin, standing
stappit, stopped
steed, stood
steek, shut, close
steen, stone
steerin, stirring
stoun, pang
stracht, straight
sweir, reluctant
syne, then, after that; ago

tae, to; toe
tap, top
tapmaist, topmost
tee, too, also
teen, taken, caught
teen: the teen, the one
than, then
thegither, together
throwcome, adventure, ordeal
throuwither, in confusion
ticht, tight

till, to
tither: the tither, the other
toonie, village
tossels, tassels
tow, rope
trance, entrance, lobby
tummle, tumble, fall
twa, two
twasome, couple
tyaav, work hard, struggle
tyangs, pincers
tỳert, tired

verra, very
vrang, wrong

waa, wall
wae, sad
waed, wood; would
wappit, wrapped
warran: I's warran, I'm certain
waull, (water-) well
wee, little
weel, well, good
ween, wind
wesh, wish
wheen, number, lot
wheepin: (leaves) whipping (off the trees)
wid, would; angry
winna, winnae, won't
wint, want
wiz, was
wiznae, wasn't
wordl, world
wyte, blame; know; wait

yarkit, jerked
yave, keep, own; **fa yaves ye?**, who is your family?

CHRONOLOGY

1785 *4 January*: Jacob Ludwig Karl Grimm is born in Hanau.

1786 *24 February*: Wilhelm Karl Grimm is born in Hanau. Jacob and Wilhelm are the sons of Philipp Wilhelm Grimm, a lawyer and court official, and his wife Dorothea Grimm, neé Zimmer. The boys grow up in the countryside.

1791 The Grimm family moves to Steinau.

1796 *10 January*: The father, Philipp Wilhelm Grimm, dies of pneumonia.

1798 The brothers are taken to Kassel, their mother's home city, where they enter secondary school (the Lyceum Fridericianum) in order to be prepared for the study of law.

1802 *30 April*: Jacob matriculates in law at the University of Marburg.

1803 Wilhelm begins to study law at Marburg. The brothers are taught by Professor Friedrich Carl von Savigny (1779–1861), who has a strong influence on them and helps them to develop the intellectual and methodological basis for their future scholarly work. They enter a circle of artists and intellectuals, today referred to as the Heidelberg Romantics (Clemens Brentano, Sophie Mereau, Achim and Bettina von Arnim, Caroline von Günderode, among others).

1805 Jacob follows Savigny to Paris where he first works on medieval manuscripts. The brothers decide to live and work together for the rest of their lives.

1806–15 Influenced by Achim von Arnim's and Clemens Brentano's folktale *Des Knaben Wunderhorn* (*The Boy's Magic Horn*), the brothers Grimm collect and edit medieval songs, ballads, legends and folktales.

1806 Jacob Grimm is employed as secretary of war (*Kriegssekretär*).

1807 Jacob writes a letter to Savigny in which he expresses his dislike for the study of law and states that he has decided to devote himself completely to the study of early German literature.

Jacob resigns from office.

Autumn and winter 1807/1808: The brothers Grimm live with Achim von Arnim and Clemens Brentano at Kassel.

1808 *27 May*: Death of the mother, Dorothea Grimm. Jacob works as private librarian for Jérome Bonaparte, Napoleon's younger brother, at Kassel in order to support his younger brothers and sister.

Publication of Jacob Grimm's first fundamental essay, *Gedanken: Wie sich die Sagen zur Poesie und Geschichte verhalten* (*Reflections: How Legends Relate to Poetry and History*) in the journal *Zeitung für Einsiedler*.

1812 Publication of the first volume of *Kinder- und Hausmärchen* (*Children's and Household Tales*), containing 86 numbered tales.

1813 Jacob Grimm is appointed as secretary to the embassy (*Legationssekretär*).

1814 Publication of the second volume of *Kinder- und Hausmärchen*, containing 70 further tales. Six more editions of the tales appear during the brothers Grimm's lifetime.

Jacob is a diplomat in Paris and, from September 1814 until June 1815, is a member of the Hessian delegation at the Congress of Vienna.

Wilhelm is employed as a library secretary at Kassel.

1816 *April*: Jacob Grimm joins his brother at Kassel and becomes a librarian. The brothers have found ideal conditions for concentrated scholarly work and further philological research.

1816–18 Publication of the two volumes of *Deutsche Sagen* (*German Legends*), containing 585 German legends.

1819 Publication of the first volume of Jacob Grimm's *Deutsche Grammatik* (*German Grammar*), which is still regarded today as a milestone in the history of European philology. Three further volumes are published by 1837.

Jacob and Wilhelm receive honorary doctorates from the University of Marburg.

1821 Wilhelm writes his important essay *Über deutsche Runen* (*On German Runes*).

1825 Charlotte (Lotte) Amalie Grimm, their sister, marries the

Hessian politician Daniel Hassenpflug and leaves the brothers' house.

Wilhelm Grimm marries Henriette Dorothea (Dortchen) Wild.

1829 Wilhelm Grimm publishes his main work *Die deutsche Heldensage* (*The German Heroic Saga*).

1829–30 The brothers Grimm are appointed as professors at the University of Göttingen.

1830–37 Jacob and Wilhelm teach at the University of Göttingen. Further philological publications.

1832 In his highly praised book *Deutsche Mythologie* (*German Mythology*) Jacob Grimm investigates pre-Christian German religious belief.

1833 Having realized that the state curtailed the rights of professors and students for no apparent reason, Jacob Grimm writes two reviews in which he defends the university's autonomous constitution.

Their sister Lotte Grimm dies.

1834 Jacob Grimm edits *Reinhart Fuchs* (*Reynard the Fox*).

1837 The brothers Grimm and five of their university colleagues (Dahlmann, Gervinus, Ewald, Albrecht, Weber) protest against the king's unlawful repeal of the constitution of Hannover. The seven professors, referred to as the 'Göttinger Sieben', are dismissed from office. Jacob moves to his brother Ludwig Emil's house in Kassel.

1838 *January*: Jacob writes his essay *Jacob Grimm über seine Entlassung* (*Jacob Grimm on his Dismissal*).
Autumn: He signs a contract with a bookseller for the edition of a historical German dictionary (*Deutsches Wörterbuch*). Wilhelm Grimm moves with his family from Göttingen to Kassel.

1840 *November*: the Prussian king Friedrich Wilhelm IV appoints the brothers Grimm as members of the Academy of Sciences and Humanities (Akademie der Wissenschaften) in Berlin. The Grimms have now reached a reasonably high standard of living, but subject to the renunciation of their political activities. Give lectures at the University of Berlin (until 1852), work on the German dictionary.

1844 On the occasion of Wilhelm Grimm's birthday, the students in Berlin join in a torchlight procession in remembrance of the Grimms' political activity at Göttingen. H. Hoffmann von Fallersleben, a professor from Breslau who has been suspended from office for political reasons, happens to be present and is praised by the students. The brothers Grimm, believing a rumour that Hoffmann had himself arranged for the students to honour him, break off contact with him. The relationship with Bettina von Arnim, who strongly resents the Grimms for having taken this step, is marred.

1846/47 Two conferences for German studies (*Germanistik*) at Frankfurt and Lübeck, both led by Jacob Grimm.

1848 Jacob is a delegate to the Frankfurt National Assembly. He pleads for a German constitution, fundamental rights, individual freedom, the abolition of slavery and of all legal inequality between the estates.

Jacob Grimm finishes his *Geschichte der deutschen Sprache* (*History of the German Language*).

1849 In his speech *Über Schule Universität Akademie* (*On School University Academy*) Jacob Grimm defends the role and importance of the Prussian Academy of Sciences and Humanities among German academic institutions.

1854 Publication of the first volume of *German Dictionary* (*Deutsches Wörterbuch*). During their lifetime the brothers get as far as the fourth volume of the dictionary (letter 'F').

1859 *16 December*: Wilhelm Grimm dies, aged seventy-three, of a carbuncle in his back.

1863 *20 September*: Jacob Grimm dies, aged seventy-eight, of a stroke.

FURTHER READING

1. Editions

Die älteste Märchensammlung der Brüder Grimm: Synopse der hand-schriftlichen Urfassung von 1810 und der Erstdruck von 1812, ed. Heinz Rölleke, (Cologne and Geneva: Foundation Martin Bodmer, 1975) (manuscript versions of the tales).

Die Kinder- und Hausmärchen der Brüder Grimm: Vollständige Ausgabe in der Urfassung, ed. Friedrich Panzer (1st edn, Wiesbaden: Emil Vollmer, 1953).

Brüder Grimm: Kinder- und Hausmärchen, ed. Heinz Rölleke, 3 vols. (Ditzingen: Reclam, 2001).

The Complete Fairy Tales of the Brothers Grimm, trans. and ed. Jack Zipes (New York: Bantam, 1987).

2. Secondary Literature
On the Brothers Grimm in General

Bluhm, Lothar, *Die Brüder Grimm und der Beginn der Deutschen Philologie: Eine Studie zu Kommunikation und Wissenschaftsbildung im frühen 19. Jahrhundert* (Hildesheim: Weidmann, 1997).

Denecke, Ludwig, *Jacob Grimm und sein Bruder Wilhelm* (Stuttgart: J. B. Metzler, 1971).

Michaelis-Jena, Ruth, *The Brothers Grimm* (London: Routledge & Kegan Paul, 1970).

Peppard, Murray, *Paths Through the Forest: A Biography of the Brothers Grimm* (New York: Holt, Rinehart and Winston, 1971).

Seitz, Gabriele, *Die Brüder Grimm: Leben-Werk-Zeit* (Munich: Winkler Verlag, 1985).

On Grimms' Folktales and Fairy Tales

Bottigheimer, Ruth B., *Grimms' Bad Girls and Bold Boys: The Moral and Social Vision of the Tales* (New Haven, CT: Yale University Press, 1987).

Ellis, John M., *One Fairy Story Too Many: The Brothers Grimm and Their Tales* (Chicago: University of Chicago Press, 1983).

Haase, Donald (ed.), *The Reception of Grimms' Fairy Tales: Responses, Reactions, Revisions* (Detroit, IL: Wayne State University Press, 1993).

Kamenetsky, Christa, *The Brothers Grimm and Their Critics: Folk Tales and the Quest for Meaning* (Athens, OH: Ohio University Press, 1992).

McGlathery, James M., *Grimms' Fairy Tales: A History of Criticism on a Popular Classic* (Columbia, SC: Camden House, 1993).

McGlathery, James M. (ed.), *The Brothers Grimm and Folktale* (Urbana, IL: University of Illinois Press, 1988).

Rölleke, Heinz, *Die Märchen der Brüder Grimm* (Zürich: Artemis Verlag, 1986).

Rölleke, Heinz, *Die Märchen der Brüder Grimm: Quellen und Studien. Gesammelte Aufsätze* (Trier: Wissenschaftlicher Verlag Trier, 2000).

Sennewald, Jens E., *Das Buch, das wir sind: Zur Poetik der Kinder- und Hausmärchen, gesammelt durch die Brüder Grimm* (Würzburg: Königshausen & Neumann, 2003).

Solms, Wilhelm, *Die Moral von Grimms Märchen* (Darmstadt: Wissenschaftliche Buchgesellschaft, 1999).

Tatar, Maria, *The Hard Facts of the Grimm's Fairy Tales* (Princeton, NJ: Princeton University Press, 1987).

Tatar, Maria, *Off with Their Heads!: Fairy Tales and the Culture of Childhood* (Princeton, NJ: Princeton University Press, 1992).

Zipes, Jack, *The Brothers Grimm: From Enchanted Forest to the Modern World* (New York and London: Routledge, 1988).

On Folktales and Fairy Tales in General

Bettelheim, Bruno, *The Uses of Enchantment: Meaning and Importance of Fairy Tales* (London: Penguin, 1991).

Lüthi, Max, *The European Folktale: Form and Nature* (Bloomington,

IN: Indiana University Press, 1982).

Zipes, Jack, *Fairy Tales and the art of Subversion: The Classical Genre for Children and the Process of Civilization* (New York: Routledge, 1991).

Zipes, Jack, *The Great Fairy Tale Tradition: From Straparola and Basile to the Brothers Grimm* (New York and London: Norton & Company, 2001).

Zipes, Jack (ed.), *The Oxford Companion to Fairy Tales* (Oxford: Oxford University Press, 2002).

Journals and Periodicals

Fabula: Zeitschrift für Erzählforschung/Journal of Folktale Studies/ Revue d'Etudes sur le Conte Populaire, ed. Rolf Wilhelm Brednich and Hans-Jörg Uther.

Marvels and Tales: Journal of Fairy-Tale Studies, ed. Donald Haase (Detroit: MI: Wayne State University).

THE STORY OF PENGUIN CLASSICS

Before 1946 ...'Classics' are mainly the domain of academics and students, without readable editions for everyone else. This all changes when a little-known classicist, E. V. Rieu, presents Penguin founder Allen Lane with the translation of Homer's *Odyssey* that he has been working on and reading to his wife Nelly in his spare time.

1946 *The Odyssey* becomes the first Penguin Classic published, and promptly sells three million copies. Suddenly, classic books are no longer for the privileged few.

1950s Rieu, now series editor, turns to professional writers for the best modern, readable translations, including Dorothy L. Sayers's *Inferno* and Robert Graves's *The Twelve Caesars*, which revives the salacious original.

1960s The Classics are given the distinctive black jackets that have remained a constant throughout the series's various looks. Rieu retires in 1964, hailing the Penguin Classics list as 'the greatest educative force of the 20th century'.

1970s A new generation of translators arrives to swell the Penguin Classics ranks, and the list grows to encompass more philosophy, religion, science, history and politics.

1980s The Penguin American Library joins the Classics stable, with titles such as *The Last of the Mohicans* safeguarded. Penguin Classics now offers the most comprehensive library of world literature available.

1990s The launch of Penguin Audiobooks brings the classics to a listening audience for the first time, and in 1999 the launch of the Penguin Classics website takes them online to a larger global readership than ever before.

The 21st Century Penguin Classics are rejacketed for the first time in nearly twenty years. This world famous series now consists of more than 1300 titles, making the widest range of the best books ever written available to millions – and constantly redefining the meaning of what makes a 'classic'.

The Odyssey continues ...

The best books ever written

PENGUIN (🐧) CLASSICS

SINCE 1946